Nature, Wellness and Sustainability in Health Tourism

Nature, Wellness and Sustainability in Health Tourism

EDITED BY

ARUNESH PARASHAR
Dev Sanskriti Vishwavidyalaya, India

AHMAD ALBATTAT
Asia Pacific University of Technology and Innovation, Malaysia

PRACHI AGARWAL
Dev Sanskriti Vishwavidyalaya, India

AND

PANKAJ SINGH CHANDEL
AAFT University of Media and Arts, India

emerald
PUBLISHING

United Kingdom – North America – Japan – India – Malaysia – China

Emerald Publishing Limited
Emerald Publishing, Floor 5, Northspring, 21–23 Wellington Street, Leeds LS1 4DL

First edition 2026

British Library Cataloguing in Publication Data
A catalogue record for this book is available from the British Library

ISBN: 978-1-83742-030-8 (Print)
ISBN: 978-1-83742-029-2 (Online)
ISBN: 978-1-83742-031-5 (Epub)

Printed and bound by CPI Group (UK) Ltd, Croydon, CR0 4YY

We humbly dedicate this book to the revered memory of Pandit Shriram Sharma Acharya ji, founder of Yug Nirmaan Yojana, and Gurumata Bhagwati Devi Sharma ji, whose vision and teachings continue to inspire us.

Contents

About the Editors

Dr. Arunesh Parashar, an eminent figure in the realm of academia and a distinguished professional in the field of culture, geography, yoga, management with specialisation in tourism and hospitality management. As the Associate Professor and Head, Department of Tourism and Travel Management at Dev Sanskriti Vishwavidyalaya, Haridwar, Dr. Parashar brings a wealth of knowledge, expertise and leadership to the vibrant academic community. He has carved a niche for himself in the specialised domain of health tourism. His academic journey is adorned with more than 50 research papers published in both national and international journals. Through extensive contributions to more than 6 books and chapters in international and national publications, he has left an indelible mark on the academic landscape, showcasing a deep understanding of the complexities within the tourism, travel and hospitality sector. Beyond the rigours of academia, Dr. Arunesh Parashar is a versatile writer with a penchant for creative expression. His prowess extends to e-books and self-learning books, reflecting a commitment to disseminating knowledge through diverse mediums. A stalwart in the academic arena, Dr. Parashar actively participates as a member of different academic bodies, industry forums and professional organisations. This multifaceted engagement underscores his dedication to advancing the discourse within the tourism and hospitality industry by organising more than 40 national and international conferences in the field of tourism and hospitality sector. Dr. Parashar's influence extends beyond national borders. His extensive camping and leadership experiences abroad have enriched his perspective and contributed to his global recognition. Notably, he has been honoured with more than 30 awards and has served as a distinguished guest of honour on numerous occasions, celebrating his outstanding contributions to the tourism and hospitality sector.

Ahmad Albattat is an Associate Professor and Program Leader in School of Global Hospitality and Tourism, Asia Pacific University of Technology and Innovation, Kuala Lumpur, Malaysia. He is a Visiting Professor and External Examiner in Medan Academy of Tourism (Akpar Medan). He received PhD in Hospitality Management 'Disaster and Emergency Planning and Preparedness' from University Sains Malaysia (USM), Malaysia. He worked as an Associate Professor in Graduate School of Management, Post Graduate Centre, Management and Science University, Shah Alam, Selangor, Malaysia. Assistant Professor, Ammon Applied University College, Amman, Jordan. Senior Lecturer and Research Coordinator in School of Hospitality & Creative Arts, Management and Science University, Shah Alam, Selangor, Malaysia, and Researcher at Sustainable Tourism Research

Cluster (STRC), Pulau Pinang, Malaysia. He was working for the Jordanian hospitality industry for 17 years. His teaching and consultancy fields include hospitality management, events management, research methodology, strategic management and final research projects. His research areas include hospitality management, hotel, tourism, events, emergency planning, disaster management, sustainable development goals and human resource. He is an active member of several Scientific and Editorial Board of International journals, reviewer, author and editor for book projects. His latest works have been published in the refereed international journals, conference proceedings, books and book chapters.

Dr. Prachi Agarwal is an Assistant Professor in the Department of Tourism Management at Dev Sanskriti Vishwavidyalaya, Haridwar, and a UGC-NET qualified scholar in Tourism Administration and Management. She holds a Master's degree in Business Administration (Tourism and Travel Management) and a Bachelor of Science in Psychology and Computer Science. Currently, she has done her PhD in the field of Health Tourism, with a research focus on Nature-Based and Sustainable Tourism Models. Dr. Agarwal has presented and published numerous research papers, books and book chapters in national and international forums. She has actively represented India as part of the Indian Youth Delegation to Palestine and completed the Kailash Mansarovar Yatra under the Ministry of External Affairs, Government of India. She got selected under student exchange programme scholarship to Lithuania. Her dedication to public service is reflected in her long-standing involvement with the National Service Scheme (NSS), through which she has received multiple honours including two Governor's Awards and the Ganesh Shankar Vidyarthi Award. With a blend of academic rigour, cultural insight and community service, Dr. Agarwal is committed to promoting India's spiritual, cultural and health tourism on both national and global platforms.

Dr Pankaj Singh Chandel is a academician and seasoned professor with over a decade of experience in higher education, hospitality management, and Tourism education. Currently serving as Assistant Professor and Head of the School of Hospitality and Tourism Management, as well as the School of Wellness at AAFT University of Media and Arts in Raipur, he holds a PhD in Tourism Management and an MBA from the Indian Institute of Tourism and Travel Management. Dr Chandel's career exemplifies relentless pursuit of academic excellence, marked by extensive publications in Scopus-indexed journals and leadership in global conferences. His scholarship intersects human resource management, homestay entrepreneurship, sustainable tourism, regenerative hospitality, and soft skills development particularly in rural contexts for regional resilience. A pivotal voice in higher education, he bridges traditional pedagogy with industry-aligned practices, integrating hospitality education with Tourism and sustainability to address 21st-century challenges. Under his guidance, student-centric programs foster creativity, critical thinking, technical proficiency, and experiential learning. By seamlessly blending theoretical knowledge with hands-on tourism and hospitality industry and research, Dr Chandel empowers the next generation of professionals, innovates curricula, and shapes the future of global hospitality, homestay, sustainability, tourism, and wellness.

About the Contributors

M. K. Amila Indika is working as a Senior Lecturer (Assistant Professor) for the University College of Ratmalana, part of the University of Vocational Technology, Sri Lanka. Having a strong interest in vocational and higher education, he contributes his valuable knowledge in the field of hospitality and tourism studies. His professional expertise and field insights contribute to the enhancement of industry-oriented education, encouraging skill-oriented learning and professional development of students.

Astha Bhanot has an experience of teaching and research for 17 years (9 years in Saudi Arabia and 8 years in India). She has contributed many research publications in national and international journals and books. She is an experienced Professor with a demonstrated history of working in the higher education industry and is skilled in Lecturing, Educational Technology, Curriculum Development, Research and Educational Leadership. Strong education professional graduated from Christ Church Jabalpur, Madhya Pradesh, India.

Ajay Bhardwaj is a faculty member at Amity University, Jaipur, India. He has extensive experience in tourism and hospitality management, with a research focus on rural sustainability, service quality and management in the tourism sector.

Tatayya Bommali is a distinguished educator, researcher, and academic leader in Finance, currently serving as a Professor & Head, Department of Management Studies, and Controller of Examination (COE), Sanketika Vidya Parishad Engineering College, Visakhapatnam, AP, India. He holds a PhD in Finance, along with MCom, MBA, and BEd, and brings 20 years of extensive teaching and research experience. A Cambridge-trained lecturer and IBDP Business Management Facilitator, Dr Bommali has taught MBA, MCA, BTech, BCom, and CA students, fostering academic excellence across diverse educational frameworks. His global academic exposure, including roles in India, Malaysia, and Dhaka, highlights his contribution to educational leadership. A prolific researcher, he has published extensively in reputed journals and contributed to books in Finance, Accounting, Banking, and Economics. His research interests focus on financial inclusion, digital finance, and sustainable investment strategies, bridging theory with practical applications through mentorship, curriculum innovation, and academic leadership.

Chafik Bouchannafa is a Senior Secondary Education Professor and Researcher specialising in Tourism Geography. He holds a PhD in Tourism, Environment and Sustainable Development with a focus on the region of Fez, and a Master's degree in Environmental Pollution, examining water resources in the same area. His research interests encompass the environmental, spatial and socio-economic dimensions of tourism, with a particular focus on therapeutic destinations such as Sidi Harazem and Moulay Yacoub. Dr. Bouchannafa has published numerous academic articles and participated in international conferences addressing sustainability, territorial development and geographic information systems. His contributions aim to promote sustainable practices within Moroccan tourism and to bridge scientific inquiry with local development challenges.

Mehdi Boukil is a tourism geographer, researcher and training supervisor at the City of Trades and Skills in Casablanca Nouaceur. He earned his PhD in Geography with a specialisation in tourism and territorial development. With over a decade of experience as a travel planner and consultant, Dr. Boukil combines practical expertise with scholarly research. His academic focus includes heritage valorisation, destination management, digital tourism and intercultural tourism experiences in Morocco. He has published in several international volumes on responsible tourism, e-reputation and cultural revitalisation. In addition to research, he is deeply engaged in training future tourism professionals and advocating for sustainable and inclusive tourism practices.

Sanjukta Chakraborty is an Assistant Professor and Head of the Department of Computer Science and Engineering at Seacom Skills University, Santiniketan, West Bengal, India. With over 11 years of teaching experience, she holds a PhD in CSE, specialising in Artificial Intelligence and Machine Learning. She has completed MTech (CSE), MCA and BSc (Physics Honours) from reputed Indian universities. Her research interests include AI, ML, Deep Learning, Cyber Security, Data Science, Sentiment Analysis, Big Data Analytics, Software Engineering and Business Intelligence. Dr. Chakraborty has published 14 research articles and 3 book chapters and has guided numerous students in their final year dissertations.

Anand K. Chaudhary is a Professor in the Department of Rasa Shastra and Bhaishajya Kalpana, Faculty of Ayurveda, Institute of Medical Sciences, Banaras Hindu University, Varanasi, Uttar Pradesh, India. With extensive experience in the field of Ayurvedic medicine, his research interests include Ayurvedic formulations, herbal drug development and the modernisation of traditional Indian medicinal practices. Prof. Chaudhary has contributed significantly to the development and standardisation of herbal medicines and plays an active role in promoting evidence-based Ayurveda. https://orcid.org/0000-0002-3914-6942

Siddhant Chaudhary is a research scholar at the Department of Psychology, Gurukula Kangri (DU). His research focuses on the impact of work experiences on career outcomes, with a particular emphasis on job crafting as a mediating factor. With five publications in journals and books, along with three conference papers, he actively contributes to the field of psychology. Beyond research, he is an experienced freelance content writer with a strong command of academic writing. Passionate about advancing psychological research, he aspires to master robust research designs and make meaningful contributions to both academia and society.

Amar Prakash Dabral currently serves as the Head of the Department of Hospitality Management at Graphic Era Deemed to be University. With extensive experience in hotel operations, he has worked with several renowned hotel brands, bringing a strong industry foundation to his academic and research endeavours. His professional journey reflects a rich blend of operational expertise and academic insight, contributing significantly to the development of hospitality education.

Sharmila Devi holds the position of Senior Lecturer at Inti International University. Her passion for HRM (Human Resource Management) has driven her to explore various facets of this discipline, including Green HRM, Women Empowerment, Women Leadership, Spiritual Intelligence, Leadership Development and Talent Management.

Anju Jangid (Corresponding Author) is a Research Scholar in the Department of Rasa Shastra and Bhaishajya Kalpana, Faculty of Ayurveda, Institute of Medical Sciences, Banaras Hindu University, Varanasi, Uttar Pradesh, India. She holds a postgraduate degree in Geography, qualified UGC-JRF in Geography and is currently pursuing doctoral research at the intersection of Ayurveda and tourism. Her research interests span across wellness tourism, medical tourism, nature tourism and heritage tourism, with a focus on integrating traditional Indian wellness practices like Ayurveda and Yoga into contemporary tourism development. She is passionate about promoting sustainable and holistic health tourism in India. https://orcid.org/0009-0003-7148-7370

Nihal Kapoor is a dedicated research scholar in the Department of Tourism, currently pursuing his doctoral studies with a focus on religious tourism in Himachal Pradesh. He has participated in various academic seminars and continues to contribute to scholarly discourse through his research, publications and fieldwork-based insights.

Sawsan Haider Khreis is affiliated to Assistant Professor/Department of Tourism and Travel. PhD in Tourism Management, Sorbonne University—France Distinction with honours. She is the recipient of many awards and grants for her valuable contributions and discoveries in major area of subject research. Her international experience includes various programs, contributions and participation in different countries for diverse fields of study. Her research interests reflect in her wide range of publications in various national and international journals.

Ravish Kukreti has been working at Graphic Era Deemed to be University for the last 16 years, where he has brought many years of academic and administrative expertise to the university. Having a solid background in hospitality and tourism management, he has been instrumental in developing the academic agenda and guiding young professionals towards realising their goals. His commitment to education, coupled with his deep subject matter expertise, has played an important role in the development and excellence of the university's hospitality education programmes.

Ashish Kumar is a Postdoctoral Fellow (ICSSR, New Delhi) at Dev Sanskriti Vishwavidyalaya, Haridwar, India. His research interests include management principles in the Indian knowledge system, sustainable tourism and organisational spirituality. He has presented and published research on tourism management, employee retention and spiritual leadership.

Manoj Kumar is a research scholar at the Centre for Promotion of Ecology, Adventure, Health and Cultural Tourism within the School of Tourism, Travel, & Hospitality Management at Central University, Himachal Pradesh in Dharamshala.

Prashant Kumar is a research scholar at the Department of Psychology, Gurukula Kangri (DU), specialising in sports psychology. He has presented his work at three academic conferences and has one journal publication to his credit. Passionate about mental health and personal development, he has a keen interest in counselling and aims to support individuals in overcoming psychological challenges. With a strong commitment to applied psychology, he aspires to bridge the gap between research and real-world mental well-being.

Rakesh Kumar is a qualified Clinical Psychologist currently holding the position in Gurukula Kangri (Deemed to be University), Haridwar. He has 34 years' experience of practicing, teaching and research in psychology. In addition to serving as supervisor for doctoral theses and publication of 110 research papers to his credit, he has authored books on hypnosis and Rorschach Inkblot Test. He has developed an innovative approach of verbal exposure popularly known as Cognitive Drill Therapy for dealing with stimulus bound anxiety present in obsessive-compulsive and phobic disorders. He is the recipient of multiple awards from National Professional Associations in recognition of his contribution to the innovative therapeutic approach. He travels widely to conduct workshops and invited lectures on hypnotherapy and cognitive-drill therapy. He is also serving as President, Psychological Association, Uttarakhand and Vice-President, Academy of Hypnosis. He has a vision to inspire young psychologists for creative thinking and novel research in the field of psychology.

B. Latha Lavanya, an Associate Professor with an impressive 24 years of professional experience, has established herself as a distinguished academic and industry expert. With a robust background that includes 7 years as a Senior HR Manager, she has seamlessly transitioned into academia, where she has made significant contributions over the past 17 years. Her academic journey is marked by a full-time PhD from the University of Madras, for which she was awarded a prestigious research fellowship by the University Grants Commission (UGC). Dr Latha Lavanya's accolades are a testament to her excellence in both teaching and research. She was honored with the Best Faculty in Management Award by Education Today in 2014, the Research Excellence Award by Indo Global Education in 2017, and the Award for Teaching Excellence by GMRAF Awards in 2019. In 2020, she was recognized with the Best Women Researcher Award, further solidifying her standing as a leading figure in her field, pursuing a Post Doc at MIT SQUARE. Academically, Dr B. Latha Lavanya holds a diverse portfolio of qualifications, including a Master's in Human Resource Management (MHRM), an MBA, and Postgraduate diplomas in Logistics & Supply Chain Management, Web Technology, and Hospital Management. Her scholarly contributions are extensive, with over 87 research papers published in esteemed journals indexed by Scopus, Web of Science, and ABDC. She is also a recognized PhD guide at the University of Madras, mentoring the next generation of researchers. A trailblazer in her field, Dr B. Latha Lavanya is the first faculty member to secure a funded internship from the Reserve Bank of India and has successfully obtained grants from the Indian Council of Social Science Research (ICSSR) to organize a national conference at MIM.

Abhishek Maikhuri is at present an Assistant Professor in the Department of Hotel Management at Graphic Era Hill University. Having a robust academic foundation and industry exposure in the hospitality and tourism industries, he has a balanced approach to teaching and research. His research emphasis lies on service excellence, sustainability and green practices in the industry, meaningfully supporting the development of hospitality education and research.

Tanmoy Majumder is an Assistant Professor at MCKV Institute of Engineering, India. Prior to joining MCKV Institute of Engineering, he served at JIS University, Kolkata. He possesses over 12 years of comprehensive experience spanning both the corporate and academic sectors. He holds a Bachelor's degree in Hospital Management from West Bengal University of Technology, a Master's degree in Hospital Administration from the West Bengal University of Health Sciences, and a Master of Business Management from West Bengal State University. He has recently completed his PhD in Healthcare Marketing Management from JIS University. His core research interests include Marketing Management and Hospital Management. Dr Majumder has made notable academic contributions through several research publications in national and international journals. He has also actively participated in numerous national and international conferences, presenting research across multidisciplinary domains such as business, technology, and social sciences.

Shila Mondol is currently pursuing her PhD at the Kalinga Institute of Industrial Technology (KIIT) a Deemed to be University, specialising in 'Social Empowerment and Microcredit in Bangladesh' under the able guidance of Senior Professor Dr. Ipseeta Satpathy. She previously has completed her Master of Business Administration (MBA) from the KIIT University. In addition to her academic endeavours, she has contributed to the university's global engagement as a key member from the International Relations Office at the KIIT University. Her role involved fostering international collaborations, coordinating exchange programs and enhancing KIIT's global outreach. With a passion for research, education and international networking, Ms. Shila Mondal is committed to advancing knowledge in her field — 'Impact of Microcredit on Women Empowerment in Bangladesh'. Meanwhile, she has published 02 (two) articles — 'Impact of Artificial Intelligence (AI) in Revolutionizing Microfinance in Bangladesh: Improving Outreach and Efficiency' and 'Impact of Microcredit on Women Empowerment in Bangladesh' in Shodha Prabha (UGC CARE Journal).

Kuzhikandathil Chirakkalthodi Murari is a Research Scholar in the Department of Tourism Studies, School of Business Studies, Central University of Kerala, India. He is an ICSSR Doctoral Fellow, researching Sustainable Cultural Tourism. He holds a Postgraduate degree from the Indian Institute of Tourism and Travel Management (IITTM) and has qualified UGC-NET in Tourism Administration and Management. With six years of industry experience in air cargo and logistics management, he brings practical insights to his research. He has presented papers at an international seminar sponsored by the Kerala Folklore Academy and a national seminar at NIT Silchar, funded by ICSSR. His research interests include Cultural Heritage, Environment, Tourism, Sustainability and Commerce.

Arpita Nayak is currently serving as an Assistant Professor, offering courses in management. She completed her PhD in Management from the KIIT School of Management. Her MBA and strong interest in Human Resource Management (HRM) led her to pursue further studies in HRM. Her passion for talent management inspired her doctoral research on 'A Comparative Study on Talent Management in Private and Public Manufacturing Industries in Odisha'. Dr. Nayak has presented research papers at both national and international conferences and has published articles in SCOPUS-listed journals. Over the years, she has taught a variety of subjects, including Human Resource Management, Principles of Management, Business Studies Management, Tribal Entrepreneurship and Organisational Behaviour. In addition to her academic career, she has several years of corporate work experience.

Subramanya Pailoor is an Associate Professor and Head of the Department of Yoga Studies at the Central University of Kerala, India. Previously, he served as an Associate Professor and Registrar at Swami Vivekananda Yoga Anusandhana Samsthana (S-VYASA), Bangalore, India. A pioneering researcher in the fields of Yoga, Meditation and Psychophysiology, Dr. Pailoor has authored over 50 research articles and more than 5 book chapters in reputed journals and publishers. He has significantly contributed to the academic integration of Yoga and has led a research project on Yoga's impact on cognitive and neuro-endocrine biomarkers, funded by the Ministry of AYUSH, Government of India. His expertise is widely recognised, making him a sought-after expert member for various universities, institutions and colleges. His work is driven by a vision to bring Yoga into the mainstream of academia while making its benefits accessible to the common person.

Monika Pandey serves as a faculty member at Dev Sanskriti Vishwavidyalaya, Haridwar, India. She specialises in human resource management, leadership and the integration of spirituality in workplace culture. Her research explores the intersection of management and ethical leadership.

Avanendu Parashar is an Assistant Professor at Dev Sanskriti Vishwavidyalaya, Haridwar, India. His research interests include adventure tourism, tourism studies and sustainable business models. He has contributed to studies on spirituality and tourism.

B. C. M. Patnaik has more than 20 years of rich experience in Educational Research, Content and Creative initiative at both postgraduate and undergraduate levels, ability to handle core administration related activities such as infrastructure, facility, human resources, training and development of staff members and organisational behaviour and organisation development. Possessing valuable insights, keen analysis and team approach to implement best practices, adept at working in high pressure environments with strict deadlines and multiple deliverables. Introduce knowledge and assist the students to develop the skills necessary for success. As a faculty of Accounts and Finance, introduced students to the principles, process, tools and techniques becoming the foundation of their ability to understand and take up challenges throughout their education and into their professional careers. Expertise in planning, organising, coordinating and monitoring all types of curricular and co-curricular activities for the overall development of personality of students. Devoted teacher striving to help students change marginal grades into good grades and supporting colleagues and administration in facilitating each child's social and intellectual growth by creating an atmosphere of mutual respect and open communication. Guided 15 Ph.D scholars and guiding 6 scholars. Published more than 150 papers including 34 papers in Scopus-indexed journals. Awarded Best Faculty 4 times.

P. K. Paul holds prestigious and unique D.Sc. in Information Science and Technology (IST) & D.Tech. in Agricultural Informatice & Management degree from Azteca University, Mexico under DAYIPF Program. He also hold PhD in IST from IIEST Shibpur, Post Doctoral Fellow Certificate (PDFC) Program in Environmental Informatics. He holds degrees like MTech. (by Research), MS (by Research) in addition to MSc (Double). He is working as Asst. Professor (IST) & Executive Director (MCIS Program) at Dept. of Computer & Information Sciences, and additionally Information Scientist Position at Raiganj University, West Bengal, India. Significantly He is also holds many National and International positions viz. Honorary Professor, Logos University International, Louisiana, USA, Chief Advisor (Innovative Program & Research Planning), Srinivas University, Mangalore, India. Credited over 35 Books in diverse areas and 400+ research/review and policy papers, Members in more than 150+ Journals and 250+ Int. Conf. Membership, organization and holds more than a dozen of Awards.

Aakanksha Prajapati is an Assistant Professor in Department of Yogic Science in University of Patanjali, Haridwar. She has completed her PhD from Dev Sanskriti Vishwavidyalaya in the field of Human Consciousness and Yogic Science which examines the relevance of ancient yogic perspectives in light of emerging models of new scientific approaches. She is also a UGC-NET qualified aspirant. She has a Master's degree in Yoga and alternative therapies and Master's in Physics. Her academic contributions include presentations at national and international conferences, as well as collaborative work in the field of interdisciplinary approach of consciousness studies. She has more than eight years of experience in teaching yoga and working in the wellness field, combining practical expertise with theoretical insights to bridge the gap between traditional knowledge systems and modern scientific discourse.

Raina is a UGC-NET Senior Research Fellow (SRF) in Psychology at Gurukula Kangri (DU), Haridwar. Her research examines the impact of Karma Yoga on psychological well-being and related variables, integrating ancient Indian wisdom with contemporary psychological science. She specialises in mixed-method studies, scale development and qualitative analysis, with expertise in various research software. Holding Master's degrees in both Psychology and Biochemistry, she brings a multidisciplinary perspective to her work and has extensive teaching experience at both university and institute levels. She has authored several research papers and presented at national and international conferences, contributing to the global discourse on culturally rooted mental health approaches. Passionate about mental health advocacy, she actively leads workshops, training programmes and digital initiatives. With deep expertise in Indian psychology, she is committed to developing indigenous interventions and therapeutic models that promote holistic well-being of mankind.

Nilanjan Ray is from Kolkata, India, and presently associated as an Associate Professor at Faculty of Management Studies, JIS University. Prior to joining JIS University, Dr. Ray was at Institute of Leadership Entrepreneurship and Development as an Associate Professor and HoD and additional responsibility as Director IQAC before that he was also associated at Adamas University as an Associate Professor of Marketing Management and Centre Coordinator for Research in Business Analytics at Adamas University in Department of Management, School of Business and Economics, West Bengal, India. Dr. Ray has obtained certified *Accredited Management Teacher Award from All India Management Association*, New Delhi, India. He has obtained his PhD (Mktg), MCom (Mktg), MBA (Mktg) and STC FMRM (IIT-Kgp). He has more than 16 years teaching and 7 years research experience, awarded 3 doctoral scholars and guided around 56 postgraduate students' project also. Dr. Ray has contributed over 100 research papers in reputed national and international referred, peer-reviewed journals, proceedings and 14 edited research handbooks from Springer, IGI-Global USA and Apple Academic Publisher CRC Press (A Taylor & Francis Group), USA. He has obtained 1 patent from Germany and 12 copyrights from India. He has also associated himself as a reviewer of Tourism Management Elsevier, Journal of Service Marketing Emerald Group Publishing

Limited, Journal of Business and Economics, Research Journal of Business and Management Accounting and as an Editorial Board Member of several referred journals.

Abinash Roy is a UGC NET-JRF qualified researcher and PhD scholar at the Central University of Kerala, India. He holds a Master's degree in Yogic Science and Naturopathy, where he was a gold medallist, and a Bachelor's degree in Science. With over five years of experience as a Yoga teacher, he has conducted numerous training programmes and camps for students, youth and special populations across various institutions. His research focuses on Yoga, Meditation, Neurocognition, Brain Waves and Psychophysiology, exploring their impact on cognitive functions and neural oscillations. He has authored two research papers in Scopus and Web of Science (WoS) indexed journals and actively integrates scientific inquiry with traditional yogic practices.

Moumita Roy is a distinguished academic and researcher with 18 years of expertise in Organisational Behaviour and Human Resource Management. Currently an Assistant Professor at JIS University, she has played a pivotal role in shaping future business leaders through her innovative teaching and research. Her expertise spans workplace dynamics, leadership strategies, employee motivation, organisational culture and change management. She has designed and delivered impactful courses that integrate theory with practical applications, ensuring students grasp modern business challenges effectively. Dr. Roy has an extensive portfolio of research publications in national and international journals, addressing critical issues such as employee engagement, work–life fusion and strategic HR practices. A frequent speaker at conferences and seminars, she is dedicated to bridging the gap between research and practice. Her commitment to academic excellence, mentorship and thought leadership continues to inspire students and professionals alike.

J. A. R. C. Sandaruwani is a Senior Lecturer attached to the Department of Tourism Management, Faculty of Management Studies, Sabaragamuwa University of Sri Lanka. With over 10 years of academic experience, she specialises in tourism and hospitality education, curriculum development, academic advising and career guidance and research and scholarly work. Her research interests span in the areas of sustainable tourism, cultural and heritage tourism, eTourism, eHospitality and tourism consumer behaviour and marketing. She has published book chapters and journal articles in reputable scientific and scholarly platforms contributing to the advancement of tourism research and policy development. She has extensively served as a resource person for community outreach programmes and capacity-building programmes organised by national tourism organisations of Sri Lanka for tourism stakeholders island wide. In addition, she has been actively involved in funded projects, particularly in the field of sustainable tourism and rural empowerment.

Srabani Sanyal is a Professor in the Department of Geography, Institute of Science, Banaras Hindu University, Varanasi, Uttar Pradesh, India. Her academic expertise lies in applied geography, urban planning and environmental studies. With a strong interdisciplinary background, Prof. Sanyal's work focuses on the spatial dynamics of urbanisation, environmental sustainability and tourism geography. She has supervised numerous research projects and publications, contributing richly to the discourse on sustainable development and regional planning.

Ipseeta Satpathy has over 22 years of experience in teaching, research and administration at KIIT University. She has authored six textbooks, including *Environment Management*, *Business Communication & Personality Development* and *Transnational Marketing Strategy*. With over 200 research papers in national and international journals, including 75 Scopus-indexed publications and ABDC category journals, she is a prolific academic. A former Visiting Professor at Lynchburg College, USA, Prof. Satpathy has presented research at international conferences in Singapore, Cambridge, and the United States, winning several Best Paper Awards, including one from Emerald Group Publishing. She has guided 25 scholars to their PhD degrees and conducted numerous management development programmes. Prof. Satpathy has been honoured with the Oxford Journal Distinguished Research Professor Award at Cambridge University and invited to address academic communities at the University of Massachusetts Dartmouth and Southampton University, UK. Recently, she was felicitated with the Times Power Women 2023 award by the Times of India Group for her contributions to academia and professional skill development.

Amrik Singh is working as a Professor and Head in the School of Hotel Management and Tourism at Lovely Professional University, Punjab, India. He obtained his PhD degree in Hotel Management from Kurukshetra University, Kurukshetra. He started his academic career at Lovely Professional University, Punjab, India, in the year 2007. He has published 57 Scopus-indexed publications. He has published 12 patents, and 01 patent has been granted in the interdisciplinary domain. Dr. Amrik Singh participated and acted as a resource person in various national and international conferences, seminars, research workshops and industry talks. He has published 10 books with IGI Global Publication on trending areas such as Food Waste, Solid Waste, Artificial Intelligence in marketing, Mountain Tourism, Virtual tourism, Guest behaviour in tourism and hospitality. His areas of research interest are accommodation management, ergonomics, green practices, human resource management in hospitality, waste management, AR VR in hospitality, etc. He is currently guiding 8 PhD scholars, and 5 PhD scholars have been awarded PhD. He is a PhD thesis external examiner for many national and international universities. He is also an editorial team member for Scopus and Web of Science journals.

Amrik Singh is an Assistant Professor at the Centre for Promotion of Ecology, Adventure, Health & Cultural Tourism within the School of Tourism, Travel, & Hospitality Management at Central University, Himachal Pradesh in Dharamshala, with a PhD in Tourism Management, a Master's degree in Tourism Administration and a Master's in Economics. Dr. Singh's academic journey is complemented by a strong foundation in economics and geography from Himachal Pradesh University, Summerhill, Shimla.

Sunil Tiwari is a Researcher and Academician by profession, working with the Department of Tourism Studies, School of Business Studies, Central University of Kerala, India, as an Assistant Professor. He was the Gold Medallist in UG and PG and holds BSc., MBA and PhD degrees with topper free-ships. Moreover, he qualified for NET-JRF and has four years of teaching, training and research experience. He authored more than 70 research papers, 2 books and 10 chapters in highly indexed journals like *Energy Economics*, *Energy Policy*, *Resources Policy*, *Sustainable Development*, *Tourism Review* and many more listed in Scopus, ABDC, ABS, SSCI, SCIE, AGRIS, CABI, CNKI, DOAJ, EBSCO, GEOBASE, FSTA, IDEAS, etc., and his research areas are energy, environment, economics, tourism and sustainability. Moreover, Dr. Tiwari specialises in qualitative, quantitative and meta-analysis and works as a reviewer and editorial board member for many well-known journals worldwide.

Saurav Uniyal is a research scholar at the Department of Psychology, Gurukula Kangri (DU), Haridwar. Mr. Uniyal is a science graduate and completed his Master's in Psychology from Doon University, Dehradun in 2020, and qualified UGC NET-JRF in 2022. His research domain includes cognitive and clinical psychology, with specialisation in cognitive flexibility, cognitive coping, cognitive distortion and psychological issues. He has made notable contributions to the academic community, presenting research papers at various national and international conferences. Mr. Uniyal has published numerous research articles and book chapters in renowned journals/book and also published a book. His future vision is to contribute significantly to the development of innovative frameworks that integrate cognitive psychology with emerging technologies to address mental health challenges and enhance human potential across diverse settings.

Foreword

The relationship between nature and health is both profound and enduring, representing an inseparable bond that has shaped human civilisation across millennia. Within this continuum, the concepts of wellness and sustainability have emerged as defining imperatives of the contemporary era. On the one hand, modern societies are increasingly encumbered by lifestyle-related disorders, stress, depression and anxiety; on the other, the degradation of ecosystems and the depletion of natural resources present parallel threats of grave magnitude. In this context, health tourism assumes significance beyond that of leisure or recreation, constituting instead a holistic framework for healing that integrates both global innovations and indigenous traditions for the benefit of individuals and communities alike.

The volume *Nature, Wellness and Sustainability in Health Tourism* is a timely and substantive contribution to this discourse. It argues persuasively that wellness tourism ought not to be conceived merely as an economic or commercial activity but rather as a multidimensional endeavour intrinsically interwoven with health, compassion, happiness, culture and ecological balance.

The principal strength of this work lies in its interdisciplinary perspective. By drawing together insights from tourism studies, medical and health sciences, environmental research and cultural heritage, it demonstrates how nature-based and wellness tourism can contribute not only to individual transformation but also to balanced societal growth and sustainable futures. The incorporation of traditional Indian knowledge systems—such as yoga, Ayurveda, naturopathy and other alternative therapies—further enriches this vision, underscoring the enduring relevance of indigenous wisdom in addressing the complexities of modern life.

The spiritual guidance of Yugrishi Pujya Gurudev Pt. Shriram Sharma Acharya ji adds an invaluable dimension to the book's message. His profound assertion remains deeply resonant: 'True health lies in the harmony of body, mind, and soul, which becomes possible through a life aligned with nature and dedicated to the service of humanity.'

These principles elevate the framework of the volume, reminding us that wellness is not solely an individual pursuit but a collective responsibility directed towards global sustainability and human flourishing. It is my considered view that this book will inspire scholars, practitioners and policymakers alike to rediscover the healing power of nature and to recognise wellness as both a personal commitment and a societal imperative. In so doing, it offers a renewed and comprehensive vision of nature-based health tourism in its fullest and most holistic expression.

Dr. Chinmay Pandya

Dr. Chinmay Pandya
(MBBS, PGDipl, MRCPsych - London)
Pro Vice Chancellor - Dev Sanskriti Vishwavidyalaya, Haridwar (Bharat)

Preface

Health tourism is one of the emerging sectors in the world. Due to its attractiveness, well-being and accountable features, it provides a holistic well-being in one's life. Since ancient times, people used to travel for their good health. Such travel helps them to regain and develop their learning capacity with their health.

This book offers a comprehensive understanding and exploration of health tourism, incorporating the intrinsic bond between human well-being, natural environments and sustainable practices. By examining the diverse dimensions of health tourism, including medical tourism, nature-based health tourism or wellness tourism and traditional healing practices, this volume highlights the pivotal role of nature in fostering physical, emotional and spiritual health. To make nature and sustainable practices as a medicine of one's overall well-being and offering it as a Global Mantra for all, the contributors to this book provided their insightful analysis of the impact of health tourism, the emergence of nature-based spa and wellness tourism, their significance of environmental sustainability, highlighting some destinations related to this, discussing different health practices in promoting holistic well-being.

As a whole, this book presents a thorough understanding of the intricate relationships between human health, tourism and the natural world, offering valuable perspectives of tourism ecosystem for scholars, practitioners, stakeholders, academicians and policymakers in the field. All the editors of the book have given their valuable contribution in analysing and presenting the chapters that aligns and revolves around the theme of this book.

Acknowledgements

The *Īśāvāsya Upaniṣad* beautifully reminds us: '*Om! That is whole, this is whole. From the whole, the whole arises. Even when the whole is taken from the whole, the whole remains. Om! Peace, Peace, Peace!*'

Life, in its essence, is a continuous journey towards wholeness. We all move along this path, striving for transformation with purity at heart. Health dimensions play a vital role in this evolution, offering meaning and depth to our existence. This book on 'Travel and Wellness: A Renaissance of Nature-based Health Tourism' seeks to shed light on the many intersections of spirituality, culture and tourism experiences.

In this spirit, we humbly dedicate this work to the Divine Source, the eternal energy that guides us. With equal reverence, we bow to the Guru principle, which awakens our inner awareness and illuminates the path of life. We also extend heartfelt gratitude to our parents, whose blessings and love have been the foundation of our endeavours.

This book would not have been possible without the encouragement, insights and contributions of many professors, researchers, explorers, travelers and friends. To all of them, we offer our sincere appreciation and best wishes.

We are especially grateful to all the contributing authors—research scholars, teachers and professors—whose thoughtful and insightful chapters have enriched this volume and reviewers who have given it shape.

Finally, we acknowledge with humility the visible and invisible forces of this universe—circumstances, experiences, energies and the shared human spirit—that have silently guided and strengthened us throughout this journey.

Chapter 1

Wellness With Conscious Nature-Based Tourism: The Art of Becoming Super Coherent

Aakanksha Prajapati[a], *Sawsan Haider Khreis*[b], *Arunesh Parashar*[a] *and Prachi Agarwal*[a]

[a]Dev Sanskriti Vishwavidyalaya, India
[b]Yarmouk University, Jordan

Abstract

Human beings and nature are not only the physical bodies that one can see. Both humans and nature are deeply interconnected subtle energy systems, but somehow, these connections have been lost. These connections were not only the ones with the physical world but the connections of coherence with nature and the natural existence of our soul. Being connected and coherent to our soul and super coherent with other species, culture, communities and environment is a basic precondition for a sustainable life on this planet. But modern day's humanity has lost the essence of it.

Our body and mind are naturally capable of being in coherence with nature, but we reach only a state of partial coherence by exploring nature from an outer perspective. We have to become aware of our inner subtle being to connect with the subtle information of nature, which emerges from nature into our consciousness. Nature itself has the immense power to revoke and awaken the subtle energy system of human beings. As nature and its components also corresponds to same subtle energy systems with their physical beauty and medicinal properties. These subtle energy systems of the nature have their own frequencies, which affect the subtle energy systems of humans due to the interference. So when we enter into the nature and spend time within it, we reach to our own super coherent state of consciousness. This aim could be achieved through conscious nature-based

Nature, Wellness and Sustainability in Health Tourism, 1–15

doi:10.1108/978-1-83742-029-220261001

tourism (CNBT) for wellness, leading forward to the state of super coherence.

Keywords: Conscious tourism; coherence with nature; nature-ourism; art of connecting; super coherence with nature

1. Introduction

In the midst of today's busy, sedentary and stressful life, travelling amidst nature is one of the activities people prefer during their holidays. The experience of spending a few days amidst the nature is a trend nowadays. We can see people travelling on their holidays and planning the adventuress to do in between the rivers, on the mountains, in the air and almost everywhere. Travelling is seen as a way to take a break from the heist of an unsettled mind, restless days and sleepless nights. It offers a chance to escape the hectic pace of daily life, to breathe in new air and to embrace unfamiliar sights, sounds and cultures. Whether it's a serene beach, a bustling city or a quiet mountain retreat, every journey holds the promise of renewal – a reset for the soul.

1.1 Background of Travelling and Living in Harmony with Nature

Travelling isn't just about changing locations, it's about shifting perspectives. It allows us to step away from the pressures of our routine, reflect and rediscover the simple joys of exploration. The road ahead, unknown and full of possibilities, can be the perfect remedy for a weary heart and a restless mind. But, the history of travelling is much deeper than this superficial reason of getting a break from routine of daily life for feeling relaxed. In the earlier time, it was aimed at achieving wellness not only happiness and feeling of relaxation.

Even though, in recent times, tourists are becoming bit aware of the reason of tour, the essence of it is still missing. As we human beings are not merely the physical bodies, we do have an energy system working inside the body which makes it possible for us to live the life. We must have the aim of tourism far beyond than fun and adventure. As we have seen in the history of our great Bharat, many great gurus enlightened us by their knowledge, and most of them have their own connections with travelling in Bharat. For example, Swami Vivekananda travelled the whole world to enlighten people with his knowledge of ultimate truth, and Prince Siddharth became the Gautam Buddha by meditating for a long time in the lap of nature. After travelling a lot, Buddha sat under the tree where he achieved his state of Samadhi and was liberated. The great sage Pandit Shri Ra Sharma Acharya also travelled a lot for enlightening his own soul and uniting so many others. The great scriptures of Bharat have so many stories of the people who travelled across Bharat and the Whole World in search for true knowledge, spreading the knowledge and achieving the higher states of consciousness to reach the enlightened state. There are many stories of great sages and enlightened people who achieved coherence with nature through their practices and travelled the world for spreading that knowledge.

Travelling across Bharat has a great history with greatest aims. In comparison to these aims, travelling for fun, adventure and relaxation is merely nothing compared with its potential. Nowadays, travelling for achieving such higher state of consciousness is not possible due to busy and sedentary lifestyle. But we can move forward toward achieving wellness in this sedentary life which is full of stress, anxiety, and helplessness. Wellness is a very complex and multidimensional concept that goes beyond the mere definition of health. It is a holistic approach to a fulfiled and balanced life. It combines physical, emotional and social aspects of well-being with the concept of balance among them (Eriksson et al., 2023). Thus, wellness speaks both of the absence of disease and, in addition, that positively incorporates the actions, choices and lifestyles leading to a total healthy state. The concept finds its application in health insurance, personal health management and tourism, each bringing in its perspectives and uses. Wellness is often equated with health, which includes a proactive approach to living a balanced life. This perspective encourages individuals to engage in practices that promote overall well-being, considering the interconnectedness of various life dimensions and the impact of external factors, such as health disparities (Pomputius et al., 2019). Considering all these things, wellness is taking us to higher states of life, that is, towards the approach of fulfilment, which can be achieved when a person is living in harmony with this nature.

1.2 Nature: The Source of Harmony

This concept of achieving fulfilment through living in harmony with nature is deeply rooted in various cultural and philosophical perspectives. This idea and practice emphasises the importance of understanding the nature and respecting it. This can lead to a more meaningful and balanced lifestyle after travelling amidst nature. By this method, aligning oneself with the natural cycles can lead to peace of mind and fulfilment to move towards the state of wellness (Frerich, 2022). In fact, nature is the source of wisdom. The Mandailing community is also promoting the concept of 'Poda Na Lima', which emphasises compassion and ecological balance, viewing nature as a source of wisdom rather than an object for exploitation (Muhajir, 2023).

Nature itself, expressed through rivers, mountains, forests, open skies, and hills, etc., serves as a vital source of energy through various renewable resources, primarily solar and telluric energy. These energy sources are essential for sustaining both natural ecosystems and human-made systems. Other than that, nature itself has the divine power in it. When someone goes amidst nature and surrenders themselves to this divine cosmic nature, it starts reflecting in the human body, which is made up of the same five elements present in the nature. With these properties of nature, we can see, observe and quantify, one of the biggest impacts of nature, its heeling capacity.

1.3 Science of Getting Super Coherent With Nature

Living beings choose data from their environment, process it according to a programme (in this situation one that will assure the highest possible chance of survival), and provide an output of organization (which subsequently serves as a source of raw materials and information for other life forms). This is a precise depiction of how living beings function, so it is not unexpected that a deeper understanding of life has coincided with the environment of them. Many research works show that spending time amidst nature has a positive impact on an individual's health and well-being (Avecillas-Torres et al., 2025; Frerich, 2022).

Nature itself is super conscious about life and living things; nothing in this nature is without any reason, as light waves carry both energy and information from the sun to the earth for all the processes of photosynthesis, carbonisation, and many more. It is no accident that the amount of energy contained in visible light is perfectly matched to the energy needed to carry out most chemical reactions in plants, human beings and other species (Watson L, 1988). Electromagnetic radiation covers a wide range of possible frequencies, but both sunlight and life are confined to the same minute section of a particular spectrum. And so, it is difficult to avoid the conclusion that everything present in nature is directly connected and dependent on the other. All of these interconnected things have some sort of frequency matching for working in harmony and enhance each other's productivity.

An electric field is a place where certain actions occur, but we can't see or hear them. When an electric charge enters this field, forces of electric field affect this new electric charge. Every atom has an electric charge, and it is influenced by the field around it. Living organisms have their own bioelectric field around them, which is the contribution of each and every cell in their body (Tuszynski, 2019). Even simple organisms, like Euglena, have their own fields that change as they build their structures from atoms and molecules. This field can be measured to understand their overall structure or specific cells and different parts of the body. Each body part works and develops its own potential based on its function (Watson, 1988).

All these minute electric fields of the organs of living organisms contribute to a measurable electromagnetic field around the living organisms, which is also known as the aura of living beings (Sizov, 2021). Semyon Kirlian was the first to capture the subtle energy field using an electronic instrument; he accidently discovered that if an object on a photographic plate is connected to a source of high voltage, small corona discharges create an image on the photographic plate. After his research, the Kirlian camera was developed, through which scientists were able to photograph the electromagnetic fields (Iovine, 1994). Even though the Kirlian photography remains a controversial topic for almost a century, now it is used as the instrument to check the electromagnetic fields around the living beings; no matter it's a plant or a human, all of the living beings are having these electromagnetic fields around them, with so many atoms contributing to this field (containing charged particles in it).

When any of the two electromagnetic fields interact with each other, there comes the role of coherence or interaction of two fields, and the resultant of these fields is going to impact both of the sources. Getting in resonance with the fields of nature is giving the state of coherence and making the living being super coherent. So, the ways of interacting with nature will improve the resonating fields of human beings who travel in the midst of nature. Hence, nature-based tourism (NBT) enhances the overall well-being of the tourists. At the same time if the tourists are not aware and connected with nature, their frequencies will be harmful for nature, and they can unconsciously deploy the fields of nature. So, the concept of CNBT leads to a path of self-realization and the overall enhancement of life quality and well-being of the tourists.

1.4 Method of Achieving Coherence with Nature

Achieving coherence with nature requires a multifaceted approach that integrates urban design, ecological principles, and community engagement amidst rapid urbanisation and environmental degradation. To ensure sustainability and resilience within urban environment and nature, we need to synthesise the strategies that will foster a harmonious relationship between humans and their natural surroundings. Similar to the Azheke village model, effective urban design incorporates traditional ecological knowledge (TEK) and biophilic design, promoting sustainable resource use and enhancing urban ecosystem health (Wu et al., 2024). Another example is the forest-based model at a tourism destination, which had a great potential to attract tourist interested in wellness, and it could have a great impact on local communities (Parashar & Agarwal, 2023). Many other research works are giving their insights on nature-based health tourism and their indulgence with youth (Boere, 2021).

Overall, NBT seems to be a new and sustainable form of tourism. There are so many case studies and research papers (Avecillas-Torres et al., 2025), showing positive effects on the well-being of tourists while they are engaged in nature-based tours. With these case studies and research studies, it is evident that NBT is a growing and trending field of tourism industry.

1.5 Conscious Nature-Based Tourism

NBT is not so much of the journey outward but it is more the journey inward amidst nature; it's an experience that grounds the tourists with their roots, mirrors all the life diversions, and reminds their place in the universe. Imagine waking up to birds singing rather than to an alarm clock, to step out into the crisp mountain air, to feel that coarse sand running through one's toes while listening to the almost silent lull of the ocean. This is what nature tourism is all about.

But CNBT takes a step further, though. It evolves the intentions of tourists and awareness of their own steps leaving marks on the large communities and whole ecosystem. We nourish ourselves on views, achieve balance by our choice and recognise that nature is not merely the setting of only adventures; it is inhabited by many as being reliant upon its equilibrium (Buckley, 2020). The essence of CNBT is that:

> It makes us realize we do not stand apart from nature; we are nature and nature is within us.

When we indulge our consciousness with the travelling, we ensure such landscapes, cultures, and delicate ecosystems should be there, waiting to welcome other wide-eyed travellers after us for more generations (Lesar et al., 2019).

Hence, the core principles of CNBT include:

- becoming coherent with nature;
- minimising negative impacts on nature and culture;
- environmentally responsible behaviour;
- generating direct income from conservation;
- educating travellers;
- maintaining ecological responsibilities and sustainability;
- use of local materials and labour;
- emphasis on experiencing nature.

The technique for achieving this coherence through tourism practice is known as CNBT.

> *Conscious Nature Based Tourism is*
>
> A subject to *learn*
>
> Experience to *gain*
>
> Spreading *awareness*
>
> Achieving *wellness*
>
> Becoming *responsible*
>
> Learning the *art*
>
> To become super coherent with *nature.*

2. Literature Review

The concept of wellness through CNBT emphasises the profound connection between nature and human well-being. Research indicates that engaging with natural environments can significantly enhance mental health, reduce stress and foster emotional resilience. This synthesis of findings highlights various pathways through which nature tourism can promote wellness, ultimately leading to a more coherent and fulfilling experience for participants. It suggests that more frequent intervention is needed for long-term effect.

2.1 Nature Connection and Well-Being

Imelda Avecillas-Torres worked with 67 university students suffering with anxiety, depression and stress disorders. The DASS-21 is used to evaluate changes in mental health before and after the intervention, which involved a tour in the Tinajillas Río Gualaceño Protected Forest, Ecuador. The results showed significant reduction in disorders and improvement in mental health whereas the 6-month follow-up report shows no long-term significance of the intervention. In this study, nature tourism was proven to be effective as a non-pharmacological treatment for patients as multiple studies show it dramatically reduces symptoms of depression, anxiety and stress in patients after their nature tourism experience (Avecillas-Torres et al., 2024, 2025).

Furthermore, studies show the different aspects of impact on well-being through NBT . This study conducted by *Rachel Clissold and team at Mt. Barney Lodge, in Queensland, Australia* displays further aspects of well-being such as physical health, psychological health as well as spiritual enriching activities. Researchers aimed to observe and quantify the various dimensions of wellness experiences in this natural setting. These data have been collected from 72 tourists, allowing for a rich exploration of their experiences and perceptions, and the findings revealed that nature can enhance physical, mental, emotional and social well-being, providing therapeutic benefits that can be harnessed through nature tourism. Researchers recommended the development of structured tourism packages that encourage consistent contact with nature and foster a sense of connectedness. Such packages should focus on self-development and transformative experiences, ultimately contributing to the lasting well-being of both people and the planet. This research highlights the importance of integrating wellness into tourism practices, showcasing how nature can play a crucial role in enhancing overall health and well-being (Clissold et al., 2022).

Emma Pope and Henna Konu in their study "*Nature Connection and Well-being in Tourism Experiences*" state that tourism is linked to meaningful and emotional experiences, which are responsible for therapeutic benefits of nature, promoting mental health, enhancing wellness, connecting more with nature, and enhancing overall wellness of the tourist. With this, they worked with an ethnographical approach for data collection and used data from tourists' interview to allow in depth understanding of qualitative personal experiences and nuances of nature connectedness. This suggests sustainable and wellness-oriented tourism options contribute to a deeper understanding of emotional and psychological benefits of tourism through nature engagement. This could pave the way for further studies exploring the intersection of tourism, nature and well-being.

The study by *Imelda Avecillas-Torres* named as 'Beyond Rest: Nature Tourism and its Measurable Effect on Mental Well-Being Through the Reduction of Depression, Anxiety and Stress' states the short-term benefits of nature tourism are well mapped, but still there is a need for further understanding of how long the benefits can be sustained from a single engagement with nature without any further assistance (Avecillas-Torres et al., 2024). This indicates an opportunity for nature-based interventions that motivate less passive and more active contacts with nature.

As the studies suggesting short-term and long-term impacts of NBT as an intervention, some of the specific studies highlight its therapeutic potential like *Role and significance of nature-based health tourism in the Himalayan region* by *Arunesh Parashar and Prachi Agarwal.* This study shows that the Himalaya region serves as an example of how natural areas can possess curative qualities. This describes the role of humanity and nature working together towards better health (Parashar & Agarwal, 2024).

2.2 Multidimensional Nature of Wellness

The concept of conscious NBT is generally described as a very holistic umbrella that includes physical, emotional, social, and spiritual well-being (Eriksson et al., 2023; Kovalova et al., 2024). It is viewed as a continuum of wellness moving away from its common understanding (Eriksson et al., 2023).

2.3 Wellness Programmes and Initiatives

Wellness programs and initiatives include a great number of fitness challenges, dietary modifications and lifestyle changes provided by the insurance companies so that their client may take this opportunity to develop healthy living. They assure a profit-sensitive statement of all the insurers as it can not only reduce the future health claims but also awards them more revenue (Roopashree & Kapadia, 2024).

2.4 Wellness in Personal Health and Lifestyle

Wellness for women means a broad infusion of physical exercise, nutrition, stress management, and mental health considerations into daily life (Kovalova et al., 2024). It includes really practical advice, such as simple exercises and healthy habits, worked out according to one's own needs (Kovalova et al., 2024).

2.5 Wellness Tourism

If Wellness Tourism focuses on staying healthy-then it is all about preventive health measures: stress- and anti-ageing-oriented programs, promoting physical and mental health in active ways (Sylchuk & Kyrpichenkova, 2023).Wellness, as such, is a service innovation in the hospitality industry, offering opportunities for better health and well-being. The mental aspect of health and wellness plays a crucial role in this framework. Also, a wellness approach philosophically integrates the mind, body and spirit in their overall quality (Hu & Hydon, 2024).

More than 20 research studies have been studied and a few studies are mentioned here. These research studies give their valuable insights on the concept of wellness, NBT and CNBT. The impact of implementation has also been discussed in some of these research articles based on different nature-based models. These studies work as evidence that the implementation of CNBT is helpful in improving the mental health and reaching to wellness.

3. Methodology

Research methodology consists of research design, research data, and analysis.

Self-elaboration:

Fig. 1.1 elaborates the research methodology in detail, with exploration of its design, data and analysis.

3.1 Design

This research is based on a systematic review, where observation methods are used, and the researcher tries to explore and describe all of the concerns regarding the research problems and objectives. Hence, the research exploratory and descriptive.

3.2 Data

The research is qualitative in nature, consisting theories, constructs and concepts as well as secondary data from journals, articles and research studies carried out in the same concerning topic.

3.3 Analysis

This research work is based on distinguishing terms, analyzing the understandings they refer to and represent them. Hence, there will be conceptual and logical analysis of all data collected. This is an exploratory study, which aims to explore:

(1) difference between health and wellness;

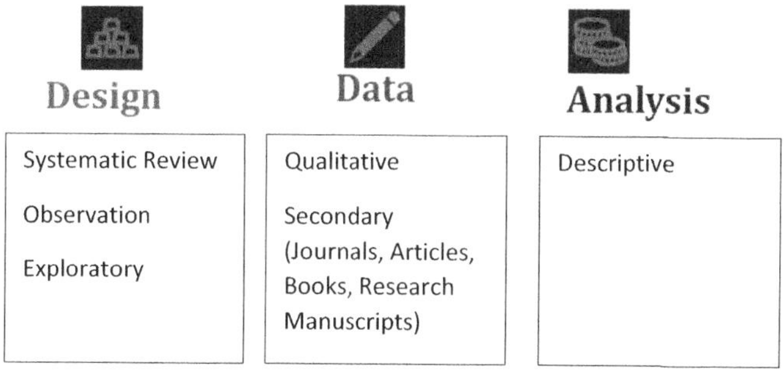

Fig. 1.1. Research Methodology.

(2) difference between NBT and CNBT;
(3) impact of CNBT to achieve wellness;
(4) wellness in contrast with super coherence with nature;
(5) importance of CNBT in achieving wellness and becoming super coherent with nature.

The researcher used different secondary resources such as books, research papers, magazines, internet etc. related to wellness, conscious tourism and coherence with nature and also tried to show the relation between wellness and NBT as a tool to become super coherent with nature.

4. Concept and Interconnection

Health, well-being, and wellness are sometimes used interchangeably; however, they do not express the same purpose. They contribute significantly to a person's overall quality of life.

Health: According to the World Health Organization (WHO), health is 'a state of complete physical, mental and social well-being and not merely the absence of disease or infirmity' (WHO, 1948). This definition makes it clear that health is more than just the absence of disease but an overall status which includes the mental, physical and social state of a person. If there are no medical challenges, an individual may then still grapple with mental health or social separation, affecting overall well-being.

Well-being: Well-being is comparatively a broader and more subjective term, embracing life satisfaction, emotional stability, and a sense of meaning. In its 2020 report, WHO defined well-being as 'the positive state of being experienced by individuals and societies', that is, quality of life with a meaningful-alive experience. Whereas health can be medically quantified through various assessments, well-being is primarily understood by the self-reported levels of happiness, fulfilment and resilience (Dodge et al., 2012).

Wellness: Wellness is the constant activities pursued for instilling habits and behaviours in oneself leading to a better quality of living. The Global Wellness Institute defines wellness as 'an active pursuit of activities, choices and lifestyles (that) lead to a state of holistic health' (GWI, 2021). Unlike health, which may take a passive form (one can be healthy and do nothing), wellness is a conscious mode, requiring deliberate steps to ensure that one regularly exercises, eats properly, reduces stress and builds social connections (Roscoe, 2009).

Conscious Nature-Based Tourism: CNBT as explained in introduction of this research is the practice of tourists in which they have to be consciously active for understanding nature and their own body system. Overall, we see CNBT is defined by this one core principle: 'Becoming coherent with nature'. All other components of CNBT are contributing in their own ways as follows:

- Minimising negative impacts on nature and culture will lead to sustainability and long-term resilience of tourism practices.

- Environmentally responsible behaviour is going to rescue our life sources, and the nature of our surroundings will be ecologically wealthy.
- Generating direct income from conservation of heritage sites, beautiful forests, natural settings of hill stations and beauty of mountains.
- Educating travellers for being responsible for their actions is the most important thing for sustainability of such CNBT practices.
- Use of local materials and labour will be worth for economic growth of the locals.
- Emphasis on experiencing nature is going to reduce the irresponsible behaviour from the behaviour of tourists and locals too.

But the one and only postulate of CNBT is the root of all these other postulates.

Self-elaboration:

Fig. 1.2 is expressing researchers understanding on the basis of literature review and findings of the root of CNBT. According to the definitions of CNBT and Wellness, it is clear that CNBT is promoting the wellness, which is having three components in it: (1) Conscious act, (2) self-directional and (3) evolving state of concise of tourist.

All these terms are used in different places for different purposes while all these are connected to tourism practices, but wellness is the term most connected to conscious tourism activities. The core principles of CNBT include environmental sustainability, health-driven experiences, integration of local context and the creation of authentic places that foster a symbiotic relationship between humans and nature, promoting well-being while conserving sensitive ecosystems. All these components of CNBT are going to lead the tourists towards the progressive state of wellness.

Wellness itself is multidimensional in nature, with positive and affirmative thoughts, but the key concept of the figure shows that the main purpose of CNBT is becoming coherent with nature and every aspect of it. Because this

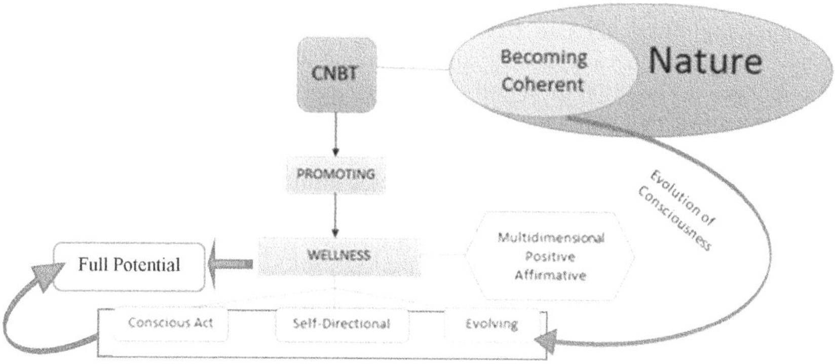

Fig. 1.2. Connection of CNBT and Wellness.

nature and we human beings are capable of being connected with each other, we just become distant apart from our roots and got disconnected with nature.

If we reconnect with our roots and build coherence with nature, we naturally elevate to higher states of consciousness. Like an internal evolution, this conscious alignment with nature enables individuals to act with greater awareness, purpose and harmony (Capra, 1996).When individuals align with nature's rhythms, they experience greater emotional stability, mental clarity, and overall well-being (Kabat-Zinn, 1990). All components of wellness – physical, mental, emotional, and spiritual – begin to manifest effortlessly when consciousness expands beyond ego-driven existence into a more connected and holistic state (Wilber, 2000).

When we perceive nature as an extension of ourselves, rather than something separate, we cultivate a sense of inner peace and ecological responsibility (Naess, 1989). This interconnectedness allows for a deeper transformation where wellness is no longer something we strive for but a natural reflection of our elevated consciousness (Wallace & Benson, 1972).

5. Findings and Conclusion

This study proposes that CNBT offers a powerful and sustainable form of tourism that enhances profound well-being, deep connectedness to nature and a more coherent relation with the environment (Hall et al., 2015). This could be a transformative opportunity for all the tourists for getting back to their roots and achieving the permanent bliss not only the temporary happiness. Unlike modern tourism, which mostly pursues transient relaxation or entertainment, CNBT can be a transformational experience that benefits both the tourist and the local communities while contributing to sustainability and conservation of the environment. First of all, this study would attract the people who wanted to be healthy and interested in achieving wellness, but they are not spending time in nature. CNBT activates the lodged wellness aspirations and strives to comprehend its psychological state in a balanced form. By inviting travellers to consciously sink down into nature's arm, CNBT awakens mental refreshment, emotional and physical balance (Kabat-Zinn, 1990). This research indicates that being in nature reduces stress, enhances immune function and boosts cognitive functioning – all essential for a holistic sense of well-being (Frumkin et al., 2017).

Furthermore, there are many economic and social benefits attainable through CNBT going beyond personal wellness. The conscious tourism trend is building up sustainable revenue for local communities among growing tourism; henceforward, opportunities are afforded eco-friendly enterprises for cultural preservation and the growth of responsible tourism. When travelers adopt local customs and environmental traditions, they deepen their respect for indigenous wisdom and sustainable living into responsible global citizens (Hall et al., 2015). Eventually, the paradigm of such a travel form is given in human life or travel styles. When experiences of an overarching 'super coherence' with nature are facilitated, a man will experience elevated consciousness, not temporary fulfilment but something deeper and lasting. Thus, CNBT poses as an indispensable way of healing for both mankind and the planet in the greater movement to a sustainable and meaningful existence.

References

Avecillas-Torres, I., Herrera-Puente, S., Galarza-Cordero, M., Coello-Nieto, F., Farfán-Pacheco, K., Alvarado-Vanegas, B., Ordóñez-Ordóñez, S., & Espinoza-Figueroa, F. (2024). *Beyond rest: Nature tourism and its measurable effect on mental well-being through the reduction of depression, anxiety and stress.* https://doi.org/10.20944/preprints202411.0831.v1

Avecillas-Torres, I., Herrera-Puente, S., Galarza-Cordero, M., Coello-Nieto, F., Farfán-Pacheco, K., Alvarado-Vanegas, B., Ordóñez-Ordóñez, S., & Espinoza-Figueroa, F. (2025). Nature tourism and mental well-being: Insights from a controlled context on reducing depression, anxiety, and stress. *Sustainability*, *17* (2), 654. https://doi.org/10.3390/su17020654

Boere, R. (2021, September 8). *Nature-based tourism: Benefits and youth involvement — Youth4Nature.* Youth4Nature. https://www.youth4nature.org/blog/nature-based-tourism-benefits-and-youth-involvement

Buckley, R. (2020). Nature tourism and mental health: Parks, happiness, and causation. *Journal of Sustainable Tourism*, *28*(9), 1409–1424. https://doi.org/10.1080/09669582.2020.1742725

Capra, F. (1996). *The web of life: A new scientific understanding of living systems.* Anchor Books. https://www.penguinrandomhouse.com/books/24149/the-web-of-life-by-fritjof-capra/

Clissold, R., Westoby, R., McNamara, K. E., & Fleming, C. (2022). Wellbeing outcomes of nature tourism: Mt Barney Lodge. *Annals of Tourism Research Empirical Insights*, *3*(2), 100077. https://doi.org/10.1016/j.annale.2022.100077

Dodge, R., Daly, A. P., Huyton, J., & Sanders, L. D. (2012). The challenge of defining well-being. *International Journal of Wellbeing*, *2*(3), 222–235. https://doi.org/10.5502/ijw.v2i3.4

Eriksson, M., Ekström-Bergström, A., Arvidsson, B., Jormfeldt, H., Thorstensson, S., Åström, U., Lundgren, I., & Roxberg, Å. (2023). Meaning of wellness in caring science based on Rodgers's evolutionary concept analysis. *Scandinavian Journal of Caring Sciences.* https://doi.org/10.1111/scs.13196

Frerich, B. (2022). *Harmony with nature* (pp. 15–49). Oxford University Press eBooks. https://doi.org/10.1093/oso/9780197574911.003.0002

Frumkin, H., Bratman, G. N., Breslow, S. J., Cochran, B., Kahn Jr, P. H., Lawler, J. J., Levin, P. S., Tandon, P. S., Varanasi, U., Wolf, K. L., & Wood, S. A. (2017). Nature contact and human health: A research agenda. *Environmental Health Perspectives*, *125*(7), 075001. https://doi.org/10.1289/EHP1663

Global Wellness Institute. (2021). *Defining wellness: The global wellness economy report.* https://globalwellnessinstitute.org

Hall, C. M., Gössling, S., & Scott, D. (2015). *The Routledge handbook of tourism and sustainability.* Routledge. https://doi.org/10.4324/9780203072332

Hu, M., & Hydon, S. (2024). *Promoting mental health and well-being* (pp. 84–92). Oxford University Press. https://doi.org/10.1093/oso/9780197603413.003.0007

Iovine, J. (1994). *Kirlian photography: A hands-on guide*. CiNii Research. https://cir.nii.ac.jp/crid/1130000798155285888

Kabat-Zinn, J. (1990). *Full catastrophe living: Using the wisdom of your body and mind to face stress, pain, and illness*. Delacorte Press. https://www.penguinrandomhouse.com/books/89344/full-catastrophe-living-by-jon-kabat-zinn/

Kovalova, N., Ieremenko, N., Kovalev, V., & Sadovskii, O. (2024). Building program "wellness" for the correction of the figure of women of the first mature age. *Naukovij Časopis Nacìonal'nogo Pedagogìčnogo Unìversitetu Ìmenì M.P. Dragomanova*, *2*(174), 76–81. https://doi.org/10.31392/udu-nc.series15.2024.2(174).18

Lesar, L., Weaver, D., & Gardiner, S. (2019). From spectrum to multiverse: A new perspective on the diversity of quality control tools for sustainable tourism theory and practice. *Journal of Travel Research*, *59*(3), 424–449. https://doi.org/10.1177/0047287519841715

Muhajir, A. (2023). Harmony with nature. *Andalas International Journal of Socio-Humanities*, *5*(2), 75–82. https://doi.org/10.25077/aijosh.v5i2.54

Naess, A. (1989). *Ecology, community, and lifestyle: Outline of an ecosophy*. Cambridge University Press. https://doi.org/10.1017/CBO9780511525599

Parashar, D. A., & Agarwal, P. (2023, December 30). *Forest-based model: A nature-based health tourism practice at tourism destinations*. https://papers.ssrn.com/sol3/papers.cfm?abstract_id=4909223

Parashar, A., & Agarwal, P. (2024). *Role and importance of nature-based health tourism in the Himalayan Region* (pp. 143–157). IGI Global. https://doi.org/10.4018/979-8-3693-0823-3.ch014

Pomputius, A., Stoyan-Rosenzweig, N., Selfe, T. K., Morgan-Daniel, J., Ansell, M., & Tennant, M. R. (2019). *Assessing need and evaluating programs for a health science center library's wellness initiative*. https://doi.org/10.29242/LAC.2018.79

Pope, E., & Konu, H. (2024). *Nature connection and wellbeing in tourism experiences* (pp. 119–136). Edward Elgar Publishing. https://doi.org/10.4337/9781803924342.00016

Roopashree, M. R., & Kapadia, D. (2024). Study on wellness programs offered by the health insurance companies. *International Journal of Preventive Medicine and Health*. https://doi.org/10.54105/ijpmh.c1043.04040524

Roscoe, L. J. (2009). Wellness: A review of theory and research. *Journal of Counseling and Development*, *87*(2), 216–226. https://doi.org/10.1002/j.1556-6678.2009.tb00570.x

Sizov, R. A. (2021). The physical aura of person during life and after death in physics with real magnetic charges. *European Journal of Applied Physics*, *3*(5), 47–50. https://doi.org/10.24018/ejphysics.2021.3.5.108

Sylchuk, T., & Kyrpichenkova, O. (2023). Wellness tourism as service innovation of the hospitality industry. *Pričornomors'kì Ekonomìčnì Studiï*, *79*. https://doi.org/10.32782/bses.79-35

Tuszynski, J. A. (2019). *The bioelectric circuitry of the cell* (pp. 195–208). Springer eBooks. https://doi.org/10.1007/978-3-030-21293-3_11

Wallace, R. K., & Benson, H. (1972). The physiology of meditation. *Scientific American*, *226*(2), 84–90. https://www.scientificamerican.com/article/the-physiology-of-meditation/

Watson, L. (1988). *Beyond supernature: A new natural history of the supernatural: Watson, Lyall: Free download, borrow, and streaming: Internet archive*. Internet Archive. https://archive.org/details/beyondsupernatur0000wats

Wilber, K. (2000). *Integral psychology: Consciousness, spirit, psychology, therapy*. Shambhala Publications. https://www.shambhala.com/integral-psychology-1495.html

World Health Organization. (1948). *Constitution of the World Health Organization*. https://www.who.int/about/governance/constitution

World Health Organization. (2020). *Mental health and well-being: A global priority*. https://www.who.int

Wu, Y., Azmi, A., Ibrahim, R., Ghafar, A. A., & Salih, S. A. (2024). Creating a sustainable urban ecosystem: The Azheke village model. *Smart and Sustainable Built Environment*. https://doi.org/10.1108/sasbe-10-2023-0292

Chapter 2

The Rise of Wellness Tourism: Bridging Wellness, Nature and Tourism

Shila Mondol, Ipseeta Satpathy, Arpita Nayak and B. C. M. Patnaik

KIIT University, India

Abstract

In this chapter, theoretical frameworks related to the concept of wellness and nature-based tourism are discussed along with the nature of its framework, its components and prospects for sustainable development. The purpose of study is to explore the current state of wellness practices and natural settings in tourism, new trends, problems and perspectives. The research uses qualitative exploratory analysis and secondary sources to explore wellness integration with nature-based tourism. Data were collected from academic sources, peer-reviewed articles and industry reports. Thematic analysis revealed patterns and theoretical links aligning with the study's goals, ensuring credibility and applicability. Aspects like community empowerment of the local people and rural development are possibilities on the flip side there are draw backs like environmental degradation and over commercialization. The findings and recommendations of this chapter can therefore be useful for policymakers, tourism developers and local communities in their attempt to develop sustainable wellness tourism models. It provides a chance to fulfil the commercial goals while being true to a company's values and respecting environment that creates the potential for improving benefits for all the involved parties. By integrating wellness and nature-based tourism within a structured framework, this chapter contributes to the discourse on sustainable and transformative tourism practices. It serves as a foundational resource for researchers, practitioners and policymakers aiming to enhance the global tourism landscape. This chapter strengthens the literature in the area of sustainable and transformative

Nature, Wellness and Sustainability in Health Tourism, 17–39

doi:10.1108/978-1-83742-029-220261002

tourism by presenting both the relationship between wellness and nature-based tourism and a clear framework.

Keywords: Wellness tourism; nature-based tourism; sustainable tourism; eco-tourism; cultural immersion; rural development; sustainable practices

1. Introduction

Wellness tourism, according to the Global Wellness Institute (GWI), is travel aimed at preserving or improving one's own well-being. With so much illness ingrained in modern travel, wellness tourism has the potential to counteract these drawbacks and transform travel into a chance to preserve and enhance our overall health. Two of the most significant trends that have evolved within the sphere of international tourism are wellness tourism and, to some extent, nature tourism (NT) that is covering both domestic and foreign travel. These two types of tourism have different but related concepts and objectives creating immense value to the individual and the environment. This chapter discusses the concept of wellness tourism and nature-based tourism and explains the increasing importance of these trends in the tourism industry and the aim and objectives of this research to help to understand these important trends in the tourism industry (Luck, 2021).

And wellness tourism is described as travel that is taken in quest of improved health in body, mind and spirit. Such type of tourism also involves taking spa treatments, yoga camps, meditating, strength training, aerobics and other related forms of body and soul enhancing procedures. The phenomenon of wellness tourism can be associated with comfortable SPA-hotel and environmentally friendly organic and Bio hotels. While nature-based tourism is coincident with travel and recreation that centres on the appreciation of nature. This ranges from trekking, bird watching, armed camping and National Park or protected area tours. This form of tourism has its origin in the desire to increase appreciation for nature, understand nature and embrace its preservation. While wellness tourism is centered on personal health and well-being, NT focuses on respect for nature and promotes healthy and sustainable practices (Andreu et al., 2021; Kim, 2015).

While the purpose of wellness and nature-based tourism is quite different, they are interconnected. Quite often, people going in search of wellness also look for comfort in nature, and various forms of NT involve aspects of wellness; this can include mindfulness practices or staying in an environmentally friendly or off-grid property. It is therefore important that both Domains pertain to modern travellers' needs – physiological, psychological and emotional (Haukeland et al., 2021).

Wellness and NT is also an indication of changes in social trends towards exercise, profound change in attitude towards nature and a more demanding approach to the idea of vacation. Today, people are often overwhelmed with the life rhythm and the number of innovations they face; thus, people search for travel experiences that make them feel relaxed and healthier. Thus, wellness tourism caters for these needs by providing isolated offerings that are packaged as relaxation, self-improvement and enhancement trips. At the same time, developing nature-based tourism has emerged as a key focus since people and populous communities begun to appreciate the importance of ecosystems, primarily engaging in activities that will support the upkeep of global well-being. In the contemporary world, tourists increasingly seek experiences that are closer to nature, leading to a growing concern for biodiversity, ecosystem conservation, and sustainability. This need is met by nature-based tourism but at the same time communicating knowledge and ideas on the balance of natural systems and conservation of nature (Agarwal et al., 2023).

The application to the case of wellness tourism and NT requires a full understanding of the object of study and the correlations between the two phenomena. To avoid confusion as to each of these concepts' role and contributions to promoting the overall travel experiences, it is necessary to demarcate these concepts. Wellness tourism involved the marketing of health tourism programmes that involved the supplementation of the physical, mental and emotional need of an individual like spa treatment, meditation and fitness programmes; nature-based tourism involves marketing of tourism that involves activities such as hiking, bird watching and visiting protected areas. In many cases, these forms of tourism intertwine because the environments that natural travel focuses on help to enrich the wellness tourism. Analyzing the relevance and trends of such tourism forms showed their relation to demographic and social changes, as well as the influence of sustainable development goals. Following the global trends towards the enhancement of the importance placed upon the state of health and the environment, these categories of tourism could be identified as the rapidly developing segments of tourism proving people's longing for meaningful and restorative tourism experiences. Economic and environmental consequences also heighten their significance because both wellness and nature-based tourism help boost income and safeguard the environment. Both of these tourism forms are revenue-generating activities that create employment and promote sustainable policies and therefore should be seen as economic enablers as well as environmental managers.

Wellness and nature-based tourism platforms provide solutions to worldwide challenges regarding mental health and environmental destruction and community concerns. Wellness tourism consists of frameworks which enable physical holistic and mental wellness through yoga retreats, meditation programmes, spa therapies and natural healing methods. The therapeutic aspect of wellness practices fights mental disorders while improving individual mental health to achieve better life outcomes which benefits entire communities. Natural tourism promotes sustainability while generating appreciation for Earth's landscapes, which protects biodiversity together with nature preservation. Tourism combines naturist-themed activities with high-end luxury accommodation to deliver happier lives together with sustainability-focused preservation of natural environments. Developed systems by policymakers should unite economic potential with sustainable elements while backing local communities alongside heritage conservation and green practice support. Tourism operators should develop experiences which follow wellness and sustainability principles to create innovative packages that offer holistic memorable journeys to travellers. The selection of wellness and nature-based tourism serves to create both beneficial social impacts alongside environmental sustainability. Travellers who practise responsible tourism gain enriching experiences, which motivates others to follow leading behavioural examples. The combination of wellness and nature-based tourism initiative creates opportunities which transform global challenges into solutions for environmental preservation and community development and mental health promotion.

2. Research Questions

- What are the key components of wellness and nature-based tourism, and how do they foster physical, mental and spiritual well-being?
- How do cultural immersion and eco-conscious practices enhance visitor engagement and promote sustainability in wellness and nature-based tourism?
- What emerging trends and challenges influence the growth and sustainability of wellness and nature-based tourism in the global tourism industry?

3. Research Objectives

- To identify and define the interconnections between wellness tourism and nature-based tourism, focusing on their contributions to sustainable development.
- To analyze the role of cultural and environmental elements in shaping tourist experiences and satisfaction in these forms of tourism.
- To examine trends, challenges and strategies for integrating wellness and nature-based tourism to ensure long-term sustainability and economic benefits.

4. Research Methodology

The research adopts a qualitative exploratory method based on secondary data to analyze wellness connections with nature-based tourism. The study started by creating three main objectives that helped choose recent peer-reviewed literature and industry reports from relevant sources. Researchers collected data from three different scholarly databases including Google Scholar as well as Elsevier and trusted reputed publishing sources. Studies focusing on wellness tourism together with nature-based experiences and sustainability and community impact were included in this review, but non-academic material and promotional content remained outside the analysis boundaries. The thematic analysis method grouped the gathered data into conceptual themes that matched the research targets to keep the inquiry-to-insight progression smooth.

5. Conceptual Foundations of Wellness and Nature-Based Tourism

Wellness and nature-based tourism theory establishes fundamental principles to study their historical development and conceptual links and academic frameworks in social and ecological settings. Sun-drenched tourist activities that date back to ancient therapeutic baths and meditative practices now handle complete physical health needs and the search to uncover natural areas has become linked with conservation work. These travel sectors unite naturally because wellness activities typically gain importance when practised within natural locations while sharing similar objectives for promoting health and sustainable stewardship of nature and active local engagement. Wellness tourism applies stress reduction models along with Maslow's hierarchy principles to its theoretical framework, and nature-based tourism implements both biophilia and human–nature connection of ecological principles. The wellness tourism sector and nature-based tourism collaborate to follow sustainable development goals through individual well-being promotion and balanced resource protection. This approach defines thoughtful practices as essential elements that enable personal wellness advancement alongside ecosystem conservation and local community advancement, thus driving sustainable development towards societal progress.

It has originated as human responses to needs for bodily health alongside mental wellness and earth connections. The origins of wellness tourism extend back to early history where Roman thermal baths existed alongside traditional Indian Ayurvedic treatments with Chinese traditional medicine practices of the same nature. The healthcare system developed these therapeutic elements to direct people towards complete mind–body–spirit balance. NT first emerged from the human desire to explore and derive value from unspoiled natural environments. Historical practices such as hiking, wildlife safaris, and forest retreats have enabled urban dwellers to relieve stress, reconnect with their senses, and develop a deeper appreciation for the beauty of nature. Therefore, nature-based tourism shares fundamental relationships with wellness practices. The therapeutic effects of wellness tourism become amplified when tourists interact with forest regions and mountainous terrains and beautiful beachfront areas. Through forest bathing, a practice originating in Japan, individuals harmonize mental clarity with contact with nature to manage stress and enhance overall well-being. Yoga retreats combine physical activity with peaceful natural landscapes to deliver holistic therapeutic encounters that fall into line with nature-based tourism principles. The collaborative link between NT and wellness tourism demonstrates how they satisfy people's increasing interest in transformative encounters which focus on both physical and ecological health (Padma et al., 2022).

A number of theoretical constructs help scholars study wellness and nature-based tourism better at a conceptual level. According to the biophilia hypothesis, humans naturally feel drawn towards nature so they gravitate towards wilderness to rest and recover. According to the theory, nature-based tourism automatically attracts visitors while delivering crucial mental health advantages. Maslow's hierarchy of needs enables the examination of wellness tourism by showing how different human requirements are met when customers access spa healing together with nourishing foods and progress towards personal fulfilment through life-changing wellness programmes. Nature-based tourism and wellness share the same fundamental human motivations along with sustainable lifestyle benefits according to these theoretical frameworks (Qiu et al., 2021).

Nature-based tourism developed as its own sector because humans always yearn to experience nature first-hand. People naturally understand and value natural environments because they provide recreational opportunities while enabling scientific exploration and helping protect wildlife populations. During the era of exploration, societies learnt to identify and value the distinctive characteristics of natural areas which led to the growing development of this touristic form. The institutionalization of nature-based tourism received its major framework during the late 19th century when Yellowstone National Park became the world's first protected area in 1872. Initial steps towards nature-based tourism developed radically to propel its widespread adoption inside national parks and reserves (Haukeland et al., 2023). During the last part of the 20th century, wellness tourism integrated deeply with nature-based travel experiences. Global environmental preservation efforts together with personal wellness approach reached peak visibility during this time. The modern traveller began choosing activities because they combined relaxation with therapeutic treatments and immersion within natural environments. The combination of wellness with NT manifested into next-wave tourist experiences which incorporated environmental consciousness and self-care needs. This product remains popular as people embrace sustainable personal-fitness-oriented genuine travel. Wellness and nature-based tourism has merged into a response which appeals to modern travellers seeking meaningful time with nature alongside their quest for physical and mental health maintenance. The emerging trend demonstrates how these tourism types stay important as they simultaneously serve individual renewal and environmental conservation needs (Björnsdóttir, 2018).

Sustainable NT follows the concept of wellness tourism as both concepts work to improve the living standards and practise environmental conservation. Wellness tourism which is largely about health enhancement distinguishes itself with such activities that have a connection with health such as yoga, spa and fitness activities while NT focusing on ecological awareness and recreation pays much attention to direct contact with nature. The similarity lies in the fact that wellness-promoting activities work most effectively when they are incorporated into natural environments. For instance, practising yoga in forest or meditating on a mountain helps recover from a stressful week in the same way that practising well-being and mindfulness does. The same is true with eco-resorts which involve services such as spa, trails and hiking which appeal to two different clienteles interested in the physical and environmental health. These connections are complemented by a focus on the compatibility of humans and their environment: a subject that is covered by both its Coptic and Old Nubian elements. Wellness tourism promotes change for the better in oneself as well as enhanced productivity, whereas nature-based tourism promotes conservation of natural resources. Combined, they help achieving sustainable tourism, ensuring the protection of wild animals, decreasing emission of greenhouse gases and benefiting people (Padma et al., 2022).

Biologist E.O. Wilson created the Biophilia Hypothesis to describe human nature's deep relationship with nature which scientists trace back to evolutionary distinct patterns. Natural environments consisting of forests, lakes and wildlife trigger both internal psychological states and physical physiological responses in people according to this hypothesis. Our fundamental attachment to nature exists not as an accidental outdoor liking but as an adaptive bond which developed throughout human evolution. During human evolutionary history, our survival depended on established domains where we could access resources and feel protected by harmonious ecosystems. Scientifically, we possess inherent mechanisms that lead us to experience positive responses when surrounded by these environments. The psychological benefits people experience from natural settings derive their explanation from this hypothesis within nature-based tourism. Through activities such as Japan's forest bathing and hiking in national parks, individuals can access the therapeutic aspects of nature by relying on this inherent environmental connection (Joye & De Block, 2011).

The recently developed frameworks on wellness and sustainability address congruency of person and environment asserting equal importance to self-actualization and protection of the environment. These models promote the sustainable action, reduction of waste, protection of the natural resources and support for communities. Both complement the principles of wellness tourism by insisting on ethical mode of consumption and concern (Burke et al., 2024).

The understanding of the history, the connections and theoretical background of wellness and nature-based tourism can help to explain the current fascination and importance of these two fields. These tourism forms meet essential needs of human health and nature seeking while supporting the sustainable development objectives through environmental preservation and community advancement. The development of these specific concepts helps the stakeholders to create experiences that would well fit travellers' requirements for fulfilling and rejuvenating travel and promote responsible tourists using the services of tourists and satisfaction of ecological and cultural resources. On this basis, wellness and nature-based tourism can further develop as innovative spheres of tourism to remain the main driving forces of the world tourism supply.

6. Key Components of Wellness and Nature-Based Tourism

The essential components of wellness and nature-based tourism emerge from plentiful natural resources which play essential roles in travel experiences. These resources present different environments where people find relief from modern pressures to relax their minds as well as restore their physical wellness. The scientific literature shows an established link between natural environments and personal wellness because nature creates therapeutic benefits for body, mind and spirit. Tourism organizations use nature's comforting resources through advertising their wildlife sanctuaries to let visitors experience restorative environments.

Nature provides serene settings throughout forests that match perfectly with forest bathing exercises (shinrin-yoku) and hiking and yoga-based retreats (Prabhakar, 2021). Natural occurrences like forest tree canopies along with leaf whispering and forest smells work together to decrease mental tension and enhance personal health. Mountains create awe-inspiring natural experiences that draw tourism participants who seek adventure and wellness experiences. Mountains provide a complete physical, mental and emotional wellness experience through their hiking passes, religious meditation locations and elevated viewpoints. Beaches form foundational attractions in nature-based tourism because they allow visitors access to ocean waves and salty air and infinite views. Scientific research proves that the rhythmic sound of ocean waves promotes relaxation, and sunbathing and swimming at the beach help people experience the natural world. Hot springs attract visitors through multiple centuries because their mineral water contains healing therapeutic properties. The geothermal sites maintain both therapeutic value for body relaxation and historic cultural meaning at various worldwide locales (Peras et al., 2021).

Nature tours choose forests as their destination because they offer peaceful rest while presenting wildlife encounters together with outdoors recreational activities. Visitors come to these dense, peaceful areas to leave behind the pressure of contemporary life since they unite humans with nature. The human body and mind find resilience while engaging with dense forest trails or while birdwatching in untouched wilderness. Japan's tradition of shinrin-yoku, known as forest bathing, demonstrates these relaxing benefits through exposure to nature which visitors find therapeutic at resorts located among forest habitats. These specialized accommodations prove excellent at shielding visitors from city disruptions while supplying silence which helps people recover mental clarity. The forest sanctuaries provide visitors peace through trees' rustling noises and birds' tweeting which create peaceful environments for self-rehabilitation. In addition to restoration activities, forests act both as educational centres and guardians of the environment. Visitors interested in ecosystem conservation and biodiversity seek out protected forest areas including both the Amazon Rainforest together with Germany's Black Forest. Education programmes and guided tours within these preserved areas provide visitors a deep understanding of wildlife ecosystems while teaching about conservation needs and climate and deforestation risks. Relaxation through natural exploration within forests teaches visitors about life systems while instilling a sense of protection for these habitats. This exposure frequently develops conservation-minded behaviours in people. Feelings from first-hand encounters with forest biodiversity deliver permanent knowledge that strengthens both support for preservation initiatives and people's commitment to greener ways of living. Tourism within forest areas creates both individual relaxation as well as sustains a worldwide shift towards preserving nature and eco-friendly life choices (Rodtook et al., 2024).

Mountains draw tourists because they have long been places for spiritual healing and meditation. Mountains offer amazing natural environments for meditation and yoga while allowing people to breathe clean fresh air and enjoy scenic views during treks and skiing expeditions. Hikers and vacationers flock to mountain regions across the globe especially in the Himalayas Alps and Rockies. Mountains benefit nature by protecting many species of plants and animals. Eco-tourists across the world visit protected mountain zones including Rocky Mountain National Park, USA, and Annapurna Conservation Area, Nepal. Each area gives tours that mix outdoor fun with learning about mountains and shows you how to visit them without harming nature (Pande, 2024).

Beaches have always been places where people achieve emotional relaxation and physical restoration so they function as key parts of wellness tourism. Millions of people travel each year to enjoy sandy beaches and relaxing sun on warm coastal areas. Wellness beach resorts offer both spa services and water recreation while teaching guests to quiet their minds in natural surroundings. Tourist hotspots such as the Maldives, Bali and Caribbean beaches work naturally to help people unwind and improve their physical health. Tourist sites at these locations combine their sustainability initiatives including coral reef restorations and waste handling to make tourism safer for ecosystems. Visitor education shows them how to protect marine environments and creates stronger respect for these essential ecosystems (Smith, 2021).

Hot springs, renowned for their natural geothermal energy and therapeutic properties, are key attractions in wellness travel. The mineral-rich waters, abundant in sulphur, calcium, magnesium and other natural compounds, offer a range of health benefits. These include alleviating arthritis pain, improving certain skin conditions and reducing stress levels. The warmth and composition of geothermal waters work to relax muscles, improve circulation and promote overall well-being, making them a sought-after destination for health-conscious travellers.

Dynamic geothermal springs around the world draw global crowds to places such as the Blue Lagoon of Iceland and Japan's onsen resorts together with Yellowstone National Park for their soothing restorative value. Visitors find relaxation by experiencing geothermal healing while exploring protected ecosystems in these dual-edge destinations. Tourists visit the Blue Lagoon in Iceland because they appreciate its distinctive milky blue waters as well as its therapeutic silica mud benefits for the skin, and they also recognize that the traditional Japanese onsen combine historical roots with holistic wellness principles. Hot spring sites typically enjoy majestic surrounding landscapes as they expand in pristine natural areas. Visitors find the connection to natural surroundings particularly essential because they experience therapeutic benefits in the waters and achieve emotional peace through their surrounding environment. Hot spring resorts create specific wellness destinations which enable people to merge therapeutic treatments and psychological restoration into one integrated experience while offering sustainability-focused operations. Businesses employ eco-friendly construction principles which incorporate boiling geothermal energy into heating systems to reduce their carbon emissions during operation. Responsible tourism flourishes through this approach which protects sensitive natural habitats surrounding attractions while also protecting the environment (Velikova, 2019). Tourists who visit such sites achieve physical recovery and experience the relationship between human health and sustainable natural conservation. The convergence of wellness and sustainability teaches the significance of natural resource respect and maintenance because health of people and earth exist as a single interconnected system (Lin & Soratana, 2023).

Protected natural regions such as national parks allow us to save plants and animals while drawing global tourists. These protected lands defend living things by letting threatened animals stay safe while protecting Earth's natural habitats. Protected areas worldwide draw large numbers of visitors every year notably in successful destinations such as the Serengeti National Park, Great Barrier Reef and Galápagos Islands to promote responsible tourism and environmental learning. Protected areas become the perfect backdrop for health and NT activities. Visitors learn about nature conservation during tours that let them experience snorkelling expeditions and explore wildlife on guided paths across natural regions. Tourism money pays for protected areas to stay protected so future generations can enjoy their unspoiled nature (Hamilton, 2024).

The practice of nature-based and wellness tourism serves both functional and protective purposes regarding natural resource management. Tourism activities centred on nature enable people to experience natural beauty as they develop enhanced knowledge about environmental beauty. Travellers who become aware of nature through tourism experiences end up practising sustainable behaviours as they head home. In addition, tourism for nature rests on two pillars which sustain environmental conservation initiatives. Tourism operators manage their financial earnings through local sustainable initiatives that protect both plant communities and wildlife and their natural habitats. Eco-tourism plans dedicate their funding to projects that establish protected areas as well as wildlife sanctuaries and reforestation activities. The financial backing directly supports natural resource preservation while establishing sustainable management practices which benefit both environmental conservation and natural resource growth. People choose alternative tourism activities running eco-tours or small hospitality services and local product sales as alternatives to timber production or fishing. Local residents benefit from stable income streams alongside environmental stewardship activities because sustainability-based tourism development brings together economic growth and protection of conservation objectives. Through responsible tourism practices, communities can statistically protect their natural environment while achieving financial success. Through their alignment of environmental protection with economic opportunities, nature-based and wellness tourism prove that ecosystem stewardship and wellness advocacy can coexist for securing a sustainable future (Diaz et al., 2023).

The main sources of health and nature-based tourism come from Earth's natural resources which include forests, mountains, beaches, hot springs and protected land. These settings let people enjoy peaceful outdoor time and exciting outdoors while naturally restoring their health through contact with nature. Preserving our natural resources needs equal attention to conservation work to stay sustainable. By running eco-friendly tourism and spreading nature education, we help keep wellness and nature-based tourism going while protecting these valuable resources for future visitors. Wellness activities form the foundation of health promotion throughout the tourism sector. Many tourists discover peace through yoga meditation and mindfulness retreats which help them stop thinking about work problems and learn about themselves. Spa services and thermal baths along with hydrotherapy sessions restore the body and mind through medical treatment. Wellness tourism connects fitness with nature when guests do hiking, forest bathing or nature treks to repair their mental and physical well-being. These wellness choices create multiple ways for travellers to relax and restore balance in their lives during their trips.

Wellness tourism thrives through adding traditional healing methods and local food preparation that help visitors improve their health. Through Ayurveda and tribal rites from various ancient cultures including American Indians, Africans and Polynesians, travellers can learn authentic ways of healthcare that reach back into distant history. In Ayurveda, patients receive custom treatments for body, mind and spirit using natural herbs yoga and nutrition. Native American ceremonies mix physical healing with cultural ways through sweat lodges and spiritual ceremonies. By trying these wellness practices at their destination, travellers can experience better health while discovering the cultural background of the place (Chang et al., 2022).

Cultural integration benefits from local food i which brings healthy regional cooking traditions to travellers from all over the world. The food shows local culture through cooking with fresh local ingredients that follow healthy sustainable practices. The Mediterranean diet stands out because it uses olive oil, fresh vegetables and lean protein to help the heart. People in Japan follow traditional diets with green tea that contains antioxidants plus they eat fermented foods that benefit their digestive system. Wellness resorts and retreats now include these food concepts to let guests discover how culture shapes their overall health experience. Guests who participate in cultural practices discover wellness traits while helping people maintain their traditional ways of life (Lai et al., 2021).

A destination's amenities and infrastructure determine how well nature and wellness tourists enjoy their trips. This sector relies on tourism properties including resorts, hotels and wellness facilities that create private environments to help guests find peace with nature. Wellness resorts combine top spa treatments with luxury services composed of modern wellness facilities and meditation spaces. Eco-lodges prioritize sustainability by using harmless materials in construction and blend perfectly with their natural surroundings while causing little harm to local environments. Wellness facilities located in busy cities and quiet environments offer programmes to detoxify your body plus hydrotherapy treatments and customized fitness plans. Travellers appreciate easier ways to reach these destinations plus updated transportation options. Travellers find wellness destinations easier to reach through well-functioning airport and transportation systems along with properly maintained roadways. Resort and eco-lodge tour operators make it simple for visitors to travel to and from local attractions (Mandić et al., 2018).

To both protect nature and benefit communities' eco-friendly operations must be present in wellness and nature-based tourism businesses. Resorts recognize that efficient resource usage depends on using renewable energy sources and implementing both water-saving systems and waste management programmes.

The main eco-friendly tools include using solar technology plus collecting rainwater and composting to decrease tourism facilities' environmental impact. Tourism must include active community partners and local residents to become long term. Tourism operations that hire local residents at resorts and buy items from nearby farmers help build wealth for people in the area while protecting their cultural traditions. Wellness centres team up with local communities to host community events and nature tours which bring tourism benefits to everyone. Wellness and nature-based tourism succeed best when organizations focus on earth-friendly habits that help both the planet and make tourism stronger in the future (Shaban et al., 2024).

7. Trends and Emerging Practices

Health tourism keeps developing because today's travellers want more options than just basic spa treatments and stay-over clinics. Tourism for wellness now extends far beyond mere spa visits because guests now seek unique adventures and technology-based wellness practices alongside digital detox periods and slow travelling methods. The evolving trends show that wellness tourism industry matches changing traveller wants by offering fresh health-focused services (Hassan et al., 2024).

Current digital connections push us to experience stress and become burned out. The rise of digital detox became popular when people wanted to stop using technology while working on their mental health. Tourism businesses focused on wellness now provide digital detox environments that guide visitors to disable technology while enjoying nature. Digital detox retreat participants practise mindfulness during meditation and nature exploration while taking workshops that build self-connection with the world. Wellness centres and resorts create special digital-free areas and design activities that help guests use technology less. Many eco-lodges near wilderness areas require guests to leave technology at home so they can enjoy their surroundings truly. The rise of slow travel combines with new tourist habits to show that visitors want immersive experiences with destinations. When you travel slowly, you get to know specific places better so you can connect deeper with local traditions and natural surroundings. Wellness tourism works well with slow travel because it helps travellers avoid stress on their journeys and relax even more easily. Launched activities like hiking at a relaxed pace lets travellers enjoy local customs and eating food that comes from the ground rebuilds their energy. The region of Tuscany draws wellness tourists because people there practise slow living through scenic views and digital separation experiences (Talukder et al., 2024).

More than just personalization companies now aim to help people achieve complete wellness through physical and mental methods. Wellness centres now go further than individual spa and meal services to give participants mental health help and life support alongside meditation instruction. People who travel want complete wellness programmes that help them handle life challenges and personal growth areas including stress relief and emotional support. Wellness centres use new technology such as genetic tests and body measurements to develop specific treatment programmes. Travellers experience real health improvements with fitness programmes that match their DNA results and nutritional counselling tools that suit their requirements. These strategies match wellness travel services to individual needs so guests develop stronger bonds with their wellness programmes.

Wellness tourism now better follows regenerative travel methods which aim to improve destinations after visitors depart. Unlike typical sustainability efforts that focus on damage reduction, regenerative travel works to rebuild natural areas and support local communities. More wellness retreat operators integrate regenerative agriculture by practising permaculture to produce natural food for visitors while repairing soils and protecting natural environments. Wellness tourism operators now lead projects that help local communities through hiring practices and education support while preserving traditional healthcare traditions. These efforts upgrade the guest travel experience while building purposeful interactions between visitors and hosts (Kazakov & Oyner, 2021).

Wellness tourism now uses biophilic design principles that combine nature into building spaces. According to the biophilia hypothesis, people naturally connect with nature. Wellness resorts bring nature into their places by designing for more natural lighting and including plants; plus, they use wood and stone as building materials to unite with natural surroundings. Yoga pavilions set in forest settings and spa areas near waterfalls at resorts create real nature experiences that calm both mind and body. Biophilic design enhances the appearance of wellness locations while creating positive health gains that lower stress levels and improve mental clarity (Zhong et al., 2021).

People now recognize social wellness as essential to their overall health because it involves building good relationships and joining community life. Wellness tourism organizes group events such as meditation groups and team-building retreats that help people create deeper relationships and feel part of something. People from different age groups now travel together to take part in wellness activities that everyone can enjoy. Destinations that host family yoga sessions and mindfulness workshops help people of all ages develop together while learning about wellness (Csirmaz, 2015).

Digital detox remains popular, but digital wellness programmes let people enjoy these services online either by choice or because travel proves impossible. You can take meditation courses, exercise lessons and speak with counsellors through digital tools from your current location. Digital wellness programmes help people who wish to practise wellness every day or test out the experience before choosing in-person classes. Digital wellness tourism now adds artificial intelligence (AI) wellness coaches and virtual reality (VR) tools to its services. Through VR and AI technology, users can access mindfulness exercises that lead them to peaceful natural scenes; plus, AI suggests individualized ways to ease stress and stay fit with proper eating habits. Digital wellness tourism combines technology with wellness to create flexible ways that tech fans can enjoy their services (Pacheco, 2021; Stäheli, 2024).

It is now focusing on traditional cultural and ancestral customs to build genuine meaningful trips for tourists. Guests can try Hawaiian lomi lomi massage or Peruvian plant medicine rituals to learn about traditional healing methods when they visit. Wellness tourism destinations use natural healing traditions that match perfectly with how people should care for their minds and bodies. Traditional wellness activities in food also include farm-to-table dining which serves recipes from the past using fresh products from nearby farms. Visitors learn about a destination's history and traditions while helping farmers and artists make a living through these special activities (Gamby et al., 2021).

The travel industry responds to modern traveller expectations and societal movements through custom-made transformative tours and digital detox spaces combined with their use of technology in wellness programmes. Wellness tourism offers customized and long-term transformational programmes as the best way to serve customer demand. The simple acts of unplugging from technology in digital detox and the practice of slow travel help us reconnect better with nature and the customs of our local community to escape from everyday life demands. Wellness programmes benefit from technology by providing important data for better results as well as tools that immerse users in wellness experiences. Wellness tourism's future depends on finding smart ways to combine technology benefits with sacred travel time. Wellness tourism will stay effective for wellness seekers when the industry follows these trends.

8. Challenges and Opportunities in Wellness and Nature-Based Tourism

Tourism sectors focused on wellness and nature are growing fast worldwide thanks to travellers who do activities that promote fitness, restore mental health and let them enjoy nature. As tourism grows fast, it faces important problems like too many visitors' damaging nature while losing authentic local culture. Wellness and nature-based tourism provide ways for rural communities to grow as they build new wealth and strengthen their local people. Strengthening both the sector's positive future performance and environmental protection requires dealing with its current challenges and maximizing its potential benefits (Elmahdy et al., 2017).

Too many visitors now stress the capacity of tourism destinations to maintain their habitats and resources. Many popular wellness destinations including tropical islands and mountain locations resist too many visitors because this crowds natural areas and consumes resources. Heavy foot traffic on trails causes land damage, while visiting coral reefs often destroys natural habitats. Too many tourists hurt nature and damage how well visitors enjoy their locations. When tourists flood popular relaxation sites and vacation spots, they destroy wellness vacationers' goal of peace and privacy. As demand for essential services grows, developers put pressure on local infrastructure systems, especially in rural places that need improvement. Several actions should be combined to solve the problem of over-tourism by setting maximum visitor numbers and promoting travel outside peak times alongside secondary vacation spots. Education efforts teach visitors about environmental protection and show them why local communities need their respect. Stakeholders who adopt responsible tourism plans help reduce over-tourism's problems while protecting the special natural and cultural features of wellness spots (Winter et al., 2019).

The spread of commercial tourism into wellness and nature experiences creates major problems for the industry. Many travellers look for authentic experiences but commercialization diminishes these benefits of destinations and services. When traditional healing practices from nations like India or Australia merge with global trends, they lose their cultural roots and spiritual importance. Luxury wellness facilities quickly dominate the market, so traditional local businesses often struggle to stay visible and active. When tourism locations become excessively similar, they lose their authentic character for tourists. Travellers who want to experience true local culture often struggle to tell real experiences apart from showy commercial versions. Tourism leaders and government figures need to find ways to give customers what they want while holding on to true cultural practices. When tourism operators partner with local people to make travel experiences, they earn both the community and visitors get to enjoy real cultural displays. Our guests will gain better insight when they understand how wellness practices came into being and what makes them special (Luck, 2021).

Wellness and nature-based tourism open new development chances for rural areas through money generation in underserved regions. The main wellness retreats and natural attractions settle in countryside areas that depend heavily on their scenic beauty and traditional local history for tourism operations. When travellers visit these areas, tourism delivers income to the region by creating local jobs and boosting nearby businesses in crafts and farming. Local communities gain better financial opportunities when eco-lodges purchase food from neighbourhood farms and connect with nearby artisans in their regions. Tourism payments help build better healthcare facilities, educational buildings and roads for local communities to live better. Wellness tourism helps local communities keep their natural and cultural resources safe because visitors come to see them. By running cultural tours, nature protection activities and traditional healing classes, residents gain jobs and deepen their connection to both their past and surroundings (Buckley et al., 2022).

As the world promotes sustainability, the growth of wellness and NT connects directly. Travellers now pick destinations that show environmental responsibility by choosing resorts that take clean energy steps plus reduce waste and harm nature. Wellness and NT gives the industry a chance to teach others sustainable principles. Wellness destinations can lower their environmental effects through new solutions including green building styles and renewable energy plus eco-transport choices. Eco-labels and business certificates help customers make responsible decisions, which drives companies to support sustainable business methods. Sustainability makes wellness travel more appealing by serving the rising number of customers who care about the environment. Wellness destinations make themselves unique while supporting environmental targets by hosting activities like organic dining and nature education programmes plus carbon-free vacation packages (Haukeland et al., 2021).

Preserving both wellness and nature-based tourism activities will draw diverse visitor demographics because they provide individual and welcoming encounters. Tourists drawn to technology will especially enjoy wellness services combining wearable health devices with virtual wellness lessons. Our wellness programmes need welcoming designs for families along with multi-age engagement to serve all client demographics. We can expand our business by targeting middle-income travellers who begin international travel in developing countries. Tourism operators must develop affordable wellness programmes which will expand their visitor base to attract different tourism sectors.

9. Strategic Implications

A growing wellness and nature-based tourism sector requires strategic guidance to achieve sustainability and value optimization through stakeholder empowerment as well as future trend exploitation. Policy recommendations for stakeholders and best practices for sustainability lie at the forefront, while technology and innovation guide the future development of the industry. These strategies create a complete instrument which helps solve future problems and advances current possibilities while developing permanent resilience for adaptive businesses. To maintain long-term sustainability in wellness and nature-based tourism, governments must establish environmental sustainability as their top priority. The accomplishment of these goals demands concrete waste management protocols alongside sustainable resource usage practices and environmentally minded construction methods. Tourism control measures requiring staffing limits within regions experiencing visitor excess exist to defend ecological habitats in protected areas. New guidelines for protected zones and tourist limits in those zones work as additional methods to protect ecosystems. Bhutan's tourism management policy features 'high-value' visitor caps alongside 'low-impact' rates which charge sustainable development fees to defend both the culture and natural heritage of the country. Environmental protection alongside enhanced visitor experience quality become two major benefits of adopting these sustainability measures (Costa, 2022).

The planning of tourism destinations must engage local stakeholders to establish their complete involvement within the industry. To achieve economic advancement and cultural maintenance, it's essential to support community tourism projects through appropriate capacity-building initiatives and fair revenue distribution systems. Tourism activities work best when locals receive direct benefits through empowerment so they can protect both their environmental assets and cultural heritage. Legacy tourism supports local economies by allowing indigenous populations to lead protected nature tours and heritage healing retreats that create job opportunities together with cultural heritage outreach opportunities. The strategic development of community empowerment through tourism creates a positive direction as an accelerator of sustainable development with social equity emphasis (Irma et al., 2021).

Governments together with private organizations driven by public–private partnerships (PPPs) create powerful solutions for developing sustainable tourist infrastructure. Through PPPs, governments and private organizations create sustainable accommodations alongside wellness centres and recreational facilities that meet both financial goals and environmental and social requirements. The combination of such funding through PPPs enables eco-lodges to build sustainable features which incorporate green systems and support both local suppliers as well as wildlife preservation programmes. Through joint ventures of public and private organizations, governments will accomplish economic expansion together with community advancement alongside environmental preservation which protects tourism as a positive influence (Romao et al., 2017).

Wellness and nature-based tourism accessibility alongside inclusivity represent essential elements in tourism policy that allow differently abled people and underserved communities to enjoy these services. State policies need to develop facilities which support different accessibility requirements by offering trails accessible to wheelchairs alongside audio description capabilities and sensory sensitive recreational options. Standards for accessibility at tourism organizations should be incentivized through government subsidies while operators receive financial support to develop sustainable projects in marginalized locations. Such social inclusion strategies through expanded wellness and nature-based tourism access allow more people to obtain the mental and physical benefits resulting from these experiences (Phuthong, 2023).

Eco-certifications alongside sustainability labels promote business environmental accountability through transparent sustainability standards for the tourism sector. Harmonized sustainability standards like Leadership in Energy and Environmental Design (LEED) alongside Green Globe and EarthCheck provide targeted benchmarks for sustainable travel which lets visitors select better options while maintaining operator compliance regarding society and environment matters. The commitment to responsible tourism finds greater appeal among eco-conscious travellers, thus providing certified businesses with a competitive marketing advantage. Through their promotion of established green practices, certification systems provide both sustainability and trust to the wellness and nature-based tourism sector (Wang et al., 2024).

Tourism which regenerates goes further than sustainability efforts through ecosystem restoration alongside community betterment. Tourism operators implement projects that restore environmental areas including forest rehabilitation schemes and coral reef preservation plus area-independent agricultural approaches to improve biodiversity. These practices both restore damage caused by excessive tourism and develop long-term destination resilience. Some eco-lodges combine their operations with rewilding initiatives which turn damaged lands into healthy active ecosystems. Tourism operators who embrace regenerative practices enable both environmental restoration and cultural resource preservation while protecting natural heritage for upcoming generations (Pan et al., 2024).

Sustainable tourism depends heavily on diminishing the amount of carbon released into the environment. Green strategies available to operators include the selection of renewable energy resources and offering packages that offset carbon emissions and the promotion of sustainable transportation methods. The modern wellness retreat promotes hiking paths along with employing electric-based transportation systems to minimize motorized scaffold sojourners. Sustainable energy management at Maldivian resorts operates through integration of solar power alongside desalination systems to supply power and water. The combined deployment of these strategies cuts environmental harm while drawing sustainable-minded visitors who desire place visits that mirror their principles (Shabili, 2018).

The relationship between tourism operations and local communities grows stronger through local purchases, which guarantees direct economic support within local communities. The partnership between wellness centres and nearby farmers brings sustainable agriculture benefits alongside fresh nutritious meals for guests. Wellness programmes become more comprehensive by integrating traditional healing techniques of indigenous peoples because this inclusion simultaneously helps protect cultural traditions plus strengthens wellness facility services. Tourism operators who choose locally sourced products foster community health as well as reduce environmental costs from distant supply chains (Bardukova, 2024).

Authorized wellness tour experiences rely fundamentally on sustaining cultural heritage talents. Local communities work with cultural experts who help prevent misrepresentation of traditional practices along with rituals and gourmet cuisine. Australian indigenous wellness retreat experiences traditionally include Aboriginal guides who provide education about their spiritual link to nature. Through these creative strategies, both visitors receive improved service while cultural communities have space to maintain and safeguard their heritage values. Tourism becomes more engaging for visitors when authenticity is recognized because it attracts positive local engagement which produces valuable memorable experiences (Widarini, 2024).

Tourism operators must install strong evaluation and monitoring systems to achieve constant sustainability targets. Tracking tourism activity impacts happens through tools which combine visitor opinion surveys along with environmental control assessments and instant data monitoring solutions. Tourism operators use regular assessments to locate areas for improvement that require modifications towards sustainability objectives. The measurement of eco-resorts' energy along with water usage enables operators to discover more efficient resource management strategies and waste reduction opportunities. Tourism businesses establish trust with their various stakeholders through transparent and accountable monitoring practices which help them maintain good faith towards sustainability goals.

10. Differentiating Medical and Wellness Tourism: An Essential Guide

In destination marketing as well as among customers, wellness tourism is frequently confused with medical tourism. Inadequate knowledge of these markets and uneven terminology use by travel destinations, governmental bodies and advertising firms are the root causes of this misunderstanding. Confusion is increased when the word 'health tourism' is used as a catch-all to refer to a variety of medical and wellness treatments and activities, ranging from dental work and open-heart surgery to yoga retreats and destination spas. In actuality, these two industries serve distinct customer demands and function primarily in different fields (Quintela et al., 2016).

DNA testing and executive exams are two examples of how medical tourism and wellness tourism might intersect. Though they may both rely on a region's core tourist and hospitality infrastructure and facilities, medical tourism and wellness tourism often differ greatly in terms of the sorts of guests, activities, services, enterprises and laws involved (Zhong et al., 2021).

According to the Global Institute of Wellness, the difference between wellness tourism and medical tourism is shown in Table 2.1.

Report from the GWI stated that people generally think wellness travellers consist only of wealthy leisure tourists who reserve their visits for yoga retreats together with meditation centres alongside luxury health resorts and destination spas. The actual wellness travelling demographic contains participants who pursue various health goals backed by distinct personal interests and faith systems. The wellness population includes adventure fans who achieve health benefits through hiking and kayaking along with working adults using mindfulness-focused retreats as stress management. Wellness travellers include entire family units taking joint vacations to experience health-led bonding moments and budget-oriented tourists checking out cost-effective wellness options. These varying visitor types demonstrate wellness tourism's power to attract travellers from all walks of life. The wellness tourism industry needs to better understand different interests to deliver more inclusive services that enable global wellness accessibility.

11. Conclusion

Travelling to wellness and natural areas brings in different tourist demographics because of creative and welcoming event options. Vacationers who depend on technology will find their wellness experiences improved by wearable health devices combined with fitness trackers and virtual wellness course offerings. Technology-oriented wellness programming lets travellers keep tabs on health indicators live and take part in fitness activities from any setting and delivers individualized support during their experiences. In order to draw wider audiences, wellness activities must cater to household members at different age ranges. Inclusive wellness tourism activities unite children of all ages with their parents and

Table 2.1. Difference Between Medical and Wellness Tourism.

Medical Tourism	Wellness Tourism
Travel to seek improvement or to obtain treatment for a diagnosed illness, condition, or affliction.	Travel to preserve, control or enhance one's health and well-being.
Driven by the need for improved access to care, better quality treatment, reduced costs and/or care that is unavailable at home.	Driven by a desire to live a healthy lifestyle, avoid illness, control bad lifestyle choices, reduce stress and/or have real experiences.
Activities are intrusive, medically essential, reactive to diseases and/or supervised by a physician.	The nature of the activities is proactive, voluntary, non-invasive and non-medical.

grandparents to share universal wellness experiences. Family-welcoming activities like yoga programmes for children and walking tours with nature elements and wellness-oriented workshops enhance destination appeal with memorable connections for families. The emerging potential of middle-income tourist travel presents an opportunity in developing nations for destination expansion. Tourism businesses who design affordable wellness programmes according to customer preferences can access growth opportunities among population segments that show increasing travel behaviour. Operators can extend their reach through affordable wellness options. The combination of inexpensive wellness retreats along with special group rates and unburden some packages enables wellness tourism to welcome people from different financial backgrounds into its realm. Premium wellness destinations that welcome all kinds of visitors help demonstrate both affordability and the importance of wellness recovery for everyone. This combination creates opportunities for markets to grow in a sustainable way.

References

Agarwal, P., & Parashar, A. (2023). Forest-based model: A nature-based health tourism practice at tourism destinations. *Himalayan Journal of Social Sciences and Humanities*, *18*, 99–110.

Andreu, M. G. N. L., Font-Barnet, A., & Roca, M. E. (2021). Wellness tourism—New challenges and opportunities for tourism in Salou. *Sustainability*, *13*(15), 8246.

Bardukova, L. (2024). Health and wellness tourism: Current trends and strategies in the Bulgarian Tourism industry. *Economics and Computer Science*, *2*, 22–36.

Björnsdóttir, A. L. (2018). *Nature based tourism trends: An analysis of drivers, challenges and opportunities*. https://static02.nmbu.no/mina/studier/moppgaver/2018-Bjornsdottir.pdf

Buckley, R. C., & Cooper, M. A. (2022). Tourism as a tool in nature-based mental health: Progress and prospects post-pandemic. *International Journal of Environmental Research and Public Health*, *19*(20), 13112.

Burke, J., Clarke, D., O'Keeffe, J., & Corrigan, S. (2024). *Positive psychology and biodiversity conservation: Health, wellbeing, and pro-environmental action*. Taylor & Francis.

Casado-Díaz, A. B., Sancho-Esper, F., Rodriguez-Sanchez, C., & Sellers-Rubio, R. (2023). Tourists' water conservation behavior in hotels: The role of gender. In *Gender and tourism sustainability* (pp. 63–83). Routledge.

Chang, W. (2022). [Retracted] An integrated development model of cultural and creative industry and rural tourism industry based on data mining. *Wireless Communications and Mobile Computing*, *2022*(1), 2351906.

Csirmaz, É., & Pető, K. (2015). International trends in recreational and wellness tourism. *Procedia Economics and Finance*, *32*, 755–762.

da Costa Guerra, R. J., dos Santos, N. N. P., & Gonçalves, E. C. (2022). Health and wellness tourism: Contributions to a local sustainable development strategy. In *Cultural sustainable tourism* (pp. 219–233). Springer International Publishing.

Elmahdy, Y. M., Haukeland, J. V., & Fredman, P. (2017). *Tourism megatrends: A literature review focused on nature-based tourism*. https://doi.org/10.13140/RG.2.2.32481.66402

Gamby, K., Burns, D., & Forristal, K. (2021). Wellness decolonized: The history of wellness and recommendations for the counseling field. *Journal of Mental Health Counseling*, *43*(3), 228–245.

Hamilton, L. S. (2024). Conserving mountain biodiversity in protected areas. In *Mountain biodiversity* (pp. 295–306). CRC Press.

Hassan, T., & Saleh, M. I. (2024). Tourism digital detox and digital-free tourism: What do we know? What do we not know? Where should we be heading? *Journal of Tourism Futures*. https://doi.org/10.1108/JTF-12-2023-0274

Haukeland, J. V., Fredman, P., Siegrist, D., Tyrväinen, L., Lindberg, K., & Elmahdy, Y. M. (2021). Trends in nature-based tourism. *Nordic Perspectives on Nature-based Tourism*, 16–31.

Haukeland, J. V., Fredman, P., Tyrväinen, L., Siegrist, D., & Lindberg, K. (2023). Prospects for nature-based tourism: Identifying trends with commercial potential. *Journal of Ecotourism*, 1–18.

Irma, R., Oka, S. I. G. A., Alam, P. S., & Suryawan, W. A. A. P. A. (2021). Main factors and analysis of wellness development strategies for the development of wellness tourism destinations in Bali. *Eurasia: Economics & Business*, *12*(54), 34–52.

Joye, Y., & De Block, A. (2011). 'Nature and I are two': A critical examination of the biophilia hypothesis. *Environmental Values*, *20*(2), 189–215.

Kazakov, S., & Oyner, O. (2021). Wellness tourism: A perspective article. *Tourism Review*, *76*(1), 58–63.

Kim, H., Lee, S., Uysal, M., Kim, J., & Ahn, K. (2015). Nature-based tourism: Motivation and subjective well-being. *Journal of Travel & Tourism Marketing*, *32* (Suppl. 1), S76–S96.

Lai, S., Zhang, S., Zhang, L., Tseng, H. W., & Shiau, Y. C. (2021). Study on the influence of cultural contact and tourism memory on the intention to revisit: A case study of cultural and creative districts. *Sustainability*, *13*(4), 2416.

Lin, M., & Soratana, K. (2023). *Environmentally sustainable development of hot spring spa: A case study of geothermal springs in Tengchong, Yunnan*. Doctoral dissertation. Naresuan University.

Lück, M., & Aquino, R. S. (2021). Domestic nature-based tourism and wellbeing: A roadmap for the new normal? In *Tourist health, safety and wellbeing in the new normal* (pp. 269–292). Springer Singapore.

Mandić, A., Mrnjavac, Ž., & Kordić, L. (2018). Tourism infrastructure, recreational facilities and tourism development. *Tourism and Hospitality Management*, *24*(1), 41–62.

Pacheco, S. M. (2021). *Ancestral healing studies: Preparing the next generation of practitioners*. https://scholarworks.sjsu.edu/cgi/viewcontent.cgi?article=1224&context=naccs

Padma, P., Ramakrishna, S., & Rasoolimanesh, S. M. (2022). Nature-based solutions in tourism: A review of the literature and conceptualization. *Journal of Hospitality & Tourism Research*, *46*(3), 442–466.

Pan, H., Mi, H., Chen, Y., Chen, Z., & Zhou, W. (2024). Measurement and evaluation of the development level of health and wellness tourism from the perspective of high-quality development. *Sustainability*, *16*(18), 8082.

Pande, K. (2024). Nepal: Exploring the synergy between wellness and tourism. In *Special interest trends for sustainable tourism* (pp. 55–93). IGI Global.

Peras, R. J. J., Pulhin, J. M., Gevaña, D. T., & Inoue, M. (2021). Natural resource base as a foundation of human security. In *Climate change, disaster risks, and human security: Asian experience and perspectives* (pp. 113–136). https://doi.org/10.1007/978-981-15-8852-5_6

Phuthong, T., Anuntavoranich, P., Chandrachai, A., & Piromsopa, K. (2023). A framework for assessing wellness tourism destination competitiveness: A perspective from the wellness tourism clusters in Thailand. *Geo Journal of Tourism and Geosites*, *49*(3).

Prabhakar, S. V. R. K. (2021). Policies and institutions shaping human security in an era of changing climate and increasing disasters. In *Climate change, disaster risks, and human security: Asian experience and perspectives* (pp. 57–84). https://doi.org/10.1007/978-981-15-8852-5_4

Qiu, M., Sha, J., & Scott, N. (2021). Restoration of visitors through nature-based tourism: A systematic review, conceptual framework, and future research directions. *International Journal of Environmental Research and Public Health*, *18*(5), 2299.

Quintela, J. A., Costa, C., & Correia, A. (2016). Health, wellness and medical Tourism–A conceptual approach. *Enlightening Tourism. A Pathmaking Journal*, *6* (1), 1–18.

Rodtook, P., Simpattanawong, D., Ruenbanthoeng, T., & Nongkhai, K. N. (2024). Forest bathing activity as a tool to promote wellness tourism in Thailand. *Humanities, Arts and Social Sciences Studies*, 428–440.

Romão, J., Machino, K., & Nijkamp, P. (2017). Assessment of wellness tourism development in Hokkaido: A multicriteria and strategic choice analysis. *Asia-Pacific Journal of Regional Science*, *1*, 265–290.

Shaban, M. M., Alanazi, M. A., Mohammed, H. H., Mohamed Amer, F. G., Elsayed, H. H., Zaky, M. E., Ramadan, O. M. E., Abdelgawad, M. E., & Shaban, M. (2024). Advancing sustainable healthcare: A concept analysis of eco-conscious nursing practices. *BMC Nursing*, *23*(1), 660.

Shablii, O. I. (2018). The main problems of healthcare and wellness tourism in Ukraine. *Journal of Geology, Geography and Geoecology*, *27*(2), 337–345.

Smith, M. K. (2021). Creating wellness tourism experiences. In *Routledge handbook of the tourist experience* (pp. 364–377). Routledge.

Stäheli, U., & Stoltenberg, L. (2024). Digital detox tourism: Practices of analogization. *New Media & Society*, *26*(2), 1056–1073.

Talukder, M. B., Kabir, F., Kaiser, F., & Lina, F. Y. (2024). Digital detox movement in the tourism industry: Traveler perspective. In *Business drivers in promoting digital detoxification* (pp. 91–110). IGI Global.

Velikova, E., & Anev, I. (2019). Value assessment of natural mineral springs water used in spa facilities. *Economic Studies*, *28*(4).

Wang, L., Damdinsuren, M., Qin, Y., Gonchigsumlaa, G., Zandan, Y., & Zhang, Z. (2024). Forest wellness tourism development strategies using SWOT, QSPM, and AHP: A case study of Chongqing Tea Mountain and Bamboo Forest in China. *Sustainability*, *16*(9), 3609.

Widarini, P. S. I., & Wijaya, M. (2022). Wellness and herbal tourism based on local wisdom as an alternative to 'New Normal' tourism. *Jurnal Komunikasi*, *14*(2), 299–321.

Winter, P. L., Selin, S., Cerveny, L., & Bricker, K. (2019). Outdoor recreation, nature-based tourism, and sustainability. *Sustainability*, *12*(1), 81.

Zhong, L., Deng, B., Morrison, A. M., Coca-Stefaniak, J. A., & Yang, L. (2021). Medical, health and wellness tourism research—A review of the literature (1970–2020) and research agenda. *International Journal of Environmental Research and Public Health*, *18*(20), 10875.

Chapter 3

Future of Health Tourism: Innovations and Emerging Trends in the Light of Industry 4.0 and Sustainability—*A Scientific Review*

P.K. Paul[a], *Tatayya Bommali*[b] *and Sanjukta Chakraborty*[c]

[a]Raiganj University, India
[b]Astha School of Management, India
[c]Seacom Skills University, India

Abstract

Healthcare is an important sector for all of us and also an emerging industry. It is widely connected with other industries, like tourism and information technology, due to the rapid growth of ICT in healthcare for the wider community development. Historically, health tourism is very much important and an old concept, and people in ancient times also traveled for the purpose of healthcare. The development of Computing Systems and ICT results in many things in healthcare, and among these, telemedicine is considered one of the important and emerging for diverse reasons, namely. patient consulting, appointment of the physician, medical monitoring, remote nursing and caring, etc. There are variety of reasons for using ICT in health tourism, and it includes reduction of the cost and exploring culture of different places and countries. There are several treatments which increase the concept of Medical Tourism, like cosmetic surgery, alternative medicine, stem cell therapy, yoga treatment, etc. There are different ongoing practices in health tourism, and it includes the enhancement of telemedicine, personalized healthcare, and monitoring. Wellness tourism is another practice in health tourism in recent past. There are many emerging technologies in health tourism practice, and this includes utilizing artificial intelligence (AI) in variety of places, including enhancing personalized healthcare, improved Healthcare 5.0 practices, etc. This chapter deals with health tourism, particularly on emerging technologies used in health tourism, practices of sustainable approaches in

Nature, Wellness and Sustainability in Health Tourism, 41–76

Published under exclusive licence by Emerald Publishing Limited
doi:10.1108/978-1-83742-029-220261003

health tourism, Industry 4.0 in Healthcare Systems, Healthcare 5.0 in Healthcare Tourism context, and so on.

Keywords: Health tourism; healthcare sector; artificial intelligence; Industry 4.0; Healthcare 5.0; telemedicine

1. Introduction

Health tourism—now often celebrated as *global healthcare mobility*—has dramatically evolved beyond its traditional roots, blooming into a vibrant, multidisciplinary phenomenon that captures the essence of our collective quest for wellness and healing. This modern expression of health tourism integrates cutting-edge technology and navigates complex international regulations. Today, it encompasses a wide range of experiences, from *medical tourism*, involving surgeries and treatments, to *wellness tourism*, rehabilitation travel, therapeutic retreats, and even preventive healthcare journeys, solidifying its vital role within the global health economy.

Amid rising *healthcare costs* in developed nations and lengthy hospital waitlists, people are turning to *cross-border healthcare* options more than ever. As gaps in healthcare access grow, individuals are increasingly seeking alternatives beyond their local systems. Meanwhile, the surge of *technological advancements,* particularly those arising from the *Fourth Industrial Revolution* (Industry 4.0), has transformed the landscape of health tourism, altering how it operates and is experienced. Innovations like *artificial intelligence (AI), big data analytics, blockchain,* the *Internet of Medical Things (IoMT), 3D printing,* robotic surgeries, and telemedicine platforms are redefining cross-border healthcare, not just by boosting operational efficiency but by reshaping its very essence.

On another front, the *sustainability discourse* has gained extraordinary traction in global policy, economics and industry frameworks, including healthcare and tourism. The merging of sustainability objectives with the groundbreaking technologies of Industry 4.0 provides an exciting opportunity to overhaul the health tourism ecosystem. *Sustainable health tourism* now champions environmentally responsible medical infrastructure, compassionate patient care, equitable resource access, and a minimal carbon footprint, successfully addressing the crucial triple bottom line of *people, planet, and profit.*

The fascinating world of health tourism is evolving at an unprecedented pace, offering many thrilling opportunities but also presenting unique challenges. We face important issues like *data privacy* and the *security of digital health records,* variations in regulations across borders, risks of *medical malpractice,* ethical questions surrounding *treatment access,* and the *uneven distribution* of healthcare innovations. These complexities demand a fresh look at our scientific approaches, a reimagination of policies, and a push for technological standards to ensure that as we innovate, we do so in a way that prioritizes ethics and equity.

In this chapter, we embark on an exciting journey to delve deeply into the realm of health tourism amid the transformative backdrop of Industry 4.0 and sustainability. Our aim is to provide a rich, multidimensional perspective enriched by scientific research, practical examples, and exemplary practices from around the globe. We will:

(1) *Contextualize the Historical Evolution and Present Dynamics of Health Tourism:* By tracing the roots and current trends of health tourism, we gain valuable insights into how this vibrant industry has come to be what it is today. This historical perspective is essential for understanding the pathways forward.
(2) *Examine How Emerging Technologies are Reshaping Healthcare Mobility:* The impact of groundbreaking technologies on how patients move through the healthcare system cannot be overlooked. We will explore innovations such as telemedicine and AI, which are redefining accessibility and efficiency in health tourism.
(3) *Analyze the Intersection of Sustainability and Digital Health Ecosystems:* Our discussion will highlight the growing importance of sustainable practices in health tourism and how digital health ecosystems can support these efforts. This intersection represents a promising frontier for both businesses and patients.
(4) *Highlight Policy, Operational, and Ethical Frameworks Necessary for Resilient, Inclusive Growth:* Effective policies and ethical considerations are crucial for fostering growth in a way that benefits all stakeholders. We aim to underline the essential frameworks that need to be in place to ensure responsible development in health tourism.
(5) *Explore Futuristic Models of Health Tourism that Balance Innovation with Responsible Care:* Looking ahead, we envision new models of health tourism that not only prioritize cutting-edge advancements but also emphasize the importance of compassionate care and ethical considerations in the delivery of health services.

As we navigate this interconnected and post-pandemic landscape, the significance of our topic has soared. With nations investing in *smart health infrastructure, digital patient management,* and *eco-conscious medical tourism models,* it is vital for academics, policymakers, investors, healthcare providers, and global travelers to grasp the emerging trends and innovative pathways shaping the future.

Ultimately, the story of health tourism is not solely about technological prowess; it hinges on our commitment to serve humanity with *integrity, inclusivity,* and *sustainability.* These vital principles will guide our scientific review and discussions within this chapter, charting a path toward a bright and responsible future in health tourism.

1.1 Problem Statement

The landscape of healthcare is undergoing a remarkable transformation, driven by the rapid globalization of services and the exciting blend of tourism with cutting-edge digital technologies. Health tourism is now at the forefront of this evolution, offering incredible opportunities to enhance *healthcare access, affordability,* and *personalization.* However, along with these promising developments comes a set of complex challenges that we must address. Although we see the potential of *Industry 4.0 technologies*—including *AI, blockchain, IoMT, big data* and *telemedicine*—being integrated into the health tourism ecosystem, there remains a crucial gap in our understanding of their practical application, particularly within diverse socio-economic and cultural settings.

Compounding these challenges is the pressing need for *standardized frameworks* that support sustainable health tourism. Persistent issues such as *data privacy, unequal access, ethical dilemmas, regulatory inconsistencies,* and *infrastructure disparities* stand in the way of realizing the full benefits that these innovative advancements could bring to global healthcare mobility. In emerging economies like India, which are poised to become major health tourism hubs, there is an exciting opportunity to critically assess existing practices, pinpoint gaps in technology and policy, and explore integrative strategies that align innovation with *ethical* and *sustainable development.*

Therefore, it is essential to conduct a thorough scientific and conceptual review that not only synthesizes the latest technological trends and sustainability practices in health tourism but also delineates the challenges, innovations, and actionable pathways crucial for fostering an inclusive, resilient, and future-ready health tourism ecosystem. This chapter is committed to fulfilling that need by delivering an in-depth analysis of *emerging trends, digital integration,* and *sustainable strategies,* setting the stage to redefine the future of health tourism through the lens of *Industry 4.0** and **Healthcare 5.0.*

2. Objective of the Chapter

This "Future of Health Tourism: Innovations and Emerging Trends in the Light of Industry 4.0 & Sustainability – A Scientific Review" chapter is not just an academic exercise but an exciting exploration into the dynamic world of health tourism! Our goal is to provide a scientific review of the innovative transformations that are significantly shaping this global industry. Here, we outline our central objectives with enthusiasm:

(1) *To Comprehensive Understanding:* We aim to offer a thorough exploration of the historical evolution, foundational concepts, and essential characteristics of health tourism. This will include its traditional roots and how it intersects with modern healthcare and wellness practices, setting the stage for a rich understanding of its journey.

(2) *To Classification and Critical Evaluation:* We will delve into the various forms and approaches within health tourism, such as medical tourism, wellness tourism, therapeutic travel, and alternative medicine-based mobility, providing a detailed classification and critical evaluation of each, which will greatly enhance our comprehension of the field.

(3) *To Scholarly Literature Review:* By examining current scholarly literature and global best practices, we aim to uncover the prevailing theories, methodologies, and research gaps in health tourism. This exploration will spotlight recent research contributions that are propelling this industry forward.
(4) *To Integration of Emerging Technologies:* We will investigate how emerging technologies like AI, blockchain, IoMT, robotics, big data analytics, and telemedicine are redefining health tourism. This emphasis on technology will highlight their crucial roles in enhancing service delivery, personalizing patient experiences, and improving outcomes.
(5) *To Impact of Industry 4.0 and Healthcare 5.0:* Our analysis will focus on the transformative effect of Industry 4.0 and Healthcare 5.0 paradigms on the health tourism landscape, illustrating how these digital revolutions are reshaping global healthcare access and operational efficiency.
(6) *To Sustainability Principles:* We'll explore the incorporation of sustainability principles in health tourism, emphasizing eco-friendly infrastructure, ethical patient care, and socially responsible tourism models that align with the UN Sustainable Development Goals (SDGs). This will underline the importance of destination sustainability.
(7) *To Contemporary Trends and Changes:* In this exciting context, we will analyze the contemporary trends, drivers, and transformational changes impacting health tourism, especially in the aftermath of the pandemic and the rising significance of digital health ecosystems. This will provide insights into the evolving landscape.
(8) *To Challenges and Ethical Considerations:* We will identify the key challenges, policy barriers, and ethical considerations related to cross-border healthcare services. Topics such as data privacy, regulatory diversity, affordability, and quality assurance will be crucial as we navigate this complex territory.
(9) *To Strategic Directions for Emerging Economies:* Finally, we'll propose strategic directions for promoting health tourism in emerging economies like India. By harnessing technological advancements, sustainable practices, and rich cultural heritage, we aim to position the country as a thriving global health tourism hub.

In conclusion, this chapter is designed to inspire and facilitate a deeper understanding of the evolving health tourism sector while contributing valuable insights for researchers, practitioners, and policy-makers alike.

3. Methods Used

The proposed chapter entitled "Future of Health Tourism: Innovations and Emerging Trends in the light of Industry 4.0 & Sustainability-*A Scientific Review*" is a conceptual work and therefore here existing works are studied theoretical basis using existing literature such as books, chapters, journals related to the health tourism and allied areas, and emerging technologies. For reviewing contemporary and on-going activities and projects, and services of health tourism related company's website have been studied.

4. Review of Existing Works

This particular piece of work has been prepared with existing related work analysis, and for this, last 10 years of significant works are studied and referred them in Existing Review work section of the Chapter. Complete in general refereed works are planned to include in the Reference section of the chapter as per scientific/applied style manual. Some of the prominent works are as follows.

The scholarly examination of health tourism's technological transformation reveals several critical developments. Bathla et al. (2024) conducted a comprehensive analysis of AI applications in health tourism, demonstrating how AI enhances diagnostic accuracy, personalized treatment plans, and operational efficiency in medical tourism. Their work particularly emphasized the dual nature of these advancements, noting significant benefits while cautioning about implementation challenges including ethical considerations and data governance issues in cross-border healthcare delivery. The foundational technologies enabling this transformation have been extensively studied. Bilotta et al. (2021) systematically mapped the evolution of Industry 4.0 technologies in tourism contexts, identifying four distinct phases of technological integration that have progressively enhanced service delivery models. Blazevic's (2016) economic analysis quantified the value proposition of smart technologies in health tourism, establishing a clear correlation between technological specialization and market competitiveness in the global healthcare tourism sector.

Region-specific studies have yielded important insights. Chaudhary et al. (2015) provided a longitudinal analysis of India's health tourism sector, drawing crucial distinctions between medical tourism (focused on surgical interventions) and wellness tourism (emphasizing preventive care). Their findings were complemented by Raj and Krishna's (2010) policy analysis, which identified structural barriers and marketing imperatives unique to emerging health tourism markets.

Technological infrastructure has received considerable research attention. Elangovan et al. (2022) demonstrated blockchain's transformative potential through case studies showing 30–45% improvements in medical credential verification efficiency and cross-border payment processing. Jangra and Gupta (2021) extended this technological focus to IoT applications, documenting measurable enhancements in patient monitoring (28% improvement in response times) and facility management through connected medical devices. Data analytics approaches have emerged as a significant research stream. Kose and Colakoglu (2023) pioneered predictive modeling techniques in health tourism, achieving 82% accuracy in forecasting patient flows using machine learning (ML) algorithms applied to historical tourism data. Kose et al. (2024) subsequently developed wearable technology integration frameworks that showed promise in real-time health monitoring for medical tourists, potentially reducing postoperative complications by 18–22%.

Theoretical contributions have shaped conceptual understanding. Panasiuk's (2018) framework for health tourism innovation identified technological readiness, regulatory alignment, human capital development, and market positioning as critical success factors. Rubino et al. (2025) employed systematic review methodology to map 127 Industry 4.0 applications in tourism, identifying healthcare tourism as the sector with highest technological adoption rates (63% implementation penetration). Contemporary infrastructure challenges have been rigorously examined. Rancea et al. (2024) analyzed edge computing architectures through comparative case studies, demonstrating 40–60% reductions in data latency for distributed healthcare tourism services while highlighting persistent security concerns in decentralized systems. The field's evolution reflects broader industry transformations. As Connell (2013) and Hall (2011) established, health tourism has progressed from simple medical travel to a complex ecosystem incorporating wellness tourism, rehabilitation travel, and preventive healthcare journeys. Economic pressures in developed nations, particularly rising costs (Crooks et al., 2017 *report* 200–300% cost differentials for comparable procedures) and extended wait times (often exceeding 6–12 months for elective surgeries), have driven cross-border healthcare mobility to unprecedented levels. Industry 4.0 technologies have fundamentally reshaped service paradigms. Büyüközkan and Göçer (2018) documented AI-driven diagnostic systems achieving 94–97% accuracy rates in preliminary assessments while Mettler (2016) and Tanwar et al. (2020) showed blockchain solutions reducing medical record exchange times from days to minutes. However, Lunt et al. (2016) identified persistent challenges, with 68% of surveyed institutions reporting data privacy concerns as a barrier to full digital transformation.

Sustainability has emerged as a central consideration. Smith and Puczkó's (2014) longitudinal study showed health tourism facilities adopting green practices achieved 15–25% better patient satisfaction scores. Han and Hyun (2017) demonstrated carbon footprint reductions up to 30% through optimized patient routing and eco-friendly facility designs while maintaining clinical outcomes. Emerging markets present unique opportunities. Agarwal et al. (2020) documented India's strategic advantages, combining cost efficiencies (procedures typically costing 60–80% less than Western counterparts) with traditional wellness practices in Ayurveda and yoga. However, Ormond and Mainil (2015) cautioned about systemic barriers, noting only 38% of emerging market facilities meet international accreditation standards. Future development pathways have been articulated by Yeoh et al. (2021), whose multi-country analysis proposed an integrated framework balancing technological innovation (particularly AI and IoT), policy harmonization, and sustainability principles to achieve equitable growth in global health tourism.

5. Health Tourism and Allied Concepts

5.1 Health Tourism vs Medical Tourism vs Wellness Tourism

The terms health tourism, medical tourism, and wellness tourism often float around in conversations *(refer* Fig. 3.1 *for more clarification),* and while they may seem similar at first glance, they actually represent unique segments of the healthcare and tourism landscape. Each of these areas caters to a specific set of traveler needs and desires, providing a variety of exciting experiences and services. This section dives deep into the distinctions among health tourism, medical tourism, and wellness tourism, clearly delineating their definitions, essential characteristics, driving forces, and challenges (Szymańska, 2016). By gaining insight into these sectors' intricacies, stakeholders can tailor their offerings to meet the diverse expectations of international patients and tourists.

5.1.1 Definitions and Key Characteristics of Health Tourism, Medical Tourism and Wellness Tourism

(1) Health Tourism

i. Definition: Health tourism is an all-encompassing term that includes both medical tourism and wellness tourism. It refers to the practice of journeying across borders in pursuit of medical treatments, wellness therapies, and a spectrum of healthcare services (Phanpanya et al., 2020).

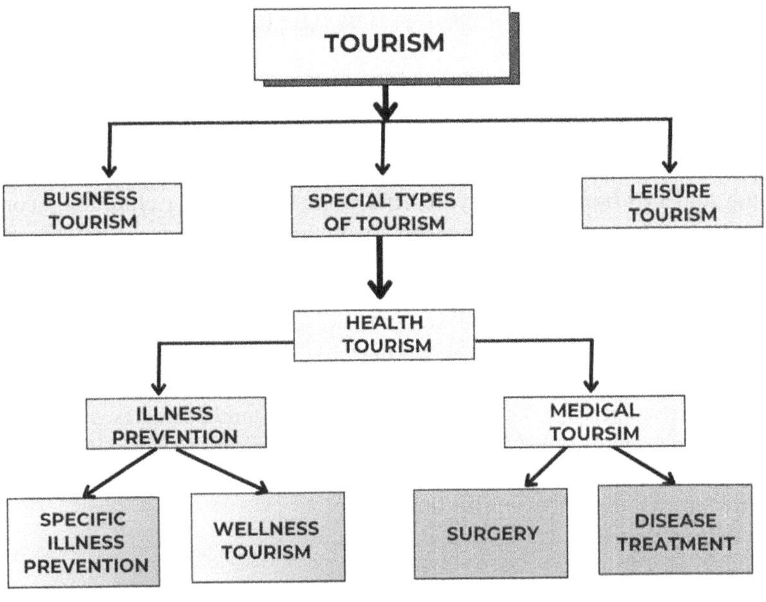

Fig. 3.1. Basic Types of Tourism and Its Sub-types.

ii. Key Characteristics

- Incorporates both curative and preventive healthcare services.
- Blends medical treatments with enjoyable wellness and relaxation experiences.
- Attracts a vibrant mix of travelers, from those seeking specialized medical procedures to individuals looking for holistic wellness solutions (Szymańska, 2017).

(2) Medical Tourism

i. Definition: Medical tourism hones specifically on traveling to another country for medical treatments and procedures (Zsarnoczky, 2018). It is primarily centered on curative healthcare services.
ii. Key Characteristics

- Involves surgical procedures, specialized treatments, and cutting-edge medical interventions.
- Motivated by factors such as cost advantages, access to advanced technology, and reduced waiting times.
- Typically includes hospitals and medical centers with internationally accredited facilities, ensuring high standards of care.

(3) Wellness Tourism

i. Definition: Wellness tourism is dedicated to enhancing health and well-being through preventive and holistic strategies. It encompasses activities and services that aim to elevate physical, mental, and spiritual wellness.
ii. Key Characteristics

- Puts a spotlight on preventive health measures, relaxation, and stress relief.
- Features activities such as spa treatments, yoga retreats, meditation, and alternative therapies.
- Appeals to individuals eager to enrich their overall quality of life and maintain long-term health.

By exploring these vibrant sectors, one can truly appreciate the exciting opportunities that lie within health tourism, medical tourism, and wellness tourism (Szymańska & Panfiluk, 2020).

5.1.2 Key Drivers of Health Tourism, Medical Tourism, and Wellness Tourism

(1) Health Tourism

- *Cost-Effectiveness:* Experience significant savings that make quality healthcare accessible without breaking the bank.

- *High-Quality Care:* Enjoy the benefits of internationally accredited hospitals and skilled medical professionals dedicated to your health.
- *Comprehensive Services:* Immerse yourself in a unique offering that merges medical treatments with wellness and relaxation for a complete healing journey.
- *Cultural and Wellness Appeal:* Discover new cultures while engaging in revitalizing wellness activities that enrich your experience.

(2) Medical Tourism

- *Affordability:* Explore medical treatments that offer substantial savings compared to what you'd pay at home.
- *Advanced Technology:* Benefit from cutting-edge medical technology and specialized treatments that are at the forefront of innovation (Paul et al., 2023).
- *Reduced Waiting Times:* Take advantage of shorter waiting periods for essential procedures, making timely healthcare a reality.
- *Specialized Care:* Gain access to highly skilled specialists and internationally accredited facilities focused on delivering top-notch treatment.

(3) Wellness Tourism

- *Holistic Health:* Embrace a focus on preventive and holistic health measures that support your overall well-being.
- *Stress Relief:* Discover opportunities for relaxation through rejuvenating spa treatments and diverse wellness activities.
- *Cultural Immersion:* Engage with traditional wellness practices while enjoying rich cultural experiences that offer more than just health benefits.
- *Long-Term Well-Being:* Prioritize your health with an emphasis on maintaining and enhancing your overall quality of life.

5.1.3 Basic Challenges of Health Tourism, Medical Tourism, and Wellness Tourism

(1) Health Tourism

- *Quality Assurance:* Strive to ensure consistent quality across a diverse range of healthcare and wellness services for every traveler.
- *Regulatory Issues:* Navigate the complex regulatory landscapes to ensure adherence to international standards that safeguard your experience.
- *Follow-Up Care:* Focus on ensuring seamless continuity of care and effective follow-up after you return home.
- *Language and Cultural Barriers:* Overcome communication challenges and cultural differences for a more enriching experience (De Arellano, 2007).

(2) Medical Tourism

- *Legal and Ethical Issues:* Understand the importance of different medical regulations and malpractice laws in various countries.
- *Post-Treatment Complications:* Stay vigilant in managing potential complications while ensuring proper follow-up care.
- *Travel Logistics:* Coordinate travel, accommodation, and medical appointments to create a smooth healthcare journey.
- *Patient Safety:* Prioritize patient safety and quality of care in foreign healthcare settings.

(3) Wellness Tourism

- *Standardization:* Address the lack of standardized practices and certifications for wellness services to ensure quality and trust.
- *Market Saturation:* Navigate the increasing competition among wellness destinations and providers vying for your attention.
- *Sustainability:* Champion sustainable practices that aim to minimize environmental impact while promoting health.
- *Cultural Sensitivity:* Respect and integrate local cultural practices and traditions for a more authentic wellness experience.

5.2 Some of the Leading Destinations for Health, Medical, and Wellness Tourism

(1) Health Tourism

- *India:* Renowned for combining top-notch medical treatments with traditional wellness practices, making it a premier destination for health seekers.
- *Thailand:* A perfect fusion of cutting-edge medical services and luxurious wellness retreats that create an unforgettable experience.
- *Germany:* Celebrated for its specialized medical treatments paired with holistic wellness therapies, offering a comprehensive approach to health.

(2) Medical Tourism

- *India:* Offers an unbeatable combination of affordability and high-quality medical treatments, particularly excelling in cardiology, orthopedics, and oncology.
- *Thailand:* A hotspot for cosmetic surgery, dental treatments, and fertility services, attracting those looking for excellence in care.
- *Singapore:* A leader in advanced medical technology, providing specialized treatments that garner international acclaim.

(3) Wellness Tourism

- *India:* Famous for its Ayurveda, yoga, and meditation retreats, this vibrant nation is a sanctuary for those seeking holistic healing.
- *Thailand:* Featuring luxurious spa treatments and wellness resorts that promise relaxation and rejuvenation.

- *Bali:* Renowned for its serene environments and holistic wellness practices, making it an ideal escape for tranquil healing.

6. Future Trends in Health, Medical, and Wellness Tourism

Tourism sector is growing in diverse scale, and as of now, there are variety of tourism kinds. This section briefly showcases some of them, briefly in contrast with health tourism.

(1) Health Tourism

- *Integration of Technology:* The future sees the adoption of Health 5.0 and Industry 5.0 technologies, paving the way for personalized and predictive healthcare.
- *Sustainable Practices:* A growing emphasis on eco-friendly and sustainable health tourism practices is shaping a greener future.
- *Global Healthcare Networks:* The development of AI-driven platforms is revolutionizing medical travel logistics for a seamless experience.

(2) Medical Tourism

- *Telemedicine:* The rising popularity of telemedicine enhances pre-treatment consultations and follow-up care, providing convenience for patients.
- *Robot-Assisted Surgeries:* The increasing use of robotic-assisted surgeries offers precision and minimally invasive options, transforming patient care (Johnson et al., 2021).
- *Blockchain for Medical Records:* Ensuring secure and transparent management of medical records, revolutionizing how health information is handled.

(3) Wellness Tourism

- *Digital Wellness:* The integration of digital health tools and apps for personalized wellness plans is reshaping the wellness landscape.
- *Holistic Retreats:* The rise of holistic wellness retreats is merging physical, mental, and spiritual well-being for a truly transformative experience.
- *Cultural Wellness Tourism:* The growing interest in cultural immersion and traditional wellness practices is making waves in the tourism sector.

Health tourism, medical tourism, and wellness tourism are not just distinct sectors; they are vibrant, interconnected realms within the global healthcare and tourism industries. Each caters to unique needs and preferences, offering invaluable experiences and services. By grasping the nuances of these sectors, stakeholders can enhance their offerings to meet the diverse demands of international patients and travelers. As we move forward, the synergy of advanced technologies, sustainable practices, and personalized care will shape the future of these sectors, ensuring a holistic and seamless experience for all adventurers on their health journeys.

7. Emerging Information Technologies in Health Tourism: A Perspective

Health tourism, an evolving sector within the global healthcare industry, has witnessed a rapid transformation driven by emerging technologies. The combination of AI, ML, big data, and the Internet of Things (IoT) refers to the process of merging these advanced technologies to enhance data processing, decision-making, and automation. This integration facilitates the development of smarter systems, capable of analyzing vast amounts of data from interconnected devices in real time, driving innovation across various sectors (Dar & Kashyap, 2023). Cloud computing and blockchain have also significantly enhanced healthcare accessibility, efficiency, and security in medical travel (Pease also refer Fig. 3.2). These technologies enhance patient care, improve the efficiency of medical procedures, and simplify healthcare workflows. They also ensure data privacy, making global health tourism more reliable and effective. This section examines how these advanced technologies are influencing the future of health tourism, emphasizing their effects on different stakeholders such as patients, healthcare providers, and policymakers (Tyan et al., 2021). This section discusses how AI, ML, big data, IoT, cloud computing, and blockchain are transforming health tourism.

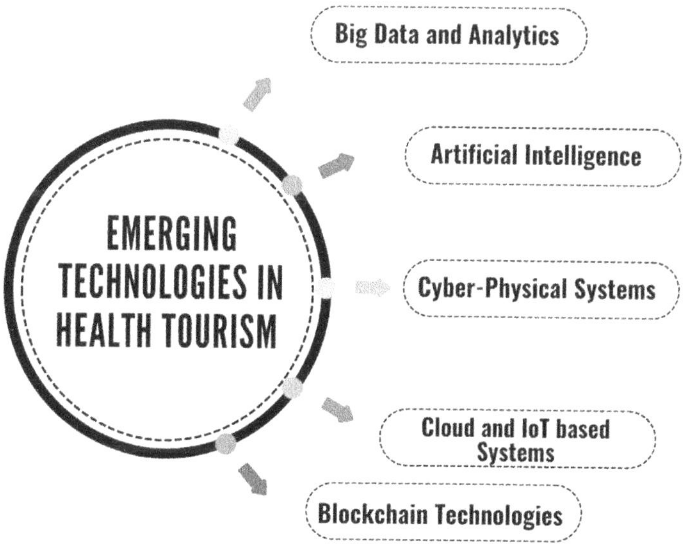

Fig. 3.2. Some Emerging Technologies Used and Rising in Health Tourism.

7.1 Artificial Intelligence (AI) in the Field of Health Tourism

AI is revolutionizing different aspects of health tourism, from personalized treatment plans to operational efficiency in healthcare facilities.

7.1.1 AI-Powered Diagnosis and Treatment

AI-powered diagnostic tools help in identifying diseases at an early stage by examining medical images, lab results, and patient histories. Machine learning algorithms, trained on extensive datasets, can accurately spot irregularities in radiology scans, minimizing diagnostic mistakes and facilitating timely interventions. AI-powered chatbots and virtual assistants provide preliminary consultations, guiding patients to appropriate healthcare destinations (Dixon et al., 2024).

7.1.2 Robotic Surgery and AI-Assisted Procedures

AI-enabled robotic systems enhance surgical precision, reduce recovery times, and improve patient outcomes. Leading hospitals offering medical tourism services employ robotic-assisted surgery for minimally invasive procedures, attracting international patients seeking advanced and efficient treatment (Gallo, 2023).

7.1.3 AI in Personalized Healthcare

AI aids in creating personalized treatment plans by evaluating genetic data, medical history, and lifestyle factors. This tailored approach enhances patient satisfaction and treatment effectiveness, making health tourism more appealing to those seeking customized healthcare options internationally.

7.2 Machine Learning (ML) in Health Tourism

ML algorithms enable predictive analytics, operational efficiency, and enhanced patient experiences in medical travel.

7.2.1 Predictive Analytics for Patient Flow Management

ML models analyze past patient data to predict peak seasons for medical tourism, optimizing hospital resource allocation. These insights help healthcare providers improve scheduling, reduce wait times, *and enhance service delivery.*

7.2.2 Fraud Detection and Risk Assessment

Medical tourism faces challenges related to fraudulent activities, such as fake treatment claims and identity theft. ML algorithms detect anomalies in medical records, financial transactions, and insurance claims, helping prevent fraud and ensuring transparency in health tourism.

7.2.3 Sentiment Analysis for Patient Feedback

Machine learning-based natural language processing (NLP) methods examine online reviews and patient feedback to assess the quality of healthcare services. This helps hospitals and wellness centers identify areas for improvement and maintain their reputation in the medical tourism sector.

7.3 Big Data and Analytics in Health Tourism

The collection, analysis, and utilization of large-scale health data enhance decision-making and operational efficiency in health tourism.

7.3.1 Data-Driven Decision Making

Hospitals and clinics use big data analytics to assess treatment success rates, cost-effectiveness, and patient satisfaction, enabling informed decision-making for both patients and healthcare providers.

7.3.2 Disease Surveillance and Global Health Trends

Big data analytics track disease outbreaks, treatment outcomes, and patient demographics, helping health tourists choose safe destinations with high-quality healthcare services. This is particularly crucial during global health crises such as pandemics (Singh & Kaunert, 2024).

7.3.3 Real-Time Data Processing for Patient Care

With real-time data monitoring, healthcare professionals can track patient vitals remotely, ensuring immediate medical intervention when required. This enhances post-treatment care for international patients returning to their home countries.

7.4 Internet of Things (IoT) Emergence in Health Tourism

IoT devices improve patient monitoring, remote consultations, and operational efficiency in healthcare facilities catering to medical tourists (Psiha & Vlamos, 2017).

7.4.1 Wearable Health Devices for Ongoing Monitoring

Wearable devices, including smart-watches and fitness trackers, monitor essential health metrics such as heart rate, blood pressure, and oxygen levels. This enables remote monitoring of international patients undergoing treatment, ensuring timely medical intervention when necessary.

7.4.2 Smart Hospital Infrastructure

IoT-enabled smart hospitals optimize energy use, automate patient check-ins, and manage medical equipment efficiently. These improvements enhance the overall experience for health tourists by ensuring seamless medical services.

7.4.3 Telemedicine and Remote Consultations

The IoT enables virtual consultations, giving patients the opportunity to communicate with healthcare providers both before and after traveling for medical treatments. This reduces unnecessary travel, lowers costs, and ensures continuity of care.

7.5 Blockchain Technology in Health Tourism

Blockchain enhances transparency, security, and trust in the medical and tourism sector, and there are huge potentialities of this emerging technologies, viz (Dasgupta et al., 2024).

7.5.1 Secure and Tamper-Proof Medical Records

Blockchain technology ensures that medical records remain immutable, preventing unauthorized modifications. Patients can securely share their medical histories with international healthcare providers without concerns about data integrity (Kasyapa & Vanmathi, 2024).

7.5.2 Transparent Payment Systems

Medical tourism involves cross-border financial transactions, which may be subject to fraud or high processing fees. Blockchain-based smart contracts enable secure, transparent, and cost-effective transactions between patients, hospitals, and insurers.

7.5.3 Ensuring Authenticity of Healthcare Providers

By maintaining a decentralized ledger of accredited healthcare providers, blockchain reduces the risk of patients falling victim to fraudulent medical tourism services. Patients can verify the authenticity of hospitals, clinics, and specialists before seeking treatment abroad.

7.6 Cloud Computing and Virtualization in Health Tourism

Cloud technology enhances data accessibility, scalability, and security in cross-border healthcare services.

7.6.1 Secure and Scalable Health Data Storage

Cloud-based electronic health records (EHRs) allow international patients and doctors to access medical histories securely from any location, improving coordination between healthcare providers.

7.6.2 Collaborative Research and Innovation

Cloud platforms facilitate collaboration between global healthcare institutions, enabling knowledge sharing and innovation in medical treatments and technologies used in health tourism.

7.6.3 Cost-Effective IT Infrastructure for Healthcare Providers

Cloud-based solutions reduce operational costs for hospitals, making high-quality treatments more affordable for international patients. This cost-effectiveness strengthens the appeal of medical tourism destinations.

8. Futuristic and Disrupted Technological Impact in Health Tourism

8.1 Uses of Edge Computing in Health Tourism

Edge computing is transforming health tourism by enhancing real-time data processing and decision-making, which is vital for timely medical interventions and personalized care. A key use of edge computing in this sector is in remote patient monitoring. As patients travel for medical treatments, real-time monitoring of their health metrics becomes vital. Edge computing allows wearable devices and sensors to collect and process data locally, providing instant feedback to healthcare professionals without the delays inherent in cloud-based solutions. This is especially crucial for managing chronic conditions that need continuous monitoring, like diabetes, heart disease, and hypertension. Moreover, edge computing contributes to improving the effectiveness of telemedicine in health tourism (Gu et al., 2021). Medical tourists frequently request consultations from remote healthcare professionals while traveling. By processing patient data locally, telemedicine platforms can offer fast, high-quality video calls and consultations, ensuring patients receive prompt and precise medical guidance. Edge computing can also enhance medical imaging services, enabling faster processing and sharing of diagnostic images like CT scans, MRIs, and X-rays, which are essential for healthcare facilities that serve international patients. Lastly, data security and privacy are heightened with edge computing, which processes sensitive patient data at the location where it is generated, minimizing the risk of exposure during transmission to centralized servers. This level of security is crucial in health tourism, where patients' medical histories, personal details, and treatment information must be safeguarded from cyber threats (Faroldi et al., 2019).

8.2 Uses of Human–Computer Interaction (HCI) and VR and AR in Health Tourism

Human–Computer Interaction (HCI) focuses on the design and use of interactive systems, which can enhance the experience of health tourists by improving patient engagement, care quality, and service delivery. In health tourism, HCI can significantly improve the way patients interact with healthcare systems, making the process more efficient and seamless. A key use of HCI in health tourism is through mobile health (mHealth) apps (Kernebeck et al., 2020). These applications enable tourists to access health information, book medical appointments, monitor treatment progress, and communicate with healthcare professionals, all from their smartphones or tablets. User-friendly interfaces and intuitive designs are essential for these applications, enabling users of varying ages and technological expertise to navigate them easily. Interactive kiosks and digital signage systems at healthcare facilities cater to international patients who may face language barriers or are unfamiliar with the facility's processes. These HCI-driven systems provide clear instructions, translations, and interactive maps, enhancing the patient's navigation journey. Virtual reality (VR) and augmented reality (AR) are also being integrated into health tourism as a part of HCI to assist in patient education and pre-surgery planning. VR can be used to guide patients through medical procedures or simulate post-surgical recovery scenarios, giving them a better understanding of what to expect. Additionally, AR can overlay real-time data on a patient's body, helping doctors in diagnostics and treatment planning, offering a more interactive and effective healthcare experience for tourists. HCI's impact on the healthcare provider–patient relationship is another important consideration (Bajwa et al., 2021). HCI-driven communication platforms allow for seamless and efficient interaction between medical professionals and health tourists, fostering a more personalized and supportive care environment (Poole, 2013).

8.3 Uses of Deep Learning and Machine Learning in Health Tourism

Deep learning and ML are key technologies driving innovations in health tourism by improving diagnosis, treatment planning, and personalized healthcare. By processing large volumes of data, these technologies can improve medical services and elevate the overall experience for health tourists. In medical diagnostics, deep learning algorithms are employed to analyze medical images such as X-rays, MRIs, and CT scans, significantly reducing the time it takes to identify potential health issues. This is crucial for medical tourists who often seek immediate and accurate diagnoses in foreign healthcare settings (Li et al., 2023). ML models can also help in predicting patient outcomes, identifying patterns in medical histories, and determining the best treatment options for specific conditions, allowing healthcare providers to offer more tailored treatments for international patients. *Predictive analytics*, powered by ML, plays an important role in managing patient flows and resource allocation in hospitals or clinics serving health tourists. By analyzing historical data, ML models can predict patient demand, ensuring that healthcare facilities have the necessary resources to accommodate an influx of medical tourists without compromising the quality of care. Furthermore, ML and deep learning are advancing the customization of health tourism experiences. These technologies can analyze patient preferences, treatment histories, and genetic data to offer more customized healthcare services. For example, they can help match patients with the right medical professionals, recommend specific wellness treatments, and offer lifestyle suggestions tailored to individual needs (Rahman et al., 2024). In summary, the incorporation of edge computing, HCI, and AI technologies, like deep learning and ML, is transforming the health tourism sector by enhancing service delivery, boosting patient involvement, and offering more tailored care. These technologies not only elevate the quality of healthcare services but also simplify the patient journey, making medical tourism more efficient, effective, and secure.

9. Emerging Technologies in India for Promoting Health Tourism

There are number of reasons of advancing health tourism using several types of Information Technologies, and here are some of such types explained in detail.

9.1 AI, ML, Robotics Emergence in Healthcare Vis-à-Vis Health and Medical Tourism in India

AI and ML are emerging as transformative technologies in healthcare globally, and India is no exception. AI is being used in diagnostics, personalized medicine, and treatment planning, all of which significantly improve the patient experience for medical tourists. In India, AI algorithms are being increasingly utilized to analyze medical data, including imaging (X-rays, MRIs, and CT scans) and patient histories, helping healthcare providers make quicker and more precise diagnoses (Maleki Varnosfaderani & Forouzanfar, 2024). These technologies are capable of identifying early indicators of conditions like cancer, heart disease, and diabetes, which is vital for timely intervention and successful treatment. The application of AI in diagnostic imaging is especially advantageous for medical tourists who require fast and accurate diagnoses upon their arrival in India. AI is also being used to create personalized treatment plans for patients. By examining factors such as a patient's genetic profile, lifestyle, and medical history, AI systems can suggest treatments that are specifically customized to the individual, improving the effectiveness of the care. For health tourists, this degree of personalization is crucial as it ensures they receive optimal care tailored to their specific needs, rather than a generic approach. Furthermore, AI-driven chatbots and virtual assistants are revolutionizing how patients interact with hospitals and clinics in India. These tools provide medical tourists with 24/7 assistance, answering questions related to their treatment, helping them navigate the healthcare system, and assisting with administrative tasks like scheduling appointments, providing directions, and offering information about the local area. *Robotics* is another key technology that is transforming the healthcare sector in India, particularly in the field of surgery. Robotic surgery, which allows for highly precise and minimally invasive procedures, is increasingly being used in Indian hospitals that cater to medical tourists (Banyai & Brişan, 2024).

These surgeries are associated with shorter recovery times, reduced risk of complications, and more accurate outcomes, making them highly attractive to international patients seeking high-quality medical care. Several renowned Indian hospitals, such as those in Delhi, Mumbai, and Chennai, have adopted robotic surgery for various procedures, including cardiac surgery, orthopedic surgery, and urology. Robotic-assisted surgeries enable surgeons to carry out intricate procedures with higher accuracy, minimizing human error and improving patient safety (Maroju et al., 2023). For medical tourists, robotic surgery provides the chance to receive advanced treatments that might not be accessible in their home countries (Parekh et al., 2023). *Robotics* also plays a key role in rehabilitation. In India, robotic exoskeletons and robotic physical therapy devices are being utilized to help patients recover after surgery (Bora et al., 2020). These technologies enable faster rehabilitation, especially for patients who require physical therapy after surgeries like joint replacements or spine surgeries. For medical tourists, this technology improves their overall experience by providing them with advanced rehabilitation options, accelerating recovery, and enhancing their well-being during their stay in India.

9.2 Blockchain and 3D Printing Emergence in Healthcare Vis-à-Vis Health and Medical Tourism in India

Blockchain technology is increasingly being adopted in healthcare as a solution to issues concerning data security, privacy, and transparency. In health tourism, blockchain can guarantee the secure transmission and storage of sensitive medical information, including patient health records, insurance information, and treatment plans, all while safeguarding patient privacy. In India, blockchain is being explored as a means to create secure, immutable medical records that are accessible by authorized healthcare providers regardless of location. This is especially crucial for international patients who might need to share their medical history with various healthcare providers in India. Blockchain can enable smooth data sharing, ensuring healthcare providers have access to precise, current information, which helps minimize errors and enhances the quality of care. Moreover, blockchain can help streamline the billing and payment processes for medical tourists by offering transparent, tamper-proof records of all transactions. This can help reduce fraud, ensure fair pricing, and improve the overall trustworthiness of the health tourism industry in India. *3D printing technology* is another emerging innovation in healthcare that is gaining traction in India, particularly in the field of prosthetics, orthopedics, and custom implants. This technology allows for the creation of highly personalized and precise medical devices, which is especially beneficial for medical tourists who may require specialized treatments or implants (Wu et al., 2023). For example, 3D printing is used to create custom prosthetic limbs, joint replacements, and dental implants that are specifically designed to fit the patient's anatomy. In India, hospitals focused on medical tourism are using 3D printing to provide customized solutions that boost treatment effectiveness and enhance patient satisfaction (Aimar et al., 2019). Additionally, 3D printing allows for faster production of medical devices, which can be crucial for medical tourists who require urgent treatments.

9.3 Wearable Health Technology and Remote Monitoring and Telemedicine in Health Tourism

Wearable health devices, including smartwatches and fitness trackers, are gaining popularity among health tourists in India. These devices enable patients to track their health parameters, such as heart rate, blood pressure, and oxygen levels, in real-time. Wearable devices can be linked to telemedicine platforms, enabling healthcare providers to remotely monitor the condition of medical tourists during their treatment and recovery process (Amin et al., 2021). For patients undergoing surgery or complex treatments in India, wearable devices can provide real-time feedback on their recovery, enabling healthcare providers to intervene quickly if any issues arise. This technology adds an extra layer of convenience and reassurance for medical tourists, ensuring that they receive continuous monitoring even after they return to their home countries.

Telemedicine, which enables remote consultations between patients and healthcare providers through digital communication platforms, is one of the most significant emerging technologies in health tourism. In the Indian context, telemedicine has become increasingly relevant as it allows international patients obtain healthcare services without having to travel immediately to India for consultations. The Indian Government has acknowledged the potential of telemedicine, with the Ministry of Health and Family Welfare introducing programs such as the National Telemedicine Network and eSanjeevani, a telemedicine platform that enables real-time consultations nationwide (Canali et al., 2022). For medical tourists, telemedicine offers a unique opportunity to consult with Indian doctors before making travel decisions. Through video calls, email consultations, and online diagnosis, patients can receive preliminary medical advice and treatment plans from top Indian healthcare professionals, which significantly reduces the uncertainty around treatment options. This technology is particularly beneficial for patients from countries with limited access to specialized healthcare or where medical treatments are prohibitively expensive. By consulting with Indian medical professionals remotely, patients can save on travel costs and plan their visits based on a clearer understanding of the treatment they require. Additionally, post-treatment follow-ups and rehabilitation sessions can be conducted through telehealth services, enhancing the overall patient experience and ensuring continuity of care (Amjad et al., 2023).

10. Health Tourism Growth With Special Reference to India

India is truly making waves as a global frontrunner in the health tourism arena, presenting an exceptional mix of top-notch medical services, affordability, and a vibrant cultural tapestry (Jangid, 2023). The nation's health tourism landscape includes medical tourism, wellness tourism, and alternative therapies, drawing millions of international patients each year, and there are different diseases which enhancing health tourism are depicted in Fig. 3.3. With its cutting-edge healthcare facilities, a pool of highly skilled medical professionals, and cost-effective treatment options, India has firmly established itself as a sought-after destination for health tourism. This chapter explores the remarkable growth, driving forces, challenges, and future possibilities of the health tourism industry in India, emphasizing its significant role in the global healthcare scene. The health tourism industry in India is on an incredible upward trajectory, showcasing exponential growth over the past decade. As reported by the Confederation of Indian Industry (CII), this vibrant

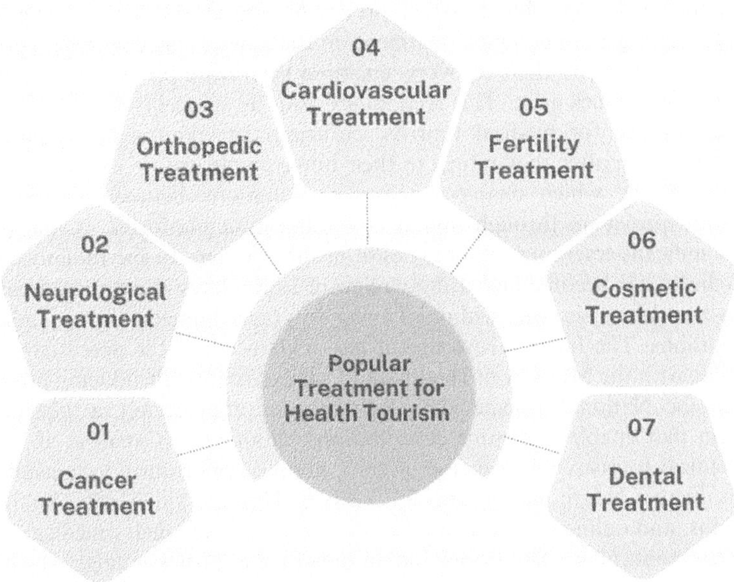

Fig. 3.3. Some Popular Treatment for Advancing and Establishing Health Tourism.

sector is poised to reach remarkable USD 9 billion by 2025, with a stellar compound annual growth rate (CAGR) of 18%. The surge in international patients stems from India's outstanding reputation for delivering world-class medical treatments at a fraction of the cost found in Western countries (Paul et al., 2024a).

10.1 Key Factors Contributing to Growth in India

Numerous factors have propelled India to a leading role in the global health tourism arena, and some of them are as follows:

- *Affordability:* Medical treatments in India are significantly more budget-friendly than those in developed nations, drawing cost-conscious patients eager for quality care.
- *High-Quality Healthcare:* The country is home to internationally accredited hospitals and a cadre of highly skilled medical professionals, ensuring superior healthcare services.
- *Advanced Medical Technology:* India is equipped with state-of-the-art medical technology and infrastructure, offering a diverse array of specialized treatments.
- *Cultural and Wellness Appeal:* The enchanting allure of India's rich cultural heritage and time-honored wellness practices, such as Ayurveda, yoga, and meditation, enhances its reputation as a prime health tourism destination.
- *Cost-Effective Treatments:* Medical procedures in India cost a fraction of what is typically charged in developed countries.
- *Internationally Accredited Hospitals:* Renowned hospitals like Apollo Hospitals, Fortis Healthcare, and Max Healthcare are accredited by prestigious international bodies such as the Joint Commission International (JCI), guaranteeing exceptional standards of care.
- *Skilled Medical Professionals:* The nation boasts a vast pool of highly trained and experienced doctors, surgeons, and healthcare specialists.
- *Wide Range of Specialized Treatments:* India offers an extensive spectrum of medical services, including cardiology, orthopedics, oncology, neurology, and fertility treatments.
- *Traditional Wellness Practices:* The rich heritage of India's ancient wellness practices, including Ayurveda, yoga, and meditation, continues to attract international visitors seeking holistic health solutions.

10.2 Key Zone and Areas Contributing to Growth in India

There are different areas and zones in which health tourism in India is becoming popular and gaining importance, and some of the prominent areas/territory and towns are as follows (Medhekar et al., 2014).

- *Delhi:* The bustling capital serves as a key health tourism hub, with renowned hospitals like Apollo and Fortis, providing an impressive range of specialized treatments.
- *Mumbai:* Celebrated for its advanced medical facilities, hospitals such as Kokilaben Dhirubhai Ambani Hospital and Lilavati Hospital are at the forefront of healthcare innovation.
- *Chennai:* Often dubbed the "Health Capital of India," Chennai is famed for its exceptional healthcare services and patient-centered approach.
- Bangalore: This city emerges as a prime destination for advanced medical care and home to esteemed institutions like Narayana Health and Manipal Hospitals.
- *Kerala:* Famous for its traditional wellness therapies, Kerala offers rejuvenating Ayurvedic treatments and serene yoga retreats, captivating international tourists seeking wellness experiences.

10.3 Indian Context Challenges in the Health Tourism Industry

The health tourism industry in India is on an exhilarating growth trajectory, yet it does encounter some noteworthy challenges that must be addressed (Upadhyay, 2011):

- *Quality Assurance:* Maintaining a consistent level of quality across healthcare facilities is essential to uphold and strengthen India's status as a premier health tourism destination.
- *Regulatory Issues:* The intricate regulatory environment can present obstacles for healthcare providers, making compliance with international standards a complex undertaking.
- *Infrastructure and Logistics:* While large cities boast top-tier healthcare facilities, there is a pressing need to enhance infrastructure and logistical support in smaller towns and rural regions (Zhao et al., 2024).
- *Language and Cultural Barriers:* Effective communication is vital for ensuring patient satisfaction, highlighting the importance of multilingual staff and cultural sensitivity training.
- *Technological Integration:* The adoption of advanced technologies such as AI, robotics, and blockchain in healthcare requires significant investment and a skilled workforce.

10.4 Government Initiatives and Policies in India for Health Tourism

The Indian Government is taking exciting strides to boost health tourism! Here are some standout initiatives:

- *Medical Visa:* With the introduction of the Medical Visa (M-Visa), the pathway for international patients seeking medical treatment in India has become much smoother.

- *Incredible India Campaign:* The vibrant tourism promotion campaign shines a light on India's remarkable healthcare offerings, drawing in international patients eager to experience world-class treatment.
- *Public–Private Partnerships:* Dynamic collaborations between government entities and the private sector are fueling impressive investments in healthcare infrastructure and cutting-edge technology.
- *AYUSH Ministry:* The Ministry of AYUSH (Ayurveda, Yoga and Naturopathy, Unani, Siddha, and Homeopathy) champions traditional wellness practices, further establishing India's reputation as a premier wellness tourism destination.

10.5 Industry 4.0, Sustainable Tourism, and Future Prospects of Health Tourism in India

Industry 4.0 is an emerging practice in Healthcare Sector, and it is dedicated in advancing several services of ICT in healthcare. Latest technologies such as cyber physical systems, cloud computing, ML and deep learning, big data analytics, and IoT enhance a new age healthcare which gives a productivity, flexibility, better supply-chain management, interconnection, intelligent decision-making, technical support enhancement, etc. (Rubino et al., 2025). The horizon for health tourism in India looks incredibly bright, with several formidable trends paving the way for growth which include *Integration of Health 5.0 and Industry 5.0, i.e.* Embracing Health 5.0 and Industry 5.0 technologies will revolutionize personalized care, boost predictive analytics, and instill sustainable practices in health tourism. *Global Healthcare Networks, i.e.* AI-driven platforms, are set to streamline medical travel logistics, ensuring everything from pre-treatment consultations to post-treatment follow-ups gets smoother than ever. *Sustainable Health Tourism,* i.e. by focusing on eco-friendly practices and responsible AI usage, India aims to cultivate sustainable health tourism hubs that attract discerning travelers (Mochlasin et al., 2024). *Immersive Medical Experiences,* with the power of VR and AR, patient education, and decision-making will be transformed, offering truly immersive medical experiences. India's health tourism sector is on track for significant growth, built on a unique mix of high-quality medical services, affordability, and rich traditional wellness practices. By tackling existing challenges head-on and harnessing technological advancements, India can strengthen its standing as a global leader in health tourism. The fusion of Health 5.0 and Industry 5.0 will be essential in crafting the future of health tourism in India, promising personalized, sustainable, and technologically advanced healthcare solutions for international patients (Wong & Sa'aid Hazley, 2021).

It is fact that the concept of Industry 4.0 is growing rapidly, and it is simply the applications and integration of the latest information technology for the Digitalization, among the technologies latest are include cloud computing, AI, big data, IoT, edge computing, fog computing, etc. for wide range of benefit in several industry and Healthcare sector is not an exception. There are variety of reasons of enhancing Industry 4.0 in healthcare tourism, and it includes the enhanced efficiency and productivity, minimizing the costs, enhancing the quality of the healthcare services, and tourism benefit while healthcare purpose. Moreover, Industry 4.0 offers effective flexibility, and as a whole, it promotes the *sustainable health tourism*, which is dedicated in the overall development of tourism and reduces negative impacts, which includes the environmental benefits, cultural advances, socio-economic developments, and complete sustainable development. There are variety of reasons for adapting health tourism, and Fig. 3.4 shows some of them (Panfiluk & Szymańska, 2017).

11. General Issues and Challenges in Health Tourism

Health tourism has risen to prominence as a vibrant sector within the global healthcare landscape, delivering exceptional medical treatments, wellness offerings, and specialized healthcare solutions at competitive prices. This dynamic field is rapidly advancing, driven by the integration of innovative technologies such as Health 5.0 and Industry 5.0. However, the journey is not without its hurdles. Challenges like ethical dilemmas, regulatory disparities, patient safety, legal complexities, and cultural differences require our attention (Panteli et al., 2021). Additionally, while technological progress brings numerous benefits, it

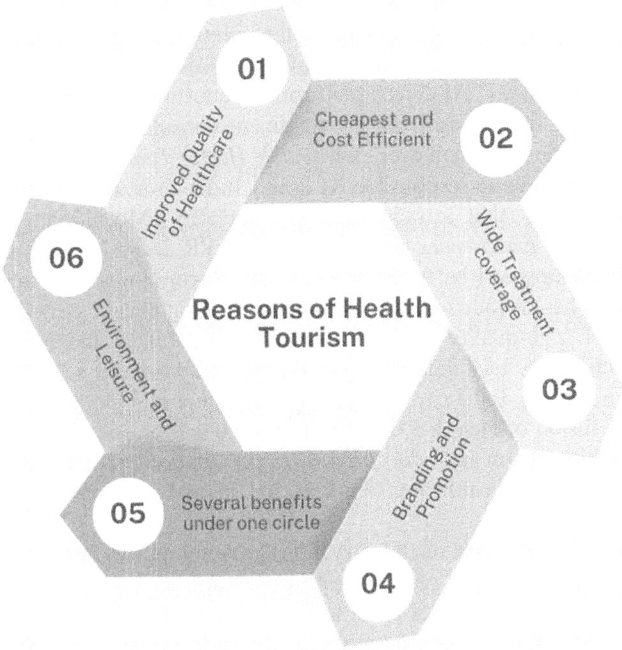

Fig. 3.4. Top Reasons of Health Tourism Growth Globally.

also introduces challenges such as cybersecurity concerns, gaps in digital infrastructure, and ethical questions surrounding AI. Addressing these challenges is paramount for ensuring the longevity and reliability of health tourism. Some of the key challenges included are as follows:

11.1 Legal and Regulatory Challenges

- *Cross-Border Legal Frameworks:* The landscape of medical regulations, malpractice laws, and patient rights varies significantly across countries, leaving international patients navigating a sea of uncertainty.
- *Medical Liability and Compensation:* In the event of complications following treatment, patients often face barriers to legal recourse due to differing jurisdictions.
- *Licensing and Accreditation:* Not all health tourism hotspots adhere to internationally recognized accreditation standards, raising concerns about the quality of care provided.

11.2 Ethical and Patient Safety Concerns

- *Informed Consent and Ethical Practices:* Language barriers and limited pre-procedure consultations can hinder patients' understanding of the risks associated with treatments.
- *Unregulated Medical Procedures:* Certain destinations promote experimental or alternative treatments lacking scientific backing, jeopardizing patient safety.
- *Organ Trafficking and Unethical Medical Practices:* The growing demand for organ transplants in some regions has sparked unethical practices, heightening moral and legal concerns.

11.3 Healthcare Quality Assurance and Continuity of Care

- *Post-Treatment Complications and Follow-up Care:* Upon returning home after procedures, patients often encounter challenges in managing post-operative care, follow-ups, and long-term treatment strategies.
- *Variability in Treatment Standards:* The inconsistency in care levels across countries complicates patients' ability to assess treatment efficacy and safety.

11.4 Financial and Insurance Barriers

- *Lack of Insurance Coverage:* Numerous health insurance policies do not extend to international treatments, compelling patients to pay out-of-pocket for their care.

- *Hidden Costs:* Despite attractive initial pricing, additional expenses related to travel, accommodation, and unforeseen medical issues can escalate the overall treatment costs.

11.5 Language and Cultural Barriers

- *Communication Challenges:* The presence of language differences between patients and healthcare providers can create hurdles, leading to misunderstandings that may affect treatment outcomes.
- *Cultural Sensitivities:* Variations in medical practices, dietary preferences, and social customs can significantly influence a patient's sense of comfort and satisfaction within the healthcare experience.

12. Technological Issues and Challenges in Health Tourism

As we embrace the revolutionary fusion of Health 5.0 and Industry 5.0, health tourism is experiencing a breathtaking transformation into a digitized arena filled with potential (Szymańska, 2015). These exciting advancements enhance accessibility, efficiency, and personalization in ways we never thought possible. However, this evolution also brings forth a set of technological challenges that demand our attention.

12.1 Cybersecurity and Data Privacy Risks

- *Medical Data Breaches:* With the rising adoption of digital health records, blockchain technology, and cloud systems, the protection of patient data from cyberattacks and hacking attempts has become paramount.
- *Lack of International Data Protection Standards:* The variation in data privacy regulations across countries complicates the task of ensuring uniform protection for patient information worldwide.
- *Ethical Concerns with AI-Based Diagnosis:* The reliance of AI-driven healthcare solutions on extensive datasets raises important questions regarding unauthorized use and the potential misuse of sensitive patient information.

12.2 Digital Infrastructure Gaps

- *Unequal Access to Smart Healthcare Technologies:* Not all health tourism destinations are equipped with the essential digital infrastructure needed to support telemedicine, AI-assisted diagnostics, and robotic surgeries (Paul et al., 2024a,b).
- *Connectivity and Interoperability Issues:* The challenge of integrating healthcare data across diverse systems and countries continues to impact the ability to provide seamless patient care.

- *Dependence on Advanced Technologies:* While AI, robotics, and the IoMT offer profound benefits, over-reliance on these technologies can create vulnerabilities in the event of system failures or technical malfunctions.

12.3 Ethical AI and Automation Challenges

- *Bias in AI-Based Treatment Recommendations:* AI-driven medical decision-making tools may operate on biased datasets, which can result in disparities in patient diagnoses and treatment options.
- *Human Oversight vs. Machine Accuracy:* Although AI enhances accuracy in diagnosis and treatment planning, an overemphasis on automation could diminish the vital role of human healthcare providers, raising significant concerns about patient trust.
- *Regulatory Delays in AI Approvals:* The absence of clear regulations governing AI-powered medical treatments in many countries slows progress and impedes international acceptance.

12.4 Robotics and Automation in Medical Procedures

- *High Cost of Implementation:* The adoption of advanced robotic surgeries and AI-enhanced healthcare often necessitates substantial financial investments, posing accessibility challenges for smaller healthcare providers in developing nations.
- *Training and Adaptability Issues:* It is essential for medical professionals to receive extensive training to operate AI-assisted surgical tools and robotic devices, presenting a notable challenge in adoption.
- *Ethical Dilemmas in Human-Machine Collaboration:* As Industry 5.0 promotes collaboration between humans and robots, ethical concerns around decision-making in critical medical procedures remain a topic of discussion (Stankov & Gretzel, 2020).

12.5 Telemedicine and Remote Health Monitoring Limitations

- *Quality of Virtual Consultations:* Telemedicine undeniably broadens access to healthcare, yet virtual consultations can sometimes fall short of the depth found in traditional in-person examinations, highlighting the need for continual improvement in digital interaction quality.
- *Digital Divide:* It's crucial to recognize that patients residing in rural or underdeveloped areas might face barriers such as limited access to high-speed internet or advanced medical devices, which hinders their ability to engage fully with remote healthcare options.
- *Regulatory Challenges in Cross-Border Telemedicine:* The absence of uniform global policies presents intriguing challenges for telemedicine practices across

various health tourism destinations, urging a collective effort to establish clearer regulations that can enhance cross-border healthcare opportunities.

The future of health tourism is bright with opportunity, yet it is imperative that we navigate these technological challenges thoughtfully and collaboratively (Shende & Wagh, 2024). Together, tackling these issues is essential for the thriving future of health tourism, fostering a safe, ethical, and effective healthcare journey for patients worldwide!

13. Future Directions: Suggestions and Overcoming Technological Challenges in Health Tourism

To tackle the pressing technological challenges within health tourism, it's essential for healthcare providers, policymakers, and leaders in the industry to drive initiatives that bolster security, efficiency, and accessibility.

13.1 Strengthening Cybersecurity Measures

- It is vital for governments and healthcare organizations to embrace cutting-edge cybersecurity protocols, such as blockchain-based medical record management and AI-driven threat detection systems, to safeguard patient information.
- There should be a focused commitment to compliance with GDPR (General Data Protection Regulation) and HIPAA (Health Insurance Portability and Accountability Act) standards to facilitate secure international medical data exchange.

13.2 Bridging the Digital Divide

- Investing in state-of-the-art healthcare infrastructure and AI-powered medical hubs in emerging health tourism regions will create equitable access to advanced healthcare services.
- Establishing public–private partnerships can fast-track the implementation of Health 5.0 technologies, which will empower smaller hospitals to harness AI and automation in healthcare delivery.

13.3 Standardizing AI and Robotics Regulations

- Developing international guidelines for AI-driven diagnostics and robotic surgeries will inspire confidence and ensure regulatory compliance across borders.
- Healthcare systems that utilize AI must prioritize the incorporation of explainable AI (XAI) to promote transparency in medical decision-making.

13.4 Enhancing Telemedicine Integration

- Countries need to unify telemedicine policies to facilitate smooth cross-border consultations, thereby minimizing legal uncertainties in virtual healthcare.
- AI-powered automated translation services can effectively bridge language gaps, resulting in improved communication between doctors and patients in the realm of medical tourism.

14. Concluding Remarks

Although emerging technologies offer numerous advantages, challenges remain, including concerns over data privacy, regulatory obstacles, and gaps in technology adoption. Governments and healthcare organizations must work together to create standardized policies that ensure ethical and secure use of technology in health tourism. Future advancements, including AI-driven robotic surgeries, decentralized health data ecosystems, and 5G-enabled telemedicine, will further revolutionize the industry. As these technologies evolve, health tourism will become more patient-centric, efficient, and globally accessible. The combination of AI, ML, big data, IoT, cloud computing, and blockchain is transforming the health tourism industry. These technologies enhance patient experiences, improve healthcare efficiency, and ensure data security, making medical travel more reliable and effective. As the sector continues to evolve, embracing these innovations will be crucial in addressing existing challenges and unlocking new opportunities in global healthcare. Emerging technologies are playing a transformative role in India's health tourism sector, enhancing the quality of care, improving patient experiences, and streamlining processes across the healthcare system. From telemedicine and AI to robotics and blockchain, these technologies are enabling Indian healthcare providers to offer world-class services that attract medical tourists from all over the globe. As these technologies continue to evolve, India's position as a leading destination for health tourism will only grow stronger, making it an even more attractive choice for patients seeking affordable, high-quality medical care. India has been a prominent destination for health tourism for many years, drawing medical tourists worldwide with its top-tier medical facilities, cost-effective treatments, and expert healthcare professionals. The rise of cutting-edge technologies in healthcare is significantly influencing the future of health tourism in India. Technologies such as telemedicine, AI, robotics, and blockchain are transforming the delivery of healthcare services to medical tourists, enhancing the efficiency, accessibility, and quality of care. This article explores the impact of emerging technological innovations on the health tourism sector in India and examines their potential to transform the industry.

References

Agarwal, P., Nath, A., & Kaushik, A. (2020). Medical tourism in India: A systematic review of the literature. *Tourism Management Perspectives*, *34*, 100631.

Aimar, A., Palermo, A., & Innocenti, B. (2019). The role of 3D printing in medical applications: A state of the art. *Journal of Healthcare Engineering*, *2019*, 5340616. https://doi.org/10.1155/2019/5340616

Amin, T., Mobbs, R. J., Mostafa, N., Sy, L. W., & Choy, W. J. (2021). Wearable devices for patient monitoring in the early postoperative period: A literature review. *mHealth*, *7*, 50. https://doi.org/10.21037/mhealth-20-131

Amjad, A., Kordel, P., & Fernandes, G. (2023). A review on innovation in healthcare sector (telehealth) through artificial intelligence. *Sustainability*, *15*(8), 6655. https://doi.org/10.3390/su15086655

Bajwa, J., Munir, U., Nori, A., & Williams, B. (2021). Artificial intelligence in healthcare: Transforming the practice of medicine. *Future Healthcare Journal*, *8*(2), e188–e194. https://doi.org/10.7861/fhj.2021-0095

Banyai, A. D., & Brişan, C. (2024). Robotics in physical rehabilitation: Systematic review. *Healthcare*, *12*(17), 1720. https://doi.org/10.3390/healthcare12171720

Bathla, G., Raina, A., & Rana, V. S. (2024). Artificial intelligence-driven enhancements in medical tourism: Opportunities, challenges, and future prospects. *Impact of AI and Robotics on the Medical Tourism Industry*, 139–162.

Bilotta, E., Bertacchini, F., Gabriele, L., Giglio, S., Pantano, P. S., & Romita, T. (2021). Industry 4.0 technologies in tourism education: Nurturing students to think with technology. *Journal of Hospitality, Leisure, Sport & Tourism Education*, *29*, 100275.

Blazevic, O. (2016). Health tourism and "smart specialisation". *UTMS Journal of Economics*, *7*(1), 85–95.

Bora, G. S., Narain, T. A., Sharma, A. P., Mavuduru, R. S., Devana, S. K., Singh, S. K., & Mandal, A. K. (2020). Robot-assisted surgery in India: A SWOT analysis. *Indian Journal of Urology*, *36*(1), 1–3. https://doi.org/10.4103/iju.IJU_220_19

Büyüközkan, G., & Göçer, F. (2018). Digital transformation in healthcare: A systematic review of current trends. *Technological Forecasting and Social Change*, *132*, 13–25. https://doi.org/10.1016/j.techfore.2018.04.016

Canali, S., Schiaffonati, V., & Aliverti, A. (2022). Challenges and recommendations for wearable devices in digital health: Data quality, interoperability, health equity, fairness. *PLOS Digital Health*, *1*(10), e0000104. https://doi.org/10.1371/journal.pdig.0000104

Chaudhary, R., Chaudhary, R., Singh, R. C., & Singari, R. M. (2015). Issues, prospects, opportunities and challenges of health tourism in India. *International Journal of Advanced Research and Innovation*, *3*(3), 547–549.

Connell, J. (2013). Contemporary medical tourism: Conceptualisation, culture, and commodification. *Tourism Management*, *34*, 1–13. https://doi.org/10.1016/j.tourman.2012.05.009

Crooks, V. A., Turner, L., Snyder, J., Johnston, R., & Kingsbury, P. (2017). Promoting medical tourism to India: Messages, images, and the marketing of international patient travel. *Social Science & Medicine*, *177*, 211–219. https://doi.org/10.1016/j.socscimed.2017.01.037

Dar, H., & Kashyap, K. (2023). Smart healthcare system (SHS): Medical tourism delivering, consumption, and elevating tool in the ages of smart technologies. *Tourism Planning & Development*, *20*(3), 397–415.

Dasgupta, S., Acharya, B., & Jamader, A. R. (2024). The advantage of security using blockchain technology for medical tourism: Approaches towards technologies for Healthcare 4.0. In *Blockchain and cryptocurrency* (pp. 208–222). CRC Press.

De Arellano, A. B. R. (2007). Patients without borders: The emergence of medical tourism. *International Journal of Health Services*, *37*(1), 193–198.

Dixon, D., Sattar, H., Moros, N., Kesireddy, S. R., Ahsan, H., Lakkimsetti, M., Fatima, M., Doshi, D., Sadhu, K., & Junaid Hassan, M. (2024). Unveiling the influence of AI predictive analytics on patient outcomes: A comprehensive narrative review. *Cureus*, *16*(5), e59954. https://doi.org/10.7759/cureus.59954

Elangovan, D., Long, C. S., Bakrin, F. S., Tan, C. S., Goh, K. W., Yeoh, S. F., Loy, M. J., Hussain, Z., Lee, K. S., Idris, A. C., & Ming, L. C. (2022). The use of blockchain technology in the healthcare sector: Systematic review. *JMIR Medical Informatics*, *10*(1), e17278. https://doi.org/10.2196/17278

Faroldi, E., Fabi, V., Vettori, M. P., Gola, M., Brambilla, A., & Capolongo, S. (2019). Health tourism and thermal heritage: Assessing Italian spas with innovative multidisciplinary tools. *Tourism Analysis*, *24*(3), 405–419.

Gallo, C. (2023). Artificial intelligence for personalized genetics and new drug development: Benefits and cautions. *Bioengineering*, *10*(5), 613. https://doi.org/10.3390/bioengineering10050613

Gu, D., Humbatova, G., Xie, Y., Yang, X., Zolotarev, O., & Zhang, G. (2021). Different roles of telehealth and telemedicine on medical tourism: An empirical study from Azerbaijan. *Healthcare*, *9*(8), 1073. https://doi.org/10.3390/healthcare9081073

Hall, C. M. (2011). Health and medical tourism: A kill or cure for global public health? *Tourism Review*, *66*(1/2), 4–15. https://doi.org/10.1108/16605371111127198

Han, H., & Hyun, S. S. (2017). Medical tourism: A sustainable approach to health and well-being? *Sustainability*, *9*(11), 1989. https://doi.org/10.3390/su9111989

Jangid, A. (2023). Insights into India's medical tourism: Growth and prospects. *Juni Khyat Journal*, *13*, 295–307.

Jangra, P., & Gupta, M. (2021). Internet of medical things (IoMT) based framework for smart healthcare tourism sector. *International Journal of Hospitality and Tourism Systems*, *14*(COVID-19 Issue), 173.

Johnson, K. B., Wei, W. Q., Weeraratne, D., Frisse, M. E., Misulis, K., Rhee, K., Zhao, J., & Snowdon, J. L. (2021). Precision medicine, AI, and the future of personalized health care. *Clinical and Translational Science*, *14*(1), 86–93. https://doi.org/10.1111/cts.12884

Kasyapa, M. S. B., & Vanmathi, C. (2024). Blockchain integration in healthcare: A comprehensive investigation of use cases, performance issues, and mitigation strategies. *Frontiers in Digital Health*, *6*, 1359858. https://doi.org/10.3389/fdgth.2024.1359858

Kernebeck, S., Busse, T. S., Böttcher, M. D., Weitz, J., Ehlers, J., & Bork, U. (2020). Impact of mobile health and medical applications on clinical practice in gastroenterology. *World Journal of Gastroenterology*, *26*(29), 4182–4197. https://doi.org/10.3748/wjg.v26.i29.4182

Kose, G., & Colakoglu, O. E. (2023). Health tourism with data mining: Present state and future potentials. *International Journal of Information Communication Technology and Digital Convergence*, *8*(1), 23–33.

Kose, G., Marmolejo-Saucedo, L., Rodriguez-Aguilar, M., & Kose, U. (2024). Wearables for health tourism: Perspectives and model suggestion. *EAI Endorsed Transactions on Pervasive Health and Technology*, *10*, 1–10.

Li, M., Jiang, Y., Zhang, Y., & Zhu, H. (2023). Medical image analysis using deep learning algorithms. *Frontiers in Public Health*, *11*, 1273253. https://doi.org/10.3389/fpubh.2023.1273253

Lunt, N., Horsfall, D., & Hanefeld, J. (2016). Medical tourism: A snapshot of evidence on treatment abroad. *Maturitas*, *88*, 37–44. https://doi.org/10.1016/j.maturitas.2016.03.001

Maleki Varnosfaderani, S., & Forouzanfar, M. (2024). The role of AI in hospitals and clinics: Transforming healthcare in the 21st century. *Bioengineering*, *11*(4), 337. https://doi.org/10.3390/bioengineering11040337

Maroju, R. G., Choudhari, S. G., Shaikh, M. K., Borkar, S. K., & Mendhe, H. (2023). Role of telemedicine and digital technology in public health in India: A narrative review. *Cureus*, *15*(3), e35986. https://doi.org/10.7759/cureus.35986

Medhekar, A., Wong, H. Y., & Hall, J. (2014). Innovation in medical tourism service marketing: A case of India. In *Innovations in services marketing and management: Strategies for emerging economies* (pp. 49–66). IGI Global.

Mettler, M. (2016). Blockchain technology in healthcare: The revolution starts here. In *IEEE 18th international conference on e-Health networking, applications and services*. https://doi.org/10.1109/HealthCom.2016.7749510

Mochlasin, M., Nurdin, N., Anwar, S., & Rusanti, E. (2024). Book review: Digital and strategic innovation for Alpine health tourism: Natural resources, digital tools and innovation practices from HEALPS2 project. *Rajagiri Management Journal*, *18*(3), 264–268.

Ormond, M., & Mainil, T. (2015). Transnational healthcare, cross-border perspectives. *Social Science & Medicine*, *124*, 284–289. https://doi.org/10.1016/j.socscimed.2014.11.014

Panasiuk, A. (2018). Theoretical aspects of innovation in health tourism. *European Journal of Service Management*, *25*(1), 213–220.

Panfiluk, E., & Szymańska, E. (2017). The measurement of the innovativeness of health tourism services using an adequacy matrix. *Entrepreneurship and Sustainability Issues*, *4*(4), 400–420.

Panteli, A., Kompothrekas, A., Halkiopoulos, C., & Boutsinas, B. (2021). An innovative recommender system for health tourism. In *Culture and tourism in a smart, globalized, and sustainable world* (pp. 649–658). Springer.

Parekh, A. E., Shaikh, O. A., Simran, M., & Hasibuzzaman, M. A. (2023). Artificial intelligence (AI) in personalized medicine: AI-generated personalized therapy regimens based on genetic and medical history. *Annals of Medicine and Surgery*, *85*(11), 5831–5833. https://doi.org/10.1097/MS9.0000000000001320

Paul, P. K., Chatterjee, R., Tiwary, K. S., Aithal, P. S., & Saavedra, R. (2023). Application & emergence of edge computing in healthcare: A conceptual study. In *Significance & emergence of computing technologies* (pp. 1–18). https://doi.org/10.5281/zenodo.7947086

Paul, P. K., Chatterjee, R., Chakraborty, S., Tiwary, K. S., Aithal, P. S., & Sharma, S. (2024). Advanced healthcare informatics practice vis-à-vis virtual reality implications—A scientific overview. In *Immersive virtual and augmented reality in healthcare* (pp. 28–49). https://doi.org/10.1201/9781003340133-2

Paul, P. K., Moumtzoglou, A., Bandyopadhyay, A., Hoque, M., Kumar, N. S., & Saavedra, R. (2024). Indian digital health information systems: Initiatives and opportunities with socio-economic perspective. *Economic Affairs*, *69*(2), 1175–1189.

Phanpanya, K., Leelapattana, W., Thongma, W., & Waiapha, Y. (2020). Tourism service factors affecting health tourism service innovation in Mae Hong Son Province. *International Journal of Innovation, Creativity and Change*, *11*(7), 34–51.

Poole, E. S. (2013). HCI and mobile health interventions: How human-computer interaction can contribute to successful mobile health interventions. *Translational Behavioral Medicine*, *3*(4), 402–405. https://doi.org/10.1007/s13142-013-0214-3

Psiha, M. M., & Vlamos, P. (2017). IoT applications with 5G connectivity in medical tourism sector management: Third-party service scenarios. In *GeNeDis 2016: Geriatrics* (pp. 141–154). Springer.

Rahman, A., Debnath, T., Kundu, D., Khan, M. S. I., Aishi, A. A., Sazzad, S., Sayduzzaman, M., & Band, S. S. (2024). Machine learning and deep learning-based approach in smart healthcare: Recent advances, applications, challenges, and opportunities. *AIMS Public Health*, *11*(1), 58–109. https://doi.org/10.3934/publichealth.2024004

Raj, T. V. R., & Krishna, P. M. (2010). Health tourism in India: Issues, challenges & marketing interventions. *International Journal of Management Prudence*, *1*(2), 79.

Rancea, A., Anghel, I., & Cioara, T. (2024). Edge computing in healthcare: Innovations, opportunities, and challenges. *Future Internet*, *16*(9), 329. https://doi.org/10.3390/fi16090329

Rubino, G., Gattuso, D., & Longo, F. (2025). Exploring Industry 4.0 technologies in tourism: A literature review. *Procedia Computer Science*, *253*, 3182–3195.

Shende, V., & Wagh, V. (2024). Role of telemedicine and telehealth in public healthcare sector: A narrative review. *Cureus*, *16*(9), e69102. https://doi.org/10.7759/cureus.69102

Singh, B., & Kaunert, C. (2024). AR and VR in health expansions and medical education: Airstrip for future-ready healthcare amenities. In *Advances in healthcare innovation* (pp. 1–16). IGI Global.

Smith, M., & Puczkó, L. (2014). *Health, tourism, and hospitality: Spas, wellness, and medical travel* (2nd ed.). Routledge.

Stankov, U., & Gretzel, U. (2020). Tourism 4.0 technologies and tourist experiences: A human-centered design perspective. *Information Technology & Tourism*, *22*(3), 477–488.

Szymańska, E. (2015). Construction of the model of health tourism innovativeness. *Procedia-Social and Behavioral Sciences*, *213*, 1008–1014.

Szymańska, E. (2016). Consumer participation in the health tourism innovation process. *Ekonomia i Zarządzanie*, *8*(4), 28–38.

Szymańska, E. (2017). Innovation systems in health tourism. *Journal of Economics, Business and Management*, *5*(1), 1–5.

Szymańska, E., & Panfiluk, E. (2020). Determinants of technological innovations in health tourism enterprises. *Business: Theory and Practice*, *21*(1), 348–359.

Tanwar, S., Parekh, K., & Evans, R. (2020). Blockchain-based electronic healthcare record system for Industry 4.0 applications. *Journal of Information Security and Applications*, *50*, 102407. https://doi.org/10.1016/j.jisa.2019.102407

Tyan, I., Guevara-Plaza, A., & Yagüe, M. I. (2021). The benefits of blockchain technology for medical tourism. *Sustainability*, *13*(22), 12448.

Upadhyay, P. (2011). Comparative and competitive advantages of globalised India as a medical tourism destination. *International Journal of Engineering and Management Sciences*, *2*(1), 26–34.

Wong, B. K. M., & Sa'aid Hazley, S. A. (2021). The future of health tourism in the industrial revolution 4.0 era. *Journal of Tourism Futures*, *7*(2), 267–272.

Wu, Y., Liu, J., Kang, L., Tian, J., Zhang, X., Hu, J., Huang, Y., Liu, F., Wang, H., & Wu, Z. (2023). An overview of 3D printed metal implants in orthopedic applications: Present and future perspectives. *Heliyon*. https://doi.org/10.1016/j.heliyon.2023.e17718

Yeoh, E., Othman, K., & Ahmad, H. (2021). Understanding medical tourists in Asia: A systematic review. *Journal of Travel & Tourism Marketing*, *38*(2), 131–147. https://doi.org/10.1080/10548408.2021.1887056

Zhao, X., Zhang, S., Nan, D., Han, J., & Kim, J. H. (2024). Human-computer interaction in healthcare: A bibliometric analysis with CiteSpace. *Healthcare*, *12*(23), 2467. https://doi.org/10.3390/healthcare12232467

Zsarnoczky, M. (2018). Novel concepts in the health tourism industry. *Vadyba*, *32*(1), 67–73.

Chapter 4

Wellness as a Development Tool: Enhancing Indian Destinations Through Tourism

Anju Jangid, Anand K. Chaudhary and Srabani Sanyal

Banaras Hindu University, India

Abstract

Wellness tourism is growing globally, with India emerging as a top destination due to its 5,000-year-old legacy of Ayurveda, yoga, meditation, naturopathy, and holistic health practices—despite a gradual decline in their distinct identity over time. However, strategic government initiatives, in collaboration with the Ministry of AYUSH and the Ministry of Tourism, have played a crucial role in reviving and promoting Ayurveda on a global scale. The "Heal in India" campaign, along with the introduction of e-medical visas for over 160 countries and the fully digitalized Online Medical Value Travel (MVT) Portal, has significantly streamlined medical and wellness tourism. Investments in advanced medical infrastructure, policy reforms, and partnerships with private healthcare providers have further enhanced the quality, affordability, and accessibility of healthcare services. India's top medical and wellness tourism hubs, including Chennai, Mumbai, New Delhi, Ahmedabad, and Bangalore, are known for their world-class healthcare facilities and cost-effective treatments. Meanwhile, destinations like Kerala, Varanasi, and Rishikesh continue to excel in traditional wellness tourism, offering authentic Ayurveda and holistic healing experiences. The Union Budget 2025–2026, with an allocation of ₹2,541.06 crore for infrastructure development, skill enhancement, and travel facilitation, further underscores the potential of this sector in driving employment-led growth. The cost advantage, availability of alternative therapies, and renowned professionals attract foreign medical tourists. Postpandemic awareness has boosted demand for wellness tourism, now

Nature, Wellness and Sustainability in Health Tourism, 77–102

doi:10.1108/978-1-83742-029-220261004

evolving through artificial intelligence (AI)-driven, personalized preventive healthcare innovations.

Keywords: Tourism; medical tourism; wellness tourism; government policies; Heal in India; ayurveda and traditional medicines

1. Introduction

Wellness tourism is the exciting intersection of two major and rising multi-trillion-dollar industries: tourism and wellness. Consumer decision-making is increasingly focused on preventative and holistic health. The Global Wellness Institute defines wellness tourism as travel associated with the pursuit of maintaining or enhancing one's personal well-being. With so much unwellness embedded in today's travel, wellness tourism brings the promise of combating those negative qualities and turning travel into an opportunity to maintain and improve our holistic health (Global Wellness Tourism Economy Report - Global Wellness Institute, n.d.). There are significant differences between wellness tourism locations in terms of scale and historical history. Certain places (like Germany, the Czech Republic, and Japan) have grown by utilizing unique natural resources that have drawn tourists for hundreds or even thousands of years while other places (like the majority of the Asian-Pacific region) are relatively newcomers to the wellness tourism scene. The scope of wellness destinations is diverse and can include single, self-contained resort complexes, frequently known as destination spas in the literature, as well as multinational or multiregional developments, entire countries, regions, islands, cities, or communities (Smith & Kelly, 2006). The relationship between tourism and well-being is explored through philosophical, psychological, and tourism study perspectives, distinguishing between hedonic well-being, which emphasizes pleasure, relaxation, and enjoyment, and eudaimonic well-being, which focuses on self-development, meaningful experiences, and personal transformation (Kay Smith & Diekmann, 2017).

The majority of the market for wellness tourism is occupied by secondary wellness tourists (Fig. 4.1) who make up 85–90% of all trips and have high travel expenses. When it comes to scheduling, working persons between the ages of 16

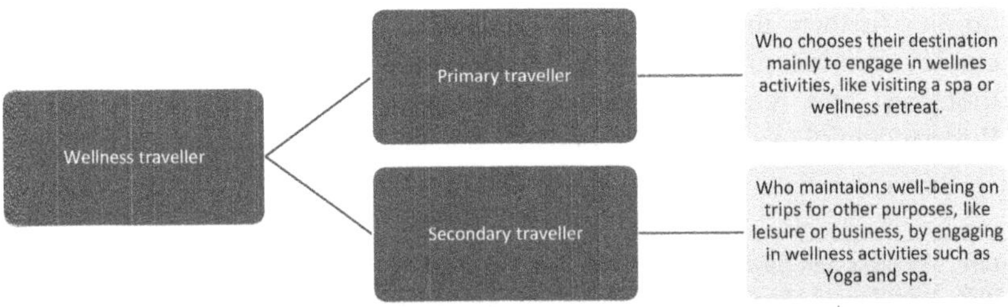

Fig. 4.1. Types of Wellness Traveler. *Source:* Tourism (2022).

and 35 usually have more flexibility than older adults who have greater work experience. They might have more time to engage in wellness-related activities or take longer vacations or breaks (Sands, 2023b). Global medical tourism is witnessing a shift from allopathic treatments to natural and traditional healing approaches, driven by concerns over the side effects of modern medicine, increasing chronic illnesses, and a growing preference for holistic well-being. Travelers are increasingly seeking preventive wellness tourism, integrating Ayurveda, naturopathy, and alternative therapies into their healing journeys (Majeed et al., 2017).

2. The Business of Wellness: Economic Value and Global Reach

A recent analysis from the Global Wellness Institute, a prominent industry association, states that wellness is a large, global market with $5.6 trillion in revenue in 2022. The business is predicted to increase by an additional 57% to reach $8.5 trillion by 2027, which is roughly twice as large as Germany's gross domestic product (GDP), from $3.4 trillion in 2013. This information comes from research conducted by the nonprofit organization (Rappaport, 2023). Since 80–85% of all wellness holidays are now spent domestically, the average cost of traveling abroad is significantly higher than that of domestic wellness travel. Domestic wellness travel is on the rise. When going internationally, the average cost is often higher because it includes the complete voyage. When traveling for wellness, both domestic and foreign visitors typically spend more on services than the typical tourist does (CVR, n.d.).

> "Millennial travelers fit the description of someone who has always defied convention and pursued novel experiences. The majority of people who travel worldwide are Millennials. Millennials are very capable of spending money, and they are drawn to real experiences and vibrant cultures. They enjoy indulging in a variety of holistic programs, including as spa gateway, food-based detoxification and cleaning, and promoting emotional and transformative health journeys. They like to share their experiences of wellness moments on social media" said Purakkal. (Kumar, 2019).

The potential for profit in wellness tourism is just too great to be overlooked. By building a top-notch tourism infrastructure and then effectively marketing it, this potential must be fully utilized (Rajasekhar, 2022). India's healthcare industry offers diverse investment opportunities across various subsectors, including hospitals, medical devices and equipment, health insurance, clinical trials, telemedicine, and medical tourism (NITI Aayog, 2022). The number of foreign tourists arriving in India for medical purposes surged from 1.83 lakh in 2020 to 6.35 lakh in 2023, drawn by world-class healthcare facilities offering advanced surgeries at significantly lower costs compared to other countries.

Additionally, India has become a popular destination for wellness tourism, especially for those seeking traditional therapies through AYUSH (Government of India, n.d.). The Asia-Pacific area is one of the major markets in the world for wellness tourism, with around 64.6 billion US dollars in revenue generated there in 2019, according to Statista. Thailand, India, Indonesia, and Japan are a few of the nations in the region that are well-known for their wellness tourism industries (*Asia-Pacific Travel And Tourism Statistics In 2023*, 2023). India is ranked 10th on the Medical Tourism Index (MTI) for 2020–2021 by the Medical Tourism Association, out of 46 global destinations, and is positioned 12th among the top 20 wellness tourism markets worldwide while ranking 5th in the Asia-Pacific region. The country boasts a large number of accredited healthcare facilities, including 55 Joint Commission International (JCI) hospitals and over 1,600 National Accreditation Board for Hospitals & Healthcare Providers (NABH) institutions. India also offers a vast pool of highly trained doctors and paramedics, many with international qualifications and fluency in English (Government of India, n.d.). 819.4 million wellness visits in 2022—nearly twice as many as before the pandemic! (Consider a worldwide yoga session involving participants from Paris to Patagonia). One in five travel dollars is now funding activities focused on well-being, with wellness trips accounting for 18.7% of all tourist expenditures. (Forget trinkets; instead, people are purchasing matcha smoothies and meditation chants). By 2027, wellness will soar to an astounding $8.5 trillion, having surpassed $6.3 trillion in 2023 (Tony, 2024). India recorded 9.24 million foreign visitor arrivals (FTAs) in 2023, up 43.5% from 6.44 million in 2022. According to preliminary estimates, FTAs contributed Rs. 2.3 lakh crores in Foreign Exchange Earnings (FEEs), which is a roughly 65% increase over Rs. 1.39 lakh crores in 2022 during the same period (PIB, n.d.). According to the IBEF Tourism and Hospitality report, 21% of foreign visitors are drawn to wellness tourism and wellness retreats because they combine traditional treatment methods with top-notch medical facilities (TOURISM & HOSPITALITY, 2024). Kerala and other southern states are most sought after by patients from Nigeria, Kenya, Iraq, UAE, and Saudi Arabia while Mumbai and Delhi and metropolis in north cater to international patients from neighboring countries like Bhutan, Bangladesh, Nepal Afghanistan, etc. (Srivastava, 2024).

Every destination offers a unique wellness experience shaped by its local culture, natural assets, and traditions. Unlike standardized travel experiences, wellness tourism is deeply connected to the distinct flavors of a place—whether through indigenous healing practices, ancient spiritual traditions, native flora, therapeutic waters, vernacular architecture, or local cuisine. Discerning wellness travelers, particularly millennials, seek authentic experiences that differentiate one destination from another. This uniqueness ensures that every location has something valuable to offer in wellness tourism (Global Wellness Institute, n.d.-b).

3. Methodology Used for Data Collection

This chapter aims to highlight Indian wellness tourism, with a particular focus on wellness tourism, its potential, growth, and associated areas. It incorporates details of popular wellness centers, data on decadal foreign medical tourist arrivals in India, and the key reasons why Indian healing practices are popular among foreign patients. The study is primarily based on secondary data, including extensive research related to medical and wellness tourism, particularly government reports published by various ministries and organizations. Resources such as worldwide peer-reviewed journals from scientific databases (e.g., Science Direct, PubMed, Web of Science, ResearchGate) were utilized. The initial step involved searching for articles using combinations of keywords such as wellness tourism, health tourism, medical tourism, nature tourism India, tourism, Government of India (GoI), foreign tourist arrivals (FTAs), Heal in India, and Medical Value Travel (MVT). Focusing on the utilization of secondary data as the research methodology, the study explores the initiatives of the GoI and policies that have redefined health and wellness tourism. A qualitative approach is employed to investigate the influence of technology on enhancing health and wellness tourism experiences. The methodology includes analyzing secondary data sources such as scholarly articles, Global Wellness Institute reports, case studies, and government publications and policies that have reshaped health and wellness tourism in India.

4. Uncovering the Key Motivations Behind the Journey to Well-Being

India is widely regarded as a spiritual hub of the modern wellness movement, offering ancient practices such as Ayurveda, yoga, meditation, rejuvenation acupuncture, naturopathy, panchakarma, and holistic health. These experiences attract wellness travelers from around the world. Popular Ayurvedic treatments, including shirodhara, pizhichil, panchakarma, and navarakizhi, are highly favored by weekend guests, while naturopathy therapies like deep tissue massage, acupressure, and hydrotherapy have gained significant success. Additionally, there is a growing trend of patients seeking treatments for conditions like spondylitis, obesity, diabetes, Parkinson's disease, and ulcers (Kumar, 2019). Consumers today have a far more nuanced and expansive definition of wellness, which goes beyond exercise and diet to include general physical and mental well-being as well as appearance. Companies can benefit greatly from rising consumer interest and purchasing power, especially as personal wellness spending has rebounded after stagnating or even falling during the COVID-19 pandemic. Six criteria, including improved health, fitness, nutrition, attractiveness, sleep, and mindfulness, are used by consumers to define wellness. More lately, better mindfulness has become more widely accepted by consumers because to apps that focus on meditation, including Headspace and Calm, as well as products that promote relaxation and meditation. Reports of mental anguish have surged worldwide during the COVID-19 pandemic; in every country we examined, over half of consumers expressed a desire to give mindfulness a higher priority. Businesses could benefit from the half of consumers who expressed a desire for more mindfulness-related goods and services (Callaghan et al., 2021). Travelers seeking to enhance and improve their physical, mental, and spiritual well-being can partake in wellness-related activities. Travelers engage in physical, spiritual, and mental pursuits by going to wellness retreats, yoga studios, Pilates studios, and meditation classes. Engaging with locals who have been to and experienced various cultures is a trend that enhances one's personal well-being (Sands, 2023). The nation has seen significant breakthroughs in healthcare, from the eradication of diseases to the implementation of groundbreaking programs. Currently referred to as the "pharmacy of the world," India has established itself as a major player in the field by becoming the world's largest supplier of vaccines and generic drugs by volume and by introducing Ayushman Bharat-PMJAY, the largest public health program in the world that aims to reach the bottom 50% of the population (Singh, 2022). A study on service quality in Indian wellness tourism analyzed customer reviews from social media to identify five critical dimensions impacting satisfaction in wellness resorts: Tangibility, Empathy, Assurance, Reliability, and Responsiveness. Tangibility, referring to physical aspects such as facilities and ambiance, was the most positively reviewed dimension while Empathy and Assurance showed more negative feedback. Common issues included insufficient attentiveness to customer complaints and a lack of friendliness among staff. Positive comments frequently praised resort aesthetics, accommodation quality, and the calming ambiance. The study concludes that enhancing staff empathy and responsiveness could significantly improve overall customer satisfaction in Indian wellness resorts (Mishra & Panda, 2021). With growing awareness of health and the need for stress relief, wellness tourism has become a popular way to enhance well-being. Health is a multidimensional concept that encompasses physical, mental, social, and environmental factors. By integrating functions such as sports, leisure, entertainment, and social interaction, wellness tourism can improve the quality of life (QOL) for participants. Additionally, enhancing natural landscapes at wellness destinations can boost health benefits by relieving mental stress (Liao et al., 2023). According to a report citing recent tourism data, there has been an annual growth of 305.4% in FTAs in 2023. In 2023, 9.23 million foreign tourists visited India. Although the FTAs arrival tally is still less than the prepandemic number of 10.93 million in 2019, experts believe 2024 numbers will surpass it (Desk, 2024). India's travel and tourism industry may be saved by wellness tourism. The study's new avenues—Safari Spa, Sand Bath, Balneotherapy, and Hot Water Springs—have the potential to boost domestic travel. Both direct and indirect employment at the suggested locations can result in income (Maitra India, 2022). These Top 10 *wellness tourism destination* in India offers meticulous experience which combines the cultural and authenticity:

(1) Ayurvedagram Heritage wellness center, Bengaluru, Karnataka;

(2) Ananda in Himalaya, Rishikesh, Uttarakhand;
(3) Shreyas Yoga Retreat, Bengaluru, Karnataka;
(4) The Leela, Kovalam, Kerala;
(5) Vana, Dehradun, Uttarakhand;
(6) Sarovaram Ayurvedic Health Center, Ashtamudi, Kerala;
(7) Devaaya, Goa;
(8) Indus Valley Ayurvedic Center, Mysore, Karnataka;
(9) Atmantan, Pune, Maharashtra;
(10) Nimba Nature Cure, Mehsana, Gujarat (Tour My India, 2018).

The decadal analysis of foreign medical tourist arrivals in India from 2015 to 2024 highlights significant trends and government initiatives driving growth. Between 2015 and 2019, arrivals grew steadily, reflecting India's rising prominence in health tourism. However, the year 2020 saw sharp decline of approximately 60–70% due to the COVID-19 pandemic. Recovery began in 2021, with a 20–30% rise as travel restrictions eased. By 2022, arrivals surged by 40–50%, nearing prepandemic levels. The upward trend continued in 2023, with further 10–15% increase. Projections for 2024 suggest a 5–10% rise, potentially surpassing 2019 figures (Fig. 4.2). Government initiatives like the "Heal in India" campaign and e-medical visas for over 160 countries have streamlined access for medical tourists. Investments in advanced medical infrastructure and partnerships with private healthcare providers have enhanced quality and affordability. These efforts, along with cost-effective treatments, have strengthened India's position as a top global healthcare destination (Fig. 4.3).

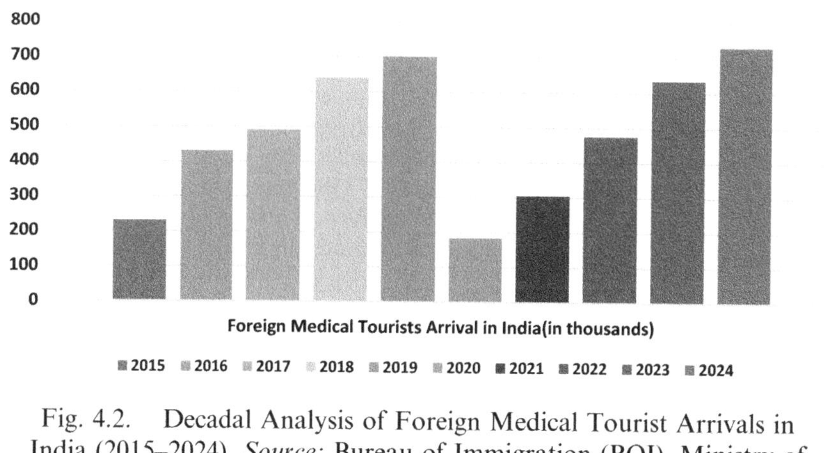

Fig. 4.2. Decadal Analysis of Foreign Medical Tourist Arrivals in India (2015–2024). *Source:* Bureau of Immigration (BOI), Ministry of Tourism, PIB.

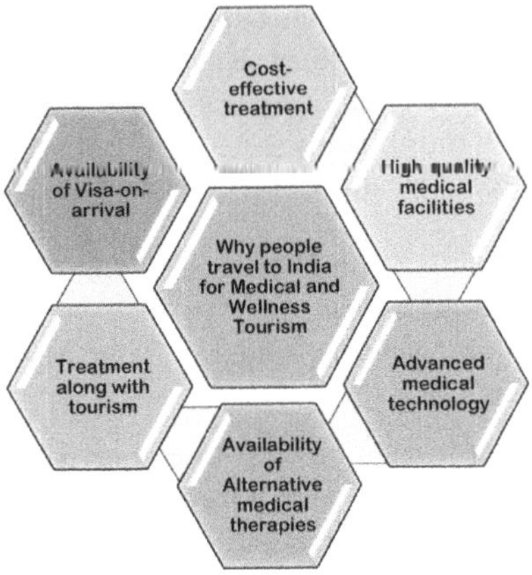

Fig. 4.3. Key Drivers to Growth of Wellness Tourism in India. *Source:* Compiled by author.

5. Policy Support and Digital Advancements in Medical and Wellness Tourism

The creation of a Ministry of Ayush specifically for Ayush on November 9, 2014, marked the first notable indication of the shift, and yoga has since been incorporated within it. With the honorable Prime Minister Shri Narendra Modi Ji's astute leadership, yoga has gotten a lot of support since 2014 (Press Information Bureau (Government of India), n.d.). Medical tourism is driven by world-class healthcare amenities and traditional healing practices, attracting 21% of international travelers to medical tourism and wellness retreats. With the signing of the *G20 New Delhi Leaders' Declaration*, India's G20 chairmanship for 2023 came to an end. It was determined by all of the leaders to step up efforts to realize the 2030 goal for sustainable development. For the first time in G20 summits, Traditional, Complementary, and Integrative Medicine (TCIM) was included in the declaration (Tillu & Chaturvedi, 2023). G-20 New Delhi leader declaration where it has been mentioned of "Recognize the potential role of evidence-based Traditional and Complimentary Medicine in health, and take note of international efforts in this direction, including WHO's global and collaborating centres, and clinical trial registries" (Minister of State for Environment, Forest & Climate Change, 2023). The *Champion Services Sector Scheme* for MVT will not only spread awareness of Ayurveda, Yoga, and other traditional medical practices in India, but it is also anticipated to draw more foreign patients, tourists, and visitors, which will likely result in increased FEEs for the nation. Along with increasing job opportunities for AYUSH, the proposed scheme aims to generate authentic data across the country for the Ayurvedic, Yoga, and other traditional medicine sectors. It also aims to expand opportunities for capacity building and skill development in these fields. The initiative aims to obtain NABH accreditation within one year of establishment, promote AYUSH systems in an ethical manner, and implement a focused strategy to attract international patients and tourists (Ministry of Ayush, 2022). The *"Ayushman Bharat – Health and Wellness Centres (AB-HWCs)"* booklet outlines India's initiative to improve primary healthcare through the establishment of HWCs, with 77,784 centers established as of September 14, 2021. Launched under the National Health Policy 2017, AB-HWCs aim to provide accessible, comprehensive healthcare that includes preventive, promotive, curative, rehabilitative, and palliative services. These centers offer a broad range of services such as maternal and child care, noncommunicable disease screenings, and wellness activities like yoga. Key features include free essential medicines and diagnostics, teleconsultation, community engagement, and IT integration for electronic health records. By transforming existing health centers, the initiative seeks to reduce out-of-pocket expenses and improve healthcare accessibility across India (MoHFW, 2021). The pandemic negatively affected global tourism but also raised public awareness of health and wellness, creating new opportunities for wellness tourism. India's rich heritage in wellness practices like Ayurveda and Yoga makes it a promising destination for wellness tourism in the post-COVID-19 era. India is currently being marketed as *"Incredible India."* The Indian Government has recognized the need of showcasing and promoting the nation's wellness offerings. In this regard, the *"Heal in India"* brand will be used to sell India in the years to come. On all international media campaigns and official digital channels, it would be regarded as a sub-brand of Incredible India (Choudhary & Qadir, 2022). To promote India as a global destination for health and wellness tourism, the Ministry of Ayush and the Ministry of Health & Family Welfare are collaborating to create a one-stop webpage called Heal in India (Press Information Bureau, 2023). India hosted the *"One Earth, One Health – Advantage Healthcare India 2023"* summit in New Delhi on April 27–28, 2023, to position the country as a global health and wellness tourism hub. With over 500 participants from 70+ countries, the event focused on promoting medical service exports and fostering networks among MVT experts. Prime Minister Narendra Modi highlighted India's traditional healthcare systems for addressing lifestyle diseases and emphasized the philosophy of "Vasudhaiva Kutumbakam," urging global investment in India's health sector, which ranks 10th on the MTI 2020–2021 (Karthikeyan, 2023). Implementing ethical standards and legal frameworks to control medical and wellness tourism and safeguard the interests of patients and regional healthcare systems is necessary if the practice is to continue (Rubagumya et al., 2024). The *"Gujrat Declaration 2023"* needs to serve as a beacon of guidance for developing strong traditional medicine policy worldwide. Through well-structured and thought-provoking talks, the Ministry of Ayush has demonstrated exceptional proficiency in promoting traditional medicine systems throughout all of its domains (Singh et al., 2024). The Indian Government has made it easier for citizens of 167 nations to go to India for medical care by granting them *e-medical visas and e-medical attendant visas* (*Lok Sabha Unstarred Question No. 147*, 2024). In order to promote MVT in Ayurveda and other traditional medical systems, the *Ministry of Ayush* and the India Tourism Development Corporation (ITDC), Ministry of Tourism, signed a Memorandum of Understanding (MoU) (Press Information Bureau, 2024). In the Ayush sector, 100% FDI is allowed via an automated process (Ministry of Ayush, Government of India, 2024). The Ministry of Tourism has formulated a *National Strategy and Roadmap for Medical and Wellness Tourism*, aiming to develop India as a brand for wellness tourism. Additionally, the strategy seeks to strengthen the ecosystem by enabling digitalization and enhancing accessibility for MVT (Tourism, 2022). Exposition of the government's Heal in India campaign, which aims to market India as a medically affordable tourism destination, includes the *Ayush Visa* category in its roadmap. An important step has been taken with the formation of a new type of *Ayush (AY) visa* for foreign nationals seeking treatment under Indian or Ayush medical systems. It will increase India's MVT. Our effort to realize our Hon. Prime Minister Shri Narendra Modi's goal of making Indian traditional medicine a worldwide phenomenon will be strengthened by this initiative. Additionally, I would like to commend Shri Amit Shah, the Union Home Minister of the GoI, for his efforts in establishing a unique category for Ayush Visas (Press Information Bureau, 2023). Any hospital or wellness center that has been approved and registered with the relevant government authority or authorities, or recognized hospitals offering Ayush services, may provide the treatment. In a similar manner, a medical attendant who is accompanying the patient can acquire an Ayush Visa (Government of India, 2024). For example, the ITDC has been designated as the Central Nodal Agency of the MVT sector by the Ministry of Tourism, which actively promotes health and wellness tourism in India. The introduction of e-visa, including triple-entry permissions for e-Medical and e-Medical Attendant Visas, has significantly streamlined MVT to India. The fully digitalized process, along with the Online MVT Portal, enhances accessibility, facilitates information exchange, and promotes India's medical and wellness tourism sector, making entry hassle-free for foreign visitors (Ministry of Tourism, 2024b). In a similar vein, the Ministry of Commerce highlights the trade potential of *MVT* and incorporates it into its larger plan for the expansion of the service industry. While the Ministry of AYUSH concentrates on enhancing India's standing as a center for traditional medicinal remedies, the Ministry of Health maintains a robust regulatory structure to preserve patient safety and credibility in Indian healthcare. In support of these initiatives, the Ministry of External Affairs streamlines the visa application procedure for medical travelers and diversifies India's MVT branding (Taneja et al., 2024). Additionally, wellness tourism service providers, such as accredited wellness facilities, are now eligible to receive *Market Development Assistance (MDA)* from the Ministry of Tourism. Currently, the MDA is also available to wellness centers that have been approved by state tourism departments. All wellness centers seeking MDA would be expected to adhere as closely as feasible to the NABH accreditation requirements whenever they are established (Ministry of Tourism, 2024a). To encourage the expansion of this industry, the Ministry of Tourism established the *National Medical & Wellness Tourism Board* in 2015.

It would strive to give industry stakeholders with grievance remedies as well as policy ideas and proposals (Invest India, 2022). To ensure and promote ethical business practices in the wellness tourism sector and to fortify, deepen, and expand collaboration across all medical service providers, including Ayurveda, Yoga, Unani, Siddha, and Homeopathy (Indian Medical Association, 2015). The Ministry of Tourism of the Government of India and the Republic of the Philippines met bilaterally in the Transport Bhawan in New Delhi on November 14, 2024. Under Secretary Ms. Maria Rica C. Bueno of the Philippines and Director General (Tourism) of India convened the meeting, which was centered on enhancing tourism relations. The India–ASEAN Year of Tourism 2025, women-led and youth tourism efforts, medical and wellness tourism, the possibility of Indian weddings in the Philippines, and luxury train services in India were among the main topics of conversation. For their mutual advantage, both parties decided to work together on these projects (Ministry of Tourism, 2024b).

6. How Destinations Leverage Wellness Assets to Establish Themselves in Wellness Tourism

Wellness tourism revolves around traditional treatments such as Ayurveda, meditation, homeopathy, naturopathy, and balanced diets, aiming to rejuvenate individuals on physical, mental, and emotional levels. Wellness retreats in India and globally offer these therapies, focusing on promoting healthful living throughout life's different stages. Beyond preventative health measures, wellness tourism also incorporates therapeutic practices to address various illnesses, contributing to overall well-being. For instance, Kerala, India, is referred to as "God's Own Country." It has positioned itself as the Land of Ayurveda, luring visitors from all over the world who are interested in well-being (Fig. 4.4). Travelers from around the world are discovering more genuine wellness experiences in the traditional therapies and routines that offer a total renewal of the body and mind. The new Wellness in Costa Rica The Pura Vida campaign has been effective in communicating well-being in an easy-to-understand way. Pura Vida, which translates to "Simple Life" or "Pure Life," represents the straightforward way of life that Costa Ricans led to perfect satisfaction. Travelers who prioritize wellness have long favored Tunisia, a small country in North Africa that is home to an abundance of thermal springs. Travelers take pleasure in both leisurely spa breaks in the hot springs and an authentic historical experience of Carthage (Jagyasi, 2024). Ayurvedic therapies, deeply rooted in the use of natural elements such as medicinal plants, herbs, milk, medicated oils, herbal powders, and curd, offer a holistic healing process known for its minimal side effects. The core of Ayurveda's healing approach is an 8-fold process, which includes therapies like Panchakarma, Abhyanga, Udwarthana, Choornaswedan, Njavarakizhi, Kaval, Vamana, and Virechana, each contributing to comprehensive wellness and rejuvenation (*Ayurveda in India, India Ayurveda Tour, Spa India, Kerala Ayurveda Tour*, n.d.).

Fig. 4.4. Regional Specializations in India's Wellness Tourism Landscape. *Source:* Tanisha (2024).

India has emerged as a leading destination for medical and wellness tourism, attracting approximately 2 million patients annually from 78 countries. Visitors primarily come from Asian and African nations, including Sri Lanka, Bangladesh, Nepal, Maldives, Indonesia, and Kenya. This influx of international tourists contributes significantly to the industry, generating \$6 billion in revenue, with projections to reach \$13 billion by 2026, driven by the government's "Heal in India" initiative. The country's top medical tourism hubs are Chennai, Mumbai, New Delhi, Ahmedabad, and Bangalore, known for their advanced healthcare facilities and diverse wellness services (Agnihotri, 2022). In 2023, the global wellness economy—which includes a variety of industries like conventional medicine, physical activity, mental health, nutrition, and personal care—was estimated to be worth \$6.3 trillion. Wellness tourism alone generated \$830 billion in 2023, according to the Global Wellness Institute, underscoring its vital significance in the larger wellness sector. Spas (\$137 billion), complementary and alternative medicine (\$553 billion), and mental well-being (\$233 billion) are all intimately related to wellness tourism. These connections highlight how modern tourists look for experiences that promote holistic well-being by combining rest, preventative medical care, and lifestyle enhancements.

Additionally, India has a great deal of opportunity to profit from this expanding industry, especially given its roots in naturopathy, yoga, and Ayurveda. By utilizing its rich history of holistic medicine, the nation's "Heal in India" campaign seeks to establish it as a top wellness travel destination. India must, however, address issues like awareness-raising, legislative frameworks that connect wellness tourism with the mainstream travel and healthcare sectors, and infrastructure shortages if it hopes to compete on a global scale. In order to meet the increasing demand for wellness-focused travel, these data emphasize the necessity of smart government interventions, corporate sector investments, and international partnerships. Wellness tourism is expected to become a dynamic and changing industry within the global economy in the future due to growing digital integration, artificial intelligence (AI)-driven wellness suggestions, and customized health retreats.

7. Pillars of Wellness Tourism in India

The Himalayas: India's Ultimate Wellness Escape—the concept of Himalayas and wellness tourism is interrelated. When considering the potential for natural wellness, the Himalayas and their resources could be used as substitutes for the opulent notion of wellness practices, such as taking morning and evening walks in verdant forests, taking a sunbath in a fresh and clean environment, spending evenings in waterfalls, eating fruits without the use of chemicals, having a bonfire in the late evening, and using rocks, natural herbs, and soil that is abundant in minerals as medicine. In Himalayan locations like Uttarakhand, Sikkim, and others, mineral springs and thermal mud are readily available for the treatment of a variety of illnesses. There are many springs in the Himalayan region that can satisfy such a person's needs. The Gasa hot springs, one of Bhutan's most well-known hot springs, provide the best illustration. These hot springs have therapeutic qualities for a wide range of conditions, including body aches and different types of skin disorders. Undertaking pilgrimages to sacred sites such as Vaishno Devi, Amarnath, Kedarnath, Mansarovar, and Badrinath, nestled in the lap of the Himalayas, fosters spiritual contemplation while simultaneously offering the opportunity to experience the region's natural beauty. These pilgrimage destinations, including the Mata Vaishno Devi and Amarnath shrines, as well as the Hemkunt Sahib in Uttarakhand, not only enrich spiritual fulfillment but also strengthen the connection between individuals and nature, contributing to overall well-being. Vipassana, or "to see things as they really are," is the best example of such a technique. Sahastradhara, often known as the "thousand springs," is the best example. It is located 16 kilometres from Dehradun. Here, sulfur is said to have therapeutic qualities and to treat skin ailments. It has been used for meditation and spiritual well-being in India for over 2,500 years. Gyuto Monastery offers such instruction. In addition, the

Himalayan regions of Tibet, Ladakh, Kashmir, and Uttarakhand are home to numerous religious monasteries, temples, and shrines that are endowed with the spirituality of gods and goddesses. Yoga has been shown in scientific studies to prevent and treat both common and uncommon ailments. There is nowhere more serene and calm than the Himalayas for yoga-based self-discovery. Due to the lack of promotion for these locations, travelers instead choose to travel to other locations, such as Kerala, for yoga and wellness treatments. Alongside preserving its authenticity and ethnicity, which are best characterized and achieved by the natural environment, wellness tourism in the Himalayan region would also aid in raising the value of traditional sources of therapies like Ayurveda. The main idea is that the wellness resources provided by Himalayan locations are not only unique but also reasonably priced and easily accessible to travelers (Manhas & Kour, 2020).

Rishikesh & Haridwar, Uttarakhand—The Yoga Capital of the World

Ananda in the Himalayas provides yoga, meditation, and around 74 body therapies. Numerous Therapies: Yoga Dhyana, Weight Loss, Detox, Ayurvedic Rejuvenation, Self-Realization Program, and Stress Management. Yoga Pavilion: A magnificent outdoor shelter with a marble floor that offers the perfect setting for one-on-one training or quiet meditation. The author came up with a plan to draw wellness travelers to the Himalayas. The existence of yoga, meditation, spiritual activities, and a spiritual environment are considered push elements in this push-and-pull model while retreats, destination spas, and the environment are considered pull factors (Charak, 2019).

Patanjali Yogpeeth "Yog Gram" has been promoting Yoga tourism since 2006 with a vision to heal tourists through Yoga and naturopathy. It is one of India's largest wellness institutes catering to both national and international visitors, offering residential facilities in a serene natural environment. Under the guidance of Swami Ramdev Ji and Acharya Balkrishna Ji, it integrates science and spiritualism, providing mental and physical rejuvenation. The institute offers four types of accommodation for wellness seekers: Rajrishi Cottage, Muniraj Cottage, Maharishi Cottage, and Tapasvi Cottage. Patanjali Yogpeeth's "Yoga Gram" provides a variety of treatments, mostly for health and wellness tourists, based on the principles of naturopathy and Ayurveda such as Hydro Therapy, Acupuncture Therapy, Yoga Therapy, Mud Therapy, Pyramid Therapy, Pranic Healing Therapy, Water Wave Therapy, Whirlpool Bath Therapy, Sand Therapy, Ozone Steam Sona Bath Therapy, Magnet Therapy, Mud Swimming Pool Therapy, Color Thermolian Therapy, Reiki Therapy, Massage Therapy, Sun Therapy, Aero Therapy, Acupressure Therapy, and Colon Irrigator Hydro Therapy (Rajeev et al., 2022).

Where Royalty Meets Wellness: Six Senses Fort Barwara's Role in India's Luxury Wellness Tourism – A comprehensive Ayurvedic healing system is provided by Six Senses Rajasthan, which incorporates meditation and personalized wellness programs founded on Eastern medicine's preventative principles with Western influences that are focused on results. The Six Senses Spa and Fitness Center, housed within the original women's palace and temple complex, features Ayurveda treatment rooms, a yoga pavilion, a meditation temple, and specialized programs such as sunset/sunrise yoga, detox therapies, and holistic lifestyle programs (Six Senses, 2025). A review of Six Senses Rajasthan highlights its personalized approach to wellness, offering Ayurvedic treatments tailored to individual body types and specific health needs. The retreat seamlessly blends authentic Ayurvedic healing with luxury, ensuring a holistic and aesthetically enriching wellness experience (Pasricha, 2023).

Kerala: The Ayurveda Capital of the World – Kerala has established itself as a leading wellness tourism destination, globally recognized for its authentic Ayurveda treatments, skilled practitioners, and natural healing environment. The state attracts a significant number of international wellness tourists due to its rich medicinal plant resources, favorable monsoon climate, and a strong network of Ayurveda resorts and hospitals. Wellness tourism significantly contributes to Kerala's economy, generating foreign exchange, employment opportunities, and growth in the Ayurveda pharmaceutical industry (Pk, 2020). Building on its wellness tourism success, Kerala is now expanding into medical wellness tourism, integrating modern healthcare with traditional healing systems. This approach focuses on preventive healthcare and evidence-based treatments, leveraging the state's advanced medical infrastructure and skilled professionals to attract global health tourists. However, challenges such as limited internationally accredited hospitals, weak coordination between tourism and healthcare sectors, and growing competition from destinations like Thailand and Singapore necessitate policy interventions and strategic branding. Kerala's evolving model presents an opportunity to integrate Ayurveda, wellness, and modern medicine into a unified health tourism framework (Grant Thornton, 2015).

Varanasi: Where Spirituality Meets Wellness Tourism—Modern medical specialties including plastic surgery, cataract surgery, and calculus surgeries are thought to have their roots in Ayurveda, which is considered to have started in Varanasi. Ayurveda and yoga's founder, Maharshi Patanjali, was also connected to the holy city of Varanasi. Since ancient times, Varanasi has also been well-known for its trade and commerce, particularly for the finest silks and brocades of gold and silver (Government of Uttar Pradesh, n.d.). Varanasi, also known as Banaras or Kashi, is the world's oldest surviving city. Because Varanasi's Ganges is said to have the ability to cleanse people of their sins, the city's numerous Ganges Ghats are explained. Varanasi is a popular tourist destination, most likely because of its distinctive culture (The Times of India, 2015).

The success of *Singapore, Bangkok, and Seoul* in establishing themselves as leading health tourism destinations offers valuable insights for India's wellness tourism development. Singapore is recognized for its world-class medical infrastructure, accreditation standards, and government-led health tourism initiatives, making it a preferred destination for high-quality medical care. Bangkok has positioned itself as a global wellness tourism hub by integrating affordable medical treatments with traditional healing practices, spa culture, and holistic therapies, attracting millions of international tourists. Seoul, on the other hand, has excelled in cosmetic surgery and traditional medicine tourism, leveraging advanced dermatology, plastic surgery expertise, and Korean herbal medicine to cater to global demand. These cities have successfully blended quality healthcare with tourism experiences, strong marketing strategies, and supportive government policies. India, with its rich heritage of Ayurveda, Yoga, and naturopathy, can take inspiration from these models to strengthen its "Heal in India" initiative, improve global branding, and develop a structured regulatory framework to enhance its position in the global wellness tourism market (Lee & Kim, 2015).

8. Post-COVID-19 Trends of Wellness

Wellness travel has grown as a result of the previous pandemic making people more conscious of their physical and mental well-being. The fundamental goal of this trend is to attain, encourage, or preserve the highest level of health and balance in one's life through pursuits like yoga retreats and spa treatments. The job market is booming once more at the same time that the hospitality and tourism industries around the world are recovering. There are a ton of opportunities for anyone who wish to work in the hospitality and tourism sector because hotels and resorts are looking for expertise to help them navigate the new era (Azzahra, 2023). The COVID-19 pandemic has reshaped wellness tourism by driving demand for nature-immersed wellness experiences and stricter health protocols at wellness resorts. There is a growing emphasis on mental well-being, stress relief programs, and personalized healing therapies. Additionally, travelers are prioritizing destinations that offer holistic health solutions while ensuring safe and regulated environments for wellness retreats (Yepez & Leimgruber, 2024). While the fast-growing demand necessitates innovative approaches to differentiate and personalize goods and services, there is also a need to address the concurrent rise in visitors' risk aversion and risk perceptions in order to slow the virus's spread. The COVID-19 pandemic has fundamentally reshaped tourists' risk perceptions and travel behavior, leading to a greater emphasis on safety, hygiene, and structured risk management in wellness tourism. Travelers are now prioritizing destinations with transparent health policies, advanced sanitization protocols, and crisis preparedness strategies. There is a growing demand for contactless services, self-contained wellness retreats, and private wellness experiences to minimize exposure risks. Additionally, health-insured travel packages and digital verification systems (such as vaccine passports and AI-driven health assessments) have emerged as crucial tools for ensuring safe wellness tourism. This shift has pushed wellness resorts and retreats to adopt adaptive crisis response models, integrating real-time risk monitoring and public health collaboration to maintain consumer trust in the postpandemic era (Rahman et al., 2021). Wellness tourism is increasingly shifting toward longevity and preventive health tourism, where travelers seek age-reversal therapies, biohacking treatments, and personalized health optimization programs rather than focusing solely on relaxation-based retreats (Piatto Clerici et al., 2023). Since wellness tourism has been outpacing all other forms of tourism for over 10 years, its share of the total tourism market has also increased. In 2022, 819.4 billion domestic and international wellness trips accounted for 7.8% of all tourism trips, a significantly higher percentage than just

10 years prior. By 2027, wellness trips are expected to account for 8.3% of all tourism trips (Global Wellness Tourism Economy Report - Global Wellness Institute, n.d.).

9. Challenges and Opportunity

Purpose-built wellness infrastructure, whether spa retreats, integrative medical tourism facilities, or wellness resorts, is lacking in many locations. Traditional tourist resorts' staff lacks sufficient training in wellness-specific services. The popularity of wellness tourism has resulted in widespread commercialization, which frequently dilutes the genuineness of conventional treatment methods. Certain locations lessen their distinctive attractiveness by packaging generic wellness experiences (such as yoga retreats devoid of cultural nuance). Seasonal variations affect many health locations, making it challenging for companies to stay profitable all year long. Economic volatility in wellness tourism industries is caused by a lack of varied options (beyond peak seasons). Water and energy resources in the area are under stress due to the growth of wellness tourism. Rather than promoting sustainability, some wellness resorts degrade the environment by overusing its natural resources. The industry is changing as a result of the use of smart tourism solutions (such as virtual wellness consultations and AI-based wellness suggestions). Customizing wellness experiences through digital platforms can boost consumer engagement. Wellness travel provides long-term sustainability and lessens reliance on mass tourism (Nel-lo Andreu et al., 2021). The largest issue facing the wellness sector is finding and keeping qualified workers. Good training facilities offering standardized and recognized courses are hard to come by. Vocational training programs frequently provide minimal practical experience along with theoretical knowledge. Despite the enormous demand, the nation has a small pool of qualified specialists. The industry has a high turnover rate, making it difficult to retain seasoned experts. There is no clear regulatory structure for the wellness services sector. Due to a lack of proper regulation, entry barriers have decreased, making it relatively simple for amateur and small businesses to enter the market. These businesses lack back-end infrastructure, standardized services, transparent pricing, pro-customer behavior, and hygiene and quality (Tourism, 2022). A significant challenge for India's wellness tourism sector is the lack of awareness about the benefits of Ayurveda and yoga among a large global audience. Enhancing awareness and creating a positive image of India as a premier wellness destination are crucial steps in boosting the country's tourism industry (Choudhary & Qadir, 2022). Low-cost travel destinations like Thailand, Malaysia, Singapore, Turkey, and South Korea are fiercely competing with India.

Kerala's Ayurvedic wellness resorts, despite attracting global tourists, face significant service quality gaps, particularly in hygiene, staff responsiveness, and personalized treatments. Tourist expectations often exceed their actual experiences, leading to dissatisfaction. Addressing these challenges requires strategic improvements in service quality, enhanced customer engagement, and better facility management to uphold Kerala's reputation as a leading wellness tourism destination (Anju and Bindu, 2024). The travel and tourism industry faces a number of complicated issues, including as geopolitical unpredictability, economic volatility, and extreme weather occurrences, according to the World Economic Forum's 2024 Global Risks Report. With problems like high seasonality, overcrowding, and rising emissions affecting long-term development, striking a balance between growth and sustainability is still a major challenge. In order to guarantee long-term industry sustainability, the chapter also emphasizes the difficulties with fairness and inclusion and the necessity of inclusive and sustainable wellness tourism policies (World Economic Forum, n.d.). The COVID-19 pandemic had a profound impact on global tourism, leading to a 74% decline in international tourist arrivals in 2020 compared to 2019. Tourism-dependent economies, particularly in developing nations, were severely affected, with small businesses facing significant financial distress. In response, governments implemented various measures, including enhanced tourism safety regulations, vaccination policies, and economic stimulus packages, to support industry recovery (Kumar & Ekka, 2024).

10. The Future of Wellness Tourism: Trends, Technology, and Policy Integration

The fact that wellness tourism is surrounded by natural benefits in every way—such as ayurvedic herbal treatments, nature walks, and Himalayan natural site seeing—makes it significant. As a result, it can serve as a marketing tool for ecotourism and sustainable tourism, which are currently the main priorities. However, as these nations are also in line with the Himalayas and may contribute to wellness tourism in a variety of ways, Himalayan wellness tourism is also expanding to other nations like China, Nepal, Bhutan, and others. All of these nations would benefit from working together and promoting the Himalayas together. Wellness tourism would significantly increase if all of these nations worked together with India to promote the Himalayas in line with Indian tourism policy. They can establish a specific agreement, make Himalayan health travel a worldwide sensation, and help to preserve its integrity between these nations. The concept's critical approach cannot ignore the fact that the tourist sector has become a deliberate process due to a number of issues, including infrastructure, economic development, sustainability, climate change, and community involvement (Manhas & Kour, 2020). In order to establish a niche in the market, spa resorts should also promote Himalayan areas as wellness travel destinations by introducing the theories of Ayurveda, yoga, and meditation. The Himalayas have enormous potential to become the go-to spa destination; therefore, it is imperative that government policies or a framework be developed to promote these unexplored locations as wellness destinations (Charak, 2019). Wellness tourism policies should integrate both hedonic (relaxation) and eudaimonic (transformational) experiences while ensuring sustainability and benefits for local communities. Governments must invest in research-driven strategies to enhance well-being through tourism. Future trends indicate a shift toward personalized wellness experiences, digital integration (AI, virtual reality [VR] meditation), and purpose-driven travel. A long-term well-being approach should be prioritized over short-term relaxation (Kay Smith & Diekmann, 2017). The future of wellness tourism lies in combining allopathic medicine with traditional healing practices like Ayurveda, naturopathy, and herbal medicine. Travelers are seeking customized health retreats, focusing on preventive care, detoxification, and long-term well-being instead of just treating diseases. More destinations are offering blended health experiences, where medical treatments are complemented by holistic wellness therapies. The future will see an increase in AI-driven health diagnostics, wearable wellness technology, virtual wellness retreats, and telemedicine services for international wellness tourists. Digital platforms will enhance personalized treatment plans, remote consultations, and wellness tracking for travelers before, during, and after their trips. Government initiatives like *"Heal in India"* will play a crucial role in making India a preferred destination for holistic health travelers (Majeed et al., 2017). Since the pandemic, the world of tourism has changed dramatically, with a greater focus on digital integration, health, and well-being. In particular, wellness tourism is changing to satisfy the growing desire for individualized, technologically advanced experiences that combine cutting-edge innovations with conventional therapy. This change is seen in the use of AI-powered wellness initiatives, online health consultations, and eco-friendly retreat models. Furthermore, travelers now prioritize safety, cleanliness, and immunity-boosting treatments, which emphasizes the importance of integrative health tourism. Sustainability and digitalization will be key factors in determining how wellness tourism develops in the future, helping to make it more efficient, accessible, and ecologically conscious (Yepez & Leimgruber, 2024).

The research of OECD suggests that governments implement policies to:

- give destinations the tools they need to effectively manage and diversify their tourist flows in order to benefit the environment and nearby communities;
- incorporate the requirements of tourism workers into more comprehensive development plans, guaranteeing that they have access to reasonably priced accommodation and transportation in isolated locations;
- assist travel agencies in obtaining funding and training to implement digital solutions, green business practices, and creative work methods (OECD, 2024).

The pandemic has accelerated tech-integrated wellness, leading to advancements in AI-driven wellness analytics, genetic testing for personalized health plans, and immersive digital wellness experiences using VR and wearable health technology (Piatto Clerici et al., 2023). As risk perception continues to shape travel decisions, wellness tourism is evolving to incorporate enhanced safety, technology, and crisis preparedness. The future will see a rise in AI-driven health monitoring, where travelers receive personalized risk assessments and wellness recommendations before and during their trips. Blockchain-based health verification systems, ensuring seamless and secure documentation of travelers' health status, will become integral to international wellness travel. Additionally, self-sustaining wellness retreats with bio-secure environments—offering controlled, nature-immersed experiences with minimal external contact—will gain popularity. The sector will also witness an expansion of travel insurance policies covering wellness and preventive healthcare, reinforcing confidence in safe, long-term wellness tourism experiences (Rahman et al., 2021). The pandemic has emphasized the critical need for adaptive strategies in tourism management. Kumar and Ekka (2024) advocate for integrating machine learning models, such as attention-based LSTMs, into tourism forecasting to improve crisis preparedness. These models can provide real-time insights into demand fluctuations, allowing policymakers and businesses to proactively adjust their strategies, rather than relying on reactive measures (Kumar & Ekka, 2024).

11. Conclusion

The tourism industry was severely affected due to the COVID-19 pandemic, and after the pandemic, people got serious about their well-being, no matter physical or mental. There are so many opportunities associated with tourism and the wellness sector and all kinds of services, infrastructure, and facilities that can help companies stand out, provide more value, and attract higher spending by travelers. India is performing well in international market in healing whether traditional or modern. The wellness tourism sector is creating abundant jobs in different sectors like hotel, travel, aviation, and food, which is directly benefiting the economy of these sectors. The pandemic has made India a go-to destination not only for travel but also to experience traditional healing practices. Ministry of Tourism and Ministry of Ayush Government of India is promoting and highlighting the value of Ayurveda and Yoga at the international platform. The Heal in India, Ayush visa, and MVT and infrastructure support are driving growth in the wellness sector, which can be seen in the number of foreign medical tourists' arrival in India after pandemic. As per the Tourism Satellite Account (TSA), 2015–2016, the percentage contribution of tourism sector to the country's GDP for 2022–2023 is 5%. The wellness tourism industry needs more support of government and strategic development policies. The Union Budget 2025–2026 has set aside ₹2,541.06 crore to improve infrastructure, skill development, and travel facilitation because of its potential for employment-led development. In India, Kerala is globally renowned for Ayurveda and yoga tourism due to its well-established traditional treatments. Likewise, Rishikesh and Varanasi are known as the lands of spirituality and healing. Statistics indicate a rising global demand for Indian healing and rejuvenation practices.

Over time, technological advancements have brought many aspects of wellness closer, such as yoga healing through video calls and AI-driven tools enhancing wellness experiences. The integration of wellness data across multiple sources, seamless communication of health-related information, and incorporation of wellness insights into daily lifestyles are shaping the future of the industry. AI-driven hyper-personalization is set to transform hospitality, wellness, and spa services by offering customized experiences tailored to individual needs. Effective destination management is crucial for the sustainable growth of wellness tourism. Developing eco-friendly wellness hubs, involving local communities, leveraging technology, and implementing standardized regulations will enhance long-term appeal and resilience in the sector. Maintaining authenticity is crucial for the sustained growth of foreign wellness tourists. In today's era, excessive commercialization is diminishing the true essence of wellness and Ayurveda. By promoting itself as a top location for Ayurveda, yoga, and holistic health, India may increase its worldwide footprint in wellness tourism. Participation in international tourism fairs, focused marketing initiatives, and worldwide partnerships with wellness groups can all help achieve this. A wide variety of travelers looking for genuine and superior wellness experiences can be drawn in by collaborating with international travel agencies, wellness resorts, and healthcare professionals. In order to strengthen India's standing as a top overseas healthcare destination, Finance Minister Smt. Nirmala Sitharaman declared that health tourism and the "Heal in India" campaign would be pushed in collaboration with the commercial sector. By utilizing advanced medical technology, world-class medical knowledge, and traditional wellness practices like yoga and Ayurveda, India hopes to draw in a greater number of foreign patients looking for high-quality, reasonably priced care. By improving infrastructure, increasing employment, and promoting a variety of tourism niches, such as spiritual, medical, and heritage tourism, the Indian Government is dedicated to making the nation a global leader in the travel industry.

Acknowledgments

The authors gratefully acknowledge the *Global Wellness Institute* for granting permission to use selected graphical materials. The inclusion of their data-driven visualizations has significantly contributed to the scholarly depth and analytical rigor of this chapter.

References

Agnihotri, A. (2022). Medical tourism in India: Top destinations, scenarios and all you need to know | Travel. *Hindustan Times.* https://www.hindustantimes.com/lifestyle/travel/medical-tourism-in-india-top-destinations-scenarios-and-all-you-need-to-know-101668163467932.html

Anju, K. P., & Bindu, V. T. (2024). What insights does service quality gap analysis offer for the wellness tourism sector in Kerala? *Atna Journal of Tourism Studies, 19*(2), 265–290.

Asia-Pacific Travel and Tourism Statistics in 2023. (2023). https://travelerwp.com/asia-pacific-travel-and-tourism-statistics-in-2023/

Ayurveda in India, India Ayurveda Tour, Spa India, Kerala Ayurveda Tour. (n.d.). https://www.incredibleindia-tourism.org/india-ayurveda-spa/. Accessed on October 12, 2024.

Azzahra, A. M. (2023). *Post-pandemic travel trends: The future of hospitality and tourism industry*. https://www.educationaltravelasia.org/post-pandemic-travel-trends-the-future-of-hospitality-and-tourism-industry/

Callaghan, S., Lösch, M., Pione, A., & Teichner, W. (2021). *The future of the $1.5 trillion wellness market | McKinsey*. McKinsey and Company. https://www.mckinsey.com/industries/consumer-packaged-goods/our-insights/feeling-good-the-future-of-the-1-5-trillion-wellness-market#/

Charak, N. S. (2019). Role of spa resorts in promoting India as a preferred wellness tourism destination–A case of Himalayas. *International Journal of Spa and Wellness*, *2*(1), 53–62. https://doi.org/10.1080/24721735.2019.1668672

Choudhary, B., & Qadir, A. (2022). Wellness tourism in India during post COVID-19 era: Opportunities and challenges. *Turizam*, *26*(3), 134–143. https://doi.org/10.5937/turizam26-34441

CVR. (n.d.). *Wellness Tourism Market Size, Share & Trends Report, 2030*. https://www.futuremarketinsights.com/reports/wellness-tourism-market. Accessed on October 8, 2024.

Desk, H. N. (2024). *Foreign tourist arrivals to India in 2024 to surpass pre-pandemic level: Experts*. Hindustan Times. https://www.hindustantimes.com/world-news/foreign-tourist-arrivals-to-india-in-2024-to-surpass-pre-pandemic-level-experts-101714385271672.html

Global Wellness Institute. (n.d.-a). *Wellness Economy Statistics & Facts. 2023*. https://globalwellnessinstitute.org/press-room/statistics-and-facts/

Global Wellness Institute. (n.d.-b). *Wellness tourism*. https://globalwellnessinstitute.org/what-is-wellness/what-is-wellness-tourism/#:~:text=What is wellness tourism?,or enhancing one's personal wellbeing

Global Wellness Tourism Economy Report. (n.d.). Global Wellness Institute. https://globalwellnessinstitute.org/what-is-wellness/what-is-wellness-tourism/. Accessed on October 07, 2024.

Government of India. (2024). *Embassy of India*. https://www.indianembassydublin.gov.in/

Government of India. (n.d.). *Journey to wellness: Medical value travel*. Invest India. https://www.investindia.gov.in/sector/healthcare/medical-value-travel. Accessed on October 11, 2024.

Government of Uttar Pradesh. (n.d.). *Varanasi tourism*. https://varanasi.nic.in/tourism/

Indian Medical Association. (2015). *Indian medical association*. https://www.ima-india.org/ima/left-side-bar.php?pid=439

Invest India. (2022). *India: A global medical and wellness tourism destination*. https://www.investindia.gov.in/

Jagyasi, Dr. P. (2024). *Guide to wellness tourism*. https://drprem.com/wellness/importance-and-advantages-of-wellness-tourism-and-its-effect-on-modern-age-travel/#wonders

Karthikeyan, S. (2023). Explained | Why is the centre promoting medical value travel? A look at the billion-dollar industry & India's growth. *The Hindu*. https://www.thehindu.com/news/national/explained-why-is-centre-promoting-medical-value-travel-a-look-at-the-billions-worthy-industry-indias-growth/article66789848.ece

Kay Smith, M., & Diekmann, A. (2017). Tourism and wellbeing. *Annals of Tourism Research*, *66*, 1–13. https://doi.org/10.1016/j.annals.2017.05.006

Kumar, A. (2019). *Wellness tourism: Taking a step forward*. www.traveltrendstoday.in

Kumar, P., & Ekka, P. (2024). Statistical analysis of the impacts of COVID-19 pandemic on the small and large-scale tourism sectors in developing countries. *Environment, Development and Sustainability*, *26*(4), 9625–9659. https://doi.org/10.1007/s10668-023-03112-4

Lee, J., & Kim, H.-b. (2015). Success factors of health tourism: Cases of Asian tourism cities. *International Journal of Tourism Cities*, *1*(3), 216–233. https://doi.org/10.1108/IJTC-08-2014-0014

Liao, C., Zuo, Y., Xu, S., Law, R., & Zhang, M. (2023). Dimensions of the health benefits of wellness tourism: A review. *Frontiers in Psychology*, *13*(January), 1–10. https://doi.org/10.3389/fpsyg.2022.1071578

Lok Sabha Unstarred Question no. 147. (2024). https://tourism.gov.in/sites/default/files/2024-11/usq.147 for 25.11.2024.pdf

Maitra India, R. (2022). New avenues of wellness tourism in untouched aspects of healing in India. *International Journal of Research in Tourism and Hospitality*, *8*(1), 1–8. https://doi.org/10.20431/2455-0043.0801001

Majeed, S., Lu, C., & Javed, T. (2017). The journey from an allopathic to natural treatment approach: A scoping review of medical tourism and health systems. *European Journal of Integrative Medicine*, *16*(July), 22–32. https://doi.org/10.1016/j.eujim.2017.10.001

Manhas, P. S., & Kour, P. (2020). Holistic approach to wellness–A case study of Himalayas. *Journal of Hospitality & Tourism Cases: An International Case Journal*, *3*(2), 38–43. https://doi.org/10.4135/9781529710854

Ministry of Ayush, Government of India. (2022). *Central sector scheme for the establishment of AYUSH super specialty hospitals/day care centres for medical tourism under champion services sector scheme for medical value travel*. Ayush NGO Portal.

Ministry of Ayush, Government of India. (2024). *A decade of transformative growth in Ayush towards holistic health for all*. https://www.ccrhindia.nic.in/WriteReadData/LINKS/Growth in Ayush(English-Final)50d5cb0a-73d9-4d8b-bb5c-60dceb0f9b1d.pdf

Minister of State for Environment, Forest & Climate Change, S. A. K. C. (2023). *Press release: Press information bureau*. PIB Delhi. https://pib.gov.in/PressReleasePage.aspx?PRID=1991441

Ministry of Tourism. (2022). *National strategy and roadmap for medical and wellness tourism*. https://tourism.gov.in/sites/default/files/2022-05/National Strategy and Roadmap for Medical and Wellness Tourism.pdf

Ministry of Tourism. (2024a). *Ministry of tourism*. Government of India.

Ministry of Tourism. (2024b). *Ministry of Tourism Annual Report 2024-25* (Issue December). https://tourism.gov.in/sites/default/files/2025-02/Ministry of Tourism Annual Report_2024-25_ENGLISH_0_1.pdf

Mishra, D. N., & Panda, R. K. (2021). How delightful is Indian wellness tourism? A netnographic study. *Advances in Hospitality and Tourism Research*, *9*(1), 132–156. https://doi.org/10.30519/ahtr.784232

MoHFW, Government of India. (2021). *Ayushman Bharat Health and Wellness Centres 2021*. https://ab-hwc.nhp.gov.in/assets/hwcpdf/Reforms_Booklet_HWC_English_updated_14th_Sep_2021.pdf

Nel-lo Andreu, M. G., Font-Barnet, A., & Espasa Roca, M. (2021). Wellness tourism-new challenges and opportunities for tourism in Salou. *Sustainability*, *13* (15), 1–13. https://doi.org/10.3390/su13158246

NITI Aayog. (2022). *Reimagining healthcare in India through blended finance* (Issue February). https://www.niti.gov.in/sites/default/files/2022-02/AIM-NITI-IPE-whitepaper-on-Blended-Financing.pdf

OECD. (2024). *Tourism continues to recover from COVID but faces renewed challenges*. https://www.oecd.org/en/blogs/2024/07/tourism-continues-to-recover-from-covid-but-faces-renewed-challenges.html

Pasricha, P. (2023). *Hotel review: Six Senses Fort Barwara, Rajasthan in India*. https://www.luxurylifestylemag.co.uk/travel/hotel-review-six-senses-fort-barwara-rajasthan-in-india/

Piatto Clerici, A., Murphy, C., & Castanheira Almeida, N. M. (2023). The future of wellness tourism after COVID-19. *European Spatial Research and Policy*, *30*(1), 103–122. https://doi.org/10.18778/1231-1952.30.1.05

PIB. (n.d.). *Tourism expansion in India*. https://static.pib.gov.in/WriteReadData/specificdocs/documents/2024/oct/doc2024103407001.pdf

Pk, H. K. (2020). *Kerala as a wellness tourism destination: Opportunities & challenges* (Vol. 70, pp. 2618–2629). https://www.semanticscholar.org/paper/Kerala-as-a-Wellness-Tourism-Destination%3A-%26

Press Information Bureau. (2023). *Government introduces a new category of Ayush visa for foreign nationals seeking treatment under Indian systems of medicine*. Press Information Bureau. https://pib.gov.in/PressReleaseIframePage.aspx?PRID=1945070

Press Information Bureau. (2024). *Government to promote AYUSH treatment through health tourism*. Press Information Bureau. https://pib.gov.in/PressReleasePage.aspx?PRID=1908019#:~:text=Government to promote AYUSH treatment through health tourism&text=Ministry of Ayush signed a,other traditional systems of medicine

Press Information Bureau (Government of India). (n.d.). *Unflinching aims of transformational reforms YOGA DAY*. https://static.pib.gov.in/WriteReadData/specificdocs/documents/2023/apr/doc2023424186001.pdf

Rahman, M. K., Gazi, A. I., Bhuiyan, M. A., & Rahaman, A. (2021). Effect of Covid-19 pandemic on tourist travel risk and management perceptions. *PLoS One*, *16*(9 September), e0256486. https://doi.org/10.1371/journal.pone.0256486

Rajasekhar, D. D. (2022). How India could become a wellness tourism hub. *The Economics Times*. https://travel.economictimes.indiatimes.com/news/destination/states/how-india-could-become-a-wellness-tourism-hub/92332108

Rajeev, R., Vikram Singh, S., Shekhar, H., & Chauhan, V. K. (2022). Factors influencing yoga tourism in Uttarakhand: A case study of Patanjali Yogpeeth. *International Journal of Trend in Scientific Research and Development*, *6*(2), 292–298. https://www.researchgate.net/publication/359603057_Factors_Influencing_Yoga_Tourism_in_Uttarakhand_A_Case_Study_of_Patanjali_Yogpeeth

Rappaport, S. (2023). The global wellness industry is now worth $5.6 trillion. *Bloomberg*. https://www.bloomberg.com/news/articles/2023-11-09/the-global-wellness-industry-is-now-worth-5-6-trillion

Rubagumya, F., Carson, L., Afolayan, D., Rugengamanzi, E., Nnko, G. A., Abdihamid, O., Vanderpuye, V., & Hammad, N. (2024). Medical tourism for cancer treatment: Trends, trajectories, and perspectives from African countries. *JCO Global Oncology, 10*. https://doi.org/10.1200/GO.24.00131

Sands, R. (2023a). *The global wellness tourism sector surpasses $814 billion market share*. https://www.forbes.com/sites/rogersands/2023/11/17/the-global-wellness-tourism-sector-surpasses-814-billion-market-share/

Sands, R. (2023b). *Wellness Tourism Market Size & Trends Analysis Report, 2030*. Grand View Research. https://www.futuremarketinsights.com/reports/wellness-tourism-market

Singh, A. (2022). India@2047 – From heal in India to heal by india…. *The Economics Times*. https://health.economictimes.indiatimes.com/news/industry/india2047-from-heal-in-india-to-heal-by-india/94337668

Singh, P. A., Bajwa, N., Hazra, S., & Chandan, A. (2024). Mapping out a direction: India's G20 presidency propels global promotion of traditional medicine. *World Medical & Health Policy, 16*(4), 783–794. https://doi.org/10.1002/wmh3.634

Six Senses. (2025). *Six Senses*. https://www.sixsenses.com/en/hotels-resorts/asia-the-pacific/india/fort-barwara/journal/myths-murder-modern-day-magic/

Smith, M., & Kelly, C. (2006). Wellness tourism A destination perspective. *Tourism Recreation Research, 31*(1). https://doi.org/10.1080/02508281.2006.11081241

Srivastava, A. (2024). Why India is a top destination for medical tourism. *The New Indian Express*. https://www.newindianexpress.com/xplore/2024/Aug/27/why-india-is-a-top-destination-for-medical-tourism

Taneja, N., Joshi, S., Rath, N., & Upreti, V. (2024). *Looking beyond Bangladesh: Making India's medical value travel sector more resilient*. https://icrier.org/publications/looking-beyond-bangladesh-making-indias-medical-value-travel-sector-more-resilient/

Tanisha, S. (2024). *What 2024 looks like for the wellness tourism in India*. India Travel Blog. Indian Holiday Pvt. Ltd. https://www.indianholiday.com/blog/wellness-tourism-in-india/

The Times of India. (2015). Varanasi: The land of spirituality. *The Times of India*. https://timesofindia.indiatimes.com/travel/destinations/varanasi-the-land-of-spirituality/articleshow/23109875.cms

Thornton, G. (2015). *Transformative evolution: From 'wellness' to 'medical wellness' tourism in Kerala* (Issue October). http://gtw3.grantthornton.in/assets/Grant_Thornton_report-Transformative_Evolution.pdf

Tillu, G., & Chaturvedi, S. (2023). G20 and traditional medicine global summit - Milestones for traditional, complementary and integrative medicine. *Journal of Ayurveda and Integrative Medicine, 14*(5). https://doi.org/10.1016/j.jaim.2023.100832

Tony, V. (2024). What's driving the explosive growth of wellness tourism in India? *The Economics Times*. https://travel.economictimes.indiatimes.com/blog/whats-driving-the-explosive-growth-of-wellness-tourism-in-india/108011163

Tour My India. (2018). *Top 20 wellness tourism destinations in India*. https://www.tourmyindia.com/blog/wellness-tourism-destinations-india/

TOURISM & HOSPITALITY. (2024). *IBEF.* (Issue May). https://doi.org/10.58532/v3bhma23p2ch4

World Economic Forum. (n.d.). *Tourism is back to pre-pandemic levels, but challenges remain.* https://www.weforum.org/press/2024/05/tourism-is-back-to-pre-pandemic-levels-but-challenges-remain/

Yepez, C., & Leimgruber, W. (2024). The evolving landscape of tourism, travel, and global trade since the Covid-19 pandemic. *Research in Globalization, 8*. https://doi.org/10.1016/j.resglo.2024.100207

Chapter 5

Nature-Based Spa and Wellness Tourism

B. Latha Lavanya[a] *and Sharmila Devi*[b]

[a]MEASI Institute of Management, India
[b]INTI International University, Malaysia

Abstract

The philosophical and practical antecedents of wellness are deeply embedded in human history, tracing back to ancient civilizations where the integration of mind and body was paramount. From a rich historical tapestry, the contemporary concept of the nature-based spa emerges, consciously echoing this ancient imperative to reconnect with the natural world. The principle of biophilia—the innate human affinity for natural systems—is central, with empirical patterns indicating a profound increase in relaxation and a significant enhancement of the tourist experience when wellness interventions are situated within a natural context. This study critically explores effects of this synthesis between biophilic design and wellness tourism. Employing a descriptive, quantitative methodology, data were accrued from a sample of 115 participants, selected via convenient sampling. Findings elucidate that the efficacy of the nature-based spa is contingent upon a tripartite foundation: the provision of highly skilled, compassionate, and professional service; a meticulously curated, serene ambiance that engages the senses; and a comprehensive menu of therapeutic services designed for holistic rejuvenation. This synergy creates an environment where customer satisfaction is intrinsically linked to profound physical, mental, and emotional restoration. These establishments offer a diverse array of tailored treatments—from advanced massages and hydrotherapy to aromatherapy and facials—that synergize traditional wisdom with modern innovation. The nature-based spa is validated as a vital sanctuary for modern tourism, reducing stress, promoting deep relaxation, and fostering an elevated state of overall well-being.

Nature, Wellness and Sustainability in Health Tourism, 103–125

doi:10.1108/978-1-83742-029-220261005

Keywords: Efficiency; kindness; competency; spa ambiance; healing benefits; wellness services

1. Introduction

Tourism is a dynamic service industry often described as the "human interaction industry." Unlike many sectors where advanced technology reduces job opportunities, tourism thrives on personal connections and human engagement, ensuring a steady demand for employment. Beyond its economic contributions, tourism plays a vital role in breaking down cultural and national barriers, fostering mutual respect, understanding, and peaceful relations among people from diverse backgrounds. The factors that influence tourism are economic development, aging population, work pressure, health awareness, and social development, which are some of the major drivers of spa tourism. The changes that took place in the economy of many countries in the 19th century indicate an increasing share of the service sector in creating national wealth. The new generation travels to maintain good health; the associated tourism activities can be defined as health tourism (García-Altés, 2005). Thermal springs, renowned for their healing and therapeutic properties, have been utilized for centuries as a vital resource for bathing and wellness. These springs are formed when underground water, often heated by geothermal activity, rises to the surface through natural openings in the earth (Huijbens, 2011; Unione Geotermica Italiana, 2010). The mineral-rich composition of thermal spring water, combined with its warmth, has long been believed to offer a variety of health benefits, including relieving aches, improving circulation, and promoting relaxation.

Recognizing these benefits, ancient civilizations developed bathing practices centered on thermal springs. Private baths became a luxury for the wealthy, offering exclusive and serene spaces for personal rejuvenation. Meanwhile, public baths were constructed for the working class, serving as communal hubs that combined hygiene with social interaction. These facilities often evolved into sophisticated complexes, featuring not just baths but also saunas, steam rooms, and spaces for relaxation and healing. The universal appeal of thermal springs reflects their enduring significance as a natural and cultural asset for promoting health and well-being.

Health perceptions are largely socially constructed, shaped by the prevailing culture and historical context of a country. The nature-based spa industry has evolved from a series of small business and cottage industries existing in parallel in many different locations around the world based on local bathing, beauty, wellness, and healing practices (Koncul, 2012; Lee & King, 2008). The industry is still evolving, and while hotel spas and day spas are becoming more established, new models are developing including specialty spas, residential spa communities, and medi-spas that are beginning to integrate western medical expertise, as well as a growing market for home spa product and services (Buxton & Michopoulou, 2021; Rancic et al., 2013). The global spa industry has seen significant growth, driven by increased consumer interest in wellness. People's beliefs about health shape their approach to wellness tourism, making it important to understand these perceptions when studying health or wellness travelers (Chen et al., 2008). Wellness tourism offers an alternative for those who don't need medical treatment but want to improve or maintain their health. Common wellness activities include spas, massages, beauty treatments, healthy eating, and exercise (Marican et al., 2021). Wellness tourism is considered a subcategory of health tourism, focusing on "healthy" individuals whose primary goal is to preserve or enhance their health. Spas can be classified into six main types: mineral and thermal springs, destination, health club, medical, resort and hotel, and day spa. While traditional spas often emerge near thermal mineral springs, modern spas typically offer a variety of beauty and wellness treatments regardless of their location (Gonzales et al., 2001).

The Burgas mineral water source, known as Aquae Calidae, is one of Bulgaria's oldest and most famous spa and balneotherapy sites, celebrated for its geothermal springs with proven healing properties. Located near Burgas city, it has been used since ancient Thracian, Roman, and Byzantine times and continues today as a modern wellness destination.

The Roman thermal Spa was built around 70 CE, the Roman Baths (Aquae Sulis) were a major public bathing and social complex. Fed by natural hot springs, producing over 1.3 million liters of mineral-rich water daily at ~40°C. Included the Great Bath and the Temple of Sulis Minerva, blending health, leisure, and religion. Served as a healing and social hub, believed to offer therapeutic benefits from geothermal waters. Today, it is a UNESCO World Heritage Site, preserved as a museum and cultural landmark, with modern spa facilities nearby.

2. Nature-Based Spa

Some of the most common health and wellness approaches included:

- Homeopathy, which uses small amounts of natural substances to heal the body.
- Hydrotherapy or hydropathy, which uses water to treat different ailments.
- Osteopathy, which is the manipulation of the muscles and joints taken from a holistic approach.
- Chiropractic, which is focusing the manipulation of the spine and other joints.
- Naturopathy, which is the thought that one can be cured without medication (Global Wellness Institute, n.d.).

Fig. 5.1: *As early as the second century AD, medical texts already identified healing spas—natural mineral water baths—(αὐτοφυῶν λουτρῶν) as opposed to common heated common water baths (λουτρόν)—without an adjective—or "artificial baths" (τῶν ἐξ ἐπιτεχνήσεως) (Antilus, in Orib. 10, 3). In this sense, in Roman times, the feminine plural word, aquae ("the waters"), was mainly used to refer to these medicinal mineral waters, as defined by Varro (Ling. 9, 41, 68–69); or, more specifically, aquae calida*

Fig. 5.1. Burgas Mineral Water Source (Ourense, Spain).

Fig. 5.2: *These are mentioned, for instance, by several authors in the compilation made by physician Oribasius (fourth century AD, Collectanae medicinalia) or the well-known works of authors such as Vitruvius (8, 3, 1), Pliny the Elder (31, 1–5) or Seneca (Nat, 3, 20–24), explicitly referring to the mineral formulation of these waters and not just to their temperature, which are linked to the health properties of these springs (s. Oro' Ferna'ndez 1996 on this topic).*

Fig. 5.3: *A bar chart showing global wellness tourism market growth from 2015 to 2025. Domestic tourism rises steadily from $569 billion to $603 billion, while international tourism increases sharply from $473 billion to $615 billion. The chart highlights the expanding demand for wellness travel worldwide).*

Health spas that used hydrotherapy continued to grow in popularity in the United States and Europe in the 18th century (Grabar, 2015). The spa buildings in Bath, along with the surrounding city, are renowned for their Palladian and Neoclassical architecture, exemplified by the iconic Royal Crescent townhouses. The Mineral Springs Spa uses natural mineral, thermal, or seawater for hydrotherapy treatments. To better understand the different types of water treatments offered at spas or wellness centers, here are two common categories: Balneotherapy: This treatment uses natural mineral waters for healing and relaxation. It involves bathing in hot or cold water, water massages, and other techniques aimed at disease prevention, care, and overall well-being (Van Tubergen & van der Linden, 2002). Thalassotherapy: This treatment uses marine water and its elements, such as seaweed wraps and mud, for therapeutic purposes. Thalassotherapy is usually offered at spas located in coastal areas, particularly on

Fig. 5.2. Roman Thermal Spa of Bath, England. *Source:* https://ourense.gal/turismo/en/termalismo/as-burgas-historic-thermal-baths/

Fig. 5.3. Bar Chart of Global Wellness Tourism.

beaches. Wellness tourism is one of the earliest forms of travel, with origins in the Romans' and Greeks' emphasis on well-being, medieval pilgrimages seeking spiritual enlightenment, and the medical seaside and spa retreats enjoyed by European elites in the 18th and 19th centuries. In recent years, however, wellness tourism has experienced a significant surge in popularity. The number of wellness centers, spas, and alternative therapies has grown substantially (Hjalager & Konu, 2011). To meet the rising demand, wellness programs now offer a variety of services, including healthy lifestyle education, fitness enhancement, nutrition counseling, preventive care, alternative treatments, and support for personal challenges such as stress and depression (Smith & Kelly, 2006; Smith & Puczkó, 2009).

Spa springs are widely distributed throughout the world, and their use in pools has been known since ancient times. The cultural and social context of the spa emphasizes issues of hygiene, public health guidelines, and water management in wellness and recreational settings. Fig. 5.4 explains about the independent and dependent variables considered for the research.

3. Reliability Analysis

"Cronbach's alpha coefficients were calculated for the scales assessing a Nature-based spa and wellness tourism variables. The analysis, based on a sample of 115 participants, revealed strong internal consistency among the scales."

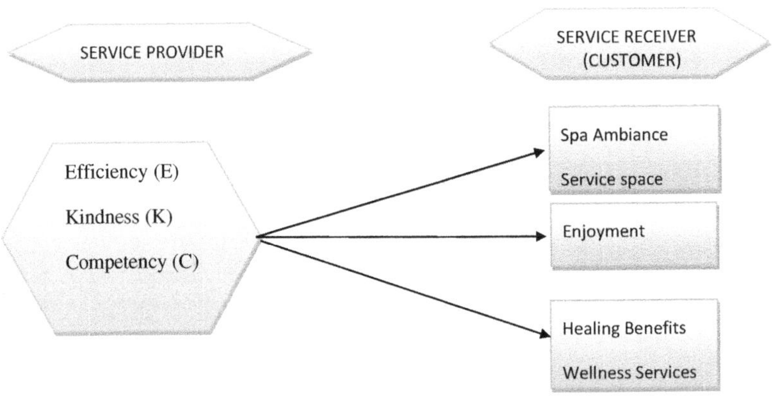

Fig. 5.4. Nature-Based Spa and Wellness Tourism Conceptual Flowchart. *Source:* Primary data. Author.

Table 5.1. Descriptive Statistics.

Factors	Mean	Std. Deviation
Efficiency 1	3.30	1.147
Efficiency 2	3.78	1.130
Efficiency 3	3.61	1.233
Kindness 1	3.13	1.056
Kindness 2	3.62	1.204
Kindness 3	3.48	1.142
Kindness 4	3.17	1.110
Competency 1	3.70	1.207
Competency 2	3.43	1.215
Competency 3	3.64	1.230
Competency 4	3.43	1.222
Spa Ambiance 1	3.54	1.110
Spa Ambiance 2	3.28	1.113
Service space 1	3.50	1.158
Service space 2	3.41	1.091
Enjoyment 1	1.92	0.947
Enjoyment 2	1.92	0.623
Enjoyment 3	1.66	0.674
Enjoyment 4	1.97	0.674
Enjoyment 5	3.17	1.037
Enjoyment 6	3.05	1.138
Enjoyment 7	3.17	1.475
Enjoyment 8	3.32	1.113
Enjoyment 9	3.35	1.093
Enjoyment 10	3.16	1.167
Healing Benefits and Wellness Services 1	3.41	1.191
Healing Benefits and Wellness Services 2	3.38	1.105
Healing Benefits and Wellness Services 3	3.50	1.079
Healing Benefits and Wellness Services 4	3.55	1.078
Healing Benefits and Wellness Services 5	3.63	1.047
Healing Benefits and Wellness Services 6	3.48	1.037
Healing Benefits and Wellness Services 7	3.27	1.111
Healing Benefits and Wellness Services 8	3.24	1.056
Healing Benefits and Wellness Services 9	3.50	1.103

Source: Primary data.

Inference: Table 5.1 explains the mean and standard deviations of the study variables.

Table 5.2. Descriptive Normality Test.

Study Variable	Statistics	Std. Error
Nature-based spa and wellness tourism	57.1209	1.24161
Skewness	−1.486	0.253
Kurtosis	2.880	0.500

Source: Primary data.

Inference: Table 5.2 disseminates the normality test done, showing the mean of nature-based spa and wellness tourism is 57.12. The skewness is −1.486 (negative), indicating left skew. The kurtosis is 2.880 (positive), suggesting a leptokurtic distribution, meaning it has heavier tails than a normal distribution.

Table 5.3. Test of Normality.

	Kolmogorov			Shapiro–Wilk		
Study	**Statistics**	**df**	**Sig.**	**Statistics**	**df**	**Sig**
Nature-based spa and wellness tourism	0.113	91	0.000	0.874	91	0.000

Source: Primary data.

Inference: The normality test for nature-based spa and wellness tourism statistics show that the data are not normally distributed. This is indicated by the Kolmogorov–Smirnov and Shapiro–Wilk tests, both of which have significant *p*-values (0.000). The negative skewness and positive kurtosis further confirm the deviation from normality which is stated in Table 5.3.

Table 5.4. The Reliability Analysis.

Cronbach's Alpha	No of Item
0.937	39

Source: Primary data.

Inference: Table 5.4 explains that the Cronbach's alpha test was performed to check the reliability of 39 items. The usual reliability coefficient ranges from 0 to 1, the greater the internal consistency of the items in the scale. Henceforth, the result states that the overall score is 0.937, indicating internal consistency of the items which states more reliability.

Table 5.5. Scale Statistics.

Mean	Variance	Std. Deviation	No. of Items
121.39	519.188	22.786	39

Source: Primary data.

Inference: The above Table 5.5 states that the scale statistics were calculated for a total of 39 items where the mean is 121.39, the variance is 519.188, and with the standard deviation of 22.786.

Table 5.6. ANOVA With Cochran's.

Factors	Sum of Squares	Df	Mean Square	Cochran's Q	Sig
Between people	1,517.62	114	13.31	1730.684	0.000
Within people between items	2,400.19	38	63.16		
Residual	3,660.22	433	0.84		
Total	6,060.51	437	1.38		
Total	7,578.13	448	1.16		

Source: Primary data.

Inference: A test of ANOVA in Table 5.6 states about the Cochran's test, which was performed since Cochran's alpha is a most common measure of internal consistency (reliability) for the questionnaire. The Cochran's Q value for demographic model is 1730.68.

4. Factor Analysis

Factor analysis is related to principal component analysis (PCA). Data were collected from all the 115 respondents of the firms with an overview to know the impact of nature-based spa and wellness tourism.

Table 5.7. Communalities.

Factor	Initial	Extraction
Efficiency 1	1.000	0.744
Efficiency 2	1.000	0.745
Efficiency 3	1.000	0.752
Kindness 1	1.000	0.674
Kindness 2	1.000	0.723
Kindness 3	1.000	0.668
Kindness 4	1.000	0.567
Competency 1	1.000	0.728
Competency 2	1.000	0.636
Competency 3	1.000	0.776
Competency 4	1.000	0.711
Spa Ambiance 1	1.000	0.653
Spa Ambiance 2	1.000	0.722
Service Space 1	1.000	0.622

(Continued)

(Continued)

Factor	Initial	Extraction
Service Space 2	1.000	0.646
Enjoyment 1	1.000	0.691
Enjoyment 2	1.000	0.530
Enjoyment 3	1.000	0.768
Enjoyment 4	1.000	0.580
Enjoyment 5	1.000	0.713
Enjoyment 6	1.000	0.763
Enjoyment 7	1.000	0.592
Enjoyment 8	1.000	0.623
Enjoyment 9	1.000	0.741
Enjoyment 10	1.000	0.766
Healing Benefits and Wellness Services 1	1.000	0.666
Healing Benefits and Wellness Services 2	1.000	0.667
Healing Benefits and Wellness Services 3	1.000	0.712
Healing Benefits and Wellness Services 4	1.000	0.631
Healing Benefits and Wellness Services 5	1.000	0.668
Healing Benefits and Wellness Services 6	1.000	0.696
Healing Benefits and Wellness Services 7	1.000	0.572
Healing Benefits and Wellness Services 8	1.000	0.686
Healing Benefits and Wellness Services 9	1.000	0.667

Source: Primary data.

Inference: The average extraction for Healing Benefits and Wellness Services is 0.67, Enjoyment is 0.67 is 0.728, Service Space is 0.63, Spa Ambiance is 0.68, Competency is 0.70, Kindness is 0.66, and Efficiency is 0.74 is tabulated in Table 5.7.

Table 5.8. KMO and Bartlett's Test.

Kaiser–Meyer–Olkin Measure of Sampling	Adequate	0.857
Bartlett's Test of Sphericity	Approx. Chi-Square	2,511.299
Sphericity	Df	741
	Sig	0.000

Source: Primary data.

Inference: Table 5.8 explains about the Kaiser–Meyer–Olkin (KMO). Measure of Sampling Adequacy is a statistic that assesses the proportion of variance in the variables that could be attributed to underlying factors. Higher values, closer to 1.0, suggest that factor analysis is likely to be effective for the data. The value of 0.857 shown in the table indicates an excellent fit for performing factor analysis with these variables.

5. Enjoyment vs Healing Benefits

Null Hypothesis: There is no association between the competency of the service providers and wellness services.
Alternative Hypothesis: There is an association between the competency of the service providers and wellness services.

6. Correlation

6.1 Hypothesis

Null Hypothesis: There is no relationship among the variables of the study.
Alternative Hypothesis: There is relationship among the variables of the study.

7. Multiple Regression

Null Hypothesis: There is no significance difference among the dimension of independent variables as predictors of in explaining the study.
Alternative Hypothesis: There is a significance difference among the dimension of independent variables as predictors in explaining the study.

$$Y = a + b$$

$$Y = -0.032 + 0.386 \tag{1}$$

$$Y = 0.043 + 0.416 - 0.071 \tag{2}$$

Model 1: Simple Linear Regression

$$\text{Equation}: Y = a + b_1 X_1$$

Where:

a (Constant) = −0.032.
b_1 (Health Benefits Coefficient) = 0.386.

$$\text{Complete Equation 1}: Y = -0.032 + 0.386X_1 \, Y = -0.032 + 0.386X_1$$

where:

Y = Dependent variable.
X_1 = Health Benefits and Well-being.

Table 5.9. Total Variances Explained.

	Initial Eigenvalues			Extraction Sums of Squared Loadings			Rotation Sums of Squarec Loadings		
Component	Total	% of Variance	Cumulative %	Total	% of Variance	Cumulative %	Total	% of Variance	Cumulative %
1	13.02	33.40	33.40	13.02	33.40	33.40	8.88	22.77	22.77
2	2.24	5.76	39.16	2.24	5.76	39.16	3.75	9.62	32.39
3	2.04	5.25	44.42	2.04	5.25	44.42	2.34	6.01	38.40
4	1.65	4.23	48.65	1.65	4.23	88.65	2.34	6.00	44.41
5	1.56	4.00	52.65	1.56	4.00	52.65	1.84	4.73	49.14
6	1.40	3.60	56.26	1.40	3.60	56.26	1.65	4.24	53.39
7	1.34	3.43	59.69	1.34	3.43	59.69	1.53	3.94	57.33
8	1.17	3.01	62.71	1.17	3.01	62.71	1.49	3.84	61.17
9	1.12	2.88	65.59	1.12	2.88	65.59	1.46	3.74	64.92
10	1.02	2.62	68.21	1.02	2.62	68.21	1.28	3.29	68.21

Source: Primary data.

Inference: The highest percentage of variance in initial Eigenvalues is 7.541% which is equal to the extraction sums of squared, and also follcwed by their cumulative percentage is 7.541%.

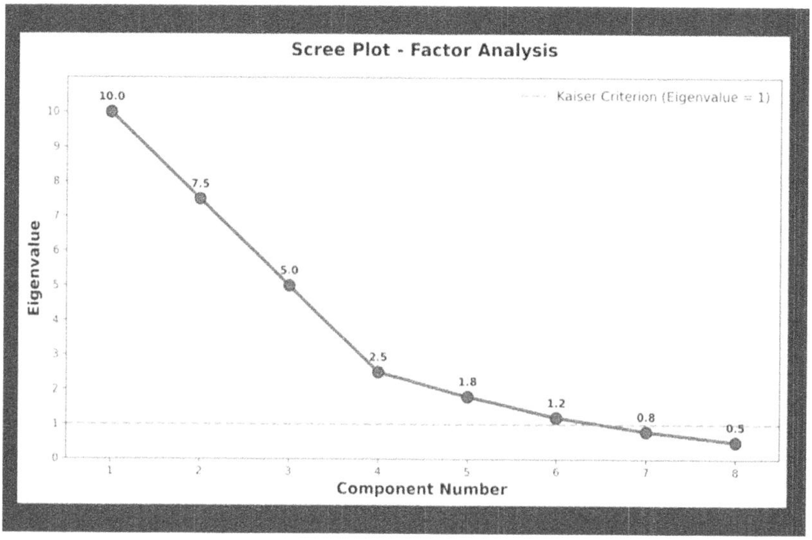

Fig. 5.5. Factor Analysis Scree Plot. *Source:* Primary data. *Inference:* In the above Fig. 5.5 plot, *X*-axis represents component number and *Y*-axis represents Eigenvalue, and its shows the items (variables) in the rotated factor space. It helps to see how the items (variables) are organized in the common rotated space.

Table 5.10. Chi-Square Test.

Factor	Value	df	*p*-Value
Pearson Chi-Square	1,144.45	1,053	**0.025**
Likelihood Ratio	281.99	1,053	1.000
Linear-by-Linear Association	0.69	1	0.792
N of Valid Cases	91		

Source: Primary data.

Inference: The Pearson Chi-Square test produced a value of less than 0.01, which is below the conventional threshold of 0.05. This indicates a statistically meaningful association between the competency of service providers and the wellness services offered. Consequently, the null hypothesis of no relationship is rejected, and the alternative hypothesis suggesting the presence of an association is accepted.

The first model establishes Health Benefits and Well-being as an exceptionally strong and significant standalone predictor. The model shows that for every one-unit increase in Health Benefits and Well-being, the dependent variable (*Y*) increases by 0.386 units. This positive relationship is highly statistically

Table 5.11. Correlations.

Study Variable	Efficiency	Kindness	Competency	Health Benefits and Wellness Services	Spa Ambiance
Pearson Correlation	1.000				
	0.397	1.000			
	0.586	0.714	1.000		
	0.392	0.388	0.737	1.000	
	−0.053	0.528	0.231	0.149	1.000

Source: Primary data.

Inference: Table 5.11, positions the data suggest that the most effective strategy for improving customer satisfaction and perceived value is to double down on staff development (both competency and kindness) rather than focusing primarily on operational efficiency or esthetic upgrades to the ambiance.

significant ($p < 0.001$), meaning there is less than a 0.1% chance that this effect is due to random variation. This single variable alone explains a substantial 58% of the variance in the outcome ($R^2 = 0.58$), which indicates it is a core driver of customer perceptions. The standardized coefficient (Beta = 0.58) confirms that this is a strong effect.

Model 2: Multiple Linear Regression

$$\text{Equation}: Y = a + b_1X_1 + b_2X_2$$

where:

a (Constant) = 0.043.
b_1 (Health Benefits Coefficient) = 0.416.
b_2 (Spa Ambiance Coefficient) = −0.071.

$$\text{Complete Equation 2}: Y = 0.043 + 0.416X_1 - 0.071X_2$$

where:

Y = Dependent Variable.
X_1 = Health Benefits and Well-being.
X_2 = Spa Ambiance.

Table 5.17 explains about the second model and introduces Spa Ambiance into the equation, creating a more complete picture. The inclusion of this

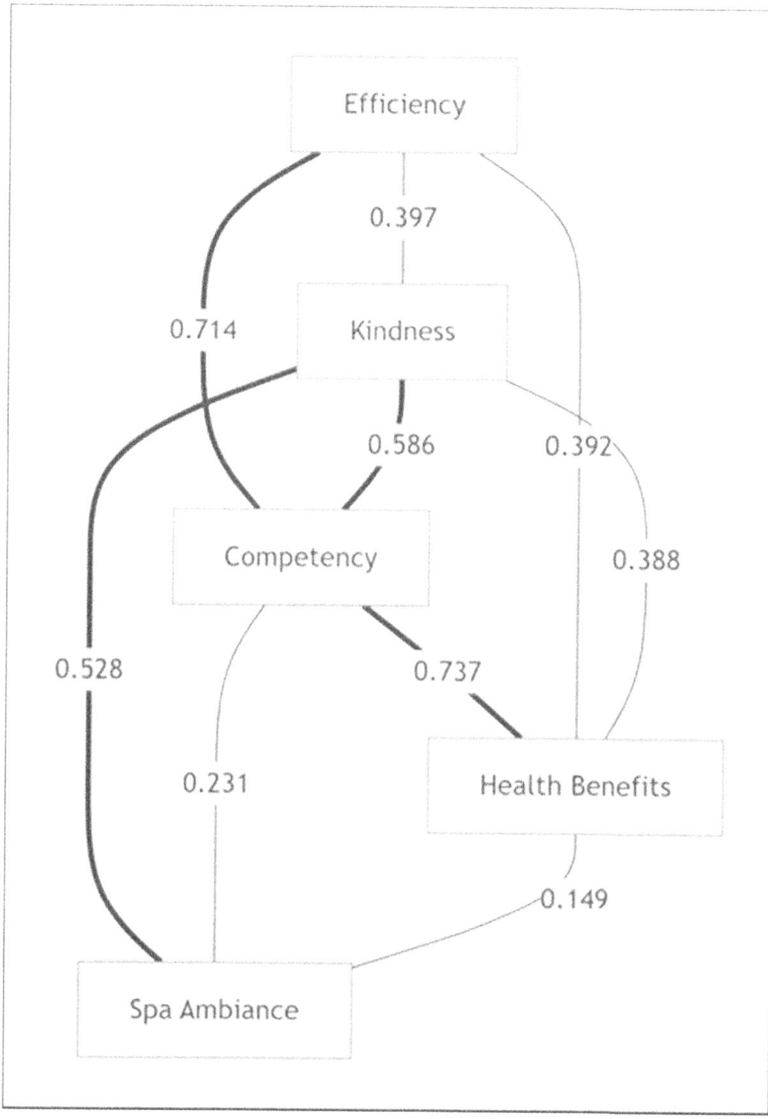

Fig. 5.6. Very Weak or Negligible Correlation.

variable slightly improves the model's explanatory power, now accounting for 61% of the variance in the dependent variable. The relationship for Health Benefits and Well-being remains robust, with its coefficient actually strengthening from 0.386 to 0.416 (Beta = 0.63), further cementing its role as the primary positive driver. However, the analysis uncovers a more complex role for Spa Ambiance. It has a statistically significant but relatively weak negative

Table 5.12. Positively Correlated.

Efficiency and Kindness	Enjoyment
Kindness and Competency	Spa Ambiance
Competency and Efficiency	Health Benefits and Wellness Services
Enjoyment and Efficiency	Wellness
Enjoyment and Kindness	Health Benefits and Wellness Services

Inference: Table 5.12 circumstances a strong link between Kindness and Competency (0.714) which means that staff training should focus on both technical skills (hard skills) and customer interaction/empathy (soft skills). They are not separate; in the customer's mind, one reinforces the other.

Table 5.13. Correlation Negatively Correlated.

Spa Ambiance	Efficiency

Source: Primary data.

Inference: Table 5.13 and Fig. 5.6 point Very Weak or Negligible Correlation:
Spa Ambiance and Health Benefits (0.149): A very weak positive relationship. The physical ambiance of the spa has almost no linear association with how customers judge the health benefits of the services.
Spa Ambiance and Competency (0.231): A weak relationship. The ambiance has a minor association with the perception of staff competency.
Efficiency and Spa Ambiance (−0.053): This is essentially no correlation. The value is very close to zero and negative, meaning there is no linear relationship between how efficient the service is and how customers rate the spa's ambiance.

relationship with the outcome ($b = -0.071$, $p = 0.02$). This suggests that when controlling for the level of Health Benefits provided, a higher-rated Spa Ambiance is associated with a very slight decrease in the overall score. This counterintuitive finding could be an example of a suppressor effect or indicate that investments in ambiance might be perceived negatively if customers feel they come at the expense of the core health services or vice-versa. It is crucial to note that multicollinearity is not a concern (Tolerance > 0.1, VIF ≈ 1.05), meaning this negative relationship is a genuine finding and not an artifact of the two predictor variables being too closely related.

The data strongly suggest that Health Benefits and Well-being is the dominant factor driving positive outcomes, and its importance is even more pronounced when Spa Ambiance is considered. The weak negative coefficient for Spa Ambiance warrants further investigation to understand the underlying customer psychology, but it does not detract from the primary conclusion that the core health-oriented services are the most critical element for success.

Table 5.14. Mutiple Regression.

Model	*R*	*R* Square	Adjusted *R* Square	Std. Error of the Estimate	Change Statistics					Durbin-Watson
					R Square Change	*F* Change	dff	df2	Sig *F* Change	
1	0.586[a]	0.334	0.336	0.14643	0.344	46.614	1	89	0.000	2.112
2	0.617[b]	0.381	0.367	0.14302	0.037	5.295	1	89	0.024	

Source: Primary data.

a. Predictors: (Constant), Efficiency, Competency, and Kindness.
b. Predictors: (Constant), Efficiency, Competency, and Kindness.

DW = 2. 112. The Durbin–Watson statistic will always have a value ranging 0–2. If DW = 2, there is no autocorrelation. If DW = less than 2, there is positive correlation. If DW = greater than 2, there is negative correlation. Here, DW = 2.112, so Durbin–Watson statistic is negative correlation.
Inference: Table 5.14 explains about the regression table, summarizing the model where *R* represents the multiple correlation coefficient with a range lying between −1 and +1. Since the R-value is 0.586, it means Efficiency, Competency, and Kindness has a positive relationship with nature-spa wellness. *R*-square represents the coefficient of determination and ranges between 0 and 1. Since the *R*-squared value is 0.334, 70% of the variation in Spa Ambiance percentage is enhanced by Efficiency and Competency.

Table 5.15. ANOVA.

Model		Sum of Square	df	Mean Square	F	Sig
1	Regression	1.00	1	1.00	46.61	0.00
	Residual	1.90	89	0.02		
	Total	2.90	90			
2.	Regression	1.108	2	0.554	27.07	0.00
	Residual	1800	88	0.020		
	Total	2.908	90			

Source: Primary data.

Inference: The ANOVA results show that the F-value is statistically significant, with a p-value below the 0.05 threshold. This indicates that there are meaningful differences in the data, suggesting that the dependent variable of Nature-Based Spa and Wellness does not demonstrate consistent reliability across the groups tested. As a result, the null hypothesis of no difference is rejected.

8. Histogram

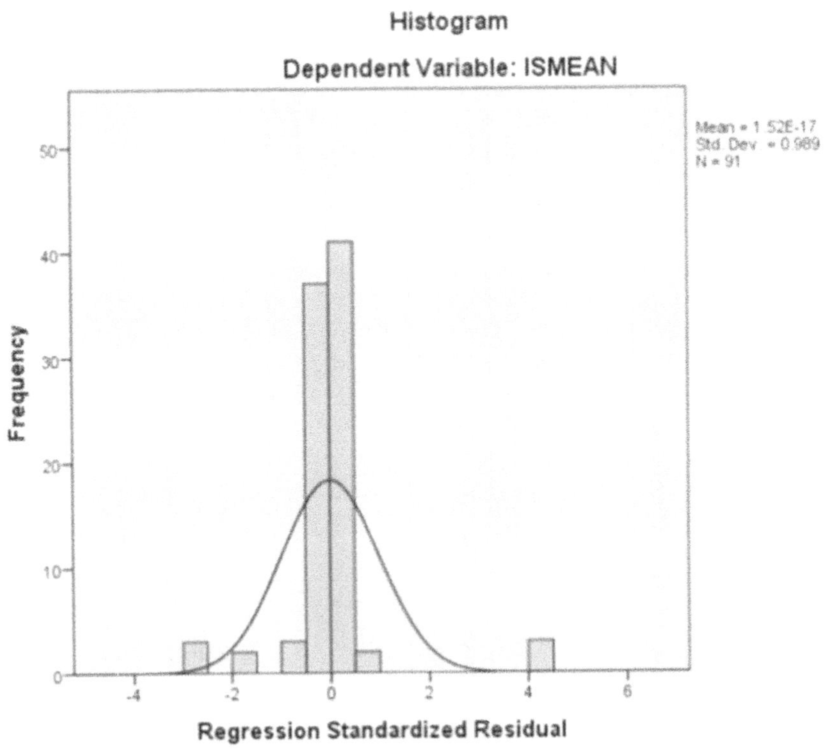

Fig. 5.7. Histogram. *Source:* Primary data.

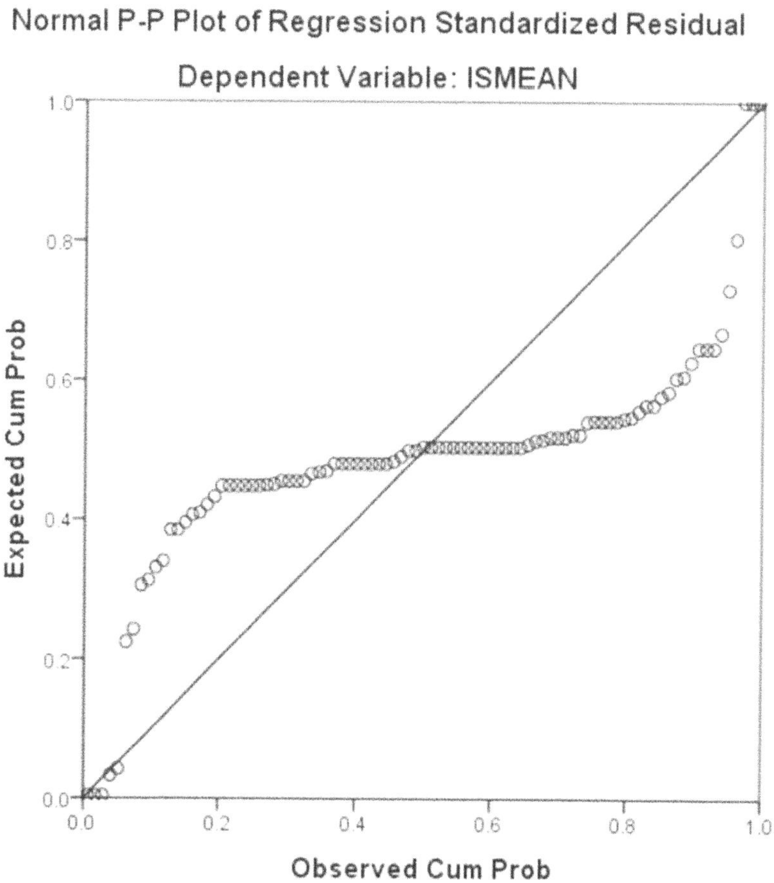

Fig. 5.8. P – Plot. *Source:* Primary data. *Inference:* Figs. 5.7 and 5.8 represent that the mean value is 1.52, standard deviation value is 0.989, and the *N* value is 91. The chart represents that the *Y*-axis is the expected cum prob and *X*-axis represents the observed cum prob. An efficient, skilled, and compassionate service provider creates a welcoming and relaxing spa environment that prioritizes customer satisfaction. By offering a thoughtfully designed ambiance and a comprehensive range of healing and wellness services, they cater to the physical, mental, and emotional well-being of their clients. Their dedication to professionalism and care ensures that each customer experiences personalized attention, rejuvenation, and a sense of tranquility, making every visit memorable and restorative.

Table 5.16. Coefficient Table.

Model	Under Standardized coefficient		Standardized Coefficients	T	Sig	Correlations		Collinearity Statistics		
(Constant)	B	Std. Er	Beta			Zero Order	Partial	Part	Tolerance	VIF
1 (Constant)	−0.03	0.01	0.58	−1.76	0.08	0.58	0.58	0.58	1.00	1.00
Health Benefits and Well-being	0.38	0.05		6.82	0.00					
2 (Constant)	0.04	0.03		1.15	0.25					
	0.41	0.05	0.63	7.33	0.00	0.58	0.61		0.94	1.05
	−0.07	0.03	−0.19	−2.30	0.02	−0.23	−0.23		0.94	1.05

Source: Primary data.

Inference: The regression model coefficient table presents the coefficients in Wellbeing, which are crucial for analyzing the influence of nature-based spa. Spa Ambiance exhibits an impactful value of less than 0.05, indicating strong statistical evidence.

Table 5.17. Model Significant.

Model	R^2	Adjusted R^2	Significant Predictors
1	0.58	0.58	Health Benefits ($p < 0.001$)
2	0.61	0.61	Health Benefits ($p < 0.001$), Spa Ambiance ($p = 0.02$)

Source: Primary data.

9. Conclusion

Health and wellness, particularly within spa environments, have been the focus of numerous studies conducted across various countries, including Finland, Greece, Jamaica, Japan, Taiwan, and the United States. These studies emphasize the significant role that spas play in promoting relaxation, reducing stress, and enhancing overall well-being (González Soutelo, 2014). Spas are often located in nature-inspired spaces, which possess a unique ability to affect individuals beyond the physical realm. These environments evoke emotions, awaken memories, and elicit immediate responses, such as a sense of awe, security, or even discomfort, fostering a deep and meaningful connection to the surroundings (Mueller & Kaufmann, 2001). The blend of natural elements with therapeutic practices enhances the restorative experience, making spas an integral part of holistic wellness worldwide. In India, the rich heritage of traditional healing therapies, such as Ayurveda and Yoga, further strengthens the connection between health, wellness, and nature. Ayurveda, one of the world's oldest holistic healing systems, emphasizes balance between mind, body, and spirit through personalized treatments, herbal remedies, and dietary guidance. Yoga, deeply rooted in Indian culture, combines physical postures, breath control, and meditation to cultivate inner harmony and improve physical and mental health. These time-honored practices continue to be globally recognized for their profound impact on overall wellness and are often integrated into spa treatments to provide a unique blend of ancient wisdom and modern care (Voigt, 2010). Together, these elements underscore the universal appeal and enduring significance of health and wellness in spa cultures around the world.

Author Contribution

The author has designed the study developed the methodology performed the analysis and written the manuscript.

Funding

This research received no external funding.

Declaration

Conflict of Interest: The author declares that there is no conflict of interest.
Ethical Approval: "Not applicable" as the study did not require ethical approval.
Consent for Publication: As per the journal guidelines and norms.

References

Buxton, L., & Michopoulou, E. (2021). Value co-creation and co-destruction: Considerations of spa servicescapes, *Tourism Planning & Development 2021*, *18*(2), 210–225.

Chen, J. S., Prebensen, N., & Huan, T. C. (2008). Determining the motivation of wellness travelers. *Anatolia*, *19*, 103–115.

García-Altés, A. (2005). The development of health tourism services. *Annals of Tourism Research*, *32*(1), 262–266.

Global Wellness Institute. (n.d.). *Guide to hydrothermal spa & wellness development standards*. (4th ed.). Global Wellness Institute. https://globalwellnessinstitute.org

Gonzales, A., Brenzel, L., & Sancho, J. (2001). *Health tourism and related services: Caribbean development and international trade.* http://www.carib-export.com/login/wp-content/uploads/2009/08/Health%20Tourism.pdf

González Soutelo, S. (2014). Medicine and spas in the Roman period: The role of doctors in establishments with mineral-medicinal waters. In D. Michaelides (Ed.), *Medicine in the ancient Mediterranean world* (pp. 200–210). Oxbow Books.

Grabar, H. (2015, November 16). *The legacy of America's water-cure towns*. Bloomberg CityLab.

Hjalager, A. M., & Konu, H. (2011). Co-branding and co-creation in wellness tourism: The role of cosmeceuticals. *Journal of Hospitality Marketing & Management*, *20*, 879–901.

Koncul, N. (2012). Wellness: A new mode of tourism. *Economic Research* [Ekonomska Istraživanja], *25*(2), 503–534.

Huijbens, E. H. (2011). Developing wellness in Iceland. Theming wellness destinations the Nordic way. *Scandinavian Journal of Hospitality and Tourism*, *11*(1), 20–41.

Lee, C. F., & King, B. E. (2008). Using the Delphi method to assess the potential of Taiwan's hot springs tourism sector. *International Journal of Tourism Research*, *10*, 341–352.

Mak, A. H. N., Wong, K. K. F., & Chang, R. C. Y. (2009). Health or self-indulgence? The motivations and characteristics of Spa-goers. *International Journal of Tourism Research*, *11*, 185–199.

Marican, N. D., Sumardi, N. A., Aziz, R. C., Simpong, D. B., & Hasbollah, H. R. (2021). The Shari'ah compliance spa for wellness and tourism context in Malaysia. *Turkish Journal of Computer and Mathematics Education*, *12*(3), 1234–1242.

Mueller, H., & Kaufmann, E. L. (2001). Wellness tourism: Market analysis of a special health tourism segment and implications for the hotel industry. *Journal of Vacation Marketing*, *7*(1), 5–17.

Rancic, M., Raljic, J. P., & Pavic, L. (2013). Spa-wellness center as part of the hotel facility. *Turizam*, *17*(2), 45–59.

Smith, M., & Kelly, C. (2006). Holistic tourism: Journeys of the self? *Tourism Recreation Research*, *31*(1), 15–24.

Smith, M., & Puczkó, L. (2009). *Health and wellness tourism.* Butterworth-Heinemann.

Unione Geotermica Italiana. (2010). Geotermia, notiziario dell'Unione Geotermica Italiana. *Aprile*, *VIII*(26).

Van Tubergen, A., & van der Linden, S. (2002). A brief history of spa therapy. *Annals of the Rheumatic Diseases*, *61*, 273–275.

Voigt, C. (2010). *Understanding wellness tourism: An analysis of benefit sought, health-promoting behaviors and positive psychological well-being.* Doctoral dissertation. University of South Australia.

Wilson, K. (2003). Therapeutic landscapes and first nations peoples: An exploration of culture, health, and place. *Health & Place*, *9*, 83–93.

Chapter 6

Nature-Based Health Tourism and Sustainability (NBHTS): A Southeast Asian Perspective

Astha Bhanot[a], *Nilanjan Ray*[b], *Tanmoy Majumder*[b] *and Moumita Roy*[b]

[a]Vishisht School of Management, Indore, India
[b]JIS University, India

Abstract

Nature-based health tourism (NBHT), an emerging segment within the wellness tourism industry, integrates natural environments with health-promoting experiences. Southeast Asia, with its rich biodiversity, indigenous healing traditions, and eco-diverse landscapes, has increasingly become a hub for NBHT activities. This chapter explores the development and sustainability of NBHT in Southeast Asia, focusing on how environmental conservation, cultural heritage, and local community involvement shape the sector's growth. It investigates the current trends, challenges, and best practices from selected countries in the region, including Thailand, Indonesia, Malaysia, and Vietnam. Through a qualitative, comparative methodology involving case studies, expert interviews, and content analysis of government and tourism board publications, the research evaluates the sustainability practices integrated into NBHT. It examines the socioeconomic and environmental impacts on host communities and identifies key success factors for responsible tourism development. Findings suggest that while NBHT contributes significantly to rural development and cultural preservation, its sustainability is often undermined by inadequate policy integration, overtourism, and insufficient community engagement. However, successful models demonstrate that when local stakeholders are empowered and traditional knowledge systems are preserved and leveraged, NBHT can serve as a tool for sustainable development. The study also highlights the role of digital transformation and health-conscious

Nature, Wellness and Sustainability in Health Tourism, 127–153

doi:10.1108/978-1-83742-029-220261006

consumer behavior in shaping future demand. This research provides critical insights for policymakers, tourism operators, and environmentalists seeking to balance economic growth with ecosystem protection.

Keywords: Nature-based health tourism; sustainable tourism development; community perspectives; ecosystem; environmental monitoring; renewable energy

1. Introduction

In recent years, nature-based health tourism (NBHT) has emerged as a significant trend within the broader wellness and ecotourism sectors. It encompasses travel activities that integrate natural environments with health-promoting practices, including traditional therapies, physical well-being, mindfulness, and environmental immersion. Southeast Asia, with its rich biodiversity, cultural heritage, and deeply rooted traditional medicine systems, presents an ideal setting for the growth of NBHT.

As global travelers increasingly seek destinations that support both physical and mental well-being while minimizing environmental footprints, the convergence of nature, health, and sustainability becomes vital. Countries like Thailand, Indonesia, Malaysia, and Vietnam have made concerted efforts to promote wellness retreats, forest bathing, hot springs, and traditional healing systems (e.g., Ayurveda, Jamu, and Thai massage) that draw from centuries-old wisdom. However, the sector also raises critical questions about ecological degradation, cultural commodification, and the need for sustainable infrastructure. Nature-based solutions (NBS) represent a novel and interdisciplinary approach to addressing pressing societal challenges, including climate change, environmental degradation, overtourism, and socio-economic inequalities. Rooted in ecological principles, these solutions draw inspiration from natural processes and ecosystems to deliver sustainable outcomes that are socially inclusive and ecologically viable. In the context of tourism, however, research on NBS remains relatively nascent. This study seeks to identify and conceptualize NBS within the tourism sector through a hybrid review encompassing tourism and hospitality literature alongside insights from agriculture, the built environment, and urban planning. The synthesis of findings from diverse disciplines facilitated the development of a conceptual framework for NBS in tourism based on six constituent dimensions: (1) empowerment of stakeholders, (2) monitoring the natural environment, (3) economic development of local communities, (4) adoption of environmentally sustainable practices, (5) fostering stakeholder cooperation, and (6) mindset transformation regarding sustainability. These dimensions reflect the multi-functional and participatory nature of NBS, positioning them as tools for enhancing resilience in tourism-dependent destinations.

Stakeholder conflict remains a persistent challenge in the implementation of sustainable tourism practices, particularly in regions where tourism intersects with traditional land uses and livelihoods. The competing demands on natural resources among tourism developers, visitors, and local communities—such as Indigenous peoples, farmers, and fisherfolk—underscore the need for integrative approaches like NBS. In terrestrial and marine protected areas, for example, the expansion of tourism can exacerbate resource conflicts and environmental stress. Tourist infrastructure, including resorts and golf courses, often redirects water resources away from agricultural use while trail erosion caused by hikers threatens the ecological integrity of mountain ecosystems. The physical and social impacts of tourism development can also trigger local discontent. The proliferation of visitor-oriented infrastructure—hotels, entertainment venues, and commercial spaces—frequently disrupts the social fabric and landscape aesthetics valued by residents (UNWTO, 2021). In this context, NBS offer a pathway for mitigating negative externalities while promoting co-benefits such as biodiversity conservation, community empowerment, and climate adaptation.

Despite these potentialities, the current study acknowledges several limitations. The conceptual framework remains theoretical and requires empirical validation through case studies and stakeholder engagement processes. Moreover, interdisciplinary convergence in NBS research must be strengthened to enhance the applicability of these solutions across varied socio-ecological contexts. Future research should investigate the operationalization of NBS in specific tourism typologies (e.g., ecotourism, community-based tourism [CBT]) and evaluate their long-term impacts on sustainability indicators.

2. Literature Review

NBHT represents a burgeoning niche within the wider sustainable tourism discourse, yet scholarly literature reveals a fragmented, often indirect engagement with the concept, particularly within the Southeast Asian context. The reviewed literature underscores an emergent but underdeveloped academic focus on Nature-Based Health Tourism and Sustainability, with most studies either conflating it with ecotourism or nature-based tourism (NBT) or neglecting its health dimension altogether.

Trupp and Dolezal (2020) articulate a foundational concern—the unclear and poorly understood role of tourism in advancing the Sustainable Development Goals (SDGs). While their work does not delve specifically into NBHT, it highlights how local tourism initiatives can promote sustainable growth and resilience, particularly through smart tourism during crises like COVID-19. This indirectly emphasizes the role of tourism in public health recovery, thereby making a case for closer integration of health imperatives within sustainable tourism frameworks. Health geography is a subfield of human geography that explores the relationship between environmental conditions and human health. It applies various theoretical approaches and analytical methods to study social and physical determinants, patterns of diseases, and the distribution and accessibility of healthcare services. The goals were to analyze the connections between human health and ecosystems and emphasize the significance of health geography in public health. The results were environments and human health outcomes are directly related in health geography. Service delivery and spatial health links are analyzed using a variety of techniques. The study's conclusion investigates the connection between environmental factors and health effects and creates policies and initiatives to promote healthy surroundings. As stated by Aneg Singh (2024), examining how individuals interact with their surroundings, health geography is a subfield of human geography that informs preventative and health policy by examining how spatial elements affect illness outcomes, health experiences, and access to healthcare. Examining how diseases and health outcomes vary geographically as well as how health affects society function and well-being were the goals. This research had implications for how preventative strategies are informed by the spatial variance of illnesses. The study of health geography looks at how people interact with their surroundings. In a more direct examination, Sabaruddin et al. (2023) provide a valuable contribution by explicitly linking NBT in Malaysia with health and well-being, particularly in the post-COVID-19 era. Their systematic review reveals that while the demand for health-driven nature tourism is rising, the conceptualization of NBT remains narrow and fragmented. This restricts its potential to be recognized as a distinct health-focused niche. The study rightly calls for a reconceptualization that captures the psychological and physiological benefits of nature immersion, thereby offering a compelling argument for positioning NBHT as a critical industry within national tourism strategies. The research conducted by Warren Y. Brockelman and Philip Dearden (1990) explores the dynamics of NBT in Thailand, with a particular focus on nature trekking activities. The authors examine how such tourism models can simultaneously promote environmental conservation and offer economic benefits to local communities. While the chapter does not specifically delve into NBHT, it provides significant insights into how structured and responsible nature tourism can act as a dual-purpose tool for ecological protection and rural development. The study finds that nature tourism, when managed properly, can serve as an important income-generating activity for people living near protected areas. By involving local communities in tourism-related services—such as guiding, lodging, and cultural exhibitions—economic opportunities are expanded beyond traditional livelihoods. The research highlights that specialized trekking programs, particularly those that are educational and conservation-oriented, foster a stronger link between tourism and biodiversity preservation. These programs attract visitors who are more environmentally conscious and willing to support sustainable practices, which in turn enhances the conservation value of the activity. The presence of tourists and trekking groups in ecologically sensitive areas may act as a deterrent to poaching and illegal resource extraction, contributing indirectly to the protection of wildlife and forest resources. The study backs up Thailand's conservation goals by using nature tourism as a tactical instrument. A sustainable model that strikes a balance between ecological integrity and socioeconomic growth can be produced by combining tourism with environmental education and community engagement. According to the research, organized trekking programs can lessen environmental risks like poaching, especially if they are created and run with input from the local population. These initiatives create financial incentives for residents to preserve natural resources in addition to promoting responsible tourism. The results suggest that long-term ecological and financial benefits can be obtained by policymakers and tourist planners through training for local stakeholders and investments in NBT infrastructure. It promotes tourist planning that incorporates conservation objectives and community empowerment in addition to visitor numbers. Joseph Asumah Braimah et al. (2023) state that health geography studies the effects of environmental and spatial elements on population health and well-being. It emphasizes the relationship between health and development in sub-Saharan Africa by concentrating on topics including infectious illnesses, maternal health, and non-communicable diseases.

Understanding demographic trends in health and well-being and advancing development and health in sub-Saharan Africa were the primary goals. Their findings showed that contagious and non-communicable diseases, as well as the reciprocal relationship between development and health, were dominant topics. The study's implications were centered on infectious diseases, maternal health, and non-communicable diseases in health geography.

In the study, Montakan Chubchuwong et al. (2015) examine the influence of NBT on fostering pro-environmental attitudes among international tourists visiting Thailand. The research emphasizes the importance of immersive experiences in natural environments and the development of emotional attachment to destinations as key drivers in shaping environmentally responsible mindsets. However, the study does not specifically address the aspect of NBHT. The study concludes that engaging with nature through tourism can significantly enhance visitors' environmental awareness and attitudes. The emotional and sensory experiences gained during such trips encourage a deeper appreciation of natural landscapes and conservation issues. However, studies by Grau (2022), Esparza-Huamanchumo et al. (2024), and Lee (2013) underscore significant conceptual and analytical gaps. Grau (2022) addresses the tension between conservation and local livelihoods, a vital issue for sustainable tourism, but stops short of examining NBHT specifically. Similarly, Esparza-Huamanchumo et al. (2024) offer a comparative analysis of sustainable tourism forms but do not isolate the health-related dimensions of nature-based experiences. Lee (2013), while insightful on environmentally responsible behavior (ERB), critiques the reliance on self-reported data and advocates for refined metrics—an area also pertinent for NBHT, where empirical evidence of health benefits is essential.

The broader regional context is further illuminated by Pongsiri and Arthakaivalvatee (2020), who advocate for an integrative view of health and environmental sustainability. Their findings stress ASEAN's recognition of the environment-health nexus, reinforcing the potential for NBHT to act as a cross-sectoral bridge toward SDG attainment. Nonetheless, the absence of direct NBHT framing limits the practical translation of these insights into policy and development strategies.

Winter et al. (2019) and Ly and Bauer (2017) add depth by discussing socio-ecological systems and ecotourism management, respectively. Both studies implicitly support the value of NBHT but lack a focused discussion. The former's exploration of adaptation and access points to equity in nature-based health interventions while the latter's emphasis on governance reveals institutional gaps that must be addressed for Nature-Based Health Tourism and Sustainability to flourish.

Finally, Seočanac (2022) introduces the transformative potential of NBT. Her exploration of nature immersion as a catalyst for pro-environmental behavior resonates strongly with NBHT goals, especially in light of heightened post-pandemic nature appreciation. However, while the psychological transformation is well-articulated, its direct health implications remain an area for future exploration.

Table 6.1 Select Literature Review (At a Glance).

Year	Authors	Objectives	Outcome	Applications
2020	Trupp, A., & Dolezal, C.	The article examines the impact of COVID-19 on Southeast Asia's tourism sector and its connection to the SDGs.	The article discusses the unclear linkage between tourism and sustainable development in Southeast Asia, indicating that whereas tourism can dramatically shape the SDGs, tourism has also been associated with detrimental impacts and disputes.	The research explores how indigenous, tourism-focused microbusinesses, such as Indonesia's Yogyakarta silver workshop enterprises, can contribute to sustainable development by employing locals and integrating them into the value chain, which will decrease poverty.
2020	Lechner et al.	With a focus on the socio-ecological challenges this biodiverse area is confronted with due to increasing urbanization, pollution, and climate change, the paper tries to bridge the literature gap regarding the application of nature-based solutions (NBS) in Southeast Asia.	The character of urbanization, the biophysical environmental and climatic context, environmental challenges and restoration problems, human–nature relationship and conflicts, and the policy and governance context are the five distinct challenges for NBS deployment in Southeast and East Asia identified in the article.	To reverse problems arising from urbanization, pollution, climate change, and loss of ecosystem services, the research investigates the application of NBS as a way of realizing a more sustainable future for low- and middle-income Southeast and East Asian countries
2022	Grau, H. R.	Through the analysis of the rapid and varied patterns of change in Asian mountain	The study stresses how NBT is developing rapidly in Asia, particularly in China, as	To redirect mass tourism to less congested areas in South Korea, the paper presents the

		ecosystems against the backdrop of globalization, the research attempts to expand the scope of knowledge of nature-based tourism (NBT) in Asia and respond to the traditionally limited attention given to western and English-speaking countries.	economic growth has led to 1.6 billion visits to forest parks each year, which creates 500,000 jobs and indirectly benefits 20 million people. Compared with this, even though national parks were established early in Taiwan and Japan, NBT has not developed much over the last few years.	evolution of modern management tools to manage visitor congestion in NBT sites. Some of these tools are dynamic pricing by carrying capacity in Huangshan, mainland China, and lottery permit systems in Taiwan.
2021	Pessot, E., Spoladore, D., Zangiacomi, A., & Sacco, M.	Through mapping and analyzing natural resources' value from multiple perspectives, the research aims to learn how these contribute to health tourism and specifically how they can facilitate well-being and assist in the development and sustainability of health tourism destinations.	The systematic review identified key research areas related to the analysis and exploitation of natural resources in health tourism. These areas were the nature-based determinants that affect tourist clustering and motivations, and the development of value propositions and marketing strategies for health tourism destinations.	Natural resource analysis and utilization in health tourism are addressed in the article, with a view to articulating the manner in which they contribute to sustainability and strengthening wellness in health tourism destinations. It underscores how critical it is that one understands the value of natural resources and related activities in pursuit of a better health tourism experience.
2019	Winter, P. L., Selin, S., Cerveny, L. K., & Bricker, K. S.	The research aims to examine how nature-based tourism, outdoor leisure, and sustainability are interrelated, with a focus on the important benefits that these activities	It discusses the impact of global factors like climate change, population growth, and urbanization on ecosystems and outdoor recreation opportunities, highlighting the	The need for multiple service delivery strategies in outdoor recreation and nature-based tourism is addressed in the paper, with an emphasis on the importance of adapting to

(Continued)

Table 6.1 *(Continued)*

Year	Authors	Objectives	Outcome	Applications
		provide to communities, society in general, and individuals. The purpose of this inquiry is to enhance knowledge of these elements' contributions towards sustainability.	need for inclusive governance and shared stewardship in managing natural spaces and the importance of adaptation strategies for long-term planning.	changing ecological, social, technological, and economic conditions to ensure sustainability and equitable access to these opportunities.
2024	Santoso, A. D., Sajida, S., & Yusnaini, Y.	The primary aim of the study is to conduct a bibliometric examination of scholarly studies on Southeast Asian forest tourism. In particular, it will analyze 174 articles in the Scopus database to identify significant themes of interest for the topic, such as ecotourism and conservation.	Ecotourism and conservation are the central areas of concern in research on Southeast Asian forest tourism, as revealed through a bibliometric analysis of 174 articles. This underscores the importance of balancing conservation with the use of natural resources in sustainable development.	In forest tourism, the research places importance on balancing the conservation and consumption of natural resources, with a focus on the need for policies and measures that facilitate the development of sustainable forest tourism in Southeast Asia.
2012	Coghlan, A., & Buckley, R.	To illustrate the vast, growing, and diversified nature of the sector, the chapter overviews a number of various types of nature-based tourism activities, destinations, and service suppliers.	Examining the widespread, growing, and heterogeneous nature-based tourism market, the chapter considers supply and demand as well as the social contexts and customs that influence tourism environments and activities.	The chapter investigates a variety of tourism activities and places that fall within the domain of nature-based tourism, focusing on the diversification and growth of the industry that involves both private and public sector providers.

2022	Seočanac, M.	Through its demonstration of the potential of these experiences to foster environmental values and behaviors in visitors, the article endeavors to present transformational nature-based tourism experiences as a means for generating a more sustainable destination.	As per the paper, the impacts of the coronavirus pandemic have grown people more aware of the significance of nature, leading to increased interest in natural sites that facilitate social distancing and have beneficial impacts on mental and physical well-being.	Against the backdrop of the impact of the coronavirus pandemic, the study investigates how nature sites can enable social distancing and enhance the well-being of their visitors both mentally and physically. It emphasizes how nature-based tourism has the capacity to motivate travelers to adopt attitudes and practices conducive to environmental conservation, thereby enhancing the sustainability of travel destinations.
2017	Ly, T. P., & Bauer, T.	The research is to highlight the differences in ecotourism management observed in Thailand, Cambodia, and Vietnam and analyze the reasons behind the gap between the theoretical concept and the real practice of ecotourism in these Southeast Asian countries.	Attributed primarily to the absence of coordination and communication between policymakers and other tourism stakeholders, the research reveals a wide gap between the conceptual idea and actual practice of ecotourism in Thailand, Cambodia, and Vietnam.	To enhance ecotourism management, the research explores the gap between the theoretical and practical application of ecotourism in Thailand, Cambodia, and Vietnam. It stresses the need for more effective communication and cooperation between policymakers and tourism players.

3. NBHT Research Trends: Pictorial Evidence

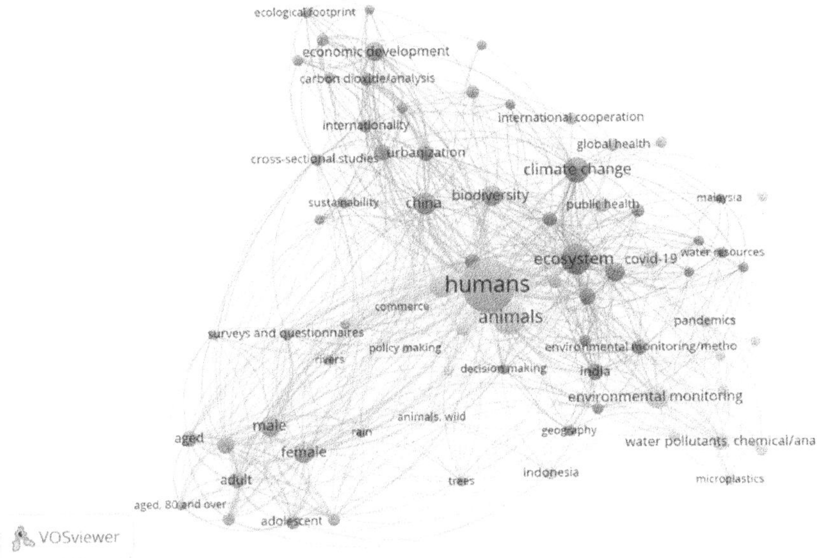

Fig. 6.1. Key Word Analysis for Research Trends.

Table 6.2. Keywords Occurrences Analysis.

Id	Keyword	Occurrences	Total Link Strength
13	Adolescent	8	69
15	Adult	11	90
22	Aged	10	79
23	Aged, 80 and over	4	41
24	Agriculture	14	51
49	Animals	45	160
50	Animals, wild	4	21
87	Asia	4	13
125	Biodiversity	16	59
165	Carbon	4	13
166	Carbon dioxide	5	23
168	Carbon dioxide/analysis	7	33

Table 6.2. *(Continued)*

Id	Keyword	Occurrences	Total Link Strength
192	Child	6	39
197	China	20	81
202	Cities	9	44
205	Climate change	25	81
228	Commerce	4	19
249	Conservation	4	5
253	Conservation of natural resources	23	114
256	Conservation of natural resources/ methods	11	44
267	Coral reefs	7	23
272	Covid-19	15	44
275	Covid-19/epidemiology	4	16
283	Cross-sectional studies	6	34
292	Decision-making	4	24
355	Ecological footprint	5	16
363	Economic development	15	67
366	Economic growth	4	15
370	Economics	4	8
372	Ecosystem	37	137
374	Ecosystem services	4	11
398	Environment	8	38
410	Environmental monitoring	21	101
411	Environmental monitoring/methods	9	36
435	Ethnobotany	4	23
460	Female	18	122
517	Geography	5	14
531	Global health	7	21
558	Groundwater	4	18
567	Health	5	8
618	Humans	107	404
632	India	10	37
639	Indonesia	7	32
672	International cooperation	6	17

(Continued)

Table 6.2. *(Continued)*

Id	Keyword	Occurrences	Total Link Strength
679	Internationality	7	29
702	Lakes	4	18
744	Malaysia	4	11
746	Male	17	113
784	Microplastics	5	24
785	Microplastics/analysis	6	33
786	Middle aged	12	95
798	Models, theoretical	5	23
886	Pandemics	6	30
939	Policy	5	21
941	Policymaking	4	25
984	Public health	9	32
996	Rain	4	26
1,012	Renewable energy	6	33
1,035	Risk factors	7	31
1,040	Rivers	5	20
1,041	Rivers/chemistry	5	26
1,053	Sars-cov-2	4	22
1,166	Surveys and questionnaires	6	43
1,167	Sustainability	5	21
1,169	Sustainable development	7	17
1,183	Thailand	5	28
1,194	Tourism	10	46
1,215	Trees	4	24
1,226	Uncertainty	4	17
1,234	Urbanization	11	48
1,253	Vulnerability	4	6
1,258	Water	4	16
1,262	Water pollutants, chemical/analysis	11	54
1,267	Water quality	5	19
1,268	Water resources	5	17
1,283	Wetlands	8	28
1,299	Young adult	6	57

Source: Author's Compilation from VoSviewer.

4. Co-occurrence Analysis of Keywords

A co-occurrence analysis was subsequently conducted to investigate patterns and keyword co-associations within the dataset. All identified keywords comprised the unit of analysis, and a minimum inclusion criterion of four occurrences was employed. Out of 1,305 keywords in total, 77 were included, a dense set of highly co-occurring concepts in the literature under investigation.

The keyword "humans" appeared with the highest frequency (n = 107) and exhibited the greatest total link strength (404), highlighting its central role in the dataset and suggesting it serves as a foundational concept across various thematic clusters. Similarly, "animals" (n = 45; total link strength = 160), "ecosystem" (n = 37; 137), "environmental monitoring" (n = 21; 101), and "climate change" (n = 25; 81) were among the most frequently occurring terms, indicating their prominence in research related to human–environment interactions.

Keywords associated with demographic groups such as "female" (n = 18; 122), "male" (n = 17; 113), "middle aged" (n = 12; 95), "adult" (n = 11; 90), and "aged" (n = 10; 79) further emphasize the human-centric focus of the literature, often linked to studies on health, behavior, and social dynamics. The presence of "children," "young adults," and "adolescents" also suggest a cross-generational perspective in research emphasis (See Table 6.2 and Fig. 6.1).

Environmental themes are well represented, as evidenced by the inclusion of terms such as "biodiversity" (n = 16; 59), "conservation of natural resources" (n = 23; 114), "ecosystem services," "wetlands," "rivers," and "forests." These terms often co-occur with topics addressing sustainability and ecological resilience, including "sustainable development" (n = 7; 17), "renewable energy" (n = 6; 33), and "carbon dioxide/analysis" (n = 7; 33), indicating integrated perspectives on environmental conservation and climate mitigation. Geographical markers such as "China" (n = 20; 81), "India" (n = 10; 37), "Indonesia," "Malaysia," and "Thailand" and regional identifiers like "Asia" highlight the global scope of the literature, with an emphasis on studies conducted in or focusing on the Global South (See Table 6.2 and Fig. 6.1).

The emergence of pandemic-related terms such as "COVID-19" (n = 15; 44), "pandemics" (n = 6; 30), "SARS-CoV-2," and associated epidemiological keywords suggests a significant research focus on public health in recent years. This is supported by the presence of "public health," "global health," and "risk factors," reflecting interdisciplinary attention to the health-environment nexus. Lastly, terms such as "policy," "policymaking," "decision-making," and "international cooperation" indicate an emphasis on governance and strategic interventions within the research corpus. These elements, combined with methodological keywords like "cross-sectional studies," "models, theoretical," and "surveys and questionnaires," reinforce the empirical and analytical approaches adopted by researchers in the field (See Table 6.2 and Fig. 6.1).

In sum, the co-occurrence analysis reveals a multidimensional research landscape centered on human and environmental systems, underpinned by regional diversity, public health imperatives, and sustainability challenges.

5. Objectives

(1) To evaluate the potential and practices of NBHT in Southeast Asia in promoting holistic well-being and environmental sustainability.
(2) To examine the challenges and opportunities for integrating sustainability principles into NBHT, with a focus on community engagement and policy support.

6. Methodology

This study adopts a qualitative and interdisciplinary research design aimed at exploring the development, sustainability, and strategic implications of NBHT in Southeast Asia. Recognizing the complexity and multidimensionality of NBHT, the researchers employed a comparative case study approach focused on four countries—Thailand, Indonesia, Malaysia, and Vietnam—selected for their ecological richness, traditional healing practices, and tourism infrastructure. The study utilized expert interviews, content analysis of policy documents, and an extensive literature review to gather both localized insights and theoretical perspectives. Thematic and comparative analyses were applied to identify patterns, challenges, and success factors across different national contexts. Furthermore, the study developed a conceptual framework integrating sustainable tourism theory, health geography, and ecopsychology to holistically address the sociocultural, environmental, and psychological aspects of NBHT. A bibliometric keyword co-occurrence analysis was also conducted on 1,305 scholarly documents, revealing key themes such as ecosystem monitoring, public health, sustainability, and demographic influences. Together, these methods provided a rich, contextualized understanding of NBHT's potential and limitations in the region.

7. Theoretical Framework: An Integrated Model for Sustainable NBHT

This present study adopts an integrated framework combining sustainable tourism theory, health geography, and ecopsychology, applied within the Southeast Asian context.

7.1 Sustainable Tourism Theory

Sustainable tourism aims to minimize negative environmental, economic, and sociocultural impacts while generating economic benefits for host communities. This theory supports the triple-bottom-line approach: People, Planet, and Profit.

7.2 Health Geography

This discipline focuses on the spatial relationships between place, health, and healthcare. In the context of NBT, it investigates how natural spaces contribute to health and how access to these spaces varies across populations.

7.3 Ecopsychology

Ecopsychology explores the psychological relationship between humans and the natural world. It supports the idea that reconnecting with nature improves psychological well-being and fosters environmental stewardship.

8. Cyclical Framework for Sustainable NBHT

The presented figure outlines a cyclical model comprising five interlinked components—*Conservation, Education, Community Involvement, Sustainable Practices,* and *Economic Benefits*—which collectively illustrate a holistic approach to sustainable NBHT. This model reflects a systems-thinking perspective, emphasizing that sustainability emerges not from isolated interventions but from reinforcing feedback loops among environmental, social, and economic elements. *Conservation* emerges as the foundational pillar, emphasizing the ecological preconditions necessary for any form of health-related tourism rooted in nature (See Fig. 6.2). The preservation of biodiversity, ecosystem services, and natural aesthetics is indispensable for sustaining therapeutic landscapes. Engagement with biodiverse environments plays a crucial role in enhancing psychological recovery and promoting overall physical well-being. However, a critical challenge lies in balancing visitor access with ecological thresholds. Without proper regulatory mechanisms, high tourist traffic can lead to degradation, paradoxically undermining the very assets the model seeks to conserve.

Education is aptly placed as the second component, serving as a bridge between conservation goals and actionable awareness. Environmental literacy among stakeholders can catalyze responsible behaviors and foster ecological stewardship. Education initiatives—ranging from interpretive guides to community workshops—build capacity at both the tourist and host community levels. Ballantyne and Packer (2011) emphasize that informed tourists are more likely to engage in

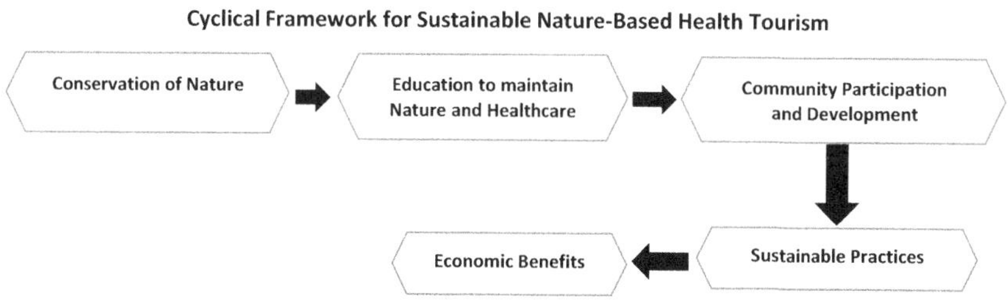

Fig. 6.2. Cyclical Framework for SNBHT.

sustainable behaviors. Nonetheless, the efficacy of education depends on cultural relevance, delivery methods, and the integration of local knowledge systems, which are often underutilized in mainstream tourism curricula. *Community Involvement* is central to the model's legitimacy and inclusivity. True sustainability demands not just ecological awareness but sociocultural alignment. When communities are genuinely engaged—as planners, custodians, and beneficiaries—the outcomes are more equitable and resilient. CBT initiatives, as explored by Scheyvens (1999), have demonstrated success in empowering local populations, preserving cultural heritage, and enhancing destination authenticity. However, tokenistic participation or externally-driven agendas can lead to community disillusionment and erode trust. Thus, the quality and depth of participation must be continuously evaluated. The inclusion of *Sustainable Practices* reflects the operational backbone of the model. These practices—such as low-impact infrastructure, renewable energy use, and waste reduction—translate values into tangible actions. From an academic standpoint, these align with the *Triple Bottom Line*, which prioritizes environmental integrity, social well-being, and economic viability. Nevertheless, sustainable practices often encounter barriers related to cost, regulation, and technical know-how, especially in rural or underdeveloped regions. Capacity-building and policy support are essential to mainstream such practices effectively.

The final component, *Economic Benefits*, underscores the importance of financial viability in sustaining the entire cycle. When local communities derive income through jobs, entrepreneurship, and revenue-sharing mechanisms, they are more likely to support conservation and sustainable practices. Stronza and Gordillo (2008) emphasize that economic incentives reinforce pro-environmental attitudes, creating a virtuous cycle. However, commercialization risks must be managed to prevent the commodification of nature and culture, which can erode authenticity and long-term resilience. In conclusion, this model presents a *regenerative tourism framework* where each component reinforces the others in a dynamic, cyclical fashion. The model resonates with the principles enshrined in the *UN SDGs*, particularly SDG 3 (Good Health and Well-being), SDG 12 (Responsible Consumption and Production), and SDG 15 (Life on Land). Its strength lies in its integrative vision; however, successful implementation hinges on context-specific adaptation, inclusive governance, and long-term commitment. For regions such as Southeast Asia, where ecological richness intersects with diverse cultural landscapes, this model offers a viable roadmap—but only if critically localized and equitably managed.

9. Application to Southeast Asia

Southeast Asia's cultural affinity to nature, spiritual traditions, and local healing systems provide fertile ground for implementing this integrated model. The framework encourages blending traditional ecological knowledge with modern sustainability strategies. Based on Table 6.1, an integrated theoretical approach to NBHT draws from multiple disciplines to create a holistic and sustainable model. Sustainable Tourism Theory serves as a foundational framework that emphasizes minimizing environmental degradation while maximizing socioeconomic benefits through the *Triple Bottom Line*, focusing on people, planet, and profit. Within the context of NBHT, this theory promotes eco-friendly infrastructure, conservation-oriented wellness retreats, and CBT initiatives that empower local populations. For instance, Thailand's Bio-Circular-Green (BCG) economy model actively integrates health tourism into its sustainability agenda while Vietnam's wellness homestays and Malaysia's herbal healing trails illustrate how local culture and biodiversity are leveraged to create wellness-focused experiences that also support environmental stewardship and local livelihoods. Health geography, another vital theoretical lens, explores the spatial dimensions of health, particularly how geographical factors affect access to natural therapeutic environments. This field emphasizes geographic equity in health resources, especially the role of natural landscapes—such as forests, springs, and highlands—in enhancing physical and mental well-being. In Southeast Asia, this is evident in initiatives like forest therapy in Sabah, Malaysia, and highland meditation retreats in Laos, which not only diversify rural tourism economies but also address health disparities by bringing wellness tourism to underserved areas. The mountain wellness tourism experiences in Sapa, Vietnam, further demonstrate how health geography principles can guide the strategic development of nature-based destinations that align with regional ecological and social contexts.

Finally, Ecopsychology contributes a psychological dimension to the model by focusing on the innate human connection with nature. It posits that nature serves as a co-therapist, providing emotional healing and spiritual rejuvenation through immersive experiences. Applications in NBHT include practices like forest bathing, yoga and meditation in natural settings, and spiritual retreats that harness the calming power of the environment. Southeast Asia offers rich examples of this theory in action, such as the spiritual retreats in Ubud, Bali; forest monasteries in Myanmar that blend mindfulness with ecological immersion; and coastal mindfulness tourism in the Philippines, which integrates traditional healing philosophies with contemporary wellness trends. These theories form a comprehensive framework that not only supports the sustainability of NBHT but also ensures its cultural and contextual relevance in Southeast Asia. They provide a multi-layered understanding of how ecological, spatial, and psychological dimensions intersect to create health-promoting tourism experiences rooted in local landscapes and traditions (See Tables 6.3 and 6.4).

10. Opportunities in Southeast Asia

- Cultural Richness and Biodiversity: Southeast Asia boasts rainforests, mountains, rivers, and coastlines, providing diverse ecosystems for health tourism. Traditional healing practices rooted in indigenous knowledge (e.g., Thai herbal compress, Jamu) offer unique selling points.

Table 6.3 Synthesis of Framework to Nature-based health tourism (NBHT).

Theory	Core Concept	Key Focus Areas	Application in Nature-Based Health Tourism	Southeast Asia Examples
Sustainable tourism theory	Minimize negative impacts and promote benefits across economy, environment, and society	Triple-bottom-line: People, planet, profit	• Eco-friendly infrastructure • Community-based tourism • Conservation-linked wellness retreats	• Thailand's BCG economy model • Community wellness homestays in Vietnam • Herbal healing trails in Malaysia
Health geography	Study of spatial relationships between place, health, and healthcare	• Access to natural healing spaces • Geographic health equity	• Location-specific wellness offerings (mountains, forests, springs) • Rural health tourism expansion	• Forest therapy in Sabah (Malaysia) • Highland meditation retreats in Laos • Mountain wellness in Sapa (Vietnam)
Ecopsychology	Psychological connection between humans and nature	• Emotional healing through nature • Nature as co-therapist	• Forest bathing • Yoga/meditation in nature • Spiritual healing through environmental immersion	• Ubud retreats in Indonesia • Forest monasteries in Myanmar • Coastal mindfulness tourism in the Philippines

Source: Author's Compilation

Table 6.4 Nature-based health tourism (NBHT) in Southeast Asia—Country Perspectives, Outcomes and Applications.

Country	Perspective/Approach	Outcomes	Applications
Thailand	• Integration of traditional Thai massage and herbal therapies • Strong government support through BCG economy model	• International reputation as a wellness hub • Community involvement in eco-wellness tourism	• Eco-resorts in Chiang Mai • Forest meditation programs • Herbal health products for tourists
Indonesia	• Emphasis on Jamu (herbal medicine) and spiritual healing • Use of nature for yoga retreats and detox programs, esp. In Bali	• Boost in wellness travel post-COVID-19 pandemic • Cultural commodification risk	• Balinese healing sanctuaries • Organic farming-tourism integration • Volcano and beach-based nature therapies
Malaysia	• Focus on forest therapy (e.g., in Sabah) • Development of healing trails within national parks	• Diversification of ecotourism offerings • Increased awareness of mental wellness benefits	• Community-run forest healing paths • Nature-guided meditation workshops • Health tourism packages
Vietnam	• Blending spiritual tourism with wellness (e.g., pagoda retreats in nature) • Promotion of herbal steam therapy (Xông hơi)	• Growth in domestic wellness tourism • Revitalization of traditional herbal knowledge	• Mountain retreats (e.g., Sapa) • Temple stays with herbal healing • Wellness river cruises
Philippines	• Coastal and island-based wellness tourism (beach yoga, reef therapy) • Use of indigenous health knowledge (hilot massage, herbal wraps)	• Expanding niche wellness market • Infrastructure challenges in remote islands	• Eco-healing island resorts • Traditional wellness homestays • Marine therapy (e.g., snorkeling + mindfulness)

(Continued)

Table 6.4 *(Continued)*

Country	Perspective/Approach	Outcomes	Applications
Cambodia	• Emphasis on spiritual healing and nature immersion near Angkor and rural villages • Untapped potential in forest-based health tourism	• Growing backpacker wellness trend • Community empowerment in rural areas	• Wellness tuk tuk tours • Yoga + local herbalism retreats • Farm-to-table health food experiences
Laos	• Nature-rich, low-impact tourism in forest and mountain areas • Focus on silence, solitude, and traditional wellness	• Low-volume but high-value tourism • Preservation of traditional healing practices	• Meditation caves and forest stays • Local herbal wellness tours • Healing huts run by monks and elders
Myanmar	• Use of sacred mountains and hot springs for spiritual and physical rejuvenation • Traditional massage and oil therapy practices	• Political instability affects potential • Interest in cross-border wellness collaborations	• Pilgrimage + healing retreats • Thermal wellness tourism • Nature wellness treks in Shan and Kachin states
Singapore	• Urban-nature integration (e.g., gardens by the bay for therapeutic use) • High-end wellness experiences with nature-based design principles	• Leadership in eco-luxury wellness • Urban green spaces as stress-reduction tools	• Nature immersion in parks for corporate wellness • Botanical therapy programs • Medical + nature wellness combos
Brunei	• Eco-wellness driven by Islamic and cultural values • Focus on forest sanctuaries and wildlife-based tranquility experiences	• Niche high-income market • Opportunities in luxury health tourism tied to conservation	• Forest reserve wellness lodges • Mindfulness and ethical lifestyle retreats • Jungle spa tourism

Source: Author's Compilation.

- Economic Empowerment through CBT: Initiatives like homestays, local healing centers, and village-based wellness retreats can empower local populations, especially women, and promote cultural pride.
- Government Support and Regional Collaboration: ASEAN's tourism development strategies emphasize sustainable and inclusive tourism. Regional branding efforts can further position Southeast Asia as a global hub for eco-wellness.

11. Challenges

- Overtourism and Environmental Pressure: Popular destinations like Bali and Phuket face issues of overcrowding, waste, and habitat degradation. There is a need to promote lesser-known destinations with capacity management.
- Cultural Appropriation and Commodification: When traditional healing practices are commercialized without community involvement or respect for heritage, it can lead to cultural dilution.
- Inadequate Infrastructure and Regulation: Many rural or natural sites lack sustainable transport, waste management, and medical standards, raising concerns for safety and hygiene.
- Climate Change Impacts: Rising temperatures, sea-level rise, and biodiversity loss threaten the very ecosystems that underpin NBHT (See Tables 6.3 and 6.4).

Waste Management in tourism: While tourism plays a considerable role in economic development all over the world and cross-cultural exchange, it also raises some serious environmental concerns. One of the most significant among them is the production of waste. Short-term population growth at tourist areas can place strains on garbage management infrastructure and lead to environmental degradation. To maintain environmental quality, public health safety, and ensure the viability of the tourism sector, efficient trash management is essential. Solid (plastics, packaging, food wastes), liquid (sewage, greywater), and hazardous (hotel chemicals, batteries) are all waste generated by tourism. Every destination and form of tourism generates varying levels and types of rubbish. As an example, ecotourism in remote areas will generate less rubbish but have greater disposal problems compared to mass tourist, which tends to leave significant plastic and food wastes in beach destinations.

12. Pictorial Evidential Facts From Select Respondents

Fig. 6.3 depicts that the analysis reveals that NBHT is primarily a periodic activity for most respondents, with 46.9% participating occasionally (one to two times per year), typically aligning their visits with holidays or time off. Another 29.7% engage rarely, likely due to constraints such as time, cost, or accessibility. Meanwhile, 18.8% of respondents are frequent participants (3+ times annually), reflecting a committed segment that prioritizes regular wellness experiences in

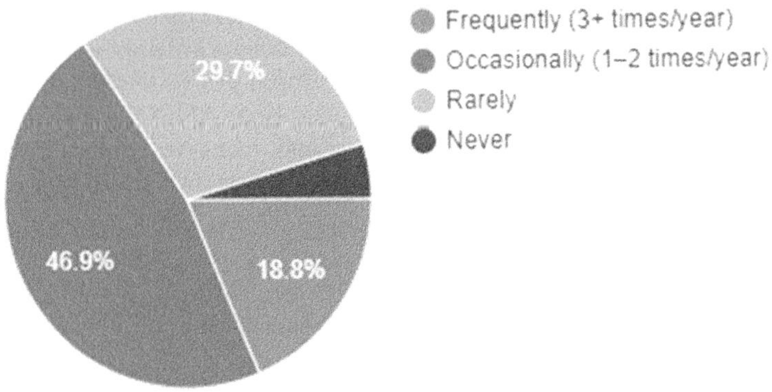

Fig. 6.3. Engage in nature-based tourism (NBT) Activities.

nature. A small group (4.7%) has never participated in NBHT, highlighting a potential area for awareness-building and market expansion.

The analysis of preferred destinations for NBHT shows that beaches and coastal areas (67.2%) and mountain retreats (62.5%) are the most favored locations among respondents, highlighting a strong attraction to scenic, tranquil environments. Forest reserves (45.3%) and rural wellness villages (32.8%) also show considerable popularity, reflecting interest in nature immersion and cultural experiences. In contrast, eco-resorts (26.6%) and hot springs/spas (6.3%) are less commonly chosen, indicating either lower accessibility or niche appeal. This suggests that NBHT planning should focus on enhancing experiences in high-demand natural settings while exploring ways to promote lesser-visited wellness destinations (See Fig. 6.4).

The chart illustrates that the primary motivation for engaging in NBHT is overwhelmingly driven by mental relaxation and stress relief (70.3%), reflecting a growing demand for wellness experiences that support emotional and psychological well-being. Environmental interest (14.1%) follows as the second most

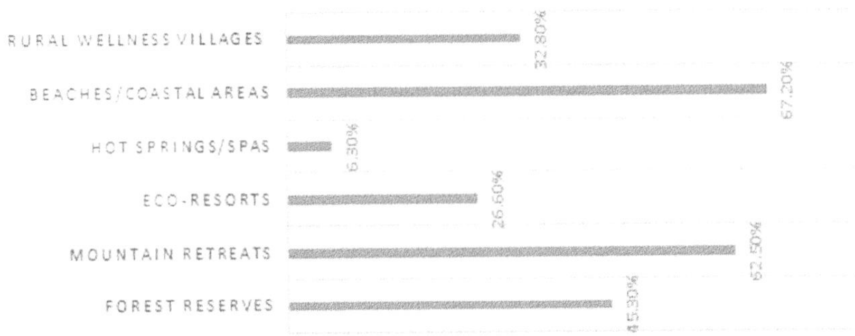

Fig. 6.4. Nature-Based Destinations Have You Visited.

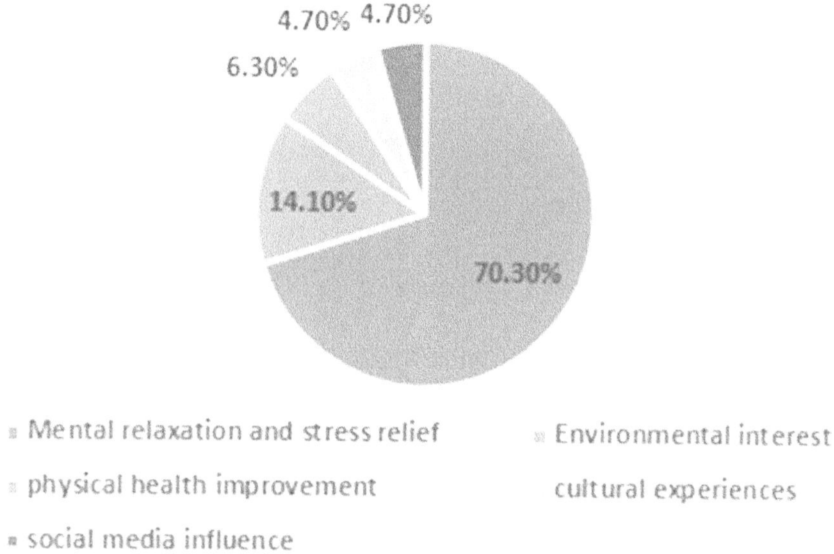

Fig. 6.5. Motivation For Choosing Nature-based health tourism (NBHT).

common motivation, indicating a significant concern for nature and sustainability among travelers. Other factors such as physical health improvement (6.3%), cultural experiences (4.7%), and social media influence (4.7%) play smaller roles. This trend emphasizes the importance of designing NBHT offerings that prioritize tranquil, restorative environments over purely physical or trend-driven elements (See Fig. 6.5).

The chart highlights key sustainability practices perceived as important in NBHT. The most emphasized factor is waste management and recycling (51.6%), followed closely by conservation of local biodiversity (50%) and organic or locally sourced food (46.9%), indicating a strong preference for eco-conscious and responsible tourism practices. Local community involvement (42.2%) and use of renewable energy (39.1%) also show significant support, reflecting a desire for tourism that benefits host communities and reduces environmental impact. *Limiting* visitor numbers to avoid overtourism (32.8%) is moderately supported, while only 1.6% value it the least, suggesting that while sustainability is a priority, measures that restrict access may be less favorable (See Fig. 6.6).

The chart outlines key improvements desired in NBHT experiences. The top priorities among respondents are improved accessibility and more sustainable practices, both selected by 53.1%, emphasizing the need for inclusive infrastructure and environmentally friendly operations. Enhanced facilities (43.8%) and better health programs (32.8%) also rank highly, indicating a demand for higher service quality and comprehensive wellness offerings. In contrast,

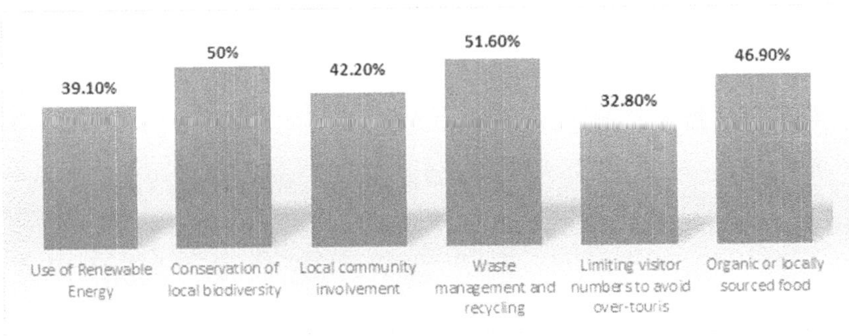

Fig. 6.6. Value Creation While Visiting a Health or nature-based tourism (NBT) Site.

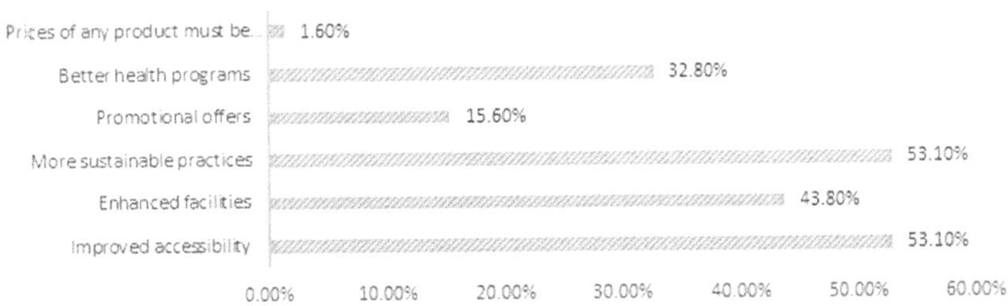

Fig. 6.7. Factors Would Increase Your Interest in Returning to a Nature-based health tourism (NBHT) Site.

promotional offers (15.6%) and affordable pricing (1.6%) are less significant concerns, suggesting that while cost may not be a major barrier, value and sustainability-driven features are more influential in shaping visitors' expectations (See Fig. 6.7).

13. Core Findings of the Study

- NBHT contributes significantly to rural development and the preservation of cultural heritage, especially through traditional healing practices and nature-integrated wellness activities.

The sustainability of NBHT is undermined by:

- Inadequate integration of NBHT in national and regional tourism policies.
- Overtourism in popular destinations, leading to ecological degradation.

- Limited community participation and empowerment, resulting in socio-cultural displacement and loss of authenticity.
- Empowered local stakeholders and the preservation of traditional knowledge systems are identified as critical success factors in achieving sustainable NBHT models.

Case studies from countries such as Thailand, Indonesia, Malaysia, and Vietnam reveal:

- Strong links between cultural heritage and biodiversity with health tourism offerings.
- Challenges such as cultural commodification and insufficient regulatory infrastructure.
- The study integrates three theoretical lenses—Sustainable Tourism Theory, Health Geography, and Ecopsychology—to propose a cyclical framework for sustainable NBHT based on:
  - conservation;
  - education;
  - community involvement;
  - sustainable practices;
  - economic benefits.
- Survey findings show that:
  - Mental relaxation and stress relief (70.3%) are the primary motivators for NBHT participation.
  - Beaches and mountains are the most preferred nature-based destinations.
  - Visitors prioritize eco-friendly practices, including:
  - waste management and recycling (51.6%);
  - biodiversity conservation (50%);
  - local and organic food sourcing (46.9%);
  - community involvement (42.2%).
- Interest in returning to NBHT sites is most influenced by:
  - improved accessibility;
  - more sustainable practices;
  - enhanced facilities and health programs.
- The COVID-19 pandemic has heightened public interest in socially distanced, nature-based wellness experiences, enhancing NBHT's relevance in contemporary tourism.
- Digital transformation and growing health-conscious consumer behavior are reshaping the demand landscape for NBHT in the region.
- Waste management and climate resilience are identified as pressing challenges, especially in ecologically sensitive and remote destinations.
- The study highlights Southeast Asia's unique advantage in blending traditional healing systems with rich biodiversity, positioning the region as a leader in sustainable NBHT development.

14. Conclusion

NBHT holds transformative potential for individuals and communities in Southeast Asia. Rooted in traditional knowledge and supported by the region's natural wealth, this form of tourism aligns well with global shifts toward wellness, sustainability, and cultural authenticity.

However, for this potential to be fully realized, sustainability must be at the heart of all planning and operations. This includes respecting local cultures, protecting biodiversity, building eco-sensitive infrastructure, and involving local communities in decision-making processes. With thoughtful integration of policy, practice, and tradition, Southeast Asia can lead the way in shaping a sustainable future for NBHT.

References

Ballantyne, R., & Packer, J. (2011). Using tourism free-choice learning experiences to promote environmentally sustainable behaviour: The role of post-visit 'action resources'. *Environmental Education Research*, *17*(2), 201–215.

Braimah, J. A., Bisung, E., & Kuuire, V. (2023). Health geography in Sub-Saharan Africa. In *Health geography in Sub-Saharan Africa: Development-health nexus* (pp. 1–10). Springer International Publishing.

Brockelman, W. Y., & Dearden, P. (1990). The role of nature trekking in conservation: A case-study in Thailand. *Environmental Conservation*, *17*(2), 141–148.

Buckley, R., & Coghlan, A. (2012). Nature-based tourism in breadth and depth. *Critical debates in tourism*, *57*, 304–307.

Chubchuwong, M., Beise-Zee, R., & Speece, M. W. (2015). The effect of nature-based tourism, destination attachment and property ownership on environmental-friendliness of visitors: A study in Thailand. *Asia Pacific Journal of Tourism Research*, *20*(6), 656–679.

Esparza-Huamanchumo, R. M., Villalba-Condori, K. O., Botezán, I., & Sánchez Jiménez, R. (2024). *Ecotourism, sustainable tourism and nature-based tourism: An analysis of emerging fields in tourism scientific literature*. University of Oradea.

Grau, H. R. (2022). *Nature-based tourism in Asia's mountainous protected areas: A trans-regional review of peaks and parks*. Springer. https://doi.org/10.1007/978-3-030-76833-1

Lechner, A. M., Gomes, R. L., Rodrigues, L., Ashfold, M. J., Selvam, S. B., Wong, E. P., Raymond, C. M., Zieritz, A., Sing, K. W., Moug, P., Billa, L., Sagala, S., Cheshmehzangi, A., Lourdes, K., Azhar, B., Sanusi, R., Ives, C. D., Tang, Y.-T., Tan, D. T., …Gibbins, C. (2020). Challenges and considerations of applying nature-based solutions in low-and middle-income countries in Southeast and East Asia. *Blue-Green Systems*, *2*(1), 331–351.

Lee, T. H., Jan, F. H., & Yang, C. C. (2013). Environmentally responsible behavior of nature-based tourists: A review. *International Journal of Development and Sustainability*, *2*(1), 100–115.

Ly, T. P., & Bauer, T. (2017). Ecotourism in Thailand, Cambodia, and Vietnam: Theory and practice. *International Leisure Review*, *6*(1), 19–31.

Pessot, E., Spoladore, D., Zangiacomi, A., & Sacco, M. (2021). Natural resources in health tourism: A systematic literature review. *Sustainability*, *13*(5), 2661.

Pongsiri, M. J., & Arthakaivalvatee, V. (2020). Addressing the environment and health nexus is a strategic approach to advance the sustainable development goals in ASEAN. In *Urban health and wellbeing programme: Policy briefs* (Vol. 1, pp. 57–63). Springer.

Sabaruddin, S. A., Jamal, S. A., & Wee, H. (2023). Redefining nature-based tourism in Malaysia: Activities and nature sites. *International Journal of Academic Research in Business and Social Sciences*, *13*(5), 224–239.

Santoso, A. D., Sajida, S., & Yusnaini, Y. (2024). Forest tourism in Southeast Asia: A bibliometric analysis. *Forest and Society*, *8*(2), 484–502.

Scheyvens, R. (1999). Ecotourism and the empowerment of local communities. *Tourism Management*, *20*(2), 245–249.

Seočanac, M. (2022). Transformative experiences in nature-based tourism as a chance for improving sustainability of tourism destination. *Economics of Sustainable Development*, *6*(1), 1–10.

Singh, A. (2024). The role of geography in the healthcare sector. *Shodh Sari: An International Multidisciplinary Journal*, *3*(3), 96–99.

Stronza, A., & Gordillo, J. (2008). Community views of ecotourism. *Annals of Tourism Research*, *35*(2), 448–468.

Trupp, A., & Dolezal, C. (2020). Tourism and the sustainable development goals in Southeast Asia. *ASEAS–Austrian Journal of South-East Asian Studies*, *13*(1), 1–16.

UNWTO. (2021). Sustainability guidelines for tourism development. *World Tourism Organization*. https://www.unwto.org

Winter, P. L., Selin, S., Cerveny, L., & Bricker, K. (2019). Outdoor recreation, nature-based tourism, and sustainability. *Sustainability*, *12*(1), 81.

Chapter 7

Reviving Ancient Traditions: Kalarippayattu and Yoga in Modern Wellness Tourism

Kuzhikandathil Chirakkalthodi Murari[a], *Abinash Roy*[a], *Subramanya Pailoor*[a] *and Sunil Tiwari*[a,b]

[a]Central University of Kerala, India
[b]Department of Economics, Indian Institute of Management (IIM) Bodh Gaya Bodh Gaya, India

Abstract

This study discovers the amalgamation of Kalarippayattu along with Yoga within wellness tourism and measures their role in promoting bodily health, phycological health, and spiritual balance. As heritage Indian practices, both Kalarippayattu, the oldest form of traditional martial art, and Yoga, a holistic discipline, offer transformative wellness experiences deeply rooted in India's cultural heritage. With the increasing demand for authentic and immersive wellness tourism, this research examines how these practices enhance the touristic experience by providing meaningful, heritage-based engagements. Using a qualitative descriptive analysis, the study employs in-depth interviews conducted at Kalarippayattu training centers and Yoga retreats. Data were collected from wellness tourism experts, Kalarippayattu practitioners, Yoga instructors, and tourists who participated in programs featuring these disciplines. Findings suggest that both Kalarippayattu and Yoga contribute to body–mind synchronization, improved flexibility, enhanced immunity, and overall vitality. Tourists engaging in these wellness programs get experiences of relaxation, rejuvenation, and deeper self-connection. Additionally, the study compares Kalarippayattu and Yoga within the wellness tourism framework and examines their distinct contributions to holistic well-being. The findings underscore the potential of Kalarippayattu and Yoga as a valuable asset in positioning India as a global destination for holistic and

Nature, Wellness and Sustainability in Health Tourism, 155–182

Published under exclusive licence by Emerald Publishing Limited
doi:10.1108/978-1-83742-029-220261007

heritage-based well-being. By integrating cultural heritage into wellness tourism, stakeholders can offer unique experiences that attract travelers seeking both health benefits and cultural enrichment.

Keywords: Cultural heritage; health; Kalarippayattu; wellness tourism; Yoga

1. Introduction

Wellness tourism has arisen as a rapidly flourishing sector in the global tourism industry, led by the growing demand for holistic health experiences that integrate traditional and alternative healing practices. Defined as travel undertaken to enhance physical, psychological, and divine well-being, wellness tourism comprises diverse cultural traditions, natural therapies, and immersive practices. India, with its rich heritage of wellness systems, offers a unique platform for travelers seeking transformative healing experiences deeply rooted in tradition (Georgiev, 2010). Among India's diverse wellness offerings, Kalarippayattu and Yoga stand out as integral components of cultural wellness tourism.

Kalarippayattu, often regarded as the oldest form of martial art, and Yoga, a widely recognized discipline for self-awareness and inner balance, both contribute significantly to holistic well-being. While Yoga is well established in global wellness tourism, Kalarippayattu remains underexplored as a potential wellness practice. Beyond its combat techniques, Kalarippayattu serves as a dynamic movement therapy that enhances flexibility, coordination, and mental resilience (Varma, 1982). Together, these practices provide an immersive and heritage-based approach to wellness tourism, attracting travelers seeking both physical rejuvenation and cultural enrichment (Chen & Petrick, 2013).

Bharath has long been a cradle of spiritual and philosophical traditions, producing a vast cluster of activities aimed at self-discovery, discipline, and holistic well-being. While Yoga is celebrated worldwide as a path to spiritual enlightenment, physical discipline, and inner harmony, Kalarippayattu embodies the fusion of physical prowess, martial discipline, and sacred knowledge (Fritz & Sonnentag, 2006). Despite their distinct methodologies, both practices share a common foundation in Indian cultural and philosophical traditions, making them valuable assets in the realm of wellness tourism. However, despite the recognized global popularity and success of Yoga, the role of Kalarippayattu remains marginalized in both academic literature and tourism practices. The lack of structured integration of Kalarippayattu into wellness tourism programs, and the absence of comparative studies examining Kalarippayattu alongside Yoga, point out a critical gap that needs scholarly and industry attention.

With the rising interest in authentic and immersive travel experiences, integrating Kalarippayattu and Yoga into wellness tourism offers an opportunity to position India as a leading destination for holistic well-being. However, while extensive research has explored Yoga's impact on wellness tourism, there exists a substantial gap in literature examining those potentials of Kalarippayattu in this domain. Moreover, limited studies have analyzed the comparative benefits of both practices in enhancing the wellness tourism experience (Mandakathingal, 2021). *Thus, there is a need to investigate how Kalarippayattu and Yoga can be leveraged to create unique, culturally rooted, and transformative wellness tourism experiences.* Therefore, this study attempts to bridge these disparities by analyzing the integration of Kalarippayattu and Yoga into wellness tourism, highlighting their distinct yet complementary contributions to bodily health, phycological well-being, and spiritual balance (Streeter et al., 2007).

The overarching research question guiding this study is—How do Kalarippayattu and Yoga contribute to enhancing wellness tourism experiences and outcomes for tourists in terms of physical, psychological, and spiritual well-being?

1.1 Research Objectives

To explore the impact of Kalarippayattu and Yoga in improving wellness tourism experiences.

To analyze the physiological, mind-related, and spiritual positive outcomes of these practices for wellness tourists.

To explore how cultural heritage leads to the authenticity and attractiveness of wellness tourism offerings in India.

To identify challenges and opportunities in integrating Kalarippayattu into mainstream wellness tourism.

To compare and contrast the impact of Kalarippayattu and Yoga on tourists' overall well-being and satisfaction.

While wellness tourism has gained significant attention worldwide, existing literature predominantly focuses on Yoga, Ayurveda, and meditation as its key components (Bilderbeck et al., 2013). Still, there is a notable absence of research on the integration of Kalarippayattu into wellness tourism despite its historical and therapeutic significance. Comparisons with martial arts tourism in countries like China and Korea highlight the absence of a structured approach to incorporating Kalarippayattu into India's wellness tourism framework. Additionally, studies rarely examine the combined impact of Kalarippayattu and Yoga on holistic well-being in a tourism setting. By addressing these gaps, this study seeks to provide empirical insights into how these ancient Indian practices contribute to the evolving landscape of wellness tourism. *Hence, this present study seeks to address these critical research gaps and propose actionable insights for enhancing wellness tourism in the Indian landscape through the integration of these ancient traditions.*

Through a cultural heritage approach, this research underscores the potential of Kalarippayattu and Yoga in positioning India as a global hub for holistic wellness tourism. By integrating these traditional practices into structured wellness tourism programs, stakeholders can offer unique, meaningful experiences that attract travelers seeking both health benefits and cultural immersion (Evans et al., 2014).

2. Methodology

This study applies a qualitative research strategy to examine the integration of Kalarippayattu and Yoga into wellness tourism. The research focuses on understanding how these ancient Indian disciplines contribute to holistic well-being and enhance the wellness tourism experience. A descriptive qualitative research design was employed to gain detailed analysis into the role of Kalarippayattu and Yoga in wellness tourism (see the Appendix 1). The study utilized direct observations, semi-structured interviews, and field visits to various centers dedicated to these practices. Data were collected through the following methods:

(1) *Field Visits and Observations*:

The researchers visited Kalarippayattu training centers and Yoga retreats to observe firsthand the practices, training methods, and engagement of participants. These visits provided a deeper understanding of how these disciplines are structured within wellness tourism programs.

(2) *Interviews with Experts and Practitioners*:

Extensive interviews were conducted with Kalarippayattu trainers, Yoga instructors, wellness tourism experts, and participating tourists, offering insights into their experiences and the impact of these practices on wellness tourism.

(3) Extensive interviews were conducted with a varied group of participants, including:

   a. Kalarippayattu masters and trainers;
   b. Yoga instructors;
   c. wellness tourism experts;
   d. tourists who participated in Kalarippayattu and Yoga programs.

(4) The interviews' aim:

It aimed to capture their perspectives on the impact of these approaches to physical, mental, and spiritual well-being, as well as their own role in enhancing the wellness tourism experience.

(5) *Tourist Experience Analysis*:

Tourists who had engaged in these wellness programs were interviewed to understand their motivations, experiences, and perceived benefits. Their testimonials provided insights into the appeal and effectiveness of Kalarippayattu and Yoga within the sector of wellness tourism and cultural heritage.

The data obtained were assessed using thematic analysis, where key themes were identified by coding responses and observations. The analysis focused on several aspects, including the physical and psychiatric benefits of Kalarippayattu and Yoga, highlighting their impact on overall well-being (Downward & Dawson, 2016). Additionally, the cultural and heritage significance of these practices was explored, emphasizing their deep-rooted traditions and historical relevance. The study also examined the role of these disciplines in shaping wellness tourism experiences, shedding light on their potential to enhance holistic travel experiences. Furthermore, the challenges and opportunities for integrating Kalarippayattu and Yoga into the wellness tourism industry were analyzed, providing insights into their future scope and sustainability within the sector (Dini, 2022).

3. Kalari Payattu: The Martial Art of Kerala

Kalari Payattu, often referred to as "God's Own Martial Art," is one of the earliest-known martial arts systems in worldwide. Deeply rooted in Kerala's history and culture, it is presumed to introduced by Lord Parasurama, the sixth form of Vishnu, who is said to have reclaimed the land of Kerala from the sea. The origins of Kalari Payattu can be traced to the *Dhanur Veda*, a section of the *Atharva Veda* that teaches the art of warfare and weapon handling. Like Yoga, Kalari Payattu is regarded as a divine gift, blending physical training with spiritual discipline.

The term "Kalari Payattu" is derived from *Kalari* (gymnasium or training ground) and *Payattu* (combat training). Some scholars link the word "Kalari" to the Sanskrit term *Khal-Urika*, meaning a parade ground where warriors are trained. Historically, Kalari Payattu was an integral part of Kerala's socio-political structure, particularly during the 12th century when the region was divided into smaller principalities. Since these smaller states could not maintain standing armies, rulers established *kalaris* (martial training centers) to train warriors in self-defense, strategic combat, and weaponry.

Kerala, known as "God's Own Country," is a southern State in India. Kerala's cultural landscape is sketched in Fig. 7.1A while its location along the Western Ghats is shown in Fig. 7.1B. This state is famous for its lush landscapes, quiet backwaters, and thriving cultural heritage. Kalari Payattu has flourished in this mystical land, evolving into a unique system of combat that incorporates elements of Yoga, Ayurveda, and meditative practices. The training begins with rigorous physical conditioning, flexibility exercises, and techniques involving unarmed combat. As practitioners progress, they master various weapons, including swords, shields, and spears. Advanced training includes *marma vidya*, the knowledge of vital pressure points, which can be used for both healing and combat.

Today, Kalaripayattu is not only a martial art but also a holistic practice that enhances agility, strength, and mental focus. It has influenced various other martial arts, including Chinese Kung Fu and Japanese Karate (Kolanad, 2022). With its resurgence in modern times, Kalaripayattu is now practiced globally as a system of self-defense, fitness, and wellness.

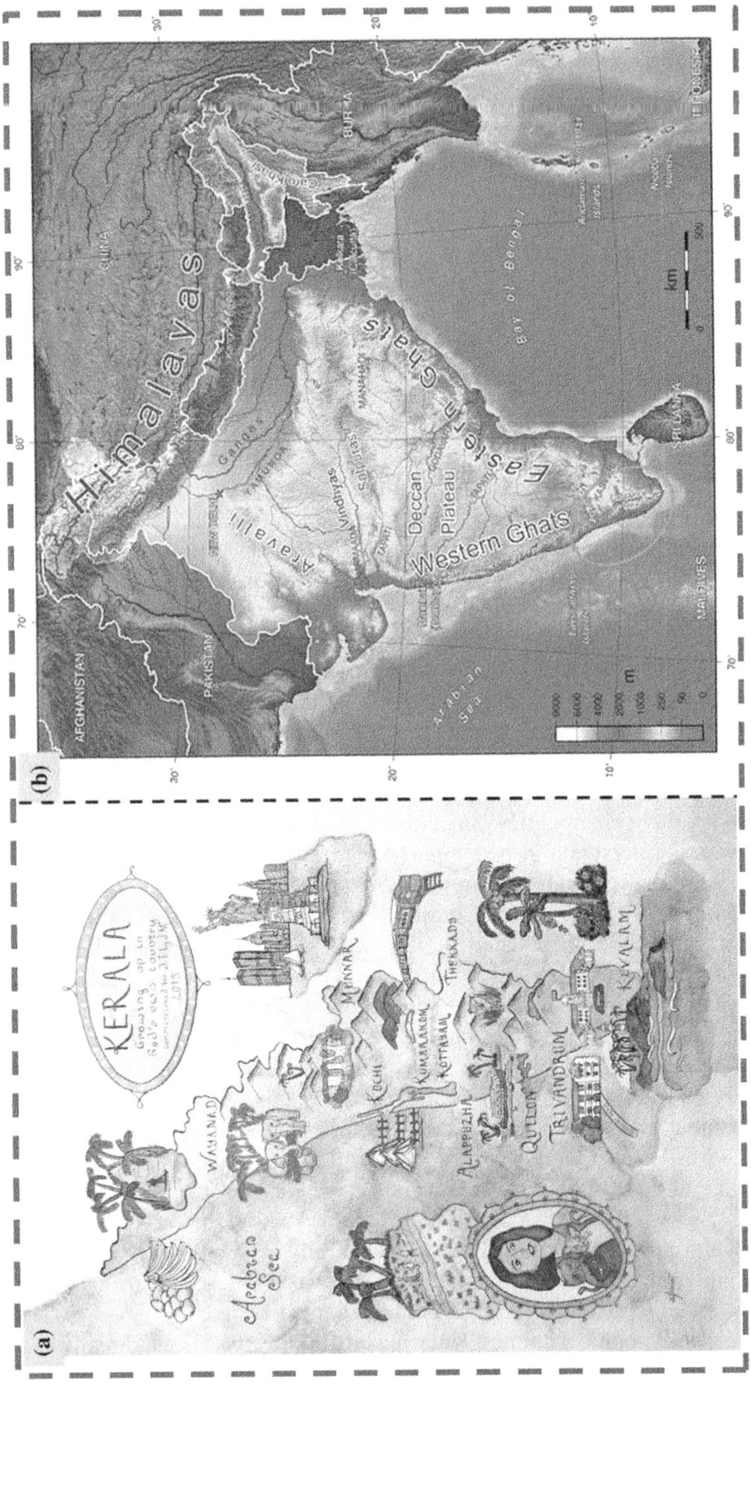

Fig. 7.1. (*A*) Hand-Drawn Map of Kerala With Key Landmarks and Cultural Elements. (*B*) Topographical Map of India Showing Kerala in the Western Ghats. https://indiamap360.com/india-geography-map

Rooted in Kerala's warrior traditions, Kalaripayattu dates back over 3,000 years. It played an essential part in the training of soldiers and was historically linked to temple rituals and Ayurveda (The full range of Kalaripayattu training weapons and the layout of a traditional Kalari are illustrated in Fig. 7.2A–F). The art form declined during British colonial rule but has since been revived, gaining recognition as an integral part of India's intangible heritage.

Kalaripayattu is not just a martial art but a holistic system for physical and mental well-being. Its rigorous training enhances flexibility, muscle strength, endurance, and agility while also improving cardiovascular health through dynamic movements (Cramer, Lauche, Hohmann, et al., 2013). The practice sharpens mind-body coordination, fostering better focus, balance, and reflexes. Additionally, Kalaripayattu includes healing techniques such as Marma therapy, which aids in pain relief and rehabilitation (Taylor et al., 2010). Beyond physical benefits, it plays a significant role in stress reduction, promoting mental resilience and emotional stability (Brown, 2005).

Recognizing its cultural and wellness potential, efforts are being made to integrate Kalaripayattu into Kerala's tourism sector. Regular cultural performances at tourism hubs attract visitors and raise awareness about this ancient art (Pati, 2010). Wellness retreats that combine Kalaripayattu with Ayurveda and Yoga further enhance Kerala's reputation as a global wellness destination. Short-term training programs and immersive experiences offer tourists hands-on engagement, helping sustain long-term interest. Additionally, digital outreach through online promotions, documentaries, and social media campaigns broadens its global appeal. Institutional support, including collaborations with tourism boards and educational institutions, ensures the structured promotion and preservation of Kalaripayattu for future generations (Govindaraj et al., 2021).

4. Yoga: The Art of Inner Harmony

Yoga, a system of spiritual and physical discipline, has been an integral part of Indian civilization for millennia. Ancient sages and seers employed Yoga as a method to explore both the external and internal worlds, ultimately seeking wisdom through sacred Indian texts such as the Vedas, Upanishads, and Shastras. Rather than being confined to religious boundaries, Yoga is perceived as an art of living, fostering inner joy and outer harmony.

The term "Yoga" derives from the Sanskrit root *yuj*, meaning "to join" or "to unite." It signifies the unity of the body, mind, and soul, as well as the connection between the individual self and the transcendental self (Balasubramaniam et al., 2013). Traditionally, Yoga has been transmitted orally from instructor to learner, with the sage Patanjali systematizing these teachings into *The Yoga Sutras*, a 2,000-year-old study. Patanjali defines Yoga as the restraint of mental fluctuations, leading to serenity and self-mastery. The path to purification, as outlined in the Sutras, involves ethical guidelines (yama and niyama), body

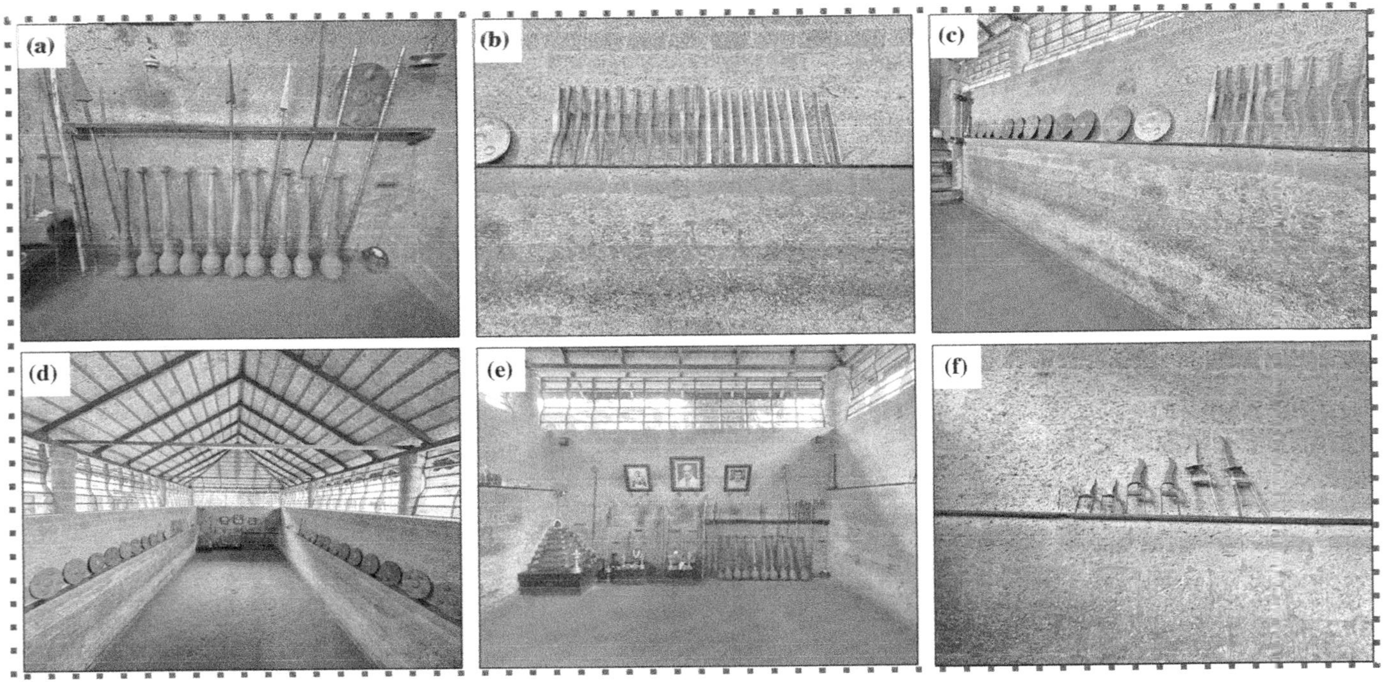

Fig. 7.2. (*A–F*) Traditional Kalari Payattu training Weapons, including Wooden Staffs, Swords, and Shields, Along With the Architecture of a Kalari training Ground.

postures (asanas), and breath control (pranayama), which together prepare the body and mind for meditation and mystical growth.

Hatha Yoga, one of the most widely practiced forms of Yoga today, was initially designed to prepare the body for prolonged meditation. The term *hatha* symbolizes the union of opposites—*ha* (sun) and *tha* (moon)—signifying balance and discipline. While many in the West view Yoga primarily as a set of physical exercises, its true purpose is self-realization and holistic well-being (Rao et al., 2021). Texts such as the *Hatha Yoga Pradipika* emphasize that Yoga serves as a vehicle for enlightenment, beyond just physical fitness (Gothe et al., 2014).

In recent decades, Yoga has gained immense popularity worldwide, particularly in the West, where it is often practiced for its health benefits. Many individuals turn to Yoga for stress relief, flexibility, and emotional stability, while health professionals recognize its therapeutic value in managing various ailments (Carlson et al., 2003). As Yoga continues to be embraced globally, it remains a profound holistic approach to cultivating physical health and mental clarity. Yoga has become a cornerstone of wellness tourism, attracting individuals from around the world seeking physical rejuvenation, mental peace, and spiritual growth. Countries like India, Thailand, and Bali have become major wellness tourism destinations, offering immersive Yoga retreats, Ayurvedic healing programs, and meditation centers that cater to a global audience.

India, the birthplace of Yoga, remains a premier destination for Yoga tourism (Dini, 2022). Locations such as Rishikesh, Mysore, and Dharamshala are renowned for their authentic Yoga schools, ashrams, and wellness resorts. Visitors engage in daily Yoga sessions, guided meditation, and holistic healing therapies, fostering a deep sense of well-being and balance.

Modern wellness resorts blend traditional Yoga practices with contemporary wellness trends, providing experiences such as Yoga therapy, detox programs, spa treatments, and nature retreats. These retreats emphasize stress reduction, mindfulness, and self-care, making Yoga tourism an essential part of the global wellness movement (Singleton, 2008).

With the increasing awareness of mental health and holistic healing, Yoga-based wellness tourism continues to flourish, bridging ancient traditions with modern lifestyles. As individuals seek refuge from the pressures of daily life, Yoga remains a timeless sanctuary, offering harmony, health, and inner peace (Brinsley et al., 2021).

5. Yoga and Kalari Payattu: A Shared Legacy

Both Yoga and Kalari Payattu emerge from India's ancient spiritual and physical traditions, deeply influenced by Vedic teachings. While Yoga primarily focuses on internal discipline and spiritual awakening, Kalari Payattu integrates martial training with meditative practices. The two disciplines share common elements, such as breath control, flexibility, and mindfulness, highlighting their interconnectedness in fostering holistic well-being (Rao, 2002).

Kalari Payattu often incorporates yogic principles in its practice, ensuring that warriors develop not only physical endurance but also mental lucidity and emotional stability. Similarly, Yoga, particularly Hatha Yoga, enhances the body's ability to endure prolonged meditation and combat training. These traditions complement each other, reflecting the holistic vision of Indian philosophy, where physical health, mental discipline, and spiritual growth are inextricably linked.

As the world continues to explore these time-honored practices, both Yoga and Kalari Payattu stand as testaments to India's rich heritage, offering timeless wisdom for physical, mental, and spiritual well-being.

6. Kalari and Yoga Philosophy

Kalari and Yoga, two ancient Indian traditions, have evolved as profound systems of physical and mental discipline that contribute to overall wellness. While Kalari, or Kalaripayattu, is a martial art emphasizing agility, strength, and self-defense, Yoga is a philosophical and spiritual system designed for inner transformation and self-realization. Despite their distinct approaches, both share deep-rooted philosophical foundations and principles that contribute to holistic well-being. By examining their similarities, differences, and shared benefits, we can better understand how each system nurtures both body and mind.

Kalari is known as the oldest martial art in the world, originating from Kerala, India. It integrates physical training, healing practices, and combat techniques in a structured manner, emphasizing discipline, flexibility, and endurance. The philosophy behind Kalari is deeply rooted in the concept of *Ayurveda* and *Dhanurveda*, ancient Indian sciences that view health and combat as interconnected. The practice involves rigorous body conditioning, controlled breathing, and mental focus, making it not just a physical discipline but also a means of self-mastery (Dhruva et al., 2012).

Yoga, on the other hand, is a comprehensive system of spiritual and physical practices aimed at achieving self-awareness and liberation (*moksha*). Rooted in the teachings of the *Upanishads, Vedas*, and *Patanjali's Yoga Sutras*, Yoga is not just about physical practices (*asanas*) but also concern ethical conduct (*yamas* and *niyamas*), breath control (*pranayama*), and meditation (*dhyana*). It is a path to transcendence that cultivates inner peace and mental clarity, leading to physical, emotional, and spiritual balance (Saraswati, 2002).

Though seemingly different, Kalari and Yoga share a common goal: the integration of body and mind. Both emphasize breath control, mindfulness, and disciplined movement, contributing to enhanced emotional stability, physical fitness and mental focus. In Kalari, breath control plays a crucial role in executing swift movements and maintaining endurance while in Yoga, *pranayama* techniques regulate energy flow, improve concentration, and calm the nervous system. The synchronization of breath and movement in both practices leads to heightened awareness and refined motor control (Folkins, 1972).

Another striking similarity is the meditative aspect present in both traditions. While Yoga directly incorporates meditation as a key element, Kalari also includes meditative techniques through its fluid movements, combat forms (*meipayattu*), and rituals. The intense concentration required in Kalari training fosters a meditative state, much like Yoga's emphasis on mindfulness and self-observation. Both practices cultivate present-moment awareness, reducing stress and enhancing mental clarity (Brems, 2015).

Despite their similarities, Kalari and Yoga differ in their primary focus and execution. Kalari is a martial art that trains individuals for combat and self-defense, requiring agility, reflexes, and quick responses. It is dynamic, involving high-intensity movements, jumps, and weapon training. Yoga, conversely, is a non-combative practice that promotes stillness, balance, and introspection. While Kalari engages in external movements to train the body for external challenges, Yoga turns inward, refining the mind and spirit. However, the underlying philosophy of self-discipline, resilience, and transformation remains a common thread.

Another contrast lies in the approach to flexibility and strength. Kalari movements develop explosive strength, quick reflexes, and dynamic flexibility, as the body moves in various planes of motion with great speed. Yoga, while also enhancing flexibility, focuses more on controlled stretching, holding postures, and gradually improving muscle elasticity. Kalari practitioners may use Yoga as a complementary practice to recover from injuries and improve their flexibility while yogis may incorporate Kalari techniques to develop greater strength and agility.

Both systems contribute immensely to wellness. Kalari enhances cardiovascular health, muscular strength, coordination, and endurance, making it an excellent form of holistic fitness. Its self-defense techniques instil confidence, discipline, and mental toughness. Yoga, in contrast, improves respiratory function, reduces stress, enhances digestion, and promotes inner peace through meditative and breathing techniques. Its therapeutic aspects address anxiety, depression, and various psychosomatic disorders, providing a holistic approach to mental and emotional well-being (Risal, 2012).

In a broader sense, both Kalari and Yoga embody the Indian philosophy of holistic health and self-realization. Kalari warriors trained not only for battle but also for personal transformation, much like yogis seeking enlightenment. The *gurukula* tradition in both systems emphasized humility, discipline, and devotion to the practice. This ancient wisdom continues to hold relevance today, as modern practitioners integrate these techniques for physical fitness, mental resilience, and spiritual growth.

By understanding and integrating both Kalari and Yoga, individuals can experience a more balanced and comprehensive approach to well-being. While Kalari empowers the body with strength, agility, and combat skills, Yoga nurtures the mind and spirit, fostering inner harmony and self-awareness (Cramer, Lauche, Langhorst, & Dobos, 2013). Together, they create a powerful synergy, demonstrating that wellness is not just about physical fitness but also about mental sharpness and emotional stability. In an era where stress and lifestyle disorders are prevalent, the combined wisdom of these traditions offers a timeless path to holistic health and inner peace.

By linking their common emphasis on mind–body integration, self-discipline, and holistic health, the analysis supports the research question regarding the interconnectedness of traditional practices of India and their relevance to modern wellness frameworks. The theoretical proposition that traditional physical disciplines also nurture emotional and spiritual well-being finds confirmation here. Thus, the findings reinforce the chapter's core argument that integrating Kalari and Yoga principles can inform contemporary models of health, cultural tourism, and therapeutic practices.

7. Kalari and Yoga Exercise and Their Relation With Cultural Tourism and Wellness Tourism

Kalari and Yoga, two traditional Indian physical disciplines, have gained international recognition for their contributions to health, fitness, and spiritual well-being. While Kalari, or Kalaripayattu, is a dynamic martial art originating from Kerala, Yoga is an ancient practice deeply rooted in Indian philosophy and spirituality (Karasinski-Sroka, 2021). Both disciplines share similarities in enhancing physical fitness, mental resilience, and overall wellness, yet they differ significantly in their approach, techniques, and objectives. The integration of these traditional practices within cultural tourism and wellness tourism has led to a growing interest in the travelers seeking authentic and transformative experiences in India.

This resonates directly with the research objectives, particularly by examining how Kalari and Yoga enhance tourist experiences in wellness tourism, promote physical and psychological benefits, and contribute to the authenticity of wellness offerings in India. The analysis also informs an assessment of the integration of into mainstream tourism and offers a comparative understanding of its impact vis-à-vis Yoga. Collectively, this inquiry addresses the core research question for how Yoga and Kalari practices enrich wellness tourism in terms of physical, psychological, and spiritual outcomes (Sullivan et al., 2018).

Kalari, often referred to as the "mother of all martial arts," is a physically demanding discipline that includes combat techniques, weapon training, and therapeutic healing methods (Büssing et al., 2012). It is deeply embedded in the cultural heritage of Kerala and is practiced not only as a form of self-defense but also as a holistic system of movement and wellness. Kalari training involves a series of dynamic movements, including leaps, kicks, and strikes, along with the use of arms such as sticks, swords, and shields. The training also includes massage therapies and medicinal treatments based on Ayurveda, which contribute to physical recovery and overall well-being (Choi et al., 2015).

On the other hand, Yoga is a multifaceted discipline that incorporates bodily postures (asanas), breathing exercises (pranayama), meditation, and ethical principles to promote holistic health (Roy & Subramanya, 2025). Fig. 7.3 captures the dynamic balance and agility typical of Yoga and Kalaripayattu are captured. Unlike Kalari, which focuses on combat skills and physical agility, Yoga emphasizes flexibility, inner peace, and spiritual growth. Various forms of Yoga,

Fig. 7.3. A Yoga Practitioner Performing a Dynamic Pose in a Traditional Setting, Illustrating the Agility, Balance, and Mindfulness Inherent in Kalaripayattu. https://timesofindia.indiatimes.com

such as Hatha, Ashtanga, and Kundalini, cater to different aspects of physical and mental well-being. Yoga practices are designed to improve body alignment, enhance relaxation, and cultivate mindfulness, making it a widely accepted approach to wellness tourism (Bielinis et al., 2018).

Despite their differences, Kalari and Yoga share fundamental principles that align them with wellness tourism. Both practices promote body awareness, balance, strength, and mental discipline. Kalari's rigorous physical regimen and therapeutic massages complement Yoga's emphasis on controlled movements and breathwork. The integration of Kalari's dynamic exercises with Yoga's meditative and restorative techniques creates a comprehensive wellness experience for practitioners and tourists alike (Cohen et al., 2017).

Cultural tourism has played a crucial role in the preserving and promoting both Kalari and Yoga as heritage practices. Many tourists visit Kerala and other parts of India to witness live Kalari performances, participate in training sessions, and explore the historical significance of this martial art (Hamilton, 2014). Similarly, Yoga retreats and ashrams attract individuals from around the world who seek to immerse themselves in the philosophy and practice of Yoga. The authenticity and rich history of these disciplines make them significant attractions for cultural tourists who are interested in India's traditional knowledge systems.

Wellness tourism, which focuses on health and rejuvenation, has further amplified the global appeal of Kalari and Yoga. Yoga retreats, wellness resorts, and Ayurvedic centers incorporate Yoga sessions and Kalari-based therapeutic treatments to provide holistic healing experiences. Tourists often engage in structured programs that include Kalari training for physical conditioning and Yoga for relaxation and mindfulness. These programs offer a balanced approach to wellness, handling both physical endurance and mental tranquility.

The rising popularity of Kalari and Yoga in the global wellness industry has also led to innovative fusion practices. Many fitness centers and wellness resorts have started integrating Kalari-inspired movements into modern exercise routines, creating unique workout regimens that combine strength training with meditative practices. Similarly, Yoga instructors have adopted dynamic Kalari movements to enhance flexibility and body control in advanced Yoga sequences. This cross-disciplinary approach appeals to fitness enthusiasts who seek both physical challenge and mental well-being in their exercise routines.

Moreover, Kalari's therapeutic aspects align well with the healing benefits of Yoga. The traditional Kalari massage, known as "Uzhichil," involves deep tissue manipulation and marma (vital point) therapy to relieve muscle tension and improve circulation. When combined with Yoga postures and relaxation techniques, this therapy enhances overall recovery and reduces stress. The synergy between Kalari's physical conditioning and Yoga's meditative approach creates a holistic framework for health and wellness tourism (Clark-Kennedy & Cohen, 2017).

In addition to their role in individual wellness, Kalari and Yoga lead to the sociocultural and economic aspects of tourism. The promotion of Kalari training centers, Yoga retreats, and cultural performances generates employment opportunities for local trainers, therapists, and wellness experts. Traditional Kalari schools (Kalari payattu gurukuls) and Yoga ashrams serve as cultural hubs where knowledge is transmitted from master to student, preserving the authenticity of these ancient practices. Furthermore, the influx of wellness tourists boosts local businesses, including eco-resorts, organic food industries, and handicrafts, thus fostering sustainable tourism.

India's tourism industry has recognized the potential of Kalari and Yoga as key components of its wellness and cultural tourism sectors. Government initiatives and private enterprises have collaborated to establish world-class Yoga and martial arts training centers to attract global tourists. International events such as the International Yoga Day and Kalari festivals have further enhanced the visibility of these traditional practices on a global scale. As a result, India has positioned itself as a leading destination for travelers seeking immersive experiences in ancient wellness traditions (Flaherty & Chua, 2018).

Despite their growing popularity, challenges remain in standardizing and preserving the authenticity of Kalari and Yoga practices. The commercialization of Yoga, especially in Western countries, has led to modifications that sometimes dilute its philosophical essence. Similarly, Kalari is often showcased as a performance art rather than a disciplined martial tradition, affecting its true essence (McDonald, 2007). To maintain authenticity, efforts must be made to promote structured training programs and accreditation systems that uphold the integrity of these ancient disciplines.

In conclusion, Kalari and Yoga, though distinct in their techniques and objectives, share a profound connection in promoting wellness, cultural heritage, and tourism. Their integration into cultural tourism allows travelers to engage with India's rich traditions while their application in wellness tourism offers holistic health benefits. By preserving their authenticity and innovatively incorporating them into modern wellness programs, these traditional practices continue to shape India's identity as a global hub for cultural and wellness tourism. The synergy between the dynamic movements of Kalari and the meditative depth of Yoga presents an unparalleled experience for tourists, fostering a deeper appreciation of India's ancient wisdom and holistic healing traditions.

8. Kalari and Yoga Therapy in Wellness Tourism

Kalari, an oldest Indian martial art form, is deeply rooted in the Kerala's cultural heritage and has evolved into a holistic wellness practice. Beyond its combat techniques, Kalari emphasizes physical conditioning, flexibility, and mental discipline (Gautam, 1999). Notably, this multifaceted system promotes internal harmony by aligning the energy pathways of the body through dynamic movement and breath awareness (Malhotra et al., 2024). It incorporates massage therapies, herbal treatments, and specialized exercises that enhance bodily strength and agility. The practice of Kalari also involves Marmachikitsa, an intricate healing system that focuses on vital energy points in the body, similar to acupuncture and acupressure (Anoop et al., 2019). This therapeutic approach, combined with rigorous training, aids in rehabilitation, pain relief, and injury prevention. The growing interest in traditional healing methods has positioned Kalari as an essential component of wellness tourism, attracting individuals seeking holistic rejuvenation (Filep, 2014).

Yoga, a scientific system of self-transformation, self-investigation, and self-realization, originated from India and has been an integral part of wellness traditions for centuries. The teachings of Yoga are rooted from the Vedas and supported by heritage texts and a rich oral tradition. It recognizes the human being's essential nature as unchanging awareness, which exists in relationship with the ever-changing empirical world. The Yoga tradition views humans as a multidimensional system, incorporating the body, breath, mind, intellect, and emotions, emphasizing their interconnected nature. Through this lens, well-being is achieved by synchronizing these dimensions in harmonious balance (Stainton et al., 2024). Yoga is founded on the principle that intelligent practice can positively influence changes in these dimensions, distinct from the individual's unchanging spirit (Gillham, 1999).

The traditional practices of Yoga include asana (postures), pranayama (breathing techniques), mantra chanting, mudras, rituals, and a disciplined lifestyle. Yoga therapy is the therapeutic application of these teachings in a structured manner to support a consistent Yoga practice (Puta & Sedlmeier, 2014). This approach aims to increase self-awareness and direct energy toward achieving specific wellness goals. The objectives of Yoga therapy include alleviating symptoms that cause suffering, boosting bodily functions, preventing illness recurrence, and enhancing overall health and well-being. *It reorients individuals toward inner resilience, providing not just relief but transformation.* Additionally, Yoga therapy helps individuals redefine their relationship with their conditions, facilitating healing beyond physical ailments.

The practice of Yoga therapy requires specialized training to establish a strong relationship between the therapist and the client, ensuring effective intervention (Karasinski-Sroka, 2021). It is informed by Ayurveda, its sister science, and continues to evolve with contemporary health sciences. With an increasing body of research supporting its efficacy, Yoga therapy is gaining recognition as a viable complementary intervention for various physical and mental health conditions, including musculoskeletal, neurological, endocrine, cardiovascular, and respiratory disorders (Chowdhury et al., 2009).

Unlike conventional medicine, which primarily adopts a biomedical approach by treating conditions in isolation through pharmaceuticals and surgical interventions, Yoga therapy considers health from a holistic perspective (Jayaram, 2013). *This integrative outlook provides a more sustainable and person-centered approach to healing.* While biomedical advancements have successfully controlled infectious diseases like smallpox and polio, they have been less effective in addressing non-communicable diseases such as heart disease, diabetes, and respiratory disorders (Bhargav et al., 2021). Many of these illnesses can be mitigated through lifestyle changes, including reduced tobacco and alcohol use, increased physical activity, stress management, and a balanced diet. Although Yoga is often perceived as a physical exercise, Yoga therapy integrates a mind–body approach, promoting overall well-being (Bitea & Luches, 2018). *Such a holistic framework enables individuals to cultivate internal resources for long-term well-being.*

The International Association of Yoga Therapists (IAYT), formed in 1989, accredits professional Yoga therapists. It defines Yoga therapy as an empowering process that improves health by altering individuals' perspectives on their conditions (Cramer et al., 2015). The primary goals of Yoga therapy, as outlined by the IAYT, include symptom management, functional improvement, illness prevention, and overall well-being. By treating health conditions as multifactorial, Yoga therapy offers a personalized approach that incorporates five key components: physical postures (asana), breathing exercises (pranayama), meditation, relaxation, and an Ayurvedic diet. *These tools work synergistically to restore equilibrium and foster conscious living.*

Yoga therapy is adapting to modern medical research standards although challenges persist due to its highly individualized nature. Despite numerous positive findings on its efficacy, research limitations in methodology, sample size, and design necessitate further exploration. Increased acceptance among medical institutions and the general public will drive more funding and advancements in research, helping to establish Yoga therapy as a mainstream therapeutic discipline. Technological developments will further enable researchers to investigate its mechanisms at cellular and molecular levels.

The revival and modernization of Yoga therapy can be traced back to the 1920s, when Indian nationalism fueled interest in traditional health practices (Bell et al., 2018). Three pioneers—Sri Yogendra, Swami Kuvalayananda, and Tirumalai Krishnamacharya—spearheaded this movement by studying Yoga's health benefits using scientific methods. Among them, Krishnamacharya gained international recognition as the Founder of Modern Yoga. His disciples, including T.K.V. Desikachar,B.K.S. Iyengar, Pattabhi Jois, and Indra Devi, further popularized Yoga therapy worldwide (Newcombe, 2009).

Since the 1980s, Yoga therapy has gained widespread acceptance, especially in Europe and the United States. A milestone occurred in 1990 when US healthcare insurance companies began covering Dean Ornish's lifestyle program, which combined Yoga, meditation, and diet to reverse heart disease. Subsequent research reinforced Yoga therapy's effectiveness, leading to its inclusion as a covered treatment under the US Medicare program in 2012.

Yoga therapy is based on balance and alignment across the five koshas (dimensions of life): anatomical, physiological, intellectual, emotional, and spiritual(Pascoe et al., 2017). A Yoga therapist conducts a detailed assessment of a client's physical, mental, and environmental factors to develop a personalized therapy plan. This plan is adaptable based on seasonal changes, daily schedules, and individual needs. Due to its highly individualized nature, Yoga therapy is typically offered in one-on-one or small group sessions, allowing for tailored guidance. Clients are often assigned a daily practice alongside weekly therapy sessions to ensure consistency and effectiveness.

The physical postures (asanas) in Yoga therapy enhance mental and physical well-being by reducing inflammation, stimulating the vagus nerve, and increasing body awareness (Bower et al., 2014). The style of Yoga therapy varies, ranging from dynamic, fast-paced movements to slow, meditative poses. Regardless of style, stability, breath control, and mindful movement remain central to its therapeutic approach (Mehta, 2010).

Breathing exercises (pranayama) in Yoga therapy controls the autonomic nervous system, strengthen respiratory functions, and promote relaxation. These exercises vary widely, involving different breathing techniques like alternate nostril breathing, deep diaphragmatic breathing, and breath retention (Ilavarasu et al., 2014). Pranayama serves as an accessible therapeutic intervention for diverse populations, including children, the elderly, and individuals with physical limitations.

Meditation, a core component of Yoga therapy, cultivates attention regulation, metacognitive awareness, and emotional resilience. Research suggests that meditation can alleviate chronic pain, cancer symptoms, and age-related cognitive decline (Simon et al., 2021). In Yoga therapy, meditation is introduced progressively, starting with simple breath awareness and gradually expanding to broader mindfulness practices. This structured approach enables individuals to develop self-awareness and emotional stability over time.

As wellness tourism continues to grow, integrating Kalari and Yoga therapy into holistic health retreats presents a unique opportunity. Destinations offering Kalari-based healing therapies and personalized Yoga therapy programs attract individuals seeking a comprehensive wellness experience (Mehta, 2010). Kerala, known for its rich tradition in Ayurveda, Kalari, and Yoga, has become a hub for such holistic retreats. Wellness tourists are increasingly drawn to programs that combine physical rejuvenation, mental relaxation, and spiritual enrichment (Bock et al., 2012).

The synergy between Kalari and Yoga therapy enhances wellness tourism by providing a multifaceted approach to health. Kalari's dynamic movements build strength and resilience while Yoga therapy's gentle, introspective practices foster inner healing. Together, they offer a well-rounded wellness experience that aligns with modern health trends, emphasizing preventive care and natural healing. The growing recognition of these traditional practices in global wellness tourism underscores their relevance in promoting sustainable health and well-being (Vinodan & Meera, 2018). As research and awareness continue to expand, combining Kalari and Yoga therapy into wellness tourism is set to redefine holistic healthcare for generations to come. *This dynamic interplay between guidance and self-practice fosters long-lasting transformation.*

9. Spirituality in Kalaripayattu and Yoga

Spirituality has been an intrinsic part of both Kalaripayattu and Yoga, shaping them beyond mere physical disciplines into profound paths of self-transformation. While Kalaripayattu, the ancient martial art of Kerala, integrates combat techniques with devotion, discipline, and reverence for higher energies, Yoga offers a holistic approach to inner realization through asanas, pranayama, and meditation (see Fig. 7.4, showing the meditative stability in Padmasana). Both practices share a deep connection with Vedic and Tantric traditions, focus on the unity of body, spirit and mind. This article explores the spiritual dimensions of Kalaripayattu and Yoga, examining their sacred rituals, meditative aspects, and their transformative impact on practitioners(Black et al., 2013).

Kalaripayattu is more than a system of self-defense; it is a disciplined way of life that embodies spiritual principles. The Kalari (training ground) is traditionally considered a sacred space akin to a temple(Cruice et al., 2003). The entrance to the Kalari is always positioned toward the east, symbolizing spiritual awakening and enlightenment. Upon entering, students step in with their right foot first and offer prayers to the Guru, Guru Thara (the seat of the master), and various deities.

Deities such as Bhadrakali, Ganapathi, and Naga Bhagavathy are venerated in the Kalari, representing strength, fearlessness, and protection. These deities are not merely worshiped in the religious sense but are perceived as cosmic energies (Shakti) that empower warriors. The rituals and prayers performed before and after training reinforce the belief that martial training is not an act of aggression but an honorable pursuit rooted in dharma (righteousness).

Training in Kalaripayattu is deeply intertwined with spiritual discipline. Each session begins with lighting the traditional oil lamp, symbolizing the dispelling of ignorance and the pursuit of wisdom. Students observe humility, respect, and

Fig. 7.4. A Yoga Practitioner in *Padmasana* With *Anjali Mudra*, Meditating in a Natural Setting to Enhance Focus, Stability, and Mindfulness. https://stock.adobe.com

devotion toward their Guru and weapons. During Navaratri and Mahanavami, Ayudha Pooja (weapon worship) is conducted to honor the tools of combat, signifying that weapons should be wielded with responsibility and righteousness (Sreenath, 2017).

Guru Thara, the seat of the master, holds a special significance in Kalaripayattu. It is believed that past Gurus guide the present generation of warriors through divine inspiration. This aligns with the broader Indian philosophy of Guru Parampara (teacher-student lineage), where wisdom is transmitted across generations. This spiritual continuity ensures that the ethical and moral dimensions of Kalaripayattu remain intact.

Among the deities revered in Kalaripayattu, Bhadrakali holds a central place. As the Goddess of war and weapons, she symbolizes both destruction and protection. Warriors invoke her blessings before combat, seeking victory and divine guidance. She is also referred to as Kalari Bhagavathi or Chamundi, embodying fierce energy and divine justice. The belief in her divine protection instils a sense of righteous combat, ensuring that warriors fight not out of malice but as a sacred duty to uphold justice.

Hanuman and Ganapathi also play vital roles in Kalari rituals. Hanuman represents immense strength, agility, and devotion, inspiring practitioners to develop endurance and perseverance. Similarly, Ganapathi is worshiped as the remover of obstacles, ensuring smooth training and mastery over techniques. These spiritual associations enrich the practice of Kalaripayattu, making it a transformative experience rather than a mere physical endeavor. Fig. 7.5 (A-E) shows the key architectural and ritual features of a Kalari – entrance murals, weapons bay, Guruthara altar, snake shrine, and deity altar.

Kalaripayattu incorporates elements of moving meditation, where breathing techniques, deep concentration, and precise movements create a harmonious flow of energy. Practitioners are encouraged to develop ekagrata (one-pointed focus), ensuring that every movement is conscious and deliberate. This integration of breath, awareness, and motion transforms Kalaripayattu into a meditative practice, aligning the practitioner's physical and spiritual energies.

Like Kalaripayattu, Yoga is strongly rooted in spirituality. Originating from oldest Indian traditions, Yoga seeks the union of the individual own with the universal consciousness. While modern interpretations often emphasize its physical aspects, traditional Yoga encompasses ethical principles (yamas and niyamas), physical postures (asanas), breath meditation (dhyana), and control (pranayama) as essential components of spiritual evolution.

Unlike Kalaripayattu, which focuses on external combat, Yoga turns inward, seeking mastery over the mind and senses. Texts like the Bhagavad Gita and the Yoga Sutras of Patanjali describe Yoga as a means to transcend physical limitations and attain self-realization. This spiritual dimension of Yoga remains central to its practice regardless of cultural adaptations across the world.

Research on Yoga and spirituality highlights variations in its practice between Western and traditional Indian settings. In the West, Yoga is often perceived as a mind–body exercise while in India, it retains its spiritual depth. Studies suggest that even physically focused Yoga enhances spirituality by fostering self-awareness, gratitude, and a sense of interconnectedness.

Yoga is known to cultivate spiritual intelligence, promoting existential thinking, meaning-making, and transcendental consciousness. Regular practitioners report higher levels of spiritual well-being, reduced existential anxiety, and a deeper sense of peace. The integration of meditation, mantra chanting, and breath control further amplifies its spiritual impact (Ravindran et al., 2018).

Mantras play a significant role in traditional Yoga, serving as vibrational tools to elevate consciousness. Chanting sacred sounds such as "Om" is believed to align the practitioner's energy with cosmic frequencies. Meditation, an integral part of Yoga, allows practitioners to detach from external distractions and

Fig. 7.5. (A) Kalari Entrance With Theyyam Murals, (B) Weapons and Training Area, (C) Guruthara (Sacred Altar) for Worship, (D) Snake Shrine (Sarpa Kavu), and (E) Kalari Deity Altar With Weapons.

experience inner stillness. Techniques like mindfulness meditation, transcendental meditation, and yogic visualization foster heightened awareness and spiritual awakening (Chandwani et al., 2014).

While most of the studies affirm the spiritual benefits of the Yoga, some findings are inconsistent. For instance, research on medical populations, such as cancer patients, has reported both positive and negligible effects on spirituality. Factors such as intervention duration, participant background, and health conditions may influence these outcomes (Gard et al., 2014). Nevertheless, long-term Yoga practice is generally associated with increased faith, meaning, and spiritual resilience.

Despite their differences in approach, Kalaripayattu and Yoga share fundamental spiritual principles. Both emphasize discipline, ethical conduct, and the pursuit of self-mastery. While Kalaripayattu channels spiritual energy through martial training and devotion to deities, Yoga fosters inner transformation through meditation and self-inquiry. The convergence of these practices highlights India's rich spiritual heritage, where physical and mental disciplines are seamlessly integrated with higher consciousness.

Spirituality remains the cornerstone of both Kalaripayattu and Yoga, distinguishing them from conventional physical practices. The rituals, meditative aspects, and ethical principles embedded in these traditions ensure that they serve as profound paths to self-realization. Kalaripayattu's reverence for divine energies and Yoga's inward journey toward enlightenment demonstrate that true mastery lies not in physical prowess alone but in mental clarity, ethical living, and spiritual awareness. As these ancient disciplines continue to evolve, their spiritual essence remains a guiding force, offering practitioners a deeper connection to themselves and the universe.

10. Conclusion

Kalarippayattu and Yoga are not merely traditional disciplines but serve as transformative tools in enhancing the physical, psychological, and spiritual well-being of wellness tourists. Kalarippayattu, rooted in devotion to deities like Bhadrakali, instils discipline and righteous combat while Yoga fosters inner transformation through meditation and self-inquiry. Despite their distinct origins, both Kalarippayattu and Yoga significantly enrich India's cultural heritage and are increasingly embraced within the realm of cultural tourism. The study indicates that each practice plays a vital role in promoting holistic well-being, resonating with the global trend toward authentic, culturally grounded wellness experiences.

Cultural tourism offers a platform for preserving these traditions, but commercialization risks diluting their spiritual depth. *However, the study also reveals that commercialization, regional inaccessibility, and reductionist portrayals (e.g., focusing only on physical benefits) pose significant challenges to authenticity.* Many programs focus on physical aspects while neglecting their meditative and philosophical dimensions. Accessibility also remains a challenge, as authentic experiences are largely confined to specific regions like Kerala.

Future research should explore how to balance commercialization and authenticity, ensuring that these traditions retain their essence. Comparative studies on traditional versus modernized training methods can provide insights into their cognitive and emotional benefits. Additionally, interdisciplinary research integrating psychology and neuroscience can examine their impact on mindfulness, resilience, and well-being. Studies on the role of cultural tourism in sustaining these practices economically while maintaining their authenticity would also be valuable.

Kerala, a hub for Kalari and Yoga, plays a crucial role in promoting India's spiritual heritage. Thoughtfully curated tourism initiatives can enhance cultural preservation and economic growth, ensuring these traditions remain relevant. By promoting responsible cultural tourism, India can share its rich spiritual legacy while maintaining the integrity of its ancient wisdom.

Acknowledgment

We sincerely express our gratitude to the Kalari and Yoga centers that generously allowed us to visit, conduct interviews, and collect valuable insights for this study. Our heartfelt thanks to Sree Krishna Kalari, Anjaneya Kalari, Hindustan Kalari Sangam, CVN Kalari, TC Chandran Gurukkal Kairali Kalari, Brahmayoga Vidyapeedam, Sree Yogadarshan, and Rudra Yoga Centre for their support and cooperation.

References

Anoop, A. K., Vaidya, A., & Gopika, P. (2019). Exploring the potentials of the intangible artform: Kalaripayattu and Kalari Chikitsa. *International Journal of Research and Analytical Reviews (IJRAR)*, *6*(2), 97–101.

Balasubramaniam, M., Telles, S., & Doraiswamy, P. M. (2013). Yoga on our minds: A systematic review of yoga for neuropsychiatric disorders. *Frontiers in Psychiatry*, *3*, 117. https://doi.org/10.3389/fpsyt.2012.00117

Bell, S. L., Foley, R., Houghton, F., Maddrell, A., & Williams, A. M. (2018). From therapeutic landscapes to healthy spaces, places and practices: A scoping review. *Social Science & Medicine*, *196*, 123–130. https://doi.org/10.1016/j.socscimed.2017.11.035

Bhargav, H., George, S., Varambally, S., & Gangadhar, B. N. (2021). Yoga and psychiatric disorders: A review of biomarker evidence. *International Review of Psychiatry*, *33*(2), 162–169. https://doi.org/10.1080/09540261.2020.1761087

Bielinis, E., Takayama, N., Boiko, S., Omelan, A., & Bielinis, L. (2018). The effect of winter forest bathing on psychological relaxation of young polish adults. *Urban Forestry and Urban Greening*, *29*, 276–283. https://doi.org/10.1016/j.ufug.2017.12.006

Bilderbeck, A. C., Farias, M., Brazil, I. A., Jakobowitz, S., & Wikholm, C. (2013). Participation in a 10-week course of yoga improves behavioural control and decreases psychological distress in a prison population. *Journal of Psychiatric Research*, *47*(10), 1438–1445. https://doi.org/10.1016/j.jpsychires.2013.06.014

Black, D. S., Cole, S. W., Irwin, M. R., Breen, E., St Cyr, N. M., Nazarian, N., & Lavretsky, H. (2013). Yogic meditation reverses NF-κB and IRF-related transcriptome dynamics in leukocytes of family dementia caregivers in a randomized controlled trial. *Psychoneuroendocrinology*, *38*(3), 348–355. https://doi.org/10.1016/j.psyneuen.2012.06.011

Bock, B. C., Fava, J. L., Gaskins, R., Morrow, K. M., Williams, D. M., Jennings, E., & Marcus, B. H. (2012). Yoga as a complementary treatment for smoking cessation in women. *Journal of Women's Health*, *21*(2), 240–248. https://doi.org/10.1089/jwh.2011.2963

Bower, J. E., Greendale, G., Crosswell, A. D., Garet, D., Sternlieb, B., Ganz, P. A., & Cole, S. W. (2014). Yoga reduces inflammatory signaling in fatigued breast cancer survivors: A randomized controlled trial. *Psychoneuroendocrinology*, *43*, 20–29. https://doi.org/10.1016/j.psyneuen.2014.01.019

Brems, C. (2015). A yoga stress reduction intervention for university faculty, staff, and graduate students. *International Journal of Yoga Therapy*, *25*(1), 61–77. https://doi.org/10.17761/1531-2054-25.1.61

Brinsley, J., Schuch, F., Lederman, O., Girard, D., Smout, M., Immink, M. A., Stubbs, B., Firth, J., Davison, K., & Rosenbaum, S. (2021). Effects of yoga on depressive symptoms in people with mental disorders: A systematic review and meta-analysis. *British Journal of Sports Medicine*, *55*(16), 992–1000. https://doi.org/10.1136/bjsports-2019-101242

Brown, S. (2005). Travelling with a purpose: Understanding the motives and benefits of volunteer vacationers. *Current Issues in Tourism*, *8*(6), 479–496. https://doi.org/10.1080/13683500508668232

Büssing, A., Khalsa, S. B., Michalsen, A., & Sherman, K. J. (2012). Yoga as a therapeutic intervention. *Evidence-Based Complementary and Alternative Medicine*, *2012*, 174291. https://doi.org/10.1155/2012/174291

Carlson, L. E., Speca, M., Patel, K. D., & Goodey, E. (2003). Mindfulness-based stress reduction in relation to quality of life, mood, symptoms of stress, and immune parameters in breast and prostate cancer outpatients. *Psychosomatic Medicine*, *65*(4), 571–581. https://doi.org/10.1097/01.PSY.0000074003.35911.41

Chandwani, K. D., Perkins, G., Nagendra, H. R., Raghuram, N. V., Spelman, A., Nagarathna, R., & Cohen, L. (2014). Randomized, controlled trial of yoga in women with breast cancer undergoing radiotherapy. *Journal of Clinical Oncology*, *32*(10), 1058–1065. https://doi.org/10.1200/JCO.2012.48.2752

Chen, C.-C., & Petrick, J. F. (2013). Health and wellness benefits of travel experiences. *Journal of Travel Research*, *52*(6), 709–719. https://doi.org/10.1177/0047287513496477

Choi, Y., Kim, J., Lee, C.-K., & Hickerson, B. (2015). The role of functional and wellness values in visitors' evaluation of spa experiences. *Asia Pacific Journal of Tourism Research*, *20*(3), 263–279. https://doi.org/10.1080/10941665.2013.877044

Clark-Kennedy, J., & Cohen, M. (2017). Indulgence or therapy? Exploring the characteristics, motivations and experiences of hot springs bathers in Victoria, Australia. *Asia Pacific Journal of Tourism Research*, *22*(5), 501–511. https://doi.org/10.1080/10941665.2016.1276946

Cohen, M. M., Elliott, F., Oates, L., Schembri, A., & Mantri, N. (2017). Do wellness tourists get well? An observational study of multiple dimensions of health and well-being after a week-long retreat. *Journal of Alternative & Complementary Medicine*, *23*(2), 140–148. https://doi.org/10.1089/acm.2016.0268

Cramer, H., Lauche, R., Hohmann, C., Lüdtke, R., Haller, H., Michalsen, A., & Dobos, G. (2013). Randomized-controlled trial comparing yoga and home-based exercise for chronic neck pain. *The Clinical Journal of Pain*, *29*(3), 216–223. https://doi.org/10.1097/AJP.0b013e318251026c

Cramer, H., Lauche, R., Langhorst, J., & Dobos, G. (2013). Yoga for depression: A systematic review and meta-analysis. *Depression and Anxiety*, *30*(11), 1068–1083. https://doi.org/10.1002/da.22166

Cramer, H., Ward, L., Saper, R., Fishbein, D., Dobos, G., & Lauche, R. (2015). The safety of yoga: A systematic review and meta-analysis of randomized controlled trials. *American Journal of Epidemiology*, *182*(4), 281–293. https://doi.org/10.1093/aje/kwv071

Cruice, M., Worrall, L., Hickson, L., & Murison, R. (2003). Finding a focus for quality of life with aphasia: Social and emotional health, and psychological well-being. *Aphasiology*, *17*(4), 333–353. https://doi.org/10.1080/02687030244000707

Dhruva, A., Miaskowski, C., Abrams, D., Acree, M., Cooper, B., Goodman, S., & Hecht, F. M. (2012). Yoga breathing for cancer chemotherapy-associated symptoms and quality of life: Results of a pilot randomized controlled trial. *Journal of Alternative & Complementary Medicine*, *18*(5), 473–479. https://doi.org/10.1089/acm.2011.0555

Dini, M., & Pencarelli, T. (2022). Wellness tourism and the components of its offer system: A holistic perspective. *Tourism Review*, *77*(2), 394–412. https://doi.org/10.1108/tr-08-2020-0373

Downward, P., & Dawson, P. (2016). Is it pleasure or health from leisure that we benefit from most? An analysis of well-being alternatives and implications for policy. *Social Indicators Research*, *126*(2), 443–465. https://doi.org/10.1007/s11205-015-0887-8

Evans, S., Lung, K. C., Seidman, L. C., Sternlieb, B., Zeltzer, L. K., & Tsao, J. C. (2014). Iyengar yoga for adolescents and young adults with irritable bowel syndrome. *Journal of Pediatric Gastroenterology and Nutrition*, *59*(2), 244–253. https://doi.org/10.1097/MPG.0000000000000366

Filep, S. (2014). Moving beyond subjective well-being: A tourism critique. *Journal of Hospitality & Tourism Research*, *38*(2), 266–274. https://doi.org/10.1177/1096348012436609

Flaherty, G. T., & Chua, C. W. (2018). High altitude travel and mental health. *Journal of Travel Medicine*, *25*, tay025. https://doi.org/10.1093/jtm/tay025

Folkins, C. H., Lynch, S., & Gardner, M. M. (1972). Psychological fitness as a function of physical fitness. *Archives of Physical Medicine and Rehabilitation*, *53*(6), 503–508.

Fritz, C., & Sonnentag, S. (2006). Recovery, well-being, and performance-related outcomes: The role of workload and vacation experiences. *Journal of Applied Psychology*, *91*(4), 936–945. https://doi.org/10.1037/0021-9010.91.4.936

Gard, T., Noggle, J. J., Park, C. L., Vago, D. R., & Wilson, A. (2014). Potential self-regulatory mechanisms of yoga for psychological health. *Frontiers in Human Neuroscience*, *8*, 770. https://doi.org/10.3389/fnhum.2014.00770

Gautam, S. (1999). Mental health in ancient India and its relevance to modern psychiatry. *Indian Journal of Psychiatry*, *41*(1), 5–18.

Georgiev, G., & Trifonova Vasileva, M. (2010). Conceptualization and classification of balneo, spa and wellness establishments in Bulgaria. *Journal of Economics*, *158*, 37–50. https://doi.org/10.1016/j.jeconom.2010.03.005

Gillham, J. E., & Seligman, M. E. P. (1999). Footsteps on the road to a positive psychology. *Behaviour Research and Therapy*, *37*, S163–S173. https://doi.org/10.1016/s0005-7967(99)00055-8

Gothe, N. P., Kramer, A. F., & McAuley, E. (2014). The effects of an 8-week Hatha yoga intervention on executive function in older adults. *The Journals of Gerontology: Series A*, *69*(9), 1109–1116. https://doi.org/10.1093/gerona/glu095

Govindaraj, R., Naik, S. S., Mehta, U. M., Sharma, M., Varambally, S., & Gangadhar, B. N. (2021). Yoga therapy for social cognition in schizophrenia: An experimental medicine-based randomized controlled trial. *Asian Journal of Psychiatry*, *62*, 102731. https://doi.org/10.1016/j.ajp.2021.102731

Hamilton, M. J. (2014). A queer and permissive text: Towards situated knowledge of CVN-Kalarippayattu. *Theatre, Dance and Performance Training*, *5*(1), 45–58. https://doi.org/10.1080/19443927.2013.873734

Jayaram, N., Varambally, S., Behere, R. V., Venkatasubramanian, G., Arasappa, R., Christopher, R., & Gangadhar, B. N. (2013). Effect of yoga therapy on plasma oxytocin and facial emotion recognition deficits in patients of schizophrenia. *Indian Journal of Psychiatry*, *55*(Suppl. 3), S409–S413.

Karasinski-Sroka, M. (2021). When yogis become warriors—The embodied spirituality of Kaḷaripayaṯṯu. *Religions*, *12*(5), 294. https://doi.org/10.3390/rel12050294

Kolanad, G. (2022). The Kalaripayattu salutation: Movement makes meaning. *Martial Arts Studies*, *12*(0), 26. https://doi.org/10.18573/mas.151

Malhotra, V., Pathak, T., Javed, D., Cidral-Filho, F. J., Suryawanshi, C., Agrawal, M., & Mittal, G. (2024). Comparative neurodynamic analysis of spinal energy enhancement in experienced yoga practitioners using various breathing techniques. *Cureus*, *16*(11), e73541. https://doi.org/10.7759/cureus.73541

Mandakathingal, A. (2021). Gender roles in martial art: A comparative analysis of Kalaripayattu practices in India. *Women's Studies*, *50*(4), 317–336. https://doi.org/10.1080/00497878.2020.1843039

McDonald, I. (2007). Bodily practice, performance art, competitive sport. *Contributions to Indian Sociology*, *41*(2), 143–168. https://doi.org/10.1177/006996670704100201

Mehta, P., & Sharma, M. (2010). Yoga as a complementary therapy for clinical depression. *Complementary Health Practice Review*, *15*(3), 156–170.

Newcombe, S. (2009). The development of modern yoga: A survey of the field. *Religion Compass*, *3*(6), 986–1002.

Pascoe, M. C., Thompson, D. R., & Ski, C. F. (2017). Yoga, mindfulness-based stress reduction and stress-related physiological measures: A meta-analysis. *Psycho neuroendocrinology*, *86*, 152–168. https://doi.org/10.1016/j.psyneuen.2017.08.008

Pati, G. (2010). Kalari and Kalarippayattu of Kerala, South India: Nexus of the celestial, the corporeal, and the terrestrial. *Contemporary South Asia*, *18*(2), 175–189. https://doi.org/10.1080/09584931003674976

Puta, M., & Sedlmeier, P. (2014). The concept of tri-guna: A working model. In S. Schmidt & H. Walach (Eds.), *Meditation—Neuroscientific approaches and philosophical implications* (pp. 317–364). Springer. https://doi.org/10.1007/978-3-319-01634-4_18

Rao, A. V. (2002). "Mind" in Indian philosophy. *Indian Journal of Psychiatry*, *44*(4), 315–325.

Rao, N. P., Ramachandran, P., Jacob, A., Joseph, A., Thonse, U., Nagendra, B., Chako, D. M., Shiri, S., Hassan, H., Sreenivas, V., Maran, S., Durgam, D., Nandakumar, K., Varambally, S., & Gangadhar, B. N. (2021). Add-on yoga treatment for negative symptoms of schizophrenia: A multi-centric, randomized controlled trial. *Schizophrenia Research*, *231*, 90–97. https://doi.org/10.1016/j.schres.2021.03.021

Ravindran, A. V., Balneaves, L. G., Faulkner, G., Ortiz, A., McIntosh, D., Morehouse, R. L., Ravindran, L., Yatham, L. N., Kennedy, S. H., Lam, R. W., MacQueen, G. M., Milev, R. V., Parikh, S. V., & the CANMAT Depression Work Group. (2018). Canadian network for mood and anxiety treatments (CANMAT) 2016 clinical guidelines for the management of adults with major depressive disorder: Section 5. *Focus*, *16*, 85–94. https://doi.org/10.1176/appi.focus.16106

Risal, A. (2011). Common mental disorders. *Kathmandu University Medical Journal*, *9*(35), 213–217. https://doi.org/10.3126/kumj.v9i3.6308

Roy, A., & Subramanya, P. (2025). The impact of meditation on sustained attention in nonclinical population: An extensive review. *Journal of Ayurveda and Integrative Medicine*, *16*(2), 101057. Advance online publication. https://doi.org/10.1016/j.jaim.2024.101057

Saraswati, S., & Saraswati, S. N. (2002). *Patanjali: Four chapters on freedom: Commentary on the yoga sutras of Patanjali*. Nesma Books.

Simon, N. M., Hofmann, S. G., Rosenfield, D., Hoeppner, S. S., Hoge, E. A., Bui, E., & Khalsa, S. B. S. (2021). Efficacy of yoga versus cognitive behavioral therapy versus stress education for the treatment of generalized anxiety disorder: A randomized clinical trial. *JAMA Psychiatry*, *78*(1), 13–20. https://doi.org/10.1001/jamapsychiatry.2020.2496

Singleton, M., & Byrne, J. (2008). *Yoga in the modern world: Contemporary perspectives*. Routledge.

Sreenath, S. (2017). Effect of Kalaripayattu on physical fitness variables among college students. *International Journal of Physical Education, Sports and Health*, *4*(4), 395–401.

Stainton, P., Danes-Daetz, C., Haworth, L., Karunanithi, S. P., & Chohan, A. (2024). Attitudes, knowledge and understanding towards mind-body practices as an asset for social prescribing in higher education. *International Journal of Health Promotion and Education*, *63*(2), 96–110. https://doi.org/10.1080/14635240.2024.2375492

Streeter, C. C., Jensen, J. E., Perlmutter, R. M., Cabral, H. J., Tian, H., Terhune, D. B., Ciraulo, D. A., & Renshaw, P. F. (2007). Yoga asana sessions increase brain GABA levels: A pilot study. *Journal of Alternative and Complementary Medicine*, *13*(4), 419–426. https://doi.org/10.1089/acm.2007.6338

Sullivan, M. B., Erb, M., Schmalzl, L., Moonaz, S., Noggle Taylor, J., & Porges, S. W. (2018). Yoga therapy and polyvagal theory: The convergence of traditional wisdom and contemporary neuroscience for self-regulation and resilience. *Frontiers in Human Neuroscience*, *12*, 67. https://doi.org/10.3389/fnhum.2018.00067

Taylor, A. G., Goehler, L. E., Galper, D. I., Innes, K. E., & Bourguignon, C. (2010). Top-down and bottom-up mechanisms in mind-body medicine: Development of an integrative framework for psychophysiological research. *Explore*, *6*(1), 29–41. https://doi.org/10.1016/j.explore.2009.10.004

Varma, V. K. (1982). Present state of psychotherapy in India. *Indian Journal of Psychiatry*, *24*(3), 209–226.

Vinodan, A., & Meera, S. (2018). Exploring the relevance of cultural resource management: A case study of Kalaripayattu. *Journal of Heritage Management*, *3*(1), 71–86. https://doi.org/10.1177/2455929618773388

Appendix 1: (Centers Visited)

Kalari Centers and Interviews Conducted

(1) Sree Krishna Kalari, Near Cheruvathur Muthappan Temple, Cheruvathur, Kasaragod—673,655. The interviewed person was Dr. Vineeth Sasi, BAMS (Mob: 8,086,612,512).
(2) Sree Krishna Kalari, Kakkayamchal, Cherupuzha, Kannur—670,511. The interviewed person was Sri Sasi Gurukkal (Mob: 94473738883).
(3) Anjaneya Kalari, Kayakunnu, Edathode, Kasaragod—671,533. The interviewed person was Sri Manikandan Gurukkal (Mob: 90612079659).
(4) Hindustan Kalari Sangam, Netaji Road, Puthiyara, Kozhikode—673,004. The interviewed person was Srimathi Rajeswari (Ph: 0495-2743659).
(5) CVN Kalari Nadakav, Nadakav, Kozhikode—673,011. The interviewed person was Sri Sunil Gurukkal (Mob: 9995929999).
(6) Kairali Kalari (T.C. Chandran Gurukkal), Town Hall Road, Opp. Crown Theatre, Mananchira, Kozhikode—673,001. The interviewed person was Sri T.C. Dheeraj Gurukkal (Mob: 7907100380).

Yoga Centers and Interviews Conducted

(1) Brahma Yoga Vidyapeedam, First Floor, Hannas Arcade, Seaport-Airport Road, Makaliyam, Irumpanam, Thrippunithura, Kochi—682,309. The interviewed staff member can be contacted at 9020806666.
(2) Sree Yogadarshan, Eroor, Tripunithura PO, Cochin—682,030. The interviewed staff member can be contacted at 9388453559.
(3) Rudra Yoga Training and Research Centre, Near Gold Souk, House No.6, Narayananasan Road, Ponnurunni, Vyttila, Cochin—682,019. The interviewed staff member can be contacted at 9447133037.

Chapter 8

Energy Conservation and Environmental Practices in Health Tourism

Abhishek Maikhuri[a], *Ravish Kukreti*[b], *M. K. Amila Indika*[c,d] *and Amar Prakash Dabral*[b]

[a]Graphic Era Hill University, India
[b]Graphic Era Deemed to be University, India
[c]University College of Ratmalana, Sri Lanka
[d]University of Vocational Technology, Sri Lanka

Abstract

This research is an inquiry into energy-saving and environmental-friendly practices in health tourism, with an emphasis on their acceptance, effects, and challenges. With rising health tourism, there is a need to balance economic profitability with ecological responsibility. The study emphasizes government policy, institutional backing, and industry players in facilitating ecotourism in healthcare. This chapter looks into energy-saving technologies—solar, wind, and geothermal—complemented by green construction practices, such as passive heating, green infrastructure, and efficient lighting. Waste and water management practices, such as recycling, composting, and hazardous waste minimization, are also explored to reduce ecological footprints. The research points out how biophilic design, healthy indoor air, and natural integration can improve patient recovery and satisfaction. It emphasizes the economic advantages of sustainability in terms of cost savings, environmentally conscious clientele, and green jobs. Major hindrances were found to be elevated up-front costs, regulatory concerns, and stakeholder knowledge gaps. Policy scenarios and case studies illustrate the need for public–private partnerships. Technology and community are essential in planning sustainable health tourism worldwide. Notwithstanding constraints such as access to data and regional diversity, this chapter recommends comparative research on renewable energy use and new green technologies in the future in the context of

Nature, Wellness and Sustainability in Health Tourism, 183–213

doi:10.1108/978-1-83742-029-220261008

health tourism. It provides pragmatic suggestions to minimize environmental footprint and maximize economic and patient results.

Keywords: Sustainable healthcare; biophilic design; green technology; renewable energy; energy conservation

1. Introduction

Health tourism, including wellness retreats, medical tourism, and holistic healing centers, has become a major industry in the world's tourism sector. With increased popularity comes an increased need to incorporate sustainable practices, ensuring long-term environmental, social, and economic sustainability. This study aims at energy conservation and environmental sustainability in health tourism, assessing their contributions toward encouraging eco-friendly development while minimizing the sector's ecological footprint.

As climate change, resource depletion, and environmental degradation have become growing concerns, energy efficiency and green practices have become key elements of sustainable tourism. The use of renewable energy sources, green building technologies, waste reduction methods, and biodiversity conservation is necessary to ensure a health tourism industry that is aligned with international sustainability objectives. Through the analysis of international trends and best practices, this research seeks to contribute to an understanding of sustainability-led development in the health tourism industry.

The intimate relationship between tourism and environmental systems requires a careful evaluation of sustainability efforts—their effectiveness, issues, and general contribution to biodiversity. Responsible tourism has the ability to conserve ecosystems, minimize carbon emissions, and positively impact local communities, whereas uncontrolled tourism growth can cause environmental degradation and socioeconomic inequality. The understanding of the beneficial and detrimental effects of sustainability efforts will allow the development of sound strategies and policies for health tourism.

This study attempts to offer a holistic view to policymakers, stakeholders in the industry, and scholars regarding the influence of energy saving and environmental responsibility on health tourism. Through empirical case studies of real-world interventions, cutting-edge sustainability models, and new trends in the industry, this study will add substance to the world debate on sustainable tourism development. Finally, it will provide guidelines that favor harmonization of economic development, environmental conservation, and social welfare and direct the health tourism sector to a greener and more resilient future.

1.1 Contextual Background

1.1.1 The Growth of Health Tourism and Its Necessity for Sustainability

International growth of health tourism is mostly driven by increasing consumer demand for wellness, holistic healing, and medical procedures that promote enduring physical and psychological well-being. Modern travelers deliberately seek relaxation, rejuvenation, and closer proximity to nature, propelling the growth of wellness retreats, medical spas, and alternative healing facilities in different destinations (Perera et al., 2023).

Health tourism benchmark destinations such as New Zealand, Costa Rica, and Thailand have, at the same time, reconciled wellness-focused tourism with environmental sustainability through the inclusion of sustainable infrastructure, energy-efficient processes, and the conservation of biodiversity (Kamalasena & Chamodya, 2021). These countries have set examples for green models of tourism, showcasing how health tourism can be enhanced without compromising on climate-responsible practices and sustainable resource management.

1.1.2 The Increasing Awareness of World Tourism for Sustainability

As health tourism becomes a global phenomenon, sustainability has become a priority area for the players in the industry. Tourism has been recognized as a high-carbon industry that can consume resources, produce immense carbon footprints, and spoil ecosystems if not controlled (Sivesan, 2021). The industry is being proactive in taking up sustainable tourism initiatives that aim at:

- Deploying responsible energy consumption using renewable energy and energy-saving equipment.
- Conservation of natural resources such as water, forest cover, and biodiversity hotspots.
- Eco-friendly waste management to avoid pollution and reduce the environmental footprint.

Sustainability in health tourism has far-reaching implications for host communities, especially in areas of high biodiversity where economic development and conservation collide. There needs to be a balance through sustainable models of tourism focusing on long-term benefits at the expense of short-term economic gain (Gössling et al., 2021).

1.1.3 The Energy Efficiency Role in Sustainable Health Tourism

For enhancing sustainability, energy-efficient practices should be implemented in the infrastructures and operations of health tourism. This entails:

- Production of renewable energy through the use of solar, wind, and geothermal energy (UNWTO, 2020).
- Green building infrastructures employing passive cooling, thermal insulation, and energy-efficient planning (Khanal, A., & Shimizu, H. 2019).
- Water-saving technologies such as rainwater harvesting, greywater recycling, and smart irrigation.
- International case studies, for example, Costa Rica's 100% renewable energy eco-resorts, prove that environmental conservation health tourism models can

still be economically sustainable while supporting environmental conservation (Khanal, A., & Shimizu, H. 2019).

1.1.4 Policy Frameworks and Governmental Role in Sustainable Tourism

Governments have an important role to play in encouraging sustainable health tourism by way of policies, regulations, and incentives. For instance, Iceland has used hydropower and geothermal energy to encourage environmentally friendly tourism (Iceland Ministry of Industries and Innovation, 2021). Bhutan's "High-Value, Low-Impact" policy of tourism guarantees that tourist revenues go into environmental as well as socioeconomic development (Royal Government of Bhutan, 2020).

India, with its immense potential in medical and wellness tourism, must assess its policies against these global standards to fill gaps and foster sustainable practices (Ministry of Tourism, Government of India, 2022).

1.1.5 Research Contribution: Analysis of Global Trends and Best Practices for India

This research analyzes global trends and best practices in health tourism to assess for India:

- Identification of innovations in sustainable health tourism (Hall, C. M., & Weiler, B. 2020).
- Identify challenges and opportunities for energy saving in India.
- Suggest policy reforms and industry adoption (Smith, M., & Puczkó, L. 2014).

By situating India's health tourism in an international sustainability context, the research seeks to lead industry players toward sustainable and environmentally friendly models.

1.2 Rationale for the Study

1.2.1 Significance of Sustainability in Health Tourism

Health tourism is naturally associated with ecosystems and cultural heritage; thus, it can be susceptible to unsustainable practices. Places such as Bali, Costa Rica, and Kerala have made viable transitions toward integrating renewable energy, waste management, and sustainable tourism policies while maintaining local culture and biodiversity (Smith, M., & Puczkó, L. 2014).

India's wellness resorts and medical tourism industry are turning more and more energy-intensive. This requires the implementation of energy-efficient models to save resources and preserve ecological balance (Ministry of Tourism, Government of India, 2022).

1.2.2 Role of Energy Conservation for Sustainable Tourism

Energy-efficient systems are the solution to:

- Reducing carbon emissions (Becken, 2017).
- Conserving ecological and cultural resources (Gössling et al., 2021).
- Enhancing economic viability through reduced operation expenses and rising green investments (World Bank, 2020).

The study will apply worldwide examples to emphasize energy conservation as a critical factor in ensuring health tourism is sustainable and resilient.

1.2.3 Institutional Influence and Policy Frameworks on Sustainable Health Tourism

Policies play a major role in shaping health tourism operations. Government incentives, eco-certification policies, and architectural regulations promote sustainable investments. For instance:

- Eco-certification of medical centers promotes credibility.
- Green infrastructure is financed by public–private partnerships (PPPs) (GSTC, 2022).

Comparing India's policies with international leaders such as Iceland and Bhutan, the study identifies policy areas that require reform in India.

1.2.4 Study Scope and Contribution

The study will address:

- Energy-efficient smart technologies (Sharma & Maikhuri, 2023).
- Traditional green practices and community participation.
- Regulatory policies that affect sustainable health tourism (Hall et al., 2021).

Its recommendations will assist in the reconciliation of economic development with environmental protection and a more energy-efficient, inclusive tourism sector.

1.3 Research Objectives

i. Analyze the situation of energy savings and environmental stewardship in the context of global health tourism today, highlighting relevant trends and successes.

ii. Identify factors that influence the adoption of energy-efficient and sustainable initiatives in health tourism, which include economic, technological, policy-related, and cultural determinants.
iii. To assess the environmental and social impact of energy conservation practices in health tourism, with specific insights drawn from destinations known for their biodiversity and wellness tourism potential.
iv. To provide actionable recommendations for strengthening sustainable energy practices and adopting innovative strategies in health tourism to ensure long-term benefits for the environment, local communities, and the industry.

1.4 Research Questions

i. To what extent are energy conservation and environmental practices integrated into health tourism worldwide, and how do implementation levels vary across regions?
ii. What are the key factors—such as governmental policies, community involvement, and technological advancements—influencing the adoption of energy-efficient practices in health tourism globally?
iii. How do implemented energy conservation and eco-friendly practices contribute to the environmental and social sustainability of health tourism in various global destinations?
iv. What challenges are commonly faced in integrating and sustaining energy-efficient practices in health tourism, and how do these challenges vary across different regions?
v. How can current energy conservation and environmental practices in health tourism be improved globally, and what innovative strategies can destinations adopt to enhance sustainability?

1.4.1 The Demand for Conservation of Energy and Environmental Accountability in Health Tourism

The increasing demand for health tourism has generated economic potential as well as environmental issues. This research is important because it responds to the urgent need to enhance energy-saving and environmental sustainability in the industry. Through a review of worldwide trends, analysis of main issues, and provision of practical evidence-based recommendations, this research intends to promote a more sustainable and responsible future for health tourism globally.

(1) Development of Health Tourism and Its Economic Importance
Health tourism has grown exponentially over the last few years, combining travel activities with medical, wellness, and rehabilitative treatments. Thailand, India, Malaysia, and Turkey have become top destinations because of their low-cost, high-standard healthcare facilities, natural wellness retreats, and holistic treatment facilities. This development has

contributed largely to: increased national and local economies through revenues from medical tourism; job creation in healthcare, hospitality, and allied sectors; and improving infrastructural growth in major tourist spots. Yet, this speedy growth imposes a huge burden on natural resources and the environment; therefore, energy-efficient and environmentally friendly measures are urgently needed.

(2) Environmental Issues in Health Tourism
Health tourism centers—such as hospitals, wellness resorts, rehabilitation centers, and medical spas—are extremely resource-hungry. These centers use vast amounts of energy, water, and other natural resources due to: 24/7 operation of medical equipment, resulting in heavy electricity consumption. Large-scale heating, ventilation, and air-conditioning (HVAC) systems, boosting carbon emissions. Water-based therapies in spas, hydrotherapy facilities, and wellness retreats. Waste creation from medical, pharmaceutical, and plastic origins, adding to environmental contamination. With growing demand for high-end healthcare and wellness services, most health tourism destinations are scaling up with energy-hungry infrastructure that does not have effective efficiency measures in place. The implications of such unbridled growth are: Large carbon footprints, fueled by fossil fuel-based electricity; air and water contamination, impacting local ecosystems; and excessive use of limited resources, resulting in unsustainable tourism practices. Since health tourism is significantly interconnected with natural habitats, ensuring clean air, water, and ecological equilibrium is imperative for the long-term success of the industry.

(3) Sustainable Solutions for Energy Efficiency and Environmental Conservation
In order to counteract these challenges, this research highlights the need to incorporate renewable energy solutions, intelligent technology, and resource-efficient methods. The implementation of green innovations in health tourism has the potential to drastically cut down on environmental damage while enhancing patient welfare and operational effectiveness. Some of the most promising interventions include:

- Renewable Energy Integration
  Implementation of solar and wind energy adoption in health tourism centers in order to lower the dependence on fossil fuels. Geothermal cooling and heating systems in wellness resorts to reduce energy usage. Microgrid and smart-grid technology for optimized energy delivery.
- Energy-Efficient Technologies
  Passive design building, incorporating natural ventilation, thermal insulation, and green roofs. Intelligent lighting controls, including LED and motion-sensing sensors, to maximize electricity usage. Artificial intelligence (AI)-based energy management, leveraging real-time data to minimize wasteful energy usage.
- Sustainable Water and Waste Management
  Greywater reuse and rainwater harvesting to lessen freshwater reliance.

Eco-friendly waste management processes, such as biowaste recycling and composting. Tight controls on pharmaceutical and biomedical waste management to avoid dangerous pollution.

(4) The Interdisciplinary Role
Successful adoption of sustainable energy options in health tourism needs multi-sectoral cooperation among: Healthcare professionals, who will have to implement sustainable medical protocols; architects and engineers, who create green, energy-sparing healthcare facilities; environmental scientists and policymakers, who enact and monitor sustainability norms; and technology entrepreneurs, who create AI-based sustainability solutions for health tourism centers.

(5) Research Scope and Contribution
The research will examine new trends in energy usage in health tourism centers, including: Best-practice examples of sustainable energy projects from top health tourism destinations; energy-efficient healthcare infrastructure innovations, such as smart hospitals and green resorts; and regulatory policy and incentive effects in promoting green tourism investments. By combining real-case examples, industrial practices, and professional opinion, this study will provide policy and practice guidelines to policymakers, business leaders, and stakeholders. Finally, it seeks to achieve harmony among economic growth, environmental preservation, and human welfare, thereby securing a resilient and sustainable health tourism sector.

1.5 Significance of the Study

This study is of great importance as it responds to the urgent call for sustainable development in health tourism through the promotion of energy conservation and environmental stewardship. With the continued expansion of health tourism across the world, there is a growing need to reconcile economic advancement with environmental conservation. This research seeks to offer a fact-based framework for appreciating the contribution of energy-saving practices and sustainable policies toward the long-term sustainability of the industry.

1.5.1 Governmental Influence: Policy Design and Regulation

Governmentally, this research supplies a background for policy formation, allowing legislators and regulatory agencies to devise policies that encourage: Energy efficiency by incorporating renewable energy resources like solar, wind, and geothermal into health tourism facilities; environmental conservation policies, such as carbon-free infrastructure planning and waste management policy; incentivization of environmental investments, such as tax reliefs, subsidization, and grants for enterprise use of eco-friendly energy uses; and compliance with international objectives of sustainability, such as the United Nations SDGs and Paris Agreement on climate change. By analyzing energy conservation initiatives in top health tourism destinations, this study presents evidence-based findings that can assist policymakers in India and across the world to develop sustainable tourism policies balancing economic development with environmental protection.

1.5.2 Industry Influence: Lessons for Health Tourism Stakeholders

This study provides key insights for health tourism operators, professionals, and investors on: Optimal energy-efficient practices, including smart HVAC systems, smart lighting, and water saving technologies; sustainable business models, demonstrating how eco-friendly practices can reduce operational costs and enhance service quality; adapting to market demand, as eco-conscious travelers increasingly prefer destinations that prioritize sustainability; and green certifications (e.g., Leadership in Energy and Environmental Design [LEED], Green Globe, and Global Sustainable Tourism Council [GSTC] standards), which enhance a facility's reputation and increase market competitiveness. By highlighting gaps in existing practices and presenting model successes, this research offers the industry a template for reducing the ecological footprint through maximizing resource efficiency, minimizing expenditures, and creating long-term resilience.

1.5.3 Environmental Impact: Minimizing the Ecological Footprint

This research is part of international efforts toward sustainability by providing pragmatic suggestions to: Offset carbon emissions by moving toward low-carbon tourism infrastructure; conserve biodiversity in health tourism destinations through the encouragement of sustainable land use and environmental-friendly facility designs; reduce waste production via recycling initiatives, biodegradable products, and eco-friendly packaging in tourism operations; and improve air and water quality, enhancing the general well-being of tourists and local people. Through focusing on energy-saving measures, the study encourages climate action and harmonizes with global sustainability movements, including the UNEP Sustainable Tourism Program and the World Tourism Organization's Green Tourism Initiative.

1.5.4 Academic Contribution: Expanding Research on Sustainable Health Tourism

From a scholarly point of view, this research is the first to bring a unique emphasis on energy conservation in the health tourism industry—a subject that is as yet under-emphasized within established literature on sustainable tourism. The study: Spans health tourism and sustainable energy management, providing innovative interdisciplinary perspectives; investigates green technology challenges, such as economic hindrances, policy loopholes, and technological limitations; examines the potential of smart technologies (AI-based energy management, Internet of Things [IoT], and automation) to increase sustainability in health tourism environments; and provides case studies of international leaders in sustainable wellness tourism, adding comparative research in tourism and sustainability studies. This information can inform future research in tourism management, environmental science, and energy-efficient building design.

1.5.5 Innovation and Future Growth in Sustainable Health Tourism

By recognizing important challenges and highlighting best practices, this research acts as an impetus for health tourism innovation. Policymakers and business leaders can apply these insights to: Create leading-edge sustainable health facilities that are integrated with green building practices; apply circular economy principles, with waste being used and resources utilized to the maximum; and develop intersectoral PPPs for promoting sustainable infrastructure development.

1.5.6 Economic and Social Impact: Addressing Demand for Responsible Tourism

As eco-friendly tourists increase, health tourism sites need to keep pace with international energy-saving standards to stay competitive. This research points out how green tourism activities draw high-spending tourists who pay a premium for green experiences. Green health tourism centers generate local jobs in green technology, renewable energy, and sustainability advisory services. Sustainability investments result in cost savings in operations, making businesses more profitable and resilient in the long term. Finally, the study highlights that energy conservation is not only an environmental imperative but also a smart economic benefit.

1.5.7 A Global Roadmap for Sustainable Health Tourism

The significance of this research goes beyond any one region—this report provides an international overview of how health tourism hotspots can gain sustainability without losing profitability. By making things pragmatic, the study: Assists governments with writing effective sustainability policies; influences businesses and investors to implement energy-conserving initiatives; arms tourism experts with information regarding sustainable operational measures; and promotes worldwide cooperation toward establishing carbon-neutral models of health tourism. To sum up, this study provides a blueprint to mainstream energy saving, sustainability, and innovation within the health tourism sector, guaranteeing the industry's boom and green mindset for future generations.

2. Literature Review

2.1 Health Tourism

Health tourism, both medical and wellness tourism, is advancing with a greater focus on sustainability. In India, wellness centers are now adopting renewable energy systems like solar panels and rainwater harvesting systems to reduce their impact on the environment. For example, green hospitals in Mumbai and Delhi have embraced green building standards, efficient equipment, and waste management to foster environmental sustainability in medical tourism (Zaveri, 2024). Moreover, spas such as Ananda in the Himalayas have added holistic wellness programs that blend traditional practices with sustainable operations, demonstrating a focus on both wellness and sustainability (Bright Ideas in Travel 2024, n.d.).

2.2 Sustainable Tourism Practices

Around the world, the tourism sector is embracing sustainable practices to mitigate its environmental footprint. The GSTC has developed criteria centered on sustainable management, socioeconomic impacts, cultural impacts, and environmental impacts, such as consumption of resources and reduction of pollution (GSTC, 2022). In India, the Ministry of Tourism has created the Sustainable Tourism Criteria for India (STCI), offering guidelines for accommodation providers and tour operators to adopt energy-conserving and environmentally friendly practices. Kerala and other states have accepted these principles with programs such as the Responsible Tourism Mission, which encourages community tourism and environmental conservation (Hospitalitynews, 2023; Ministry of Tourism India, 2023).

2.3 Energy Conservation and Environmental Practices in Tourism

Energy saving is an important part of sustainable tourism. Resorts and hotels are relying more and more on renewable energy and smart devices to make the best use of energy. A research using artificial neural networks showed the application for energy forecasting and controlling in hotels and increasing efficiency with a decrease in environmental footprint (Trull et al., 2024). In Kerala, 25 places have been chosen as "Green Tourism Destinations" under the "Malinya Muktham Nava Keralam" initiative, with the goal of adopting sustainable waste management and conservation methods on favorite tourist spots (Safari India, n.d.).

2.4 India's Tourism Landscape

India's multicultural geography and rich heritage make it an ideal health tourism destination. The Rs 385 crore allocation by the Kerala Government in the 2025–2026 budget highlights commitment to wellness-tourism growth and the creation of green-friendly infrastructure. Measures encompass repurposing vacant homes as homestays and improving inland waterways, a sign of an overarching approach to sustainable tourism development (Thiruvananthapuram News – The Times of India. n.d.).

2.5 Governmental and Institutional Support for Sustainable Tourism

Institutional backing is crucial in encouraging sustainable tourism. The Kerala Government's sanction of Rs 6.64 crore for Responsible Tourism initiatives during 2024–2025 is intended to improve sustainability and local participation in major destinations. These projects address how to incorporate digital marketing, artificial intelligence (AI), and training modules to develop environmentally friendly tourism activities (Hospitalitynews, 2023; The New Indian Express, 2024). In addition, the GSTC has collaborated with Indian states to advance sustainable tourism through training and certification schemes, supporting the implementation of globally accepted best practices in environmental sustainability (GSTC, 2022).

2.6 Challenges and Opportunities in Energy Conservation

Although the use of energy-efficient technology offers a window of opportunity for eco-friendly tourism, the initial cost of investment and resistance to change remain challenges. Nevertheless, PPPs and government incentives can overcome these obstacles. For instance, the Uttar Pradesh Government provides a 50% refund of the certification cost to tour operators who acquire GSTC-accredited certifications, encouraging sustainable operations (GSTC, 2022).

Technological innovations in digital energy management systems aided by AI and the IoT provide real-time monitoring and energy consumption optimization in tourist facilities, improving efficiency and minimizing environmental footprint.

2.7 Impact Assessment of Energy Conservation in Tourism

Measurement of the effect of energy conservation initiatives is vital for ongoing improvement. Resorts and hotels are adopting sustainability reporting and carbon accounting methods to track energy savings and environmental footprint. These measurements guide policymaking and investment decisions, making energy-efficient solutions environmentally and economically sustainable. The growing popularity of sustainability certification programs such as LEED and India's Eco-Tourism Certification has led health tourism operators to conduct energy audits and monitor sustainability performance, which improves their market reputation and attractiveness to environmentally aware travelers. This literature review introduces the convergence of energy conservation and environmental practices in health tourism, focusing on recent trends and initiatives in India and worldwide. The intersection of health tourism and environmental sustainability offers opportunities for economic development alongside the conservation of natural resources and responsible travel.

3. Energy Use in Health Tourism Facilities

Health tourism establishments, such as hospitals, spa retreats, and rehabilitation facilities, are some of the most energy-intensive in the tourism industry. They consume vastly high levels of energy for heating, cooling, lighting, water heating, operation of equipment, and provision of various services to patients. As opposed to traditional hotels, health tourism establishments are usually run round-the-clock, require the use of constant power for special medical equipment and for air-conditioning, among other things. The environmental consequences include high carbon emissions, excessive water usage, and the production of both medical and nonmedical waste, all of which need to be managed sustainably. Energy consumption in health tourism varies based on several factors, including the size of the facility, the type of medical or wellness services offered, location (urban, rural, or coastal), climate conditions, patient demographics, and operational strategies.

Health tourism establishments can be divided into three primary energy-consuming zones:

- *Patient and Guest Areas:* This includes patient rooms, therapy suites, and wellness accommodations. These areas often have high energy demands due to the need for climate control, continuous lighting, and the operation of medical equipment.
- *Public and Common Areas:* Reception halls, lounges, therapy pools, fitness centers, and dining areas require significant energy for lighting, heating, and cooling. These spaces experience varying occupancy levels, which influence energy consumption patterns.
- *Service and Technical Areas:* Operating rooms, diagnostic labs, kitchens, laundry services, administrative offices, and mechanical rooms are highly energy-intensive, necessitating advanced air handling, sterilization, and medical waste processing systems.

Research shows that electricity serves as the main energy source in health tourism facilities, with HVAC systems, representing the largest portion of energy use. Additionally, water heating for patient care, therapy pools, and sanitation is another significant energy-consuming process. However, numerous facilities do not have comprehensive monitoring of energy flows, which complicates the implementation of focused conservation strategies.

4. Energy Efficiency and Sustainability Strategies

To lessen environmental impact and boost energy efficiency, health tourism facilities can implement a variety of sustainable practices:

- *Renewable Energy Integration:* By using solar thermal systems for water heating, photovoltaic panels for electricity generation, and geothermal energy for heating and cooling, facilities can significantly decrease their dependence on fossil fuels.

- *Passive Design Strategies:* Enhancing building orientation, insulation, natural ventilation, and shading techniques can lower the need for artificial heating and cooling.
- *Smart Energy Management Systems:* The use of automated lighting, occupancy sensors, and advanced HVAC controls can improve efficiency and cut down on unnecessary energy use.
- *Water Conservation Measures:* Rainwater harvesting, low-flow fixtures, and wastewater recycling reduce water waste. Simultaneously, it will reduce the demand for energy required to heat up water.
- *Sustainable Waste Management:* Effective segregation and treatment of medical and nonmedical waste and embracing circular economy principles can help in environmental sustainability.

5. Efficient Planning for Higher Energy Efficiency

The idea of energy-efficient healthcare facilities seems to attract many stakeholders; however, putting these into practice is a difficult job that needs to be considered in the larger framework of sustainable health tourism planning.

Unfortunately, health tourism is in many regions neglected within public planning, which is pivotal for effectively influencing, organizing, and managing health tourism as well as its intricate implications and effects. Only the presence of suitable planning and management functions can guide and monitor the growth of health tourism, making planning successful. It also requires the willingness of all the stakeholders to adopt a collaborative approach in development of that important sector.

It is a common notion that substantial energy reductions in health care facilities can only be achieved through the installation of complex, high-maintenance, and overpriced technologies. Although this may be the case in some instances, considerable energy savings can often be achieved through a far more straightforward approach that does not require specialized knowledge or significant investments. This is particularly true in cases where principles of energy efficiency and resource conservation are implemented in the planning and design stages of health tourism facilities. A critical review of the sustainability of any site in question should involve regional land planning, suitable site selection, and eco-friendly design of the facility in question.

Critical considerations in planning/design for Health Tourism Facilities for Energy Conservation and Efficiency include the following:

- suitable site selection;
- local building materials and renewable energy sources;
- impact on patient and visitor behavior, services offered, and operational cost;
- sustainable design features.

5.1 Appropriate Site Selection

The ecological, social, cultural, and economic factors of the surrounding area all need to achieve a balance when developing a sustainable healthcare facility with the ecological system. Developers require a comprehensive knowledge of the specific characteristics of their chosen site. The local climate and topography also have key roles in ascertaining facility energy requirements, as well as the availability of necessary materials and renewable energy.

Implementing environmentally friendly site selection, using sustainable building materials, optimizing renewable or passive heating, cooling, shading, and lighting technologies, and reducing internal transportation needs are some effective bioclimatic design strategies to lower energy consumption. For instance, the Crestwood Corporate Centre Building No. 8 in Richmond, B.C., Canada, was designed and built to adhere to stringent energy-saving and environmental standards, currently operating at less than 50% of the annual energy usage of a similar standard facility.

When choosing a location for a healthcare tourism facility, it's important to take into account cultural and ecological sensitivity, accessibility, carrying capacity, and the availability of supporting services and amenities.

5.2 Availability of Local Resources

Renewable energy sources like solar, wind, hydro, and biomass present effective options for enhancing energy use while minimizing environmental impact. It's important to compare estimated energy needs with the resources available locally to identify the most appropriate technologies. Although renewable energy solutions are becoming more common in health tourism—such as using solar energy for water heating and powering critical medical equipment—there is still a vast amount of untapped potential.

The choice of renewable energy technologies is influenced by the availability of local resources. Today, solar (both thermal and photovoltaic), wind power, biomass systems, and micro-hydro plants are among the most widely utilized. Looking ahead, we may see the adoption of advanced fuel cell systems, ocean thermal energy conversion (OTEC), geothermal energy, or wave and tidal energy systems. For example, Hawaii, a key destination for health tourism, has the potential to fulfill nearly all its energy requirements through renewable sources, yet over 90% of its energy still relies on fossil fuels.

Combined heat and power generation in healthcare facilities offers a variety of energy-efficient solutions.

5.3 Implications on Overall Cost and Services Provided

Energy conservation measures should be put in place without sacrificing patient safety, comfort, or the quality of services. This depends on the type of health tourism services being offered. Some energy-saving initiatives may be more practical than others. While eco-conscious travelers would be willing to make some changes in services for the sake of sustainability, high-end medical tourists expect rooms that consume more energy and more welfare.

Energy conservation in healthcare facilities is going beyond technical measures, as it also includes behavioral and educational dimensions. Education of all parties, be it the patient, the staff, or the management, leads to sustainability over time. These messages should focus on environmental friendliness, economic feasibility, and the merits of energy conservation for health tourism in general.

5.4 Design Aspects

Proper architectural and operational design could cut energy by substantial amounts. Even zoning with autotemp in the air condition system cuts use by de-energizing the rooms where no person has been around while sensors can cut 35–45% of energy waste from lighting usage, reducing light energy even more with maximization of natural daylight.

Adequate thermal insulation with minimal thermal bridges together with energy-efficient glazing can limit the need for heating and cooling. Healthcare buildings should therefore be designed to minimize loss of heat. Space conditioning ought to make use of passive as well as renewable sources including natural ventilation, natural passive heating and cooling, and optimized daylight.

Interactive energy management and smart monitoring systems can equally contribute to further reductions in consumption by health tourism facilities, offering sustainable and economic operations.

6. Economic Benefits of Energy Conservation and Environmental Practices in Health Tourism

This type of tourism has rapidly become an expanding part of the global industry and is further fueled by the clean, energy-efficient, and environmentally responsible nature of facilities. Between 1989 and 1998, the tourism industry expanded significantly. It is estimated that this pattern will continue. For example, from 2020, a projected annual increase of about 4.1% is anticipated. In the emerging market of health tourism, facilities that target energy conservation and sustainability will emerge with significant economic benefits.

Even though the energy-saving and environmentally friendly operations currently form a small portion of health tourism activities, they are rapidly turning into one of the fastest-growing sub-markets. As travelers grow in awareness and demand for environmentally friendly accommodations grows, health tourism facilities with energy-saving practices will attract many of the conscious and aware eco-consumers. Such trends imply that environmentally friendly health tourism is beneficial to the planet and creates an enormous opportunity for business growth.

Some developers argue that implementing such practices may raise the initial capital costs and add complexity to the project planning. However, in proper design and execution, energy-efficient health tourism facilities may decrease construction and operation costs and bring higher profit margins. Long-term savings in terms of energy and maintenance usually exceed the slight extra costs associated with sustainable design.

The economic benefits that are associated with the preservation of energy and green environment in health tourism include:

6.1 Economic Development Opportunities

Health tourism is among the fastest-growing industries in the world, making an important contribution to regional and national economies through income generation, employment, and the development of infrastructure. As destinations for health tourism increase, they create employment in hospitality, healthcare, wellness services, and ecotourism management, impacting both skilled and unskilled labor. Through the application of resource-saving technologies and local renewable resources, health tourism facilities can maximize their economic contribution while keeping operating costs at bay. Solar power, energy-conserving water heating, and intelligent waste management lower long-term costs and improve profitability such that more of the income will be retained in the local economy. Additionally, utilization of locally available sustainable materials, locally grown organic food, and green transportation solutions provides economic stimulation to neighboring communities. Beyond its direct economic return, green infrastructure projects associated with sustainable health tourism also promote collective community development. Investments in clean and energy-efficient accommodations, effective water management structures, and low-carbon emission transportation systems improve the general health and well-being of tourists as well as host communities. As an example, wellness retreat centers in India's Kerala, Rishikesh, and Goa have adopted nature-friendly designs for the benefit of both tourism-focused businesses and their surrounding communities. In addition, tourist entry charges, ecotourism fees, and conservation fees contribute to the funding of environmental protection projects. These resources can be cycled back into biodiversity conservation efforts, waste management projects, and renewable energy ventures to ensure that natural attractions are sustained. With an environmentally sound strategy, health tourism sites are able to keep their appeal for global visitors intact while protecting the very environments that render them attractive in the first place. Therefore, the economic value of sustainable health tourism goes beyond direct monetary gains—it sustains local industries, fosters green entrepreneurship, and maximizes the long-term sustainability of both tourism and natural resources. By aligning economic growth with environmental protection strategically, nations such as India can optimize the benefits of health tourism while strengthening sustainability objectives.

6.2 Enhanced Guest Comfort and Operational Efficiency

It is crucial that health tourism find a balance between guest comfort and environmental sustainability if it is to succeed. Fitting energy-conserving technologies, such as energy-efficient HVAC equipment, smart lights, and clean energy systems, into facilities such as wellness resorts, health spas, and medical tourism centers serves to lower expenses but also offers greater overall satisfaction for guests. With these integrated technologies, resort managers can assure better indoor air quality, room temperature, and customized comfort for their guests. An effectively planned, energy-conserving building can considerably enhance the guest quality of stay. To illustrate, intelligent climate control systems adapt room temperature in relation to occupancy, whereas motion-sensing LED lighting produces an optimal environment without waste. In addition, natural ventilation and passive cooling measures can limit artificial air-conditioning use, which in turn improves guests' well-being. In addition to guest comfort, another major benefit of energy conservation in health tourism is operational efficiency. In implementing automated energy management systems, facilities can track and maximize energy use in real time, minimizing waste and increasing cost-effectiveness. More resorts and wellness centers nowadays incorporate solar water heating, rainwater collection, and energy-efficient building design, minimizing their use of traditional energy sources. Together with cost savings and improved guest experience, sustainability becomes a competitive edge for the health tourism industry. Guests today increasingly opt for green accommodations, and energy-efficient operations can brand a facility as a premium, sustainable destination. In the end, incorporation of energy-efficient practices not only lessens environmental impact but also improves reputation and appeal of health tourism facilities, making them more resilient, profitable, and future-proof.

6.3 Improved Work Environment and Increased Productivity

Energy-saving and ecologically designed health tourism centers not only provide advantages to visitors but also provide a healthier and more productive workplace for workers. Green buildings with improved air quality, optimal lighting, and pleasant indoor temperatures reduce workplace stress, minimize fatigue, and lower staff-related health-absences. Research has shown that improved indoor environmental quality results in increased job satisfaction and improved employee retention rates, which is particularly important in service-focused health tourism. For example, buildings that incorporate natural ventilation systems, air cleaning technologies, and ergonomic workspace create an environment that encourages well-being. Workers in energy-efficient buildings are exposed to fewer toxins and less suffer from symptoms of sick building syndrome (SBS), including headaches, respiratory discomfort, and eye irritation. Moreover, daylight-optimized interiors also result in improved mental health and alertness, leading to enhanced overall productivity. Apart from physical well-being gains, involving employees in energy management programs also instills a sense of ownership and accountability toward sustainability measures. Employees who are educated on energy-saving practices, like optimized resource management and waste minimization techniques, will be inclined to take an active role in improving day-to-day functions. Not only does this boost job satisfaction but it also promotes greater efficiency in day-to-day activities. From a financial point of view, better work environments mean real bottom-line impacts. Healthier and happier employees mean reduced turnover rates, fewer recruitment and training expenses, and better guest service quality. These impacts are added to the energy savings that green technologies provide, making sustainability investments very worthwhile not only from the environmental and operational perspectives but also from people development and business profitability standpoints.

6.4 Competitive Advantage in the Marketplace

Health tourism facilities that integrate energy conservation and environmental sustainability into their operations have a massive competitive edge in the market. As the world becomes more environmentally conscious, eco-friendly tourists actively seek out destinations that align with their values, where sustainability is given equal importance as health and wellness services. This shift in consumer behavior has generated a high demand for energy-saving and eco-friendly health tourism facilities, and such facilities are a market favorite. Properties can differentiate themselves from their peers by adopting green technology, sustainable materials, and efficient use of energy. This not only attracts eco-friendly travelers but it also enhances corporate relations with the local authority and government bodies. Governments and tourism boards increasingly favor properties that align with sustainable objectives, commonly fast-tracking licenses, certifications, and grant approvals for green properties. The marketing advantage of being recognized as an ecologically sustainable health tourism destination is the primary source of competitive strength. Hotels that publicize their efforts at energy saving—through certifications like LEED, Green Key, or EarthCheck—enhance their reputation and build brand equity. In some cases, the adoption of sustainability initiatives has had a tangible impact on business performance. A well-being retreat in India, for example, experienced a 25% increase in occupancy following vigorously marketing its energy-saving efforts, use of renewable energies, and green wellness initiatives. In addition to the direct appeal to clients, good media coverage and word-of-mouth promotion also increase the market visibility of a facility. Green health tourism facilities are normally advertised in travel magazines, backed by green organizations, and endorsed by world tourism authorities, all of which build visibility and confidence. Sustainability investments over time increase profitability while also offering resistance to future regulation changes. With governments around the world imposing more stringent environmental laws, facilities that proceed with green practices will reap compliance cost savings, lower operating expenses, and remain competitive within their industries. By embracing leadership in health tourism sustainability, energy-efficient facilities are able to enjoy customer loyalty, increased market share, and long-term business sustainability.

6.5 Greater Profits Through Operational Savings

Energy efficiency and sustainable design in health tourism centers result in substantial cost reductions, which make operations more financially sustainable in the long term. Although the green building materials and energy-efficient technologies might be more expensive in the short term, the long-term utility bill, maintenance, and resource savings are far greater than the upfront cost. Studies indicate that for every ₹1 invested in energy-efficient technology, buildings can reap ₹525 in the form of energy savings, waste reduction, and operating efficiency. By conserving energy through the sun's power, LEDs, intelligent HVAC, and low-flow fixtures, overhead costs are directly cut, allowing the company to recycle the savings in customer experience and innovation in services. Besides cost reduction, increased guest satisfaction and employee productivity also translate into overall profitability. Guests like green practices and most would opt for sustainable health retreats rather than traditional ones, resulting in increased occupancy. Meanwhile, employees who work in properly ventilated, energy-efficient conditions are more productive and motivated, decreasing turnover and related recruitment costs. Finally, energy-efficient health tourism facilities not only enhance margins but also their long-term business viability so that they can maintain competitiveness in a dynamic market.

6.6 Increased Property Value and Investment Appeal

Green health tourism facilities not only cut expenses on maintenance but are also extremely appealing to property investors and owners. As the demand for green tourism rises, properties that incorporate green buildings, renewable energy infrastructure, and resource efficiency appreciate at a faster rate than traditional properties. Increasing numbers of tourists are drawn to eco-friendly, health-oriented hotels, so energy-saving health tourism hotels are more appealing. Low operating costs, high guest satisfaction, and high environmental credentials combine to make them appealing investments. In terms of the investor, energy-efficient buildings are safer long-term assets as they tend to be immune to regulatory uncertainties and qualify for government incentives as well as tax credits. Also, green-certified buildings earn greater rental income and resale value, offering assured returns. With increasingly stringent global and national sustainability laws due to global warming, health resorts with energy-saving characteristics will benefit economically. Their long-term viability, lower risk, and increasing demand in the marketplace make them a high-value product for India's real estate and hospitality sectors.

7. Policy and Institutional Support

Encouragement of green and energy-efficient tourism in India's healthcare tourism sector requires a strong policy framework, fiscal incentives, and institutional backing. Advances in clean energy technologies, digitalization, and smart infrastructure have facilitated the development of next-generation green tourism practices that the Indian Government, as well as international organizations, is actively supporting.

7.1 Government Policies and Regulations

The Government of India has launched a range of policy initiatives and regulatory measures to enhance green health tourism by integrating green energy technologies and climate-resilient infrastructure in wellness destinations. These initiatives are:

(1) *Sustainable Tourism Criteria for India (STCI):* STCI establishes energy saving, carbon minimization, and environmentally friendly waste management practices tuned to hotels, wellness resorts, and Ayurveda retreats. BEE (Bureau of Energy Efficiency)

(2) *Energy Efficiency Regulations:* Encourages tourism infrastructure to follow Energy Conservation Building Code (ECBC) standards, leading to the conservation of 30–50% of energy in hotels and resorts.

(3) *Green Building Incentives and Certifications:*

- Green Rating for Integrated Habitat Assessment (GRIHA) and LEED certification offers incentives through tax rebates, fast-track approvals, and carbon credit trading for ecologically sustainable health tourism facilities.
- Indian Green Building Council (IGBC) standards promote solar roofing, thermal insulation, natural ventilation, and waste-to-energy systems in hotels.

(4) *Renewable Energy Adoption Policies*

- The Ministry of New and Renewable Energy (MNRE) is giving grants and subsidies for health resort solar PV systems, bioenergy power stations, and hybrid wind-solar power systems.
- The Faster Adoption and Manufacturing of Electric Vehicles (FAME-II) scheme is promoting electric vehicle (EV) infrastructure for eco-friendly travel between wellness destinations.

(5) *Financial Incentives for Green Tourism:*

- Soft loans and priority sector lending are provided by Small Industries Development Bank of India (SIDBI) and Green Energy Finance Schemes to enable smart energy solutions adoption by tourism enterprises.
- Tax relief and GST concession on energy-efficient air-conditioning, smart metering, and solar hot water systems reduce the initial costs of businesses.

(6) *Eco-Tourism Sites and Permitting Regulators*

- The government is making it simpler to sanction energy-saving eco-tourism zones to enable new spas to implement green building practices starting from the planning stage.
- Waste-to-energy implementation is obligatory to make sure that biogas digesters and segregation units are employed in large spas and wellness centers in order to reduce landfill waste.

7.2 Institutional Support and PPPs

Successful institutional support and coordination between government agencies, private investors, and environmental organizations are needed in the development of energy-efficient health tourism.

(1) *Public–Private Investment Programs:*

- World Bank and International Finance Corporation (IFC)-supported Tourism Sustainability Funds are funding solar microgrids and energy storage for off-grid health retreats.
- Corporate Social Responsibility (CSR) partnerships call on ecotourism company managers to implement AI-driven energy tracking, green waste disposal, and sustainable food procurement.

(2) *Sustainability Capacity Development and Training:*

- The Indian Institute of Tourism and Travel Management (IITTM) has also collaborated with foreign institutions to educate tourism professionals in green operations, energy conservation, and eco-friendly waste management.
- Government-sponsored initiatives in intelligent energy solutions, IoT-based building automation, and climate management with AI are equipping tourism managers with the appropriate expertise to run energy-efficient resorts.

(3) *International Collaborations against Climate Change*

- India is collaborating with the UN World Tourism Organization (UNWTO), GSTC, and World Travel and Tourism Council (WTTC) to introduce net-zero initiatives in the tourism sector.
- Collaborations with the German GIZ and the Japanese JICA are facilitating low-carbon tourism destinations to be developed using intelligent grid systems and green architecture.

(4) *Eco-Certification and Consumer Awareness Programmes:*

(5) *Green labels such as "Eco-Friendly Hotel Certification" and "Responsible Tourism Mission Accreditation"* are helping health tourism businesses construct their sustainability branding.

(6) *Awareness campaigns under the Incredible India 2.0* are making tourists aware of responsible tourism, conservation of energy, and waste reduction at health resorts.

7.3 Deployment of Next-Generation Green Technology

(1) *AI-Driven Intelligent Energy Management:*

- Hotels and spas are employing AI-based energy monitoring systems to maximize power usage and reduce wastage of energy.

- Smart sensors with IoT power HVAC systems, lights, and water consumption automatically to maximize efficiency without sacrificing guest comfort.

(2) *Net-Zero Energy Wellness Retreats:*

- The next-generation Indian net-zero resorts, including in Goa, Rishikesh, and Kerala, are now planned with carbon-zero infrastructure and operated on solar, wind, and geothermal energy.

(3) *Green Hydrogen and Biomass Energy:*

- Some of the high-end wellness resorts are trying out green hydrogen fuel cells and biomass energy stations to substitute diesel generators and minimize carbon footprints.

(4) *Waste-to-Energy and Water Recycling Innovations:*

- Advanced waste-to-energy technology generates electricity and biogas from organic waste, reducing landfilling.
- Intelligent water recycling facilities with IoT-controlled greywater treatment are helping health resorts save water and maintain sustainability values.

(5) *Electric Mobility and Sustainable Transportation:*

- Solar-powered charging centers for electric automobiles are being implemented at tourist facilities to supplement renewable transport mediums.
- Wellness centers are promoting E-rickshaws, electric shuttle buses, and bicycle-sharing schemes to offset transport emissions.

8. Methodology

8.1 Research Approach

This research applies a mixed-method approach to obtain in-depth understanding about energy conservation and environmental practices globally in health tourism, especially taking India as a case study. By incorporating both quantitative and qualitative methodologies, this study is able to evaluate the current status of sustainable practices, identify significant factors that are considered influential, and assess the environmental and social effects of energy-saving measures in health tourism.

The quantitative phase involves gathering and analyzing large-scale data through surveys and statistical evaluations. These questionnaires are designed to gather information from various stakeholders such as health tourism facility operators, policymakers, environmentalists, and tourists. This stage measures the rate of adoption of energy-efficient technologies, evaluates efforts at waste management and water conservation, and identifies what obstacles there are to sustainable behaviors. Statistical analysis and data analytics are applied to comprehend the energy consumption patterns, operational efficiencies, and sustainability initiatives–cost-effectiveness nexus in health tourism facilities globally. The qualitative phase is the last phase after quantitative analysis to present more insights into the pragmatic challenges and opportunities for energy conservation in health tourism.

This comprises extensive interviews with industry stakeholders, healthcare officials, and sustainability experts to glean their opinions about incorporating sustainability. Case studies of pioneering health tourism facilities—Indian and international—are undertaken to review exemplary models for the utilization of renewable energy sources, passive design in architecture, and efficient usage of resources. These case studies depict best practices, innovative strategies, and valuable lessons from trailblazing institutions in the field. Cross-pollination through collaboration across all fields, ranging from academia and industry stakeholders to policymakers, underlines this study approach. Pooling experts on architecture, engineering, environmental science, and health care, it seeks a wholesome assessment of health tourism sustainability. Policy analysis would also be employed to assess whether government initiatives are supportive or oppressive of institutional frameworks and regulatory measures that either inhibit or facilitate energy-saving practices within the industry.

In order to make sure that the findings are credible and relevant, the research follows a structured methodology, which features data triangulation, comparative analysis, and thematic coding for qualitative insights. It balances empirical data with expert opinions on the challenges and opportunities for the adoption of sustainable energy solutions within health tourism.

This research, in the end, contributes to the growing knowledge base on environmental responsibility in health tourism, offering data-driven recommendations to improve energy efficiency, reduce carbon footprints, and promote environmentally friendly medical and wellness tourism destinations.

8.2 Data Collection Methods

a. *Quantitative Phase:*

- *Surveys:* A standardized questionnaire was designed to collect quantitative data regarding the practices of environmental sustainability and energy saving that had been implemented, the drivers of their implementation, and their perceived impacts. The survey was aimed at health tourism units of established wellness places all over the world, such as India, Bali in Indonesia, Costa Rica, Thailand, and the Maldives. This international sample enabled comparisons and gave a complete picture of the sustainability efforts of the sector (Ranasinghe et al., 2020).
- *Document Analysis:* Government policies, industry guidelines, and sustainability reports of prominent tourism organizations were examined for contextual insight. The influence of government policies, global regulations, and industry standards on energy saving and environmental practices in health tourism was evaluated through these documents.

b. *Qualitative Phase:*

- *In-depth Interviews:* In-depth interviews were conducted with key stakeholders in the global health tourism sector, such as wellness center managers, government officials, sustainability experts, and local leaders. They were asked about the challenges and opportunities, as well as region-specific context factors, which influenced the adoption and implementation of energy-efficient and sustainable practices (Braun & Clarke, 2014; Fernando et al., 2021).
- *Case Studies:* In-depth case studies were undertaken in the world's major wellness centers like India, Bali, Costa Rica, and New Zealand. They gave deep, rich contextual data about how energy conservation and environmental sustainability were integrated into health tourism enterprises and the subsequent environmental, social, and economic consequences of doing so.

8.3 Population and Sample

The research was grounded on health tourism facilities from various sources worldwide. The sample included wellness centers, Ayurveda resorts, yoga retreats, and ecotourism resorts providing health and wellness services. Stratified random sampling was used to divide facilities by type, like spa resorts and yoga retreats; location, such as coastal, rural, and urban regions; and size. A representative population for both interviews and qualitative questionnaires was selected to have an ample and representative sample of the sector, representative of the several regional contexts where the various steps of energy and environmental sustainability take place.

9. Data Analysis and Results

Regression analysis was used to analyze the determinants of satisfaction with energy-saving practices in health tourism facilities. The findings show that the use of energy-efficient practices has the most significant positive effect on satisfaction ($\beta = 0.4322, p < 0.001$). This implies that when facilities implement and utilize energy-saving technologies, including smart lighting, efficient HVAC systems, and renewable energy, visitors are likely to report greater satisfaction with their visit.

Further, knowledge of environmental practices ($\beta = 0.1506, p = 0.026$) and the efficacy of carbon emission lowering measures ($\beta = 0.1556, p = 0.033$) emerged as significant determinants of satisfaction. This reveals that when customers are well-versed with respect to a facility's sustainability activities and feel them to be successful in lowering the environmental footprint, their overall satisfaction with energy-conserving measures grows.

In contrast, guest participation in conservation activities ($\beta = 0.1169$, $p = 0.059$) and perceived sustainability practice impact ($\beta = 0.0917, p = 0.219$) did not exhibit statistically significant influences on satisfaction. What this suggests is that although knowledge of sustainability initiatives is crucial, actual participation in energy conservation activities might not necessarily lead to increased guest satisfaction. Equally, a general perception that sustainability practices lead to less energy usage does not automatically imply increased satisfaction levels.

Further, the perception that sustainability practices help decrease energy usage significantly ($\beta = 0.0172$, $p = 0.824$) did not have a significant impact on satisfaction, which indicates that customers appreciate tangible implementations of energy savings over mere claims of sustainability.

The general model accounts for 47.7% of the satisfaction level variance ($R^2 = 0.477$), and the relationship is moderate to strong between the independent variables and the level of guest satisfaction. The F-statistic (21.78, $p < 0.001$) indicates that the regression model is significant statistically, affirming the significance of predictors used.

The findings emphasized that direct implementation of energy-efficient practices is the most critical factor in enhancing guest satisfaction. While raising awareness and ensuring effective carbon-reduction efforts contribute positively, merely involving guests in conservation activities or promoting general sustainability claims may not significantly improve their satisfaction. These insights suggest that health tourism facilities should prioritize visible, effective, and well-communicated energy-efficient strategies to enhance guest experiences and sustainability perceptions.

9.1 Regression Analysis Results

Dependent Variable: Satisfaction With Energy-Saving Measures

$R^2 = 0.477$ → The model accounts for 47.7% of the variation in satisfaction levels.

F-Statistic = 21.78 ($p < 0.001$) → The overall model is significant.

9.1.1 Key Findings (Coefficients and p-Values)

Fig. 8.1 shows the heatmap shows that guest satisfaction in health tourism is strongly linked to effective environmental practices, energy-efficient measures, and guest involvement in conservation efforts. In contrast, simple awareness of sustainability practices has little impact, highlighting the need for active engagement and visible actions to enhance guest satisfaction.

10. Conclusion

Health tourism facilities now have a key challenge: balancing operation efficiency with environmental sustainability. Spa resorts, rehabilitation centers, and hospitals are energy-intensive establishments by nature. To reduce their ecological footprint, these facilities have to implement overall sustainable energy measures. Through the incorporation of energy-efficient technologies, renewable

Table 8.1. Display the Energy Conservation and Environmental Practices in Health Tourism Survey Analysis.

Predictor Variable	**Coefficient (Effect Size)**	***p* Value**	**Significance**
Implementation of energy-efficient practices	0.4322	<0.001	✓ Significant
Awareness of environmental practices	0.1506	0.026	✓ Significant
Effectiveness of carbon emission reduction	0.1556	0.033	✓ Significant
Guest involvement in conservation efforts	0.1169	0.059	✗ Not significant ($p > 0.05$)
Perceived impact of sustainability practices	0.0917	0.219	✗ Not significant
Belief in energy reduction by sustainability practices	0.0172	0.824	✗ Not significant

Interpretation (Table 8.1): (1) Most influential factor: *Implementation of energy-efficient practices* ($\beta = 0.4322$, $p < 0.001$) has the strongest impact on satisfaction. (2) Awareness and effectiveness matter: *Awareness of environmental practices* and *effectiveness in carbon reduction* also significantly influence satisfaction. (3) Guest involvement and general beliefs have weak or nonsignificant effects, meaning people may appreciate sustainability, but direct implementation matters more.

energy, and resource optimization techniques, these facilities can best lower their carbon footprint—without adversely affecting patient comfort or care standards.

With the global trend of sustainability impacting all sectors, the convergence of healthcare and tourism has become an evolving arena. Health tourism is no longer just about delivering medical and wellness services; it now includes green-friendly travel experiences. An increasingly large part of environmentally conscious tourists is looking for destinations that focus on energy efficiency, waste management responsibly, and the preservation of resources. This change has speeded up the growth of health tourism destinations that are not just scenically elegant and culturally vibrant but also ecologically sound.

Renewable energy is a foundation of sustainable health tourism. In coastal and tropical areas, numerous establishments have fitted solar panels on their rooftops to provide for their energy requirements, cutting down the use of fossil fuels. Geothermal energy is also becoming popular in spas and wellness centers to warm hydrotherapy pools in a carbon-free manner. These technologies have the dual advantage of cutting down operating expenses while contributing to the worldwide carbon-reduction targets.

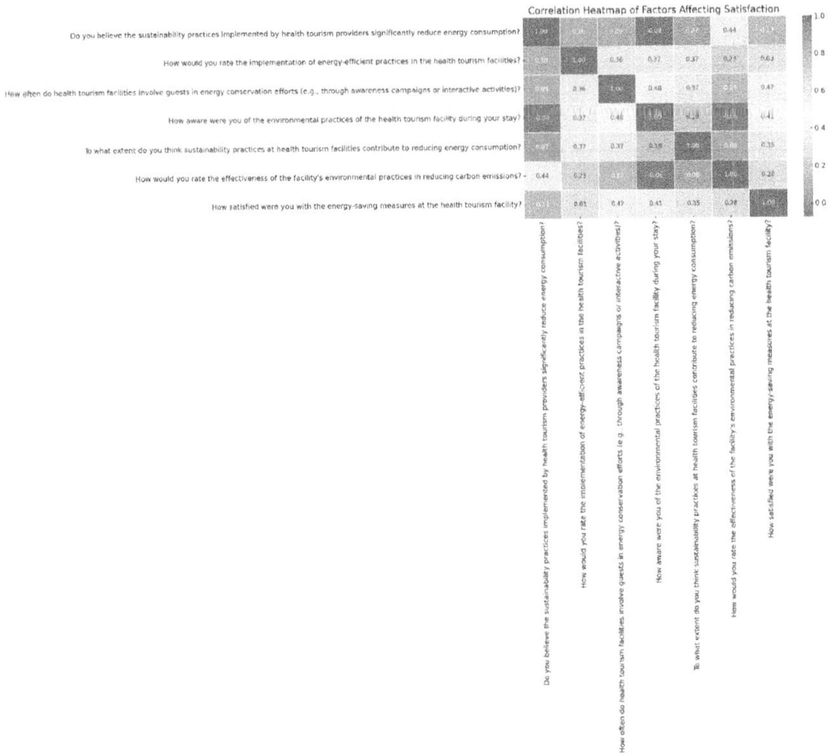

Fig. 8.1. Shows the Correlation Graph.

Passive design techniques also contribute significantly to energy savings. Contemporary architectural advancements involve maximizing natural lighting and ventilation by positioning buildings in ways that optimize passive solar gain and orientation, employing energy-efficient building materials, and integrating elements like green roofs, shaded outdoor spaces, and water-conserving landscaping. These are not only environmentally beneficial but also add to a peaceful, holistic healing environment conducive to recovery and well-being.

Water saving and efficient waste management are also of paramount importance. Wellness and health centers normally utilize a lot of water. Use of water-saving technologies like rainwater collection systems, greywater reuse, and low-flow devices can significantly lower the water needed. At the same time, taking up strong biomedical waste segregation, recycling systems, and environmentally friendly disposal solutions ensures health regulations adherence while reducing environmental footprints.

Technological innovation is quickly changing energy management in health tourism. Smart energy systems now offer real-time monitoring and automatic control of lighting, heating, and air-conditioning according to occupancy levels.

AI and IoT-based solutions optimize energy efficiency and minimize waste. Additionally, the growth of telemedicine and virtual wellness programs helps ensure sustainability by minimizing the demand for patient travel, hence lowering emissions associated with it.

In spite of these developments, some barriers continue to hamper the universal adoption of sustainable processes. Financial constraints, poor technical know-how, and resistance to change are still major challenges, especially among small and mid-range facilities. To address these, government interventions like subsidies, tax credits, and grants can be crucial. These policy instruments can drive the take-up of green technologies and support sustainable business models.

The journey toward a sustainable health tourism industry demands interdisciplinary partnership. Architects, engineers, healthcare professionals, environmental scientists, and policymakers are needed to collaborate and create innovative solutions through planning and policymaking. Academic institutions and research institutions can also facilitate this change through provision of evidence-based approaches and green technologies.

In the future, the dynamics of health tourism will be driven by changing environmental regulations, the growth of green technologies, and the desire for sustainability by consumers. Such facilities will not only save on operating expenses and regulatory penalties but also become competitive through their appeal to environmental-friendly tourists. Incorporating circular economy approaches—recycling materials and resources back into production and eliminating or minimizing waste—can make sustainability efforts even better.

Essentially, energy conservation and green responsibility are no longer choices in health tourism but a necessity. A sustainable model for health tourism needs to be integrated, with renewable power, green infrastructure, efficient water and waste management, and advanced technologies. With multi-disciplinary collaboration and the support of enabling policy environments, the industry can change to achieve the twin objectives of human health and environmental conservation.

By committing to sustainability today, health tourism can contribute meaningfully to global energy conservation efforts and secure a resilient future for both people and the planet.

References

Becken, S. (2017). Energy efficiency in tourism: Motivations and best practices. *Sustainable Tourism Research Journal*, *5*(4), 289–305.

Braun, V., & Clarke, V. (2014). What can "thematic analysis" offer health and wellbeing researchers? *International Journal of Qualitative Studies on Health and Well-Being*, *9*(1), 26152.

Bright Ideas in Travel 2024. (n.d.). Condé Nast Traveler. https://www.cntraveler.com/story/bright-ideas-in-travel-2024

Fernando, Y., Wah, W. X., & Shaharudin, M. R. (2021). The role of environmental sustainability in the governance of tourism: A stakeholder perspective. *Environmental Science and Pollution Research*, *28*, 30608–30628.

Global Sustainable Tourism Council. (2022). *Criteria for sustainable tourism: Industry and destination standards.* https://www.gstcouncil.org/wp-content/uploads/GSTC-Destination-Criteria-v2.0-2022.pdf

Going Green: Promoting Environmental Sustainability in Medical Tourism. (n.d.). Retrieved from https://www.indiheal.com/post/environmental-sustainability-in-medical-tourism

Gössling, S., Scott, D., & Hall, C. M. (2021). Tourism and carbon emissions: Mitigation strategies and policy imperatives. *Journal of Sustainable Tourism, 29*(9), 1420–1438.

Hall, C. M., Gössling, S., & Weaver, D. (2021). *Sustainable tourism futures: Perspectives on systems, restructuring, and innovations.* Routledge.

Hall, C. M., & Weiler, B. (2020). *Sustainable tourism development: Best practices and case studies.* Channel View Publications.

Hospitalitynews. (2023). https://responsibletourismpartnership.org/kerala-responsible-tourism-declaration-2023

Iceland Ministry of Industries and Innovation. (2021). *Sustainable tourism plan: 2021–2025.* https://www.government.is

Kamalasena, S., & Chamodya, D. (2021). Sustainable wellness tourism: Lessons from leading destinations. *International Journal of Sustainable Tourism Research, 9*(2), 78–91.

Khanal, A., & Shimizu, H. (2019). Eco-resorts and renewable energy use: The case of Costa Rica. *Renewable Energy and Tourism Journal, 8*(1), 65–75.

Ministry of Tourism, Government of India. (2022). *Draft national strategy for sustainable tourism.*

Perera, H., Jayawardena, C., & Gamage, A. (2023). Wellness tourism in the post-COVID era: Trends and sustainability considerations. *Journal of Tourism and Health, 15*(1), 45–59.

Ranasinghe, R., Damunupola, A., Wijesundara, S., Karunarathne, C., & Weerasinghe, T. D. (2020). Tourism after Corona: Impacts of COVID-19 pandemic and way forward for tourism, hotel and MICE industry in Sri Lanka. *South Asian Journal of Social Studies and Economics, 7*(1), 1–15.

Royal Government of Bhutan. (2020). *High-value, low-impact tourism policy.* Bhutan Tourism Council.

Safari India. (n.d.). *Kerala will transform 25 locations into "Green Tourism Destinations".* https://safariindia.com/travel-industry/25-places-in-kerala-to-become-green-tourism-destinations-7058535

Sharma, A., & Maikhuri, A. (2023). Smart technologies and sustainability in Indian wellness tourism. *Indian Journal of Tourism Studies, 12*(2), 101–115.

Sivesan, S. (2021). The role of sustainable tourism in environmental protection: A global overview. *Journal of Environmental Management and Tourism, 12*(3), 812–819.

Smith, M., & Puczkó, L. (2014). *Health, tourism and hospitality: Spas, wellness and medical travel.* Routledge.

The New Indian Express. (2024). *Kerala government approves INR 6.64 crore for responsible tourism projects.* https://www.newindianexpress.com/cities/thiruvananthapuram/2024/Oct/23/kerala-govt-okays-rs-664-crore-for-responsible-tourism-projects

Thiruvananthapuram News – The Times of India. (n.d.). Kerala budget 2025: Boost to tourism with Rs 385 crore allocation. https://timesofindia.indiatimes.com/city/thiruvananthapuram/boost-to-tourism-with-385-crore-allocation/articleshow/118033827.cms

Trull, O., Peiro-Signes, A., Garcia-Diaz, J. C., & Segarra-Ona, M. (2024). Prediction of energy consumption in hotels using ANN. *arXiv*. https://doi.org/10.48550/arXiv.2405.18076

United Nations World Tourism Organization. (2020). *Tourism and sustainable energy: Enhancing energy efficiency and renewable energy use in the tourism sector*. United Nations World Tourism Organization.

World Bank. (2020). *Sustainable energy for all: The role of tourism in achieving energy efficiency goals*. https://www.worldbank.org/en/publications

Zaveri, M. (2024). *Going green: Promoting environmental sustainability in medical tourism*. https://www.indiheal.com/post/environmental-sustainability-in-medical-tourism

Chapter 9

Exploring the Experiences of Private Sector Employees in Panch Kedar Treks: A Study on Well-Being and Health Tourism

Siddhant Chaudhary, Saurav Uniyal, Prashant Kumar, Raina and Rakesh Kumar

Gurukul Kangri (Deemed to be University), Haridwar, India

Abstract

Despite the increasing popularity of nature-based health tourism, there is limited research exploring its holistic benefits, particularly among private sector employees. Understanding how trekking experiences at Panch Kedar influence their mental, spiritual, and physical well-being can provide valuable insights into coping mechanisms for urban work stress. Building on this idea, the current study interviewed 10 participants using a structured interview schedule. The interview transcripts were analyzed using thematic analysis using ATLAS.ti software. This study identified three major themes related to the effects of trekking: (1) Physical Effects, (2) Mental Effects, and (3) Spiritual Effects. Physically, participants experienced exhaustion lasting 2–10 days yet reported a strong sense of accomplishment after completing the trek. Mentally, trekking contributed to stress relief, mental clarity, and lasting positive memories, highlighting its potential as an effective intervention for mental relaxation. Spiritually, experiences varied; while many reported spiritual transformations, some did not experience any significant spiritual effects. These findings suggest that trekking offers physical challenges, psychological benefits, and potential spiritual growth, making it a holistic activity for well-being.

Keywords: Panch Kedar; tourism; health tourism; well-being; mental well-being; spiritual experiences

Nature, Wellness and Sustainability in Health Tourism, 215–250

doi:10.1108/978-1-83742-029-220261009

1. Introduction

Stress in the workplace has grown to be one of the biggest issues over the past decade, especially for employees in the private sector. According to Global Workplace Report 2021, an unprecedented 43% of the world's workforce reported a feeling of stress on a daily basis. Such stress is linked to excessive workloads, extremely tight deadlines, lack of autonomy, ambiguity, and poor working environments (Bhui et al., 2016; Mitchel, 2025; Tandon, 2025). These results align with studies done in India, where workers in the private sector displayed considerably more stress than employees in government jobs. A study conducted to evaluate occupational stress in the city of Delhi found that around 75% of employees working in the private sector are moderately stressed while 11.7% are highly stressed. The variables contributing to stress included vague job expectations, excessive job responsibilities, and low levels of involvement in organizational decision-making (Biswas & Kumar, 2021). The existing literature outlines workplace stress as the predominant factor contributing to mental health issues like anxiety, depression, as well as burnout (Biswas & Kumar, 2021; Gallup, 2024). Burnout, which can be described as feeling emotionally drained and ineffective, tends to be much more common for employees in high-stress working conditions. A research study conducted in the information technology (IT), insurance, and banking industries in Kerala found that executives experienced stress mainly due to long working hours and monotonous work. This stress had severe psychological consequences like anxiety and low self-esteem. Moreover, stress-related fatigue and headaches were commonplace (Jayarajan & Vasanthagopal, 2017). In Europe, evidence demonstrates that job-related stress has detrimental effects on mental health as well as cardiovascular disease and musculoskeletal disorders (Bhui et al., 2016).

In India, the prevalence of workplace stress is a growing concern, affected by the rigid working hour requirements and constant interconnectivity of the IT and finance sectors (Biswas & Kumar, 2021; Deloitte Global Report Team, 2022). One emerging problem in the private sector is overdependence on technology, known as technostress. Marchiori et al. (2019) show that IT specialists suffer from technostress due to diminished productivity and increased emotional fatigue. Also, organizational change and fear of unemployment have been noted as relevant causes too. Government and private sector employees were compared on an invasive job stress survey, and it was found that the job-related stress levels of private sector employees were much higher because of insufficient job security, paying job requirements, and other related factors (Vichhiya, 2017). Some instances show how work-related stress can lower productivity and negatively influence decision-making ability. Employees under stress become prone to angry outbursts, emotional swings, and nervousness, which destroy workplace relationships (Mensah, 2021). Aside from that, stress-induced sickness leaves are becoming more of a problem for unwanted attention from the organization. Investigations carried out in Eastern Africa showed that work overload, in conjunction with role ambiguity, leads to absenteeism and lower staff morale (Munisi, 2025). In the same vein, studies from India reveal the damaging consequences of occupational stress on productivity as well as the health of employees (Biswas & Kumar, 2021). Even with traditional mental health programs within workplaces aimed at alleviating stress, these interventions often neglect the comprehensive mental and emotional requirements of employees. For instance, stress symptom yoga classes or mindfulness training do not solve the fundamental problems of poor organizational communication or unrealistic workloads (Tetrick & Winslow, 2015). Specified focus on structural improvements, like fostering peer support networks and encouraging a work–life balance, are now acknowledged as effective means for promoting employee well-being (Shapiro et al., 2020). Therefore, the overwhelming focus on such mental health programs is indicative of the desperate need for new strategies that focus on managing employee well-being.

1.1 Growing Popularity of Nature-Based Health Tourism

Nature-based health tourism describes travel that involves the combination of physical, mental, and spiritual recovery in conjunction with immersion in nature. This type of tourism facilitates natural stress relief as well as rejuvenation, improved cardiovascular health, enhanced emotional resilience, and facilitated aging (Somanchi et al., 2023). It includes forest bathing, hiking, wildlife observation, and water recreation activities that utilize the health-promoting effects of green spaces and waterbodies (Li & Trivic, 2024). For example, the forest therapy model structures provide visitors with natural wellness experiences geared toward fostering recovery and mental clarity (Kil et al., 2023). Moreover, health tourism has been recognized to advance biodiversity conservation, support local communities by providing eco-friendly accommodation, and preserve culture, making it an increasingly attractive sustainable practice (Maniktala & Sharma, 2024).

1.2 Emerging Trends in Nature-Based Health Tourism

The recent surge of health tourism integrating nature reflects its popularity in combating occupational stress and enhancing productivity. Overall, health and wellness tourism is expected to outgrow USD 1.3 trillion by 2025 as more people adopt holistic approaches to health (Global Wellness Institute, n.d.). In recent years, empirical studies also pointed out that alleviation of anxiety and depression, cognitive/emotional functioning, and general well-being are improved by spending time outdoors (Jimenez et al., 2021). For instance, forest bathing which involves the practice of mindfulness in forest settings has been documented to lower blood pressure and cortisol while enhancing heart rate variability (Yau & Loke, 2020). Alongside the tranquil and rejuvenating effects of islands and beaches, coastal places promote relaxation. According to Agarwal and Parashar (2024), The Island and Beach Based Model incorporates wellness activities alongside coastal settings, improving well-being on physical, mental, spiritual, and emotional levels.

1.3 Postpandemic Acceleration

The pandemic heightened the existing interest in health tourism with a nature-based approach. People traveling for personal growth prefer wellness tourism. Such tourism is gaining prominence due to the rise in ecotourism (Gounden et al., 2024). After the pandemic, there was a rise in interest in "detox" tourism, tourism with no technological devices aimed at improving the physical and mental health of the person through contact with nature. Such activities improve the ability to think clearly and manage feelings by providing a break from the stress caused by constant connectivity to the outside world (Quaye, 2025). Nature-based health tourism emerged as one of the postpandemic recovery strategies aimed at the improvement of the population's mental health. Protected areas and national parks are places where nature therapy aimed at improving productivity psychosocially through enhanced mental health is facilitated (Weir, 2020).

1.4 Therapeutic Benefits

Health tourism, which is linked to nature, provides various therapeutic solutions for holistic well-being. Activities like hiking or pursuing water-related activities aid in relaxing the cardiovascular system and reap muscular benefits while also inducing calm (Knauf, 2024). Contact with green areas improves immunological response due to lower inflammation markers and faster recovery from illnesses (Rook, 2013). The benefits of mental health encompass relief from depressive symptoms and anxiety while enhancing self-awareness and mindfulness (Davis & Hayes, 2012). Forest therapy strategies are particularly effective in aiding the development of emotional resilience through gentle forms of guided introspection in nature (Physio-pedia, n.d.).

1.5 Sustainability in Nature-Based Health Tourism

By assisting local economies and promoting conservation efforts, nature-based health tourism contributes significantly to Sustainable Development Goals (SDGs). The forest-based models accentuate sustainable practices such as eco-friendly accommodations and renewable energy-powered waste management systems (Li et al., 2023). These models also promote interactions between travelers and residents of regions that coexist with nature. Nature-based health tourism helps in global stewardship by encouraging the conservation of biodiversity through active participation and creating awareness of environmental issues (Geeta University, n.d.).

1.6 About Panch Kedar

Although Uttarakhand is a geographical marvel itself, it is not all about the geographical features of the state. Uttarakhand is special as its landscapes are where spirituality intertwines with nature.

With numerous temples and spiritual realms, Uttarakhand is also home to the Panch Kedar temples. The Panch Kedar temples hold an unparalleled significance, drawing both pilgrims and adventurers into their mystical embrace.

These five temples—Kedarnath, Madhyamaheshwar, Tungnath, Rudranath, and Kalpeshwar—are dedicated to Lord Shiva and are deeply embedded in Hindu mythology, particularly the legend of the Pandavas from the Mahabharata.

The unique aspect of the Panch Kedar temples is that they are not just pilgrimage sites for Hindus. Located at high altitudes and remote places, visiting these temples tests endurance, strengthens faith, and rewards seekers with breathtaking beauty and divine energy. That is one of the reasons why they are a perfect place for nature-based health tourism. The journey to these temples is not merely a trek through rugged terrain but a transformative spiritual voyage.

1.6.1 Mythological Significance of Panch Kedar

While the Panch Kedar temples have difficult trekking routes which is attractive to many trekkers and adventurers, it is not solely a trekking destination. The Panch Kedar temples hold deep spiritual and mythological significance in the Hindu dharma.

According to Hindu legend, the origin of Panch Kedar is closely tied to the Pandavas. After the great Kurukshetra War, the Pandavas had the burden of the sins of fratricide and killing Brahmins. To find some clarity, they sought atonement and forgiveness from Lord Shiva. Bhagwan Krishna advised the Pandavas to travel to Kashi (the modern-day city of Varanasi) as it is the abode of Lord Shiva. However, Lord Shiva was angry with the war and the killing of so many people, and he evaded Pandavas. Lord Shiva transformed into a bull (Nandi) and went into hiding in the Garhwal Himalayas, now known as Guptkashi (meaning Hidden Kashi).

However, the Pandavas were determined and pursued Lord Shiva to seek his forgiveness. In the Himalayas, Bhima, one of the Pandavas, noticed and recognized that it was Lord Shiva in the form of a bull, and he pursued the bull. As soon as Bhima grabbed its hump, Shiva, in the form of the bull, began to sink into the ground. Lord Shiva reappeared in five distinct parts of the bull's body at different locations in the Garhwal region. The five parts of the bull's body (form of Lord Shiva) are believed to be manifested as the hump at Kedarnath, the navel at Madhyamaheshwar, the arms at Tungnath, the face at Rudranath, and the hair (jata) at Kalpeshwar (Thapliyal, 2022). These five sites collectively became known as Panch Kedar, where the Pandavas built temples to honor Shiva and seek his blessings. The reason it's called Panch Kedar is because "Panch" means five, which denotes the five different body parts of Lord Shiva, and the word Kedar has many meanings, one of them being the name of Lord Shiva. Hence, the word Panch Kedar simply denotes the five names of Lord Shiva (Uttarakhand Tourism, n.d.c).

1.6.2 About Kedarnath

Kedarnath is easily the most popular temple in the Panch Kedar circuit. It is not only one of the Panch Kedar temples but also part of the mini Char Dham Yatra of Uttarakhand alongside Badrinath, Gangotri, and Yamunotri. It is also one of the 12 Jyotirlingas of Lord Shiva, the holiest shrines of Lord Shiva. Due to its religious and spiritual significance, Kedarnath is one of the most important temples in Uttarakhand. As per the data, in 2024 alone, the Kedarnath Dham was visited by 16,52,076 pilgrims between May 10 and November 3 (ANI, 2024). In terms of geographical features, the Kedarnath temple is located at an altitude of 3,586 m in the Rudraprayag district of Uttarakhand (Government of Uttarakhand, 2024). The name itself is derived from Sanskrit, where "Kedara" means field and "Nath" means lord, signifying Shiva as the Lord of the Sacred Field.

The temple holds a lot of significance as it is believed to be over 1,000 years old. The temple itself is constructed using massive gray stone slabs in the Rekha-Shikhara architectural style (Thapliyal, 2022). Kedarnath is the place where it is believed that Bhima, after a long pursuit, caught the hump of Lord Shiva who was in a bull form. The Shivling in the temple confirms this legend as it is in a form of a hump.

Since this temple is part of other pilgrimages apart from the Panch Kedar, it is also the most commercialized among the Panch Kedar temples. It has a 17-km trekking route from Gaurikund, and one can also get mules and helicopters to reach the temple. The route is full of temporary cafes and restaurants selling food items, such as fruits, packaged foods, water, and more. For those who decide to take the trekking route, the trek is both physically demanding and spiritually uplifting. The trek can take 6–8 hours to complete, but the rewards are worth it. The Aarti at Kedarnath is considered one of the most powerful and resonating experiences for Shiva devotees, capable of sending shivers down one's spine.

The temple opens at the beginning of summer and closes near Diwali every year. With the increase in tourism, Kedarnath has seen a dramatic increase in the number of visitors. While this might be good from a tourism perspective, it has also led to some issues. Since it is situated in the Kedarnath Wildlife Sanctuary, it is ecologically sensitive, and the over-construction and commercialization of the trekking route raise many issues among the locals and environmentalists.

Beyond the temple, trekkers can visit Vasuki Tal, a pristine alpine lake where Lord Vishnu is believed to have bathed on Raksha Bandhan. Another significant site is Bhakund Bhairav, located 3 km from Kedarnath, which is revered as the guardian deity of the region.

In terms of transportation facilities, visitors can get there by road, with both buses and taxis available regularly from Haridwar, Rishikesh, and Dehradun. The nearest train station is Yoga Nagri Rishikesh, situated in Rishikesh, and the nearest Airport is Jolly Grant Airport in Dehradun (Government of Uttarakhand, 2024).

The best time to visit the temple is right around May when it opens and after the monsoon season as trekking and traveling to mountains during monsoon has many risks.

1.6.3 About Madhyamaheshwar

The second Kedar in the Panch Kedar circuit is Madhyamaheshwar, which is situated at 3,490 m in the Rudraprayag district of Uttarakhand. It is also located in the Kedarnath Wildlife Sanctuary. This temple is a treat for trekkers as it offers a scenic trek of around 24 km (Uttarakhand Tourism, n.d.b). The nearest town is Ukhimath, where one can get buses and shared taxis as forms of public transport. The starting point of the trek is Ransi village.

Reaching the Madhyamaheshwar temple requires a 22-km trek, and pilgrims can either walk or take ponies. Along the way, one encounters beautiful waterfalls and panoramic views. Two km from the Madhyamaheshwar temple is the Buda Madhyamaheshwar, a high-altitude shrine that has a lake, and if the weather is right, one might also see the mighty Chaukhamba peak and its reflection in the lake from this location.

It is also the place where the Brahma Kamal, Uttarakhand's state flower, blooms in abundance. It is believed that from this region, the Pandavas ascended to Badrinath and eventually to Baikunth (heaven). The best time to visit this temple is from May to October. It is one of the Panch Kedars where trekkers go primarily for trekking, and the spiritual significance is an additional benefit.

1.6.4 About Tungnath

Next to the Panch Kedar is the mighty Tungnath. Located at 3,680 m, the temple holds the distinction of being the highest temple of Lord Shiva in the entire world (Times of India, n.d.). The temple is situated in the Rudraprayag district of Uttarakhand, and the starting point of Tungnath is Chopta, which is a hill station also known as the mini Switzerland of Uttarakhand (Uttarakhand Tourism, n.d.a). The trek to Tunganath temple is short, about 4 km, but steep and takes 2–3 hours to complete. This trekking destination is rewarding in all seasons as it offers different sceneries across seasons. During the onset of summer, one can witness the entire route covered with rhododendron forests and beautiful flowers blooming. During the monsoon season, one can witness the green scenery, and in peak winters, one can witness knee-deep snow. The temple architecture follows the Nagara style, built using stone and wood, with a statue of Nandi at the entrance.

A further 2-km trek from the temple takes visitors to Chandrashila Peak. It is believed that Lord Rama meditated here after defeating Ravana. Also, if the weather is just right and there are no clouds, one can get a 360° panoramic view of the Himalayan range. Because of the versatility of views in different seasons, easy connectivity, and the low-effort-high-reward nature of the trekking route, it is slowly becoming a popular choice for newbie trekkers. Although the Tungnath temple is closed during the Winter season, the trek stays open throughout the year. The nearest town is Ukhimath, and one can easily get shared taxis and buses to reach the town. The best time to visit is between April and October.

1.6.5 About Rudranath

Rudranath is situated at 3,600 m in the Chamoli district of Uttarakhand. Out of the Panch Kedar temples, this is the most arduous of the Panch Kedar treks. The trek has a difficult and remote 24-km terrain with steep elevation gain through dense rhododendron forests and lush alpine meadows. Here, the face (Mukha) of Shiva is worshiped.

The trek begins from Sagar village, but an alternative, even tougher, route exists from Mandal village near Ansuya Mata Temple. The landscapes along the way include meadows like Punar Bugyal and Panch Ganga, where five streams merge. The final stretch, known as Devdarshini, offers the first glimpse of the temple, making the strenuous journey immensely rewarding.

Surrounding the temple are sacred water pools or kunds, such as Surya Kund, Narad Kund, and Saraswati Kund. In the backdrop stand iconic Himalayan peaks like Nanda Devi, Trishul, and Nanda Ghunti. The best time to visit the temple is from May to September and the nearest town is Gopeshwar.

1.6.6 About Kalpeshwar

Finally, there is Kalpeshwar, which is a bit different from the other Panch Kedar temples. That is because, unlike other Panch Kedar temples, Kalpeshwar is located at 2,200 m in the Urgam Valley. It is easily accessible by a motorable road with just a 1 or 2-km walk. Since it is easily accessible, it is open throughout the year. Out of all the Panch Kedar temples, this is also the easiest one to access.

This is where Lord Shiva's hair (jata) is worshiped, naturally imprinted on a stone. The region is abundant with natural beauty, including rivers, terraced fields, and waterfalls. Unlike the other temples, which require long treks, Kalpeshwar allows even those with limited physical ability to experience the divine presence of Shiva in the Himalayas.

1.6.7 Summary of Panch Kedar

Uttarakhand is also known as "Devbhoomi," which means "Land of Gods," and has many destinations that hold high spiritual significance in the Hindu religion. The Panch Kedar is right in the heart of Devbhooomi, and these divine shrines of Lord Shiva are not only spiritually and religiously significant, but they are also perfect destinations for nature lovers, trekkers, and seekers from across the globe. The beautiful trekking routes of Panch Kedar have great potential for people who are looking for spiritual, mental, or physical upliftment through nature-based tourism. Table 9.1 summarizes the key features of Panch Kedar.

Table 9.1. Summary of all Panch Kedar Temples.

Panch Kedar Temple	**Elevation (in Meters)**	**District**	**Significance**	**Trekking Start Point and Distance**	**Best Time to Visit**	**Unique Features**
Kedarnath	3,586	Rudraprayag	Hump of lord Shiva	17 km from Gaurikund	May–October	One of the 12 Jyotirlingas; part of mini Char Dham Yatra; most visited temple of panch Kedar
Madhyamaheshwar	3,490	Rudraprayag	Navel of lord Shiva	22 km trek from Ransi village	May–October	Offers stunning views of Chaukhamba peak; nearby Buda Madhyamaheshwar has a high-altitude lake
Tungnath	3,680	Rudraprayag	Arms of lord Shiva	4 km trek from Chopta	April–October	Highest Shiva temple in the world; leads to Chandrashila peak with 360° Himalayan views
Rudranath	3,660	Chamoli	Face of lord Shiva	24 km trek from Sagar village	May–September	Most difficult trek of Panch Kedar; scenic route through alpine meadows and rhododendron forests
Kalpashewar	2,200	Chamoli	Hairs (Jata) of lord Shiva	1–2 km walk from Urgam Valley	All year	Only Panch Kedar temple accessible throughout the year; natural stone imprint of Shiva's hair

1.7 Well-being in Tourism Research

Well-being integrates various aspects such as physical health, mental health, and spiritual wellness, which collectively make a person feel healthy and satisfied in life. The Panch Kedar treks in Uttarakhand provide a unique platform for engaging with the physical, mental, and spiritual aspects of well-being simultaneously. These treks combine physical challenge and mental refreshment with spiritual contemplation, which makes them ideal for examining holistic health outcomes for private sector employees wanting a break from work-related stress.

1.7.1 Physical Well-being

Physical health refers to the optimal operation of body systems, which ranges between good nutrition, steady physical activities, balanced exercise, disease prevention, and good physical fitness (Australian National University, n.d.). Also, it is one of the primary health components that affect us in achieving daily tasks as well as coping with their stressors. Furthermore, physical well-being is crucial for the outcomes of trekking activities like Panch Kedar, as it includes high levels of cardio activities like hiking, climbing, and moving at high altitudes. These actions are constructive toward the development of cardiovascular health, muscular strength, and physical fitness (Johns Hopkins Medicine, n.d.). The ecosystem of the Himalayas offers clean air and seclusion, which could maximize these benefits by minimizing urban pollutants and augmenting respiratory functions (World Health Organization, 2021). Research illustrates that trekking in natural settings such as Himalayan Uttarakhand aids in reducing blood pressure and cortisol levels and equally serves to better heart rate variability (Kobayashi et al., 2019). The trekking of Panch Kedar in particular involves moving through thick forest, alpine meadows, and snowed-capped peaks, which can offer the participant a challenging feat but one greatly beneficial to physical health (India Hikes, n.d.). Experts have stated the reason why Uttarakhand is highlighted is because it has not been fully uncovered as a nature-based health tourism destination. Economics Economic Times, 2023 highlights President Droupadi Murmu's emphasis on the state's unparalleled prospects for medical tourism and nature-based healing practices. The President noted the state's potential due to its clean environment and naturopathy centers. These facilities are usually combined with trekking activities which offer yoga and Ayurveda-oriented recovery treatments enabling additional healing after the trek.

1.7.2 Psychological Well-being

It is defined as a self-sustaining equilibrium that allows a person to function on a productive level in relation to society's expectations. This involves an individual having emotional coping skills, appropriate and productive behavioral response, absence of negative symptoms, anxiety and depression, and the ability to relate to others as well as deal with everyday life in a balanced manner (Gautam et al.,

2024). In complete harmony with the definition provided by the World Health Organization, mental health is "within the context of the absence of mental disorder, encompasses the individual's emotional and psychological wellbeing and functioning" (World Health Organization, n.d.). The concept of mental well-being has also been further advanced by researchers by introducing eudaimonic well-being, which is centered on the cultivation of purposeful life as well as self-acceptance (Waterman et al., 2010). The peaceful Himalayan setting can be considered a natural antidote for stress as it fosters emotional resilience while alleviating anxiety and depressive symptoms. Interaction with natural environments has been shown to enhance attention and decrease mental fatigue as explained in Attention Restoration Theory (Environmental Change and Human Health, n.d.). For stressed private sector workers, the life experience of trekking in the picturesque landscapes of Uttarakhand is offered as an escape from work-related stress while enhancing their focus and calmness. The tranquil nature of the trek is associated with the Panch Kedar temples. Many pilgrims report a sense of peace as well as deep thought while trekking to these sacred areas. Studies suggest that emotions are better regulated when combining physical activity with spirituality, especially during journeys, and that such activity elicits positive feelings like gratitude (Gautam et al., 2024). In addition, increased trekking has been linked to lower levels of stress, which improves mood due to the increased release of endorphins (Mayo Clinic, n.d.).

1.7.3 Spiritual Well-being

Another critical dimension that involves finding meaning and purpose in life is through introspection or connecting with oneself on higher levels. It contains both religious and existential components: religious well-being concerns the individual's relationship to a higher power or presence, while existential well-being pertains to the meaning and purpose in life regardless of fundamental religious frameworks (Hernández & Aguilera, 2011). Spiritual health enhances integration at the level of a human's being (physical, psychological, and social) by fostering pleasant feelings of hope, vitality, empowerment, and the absence or elimination of negative feelings, like sadness and anxiety (Ghaderi et al., 2018). A wide range of practices, not limited to meditation retreats, such as pilgrimage journeys, are capable of improving spiritual well-being through self-reflection, connections with nature, or other higher purposes (Fazlan Nature's Nest, n.d.). The spiritual dimension of well-being is closely related to the Panch Kedar trek. With regard to the Shiv Kedar pilgrimage, it combines trekking with spiritual reflection as prayers visit sacred places such as Kedarnath and Tungnath, which brings the individual closer to the divine (Walking the Himalayas, 2021). Meaningful meditation retreats or even a simple pilgrimage help achieve one's spiritual well-being (Swastik Wellbeing, n.d.). This is made possible by the Panch Kedar trek, which offers a combination of stunning nature and spirituality. Historically, Uttarakhand has been considered one of the shrines of peace and healing. The Himalayas is a region that is considered very sacred in the Indian culture. Many sages have sought out knowledge and enlightenment by hiding in the deep caves of these mountains. This unique culture is one of the reasons of the increased attraction of the treks like Panch Kedar. Some traits of pilgrimage tourism suggest that such journeys foster self-transcendence because participants need to think about their goals and value systems while taking part in meaningful rituals (Polus & Carr, 2023). Another astonishing thing that has become an addition to trekking is forest bathing, one of the activities that stimulates the sensation of "awe" and connection with nature. The principles of spiritual wellness are followed through the cultivation of mindfulness and a sense of purpose (Keller et al., 2023). These experiences for private sector workers on vacation from the stressors of the city allow for deep personal reflection alongside a broader understanding of their occupational difficulties.

The holistic practice of healthcare considers the interdependence of the physical, mental, and spiritual components of a person's well-being. Taking nature therapy as an example, it has been demonstrated that being outdoors contributes to physical fitness, such as through trekking while simultaneously reducing stress, enhancing spiritual fulfillment, and boosting overall contentment through immersion in natural environments (UC Davis Health, 2023). This dynamic is also captured in greenspace visitation studies, where individuals with a strong affinity to nature reported experiencing a greater reduction in stress and anxiety while eudaimonic well-being was higher compared to those with weaker connections (Chang et al., 2024). These findings illustrate the moderating impact that personal perceptions can have on the nature-related benefits an individual is able to obtain. The body of literature regarding the health outcomes having been ever-increasingly documented with nature in regard to its exposure to humans is quite vast. Hiking is beneficial to one's health by alleviating symptoms of depression and anxiety, improving cognitive function, and boosting immune response (Jimenez et al., 2021). Even unplanned trips to natural areas have the potential to boost a person's emotional well-being (University of Minnesota, n.d.). According to Liu and Guo (2022), forest therapy models have been found to enhance cardiovascular health by lowering blood pressure and decreasing heart rate variability. There is a distinctive type of tourism that combines devotion and reverence for a particular shrine where the holistic natural setting provides psychological restorative benefits. Such journeys evoke positive feelings of appreciation while promoting deeper self-evaluation and satisfaction in life (Talk to Angel, n.d.). Transformative values gained from pilgrimage are known to profoundly strengthen psychological aspects such as engagement, relationships, meaning, accomplishment, and positive emotions (Zhang et al., 2023).

1.8 Alignment With SDGs

The Panch Kedar trek in Uttarakhand combines seamlessly with multiple SDGs of the United Nations such as SDG 3 (Good Health and Well-being), SDG 8 (Economic Growth), SDG 12 (Responsible Consumption), and SDG 15 (Life on Land). These treks are enhancing the tourists' experience on a physical and spiritual level while simultaneously fostering sustainable tourism, local development, and environmental protection.

1.8.1 SDG 3: Good Health and Well-being

The Panch Kedar trek integrates physical, mental, and spiritual facets of an individual's well-being. Cardiovascular function, muscle strength, and endurance improve from the trekking activity, which includes navigating difficult landscapes, dense forests, and high-altitude meadows (Kang, 2024). Moreover, stress reduction and relief from anxiety and depression promote emotional resilience and mental clarity. Restoration in natural environments has been associated with improved focus and a notable enhancement in mental health (White et al., 2019). Visits to sacred shrines such as Kedarnath and Tungnath help nurture spiritual wellness as participants reflect and perform temple rites, fostering a profound sense of purpose alongside connection to higher powers. The trek serves as an urban stress remedy, highlighting congruence with SDG 3.

1.8.2 SDG 8: Decent Work and Economic Growth

The Panch Kedar trek generates employment opportunities in remote villages all along the trekking route, thereby contributing significantly to the local economy. Community members are provided with employment in guiding, accommodation, food vending, transportation, and entertainment services. Trekking initiatives also enhance local residents' skill levels, allowing the development of sustainable tourism. For example, villagers' homestays offer trekkers insightful tourism and equitable sharing of tourism revenue. In addition, these practices of tourism use and development encourage long-term tourism economic growth by increasing the inflow of both domestic and foreign tourists who seek eco-friendly destinations. Tourism is regarded as a constituent pillar for balanced economic advancement in the state as mentioned in Uttarakhand Vision 2030 together with the creation of decent work opportunities for state residents (Institute of Human Development, 2020).

1.8.3 SDG 12: Responsible Consumption and Production

The Panch Kedar trek is an example of eco-friendly consumption and production patterns on account of its trekking operations, which implement green policies. Accommodations on the routes provide waste management systems and renewable energy and promote biodegradable products, which aid in the step's minimal environmental impact (Program for the Endorsement of Forest Certification, n.d.). Along the trekking routes, strategic sustainable forest management provides locals with renewable resources while maintaining natural resources. Moreover, participants are taught about sustainable living and encouraged to sustain responsible behavior during the trip with the help of awareness programs. For instance, trekkers are told to refrain from littering and use reusable water bottles (Moxtain, 2023). Such actions contribute toward accomplishing SDG 12 by "doing more with less," as these steps enhance life quality while consuming resources in a lesser quantity.

1.8.4 SDG 15: Life on Land

The Panch Kedar trek promotes conservation work in the fragile Himalayas of Uttarakhand, which helps to achieve SDG 15. Also, the trekking paths go through thick ecosystems which include forests, alpine meadows, and other regions rich with unique flora and fauna. The ecosystem is protected from the impact of over-tourism or irresponsible behavior through sustainable tourism practices. Local communities participate in conservation efforts by volunteering in reforestation programs and maintaining trekking paths to control soil erosion (United Nations, n.d.). Additionally, educational activities conducted during the trek help in raising awareness about biodiversity conservation. For example, trekkers are taught about the need to protect endemic species like the Himalayan monal and musk deer that are present along the trails (Program for the Endorsement of Forest Certification, n.d.). All these efforts help reduce biodiversity loss while enhancing the protection of the terrestrial ecosystems.

The Panch Kedar trek demonstrates how nature-oriented tourism aligns with the given SDG targets, aiding sustainable cultural and biodiversity conservation.

1.9 Research Objectives

This study aims to explore the impact of Panch Kedar trekking experiences on the physical, mental, and spiritual well-being of private sector employees.

2. Methods

2.1 Research Design

Due to the lack of existing literature on the topic, the current study used an exploratory approach. The current study is a qualitative study that integrates elements of grounded theory and narrative analysis to capture and interpret the lived experiences of participants. Grounded theory was used to generate conceptual insights from participants' narratives, while the narrative approach helped in understanding personal accounts of transformation through trekking.

2.2 Sampling and Participants

2.2.1 Inclusion Criteria

The current study selected the participants based on the following criteria:

- Private sector employees who are working for at least eight hours a day for five days a week.

- Participants with age range from 20 to 35 as this demographic is more likely to undertake challenging treks.
- Participants who completed the trek to Kedarnath, Madhyamaheshwar, Tunganath, or Rudranath without using aids such as helicopters, ponies, or luggage carriers in the last year.

2.2.2 Exclusion Criteria

Participants were excluded if they:

- had medical conditions preventing strenuous physical activity;
- visited Kalpeshwar, as this site lacks a significant trekking challenge.

2.2.3 Sampling Method

The current study utilized a combination of convenience sampling and snowball sampling to recruit participants. Initially, the participants were identified using personal networks and trekking groups, as the researchers are also keen trekkers. Furthermore, these individuals then referred others who met the study's criteria, ensuring a diverse yet relevant participant pool.

2.2.4 Sampling Size and Saturation

For the current study, the researchers conducted interviews with 10 participants, out of which 8 were males and 2 were females with an average age of 28.5 (SD = 1.90). The data collection was terminated upon reaching saturation—the point at which no new themes or insights emerged from additional interviews.

2.2.5 Participant Trekking Details

Table 9.2 describes which participants trekked to Panch Kedar to help understand the experiences of the trekkers in the findings section.

2.3 Data Collection Methods

2.3.1 Interview Procedure

Data were collected through in-person interviews. The interviews were recorded using a voice recording app for accuracy. Each interview was structured yet open-ended, allowing participants the freedom to narrate their experiences while ensuring key themes were covered.

Table 9.2. Participant Code and the Panch Kedar Site They Visited.

Participant Code	Panch Kedar Visited
Participant 1	Tungnath
Participant 2	Tunganath
Participant 3	Tungnath
Participant 4	Kedarnath
Participant 5	Kedarnath
Participant 6	Tungnath
Participant 7	Rudranath
Participant 8	Madhyamaheshwar
Participant 9	Rudranath
Participant 10	Tungnath

2.3.2 Transcription and Anonymization

Interviews were transcribed into text files using Google Docs. For seamless transcription, the responses were transliterated to Hinglish. To maintain anonymity, participants' names were not recorded. Instead, pseudonyms were assigned during transcription.

2.3.3 Interview Schedule

The current study utilized an interview schedule that had 10 open-ended questions. Each question was translated into Hindi and back-translated to make sure that the participants could understand and answer each question clearly. The questions revolved around the trekking experiences of the participants regarding their overall experience, physical challenges and aftereffects of the trek, spiritual experiences, accommodation, and more. Here is the complete interview schedule that was used in the current study:

- Kindly describe your overall experience of completing your last Panch Kedar pilgrimage.
- How do you feel when you are trekking in a natural environment away from an urban setting?
- How did interacting with fellow trekkers, locals, or temples along the route influence your experience?
- How did trekking through the Panch Kedar route impact your physical health during and after the journey?
- As a private sector employee, your work may involve routine stress. Did the pilgrimage help in relieving stress? If so, can you describe how?

- Did you experience any spiritual or transformative moments during the trek and when you reached the destination? If so, can you describe them?
- How would you describe your experience with food, accommodation, and overall logistical aspects of the trek?
- What challenges did you face during the pilgrimage/trek, and how did you overcome them?
- After returning to your normal routine, how long did the physical, mental, or spiritual effects of the pilgrimage last?
- If you had to summarize how the Panch Kedar pilgrimage has influenced your life, what would you say?

2.4 Data Analysis

2.4.1 Thematic Analysis

For the current study, the researchers used a thematic analysis approach to identify and interpret recurring patterns in the data (Braun & Clarke, 2006). The steps included:

- Familiarization with Data: Reading and re-reading transcripts to gain an initial understanding.
- Initial Coding: Assigning labels to meaningful excerpts using ATLAS.ti.
- Theme Development: Grouping codes into broader themes based on conceptual similarities.
- Refinement and Interpretation: Reviewing themes to ensure coherence and alignment with research objectives.

2.4.2 Software Used

To manage and analyze the data, Google Docs was used for preparing and reviewing interview transcripts, and ATLAS.ti was used for systematic coding and thematic development.

2.5 Ethical Considerations

2.5.1 Informed Consent

Participants were informed about the study's objectives and their voluntary participation. They were also informed that the transcript of their interviews might be shared with the publisher and other researchers after removing any personal identifiers (if any). Verbal consent was obtained before each interview.

2.5.2 Confidentiality Measures

The following confidentiality measures were taken for the study:

- No personal identifiers were recorded.
- Pseudonyms were assigned to ensure anonymity.

2.5.3 Participant Compensation

No monetary or material compensation was provided. Participants were sincerely thanked for their time and insights.

3. Findings and Discussion

3.1 Theme Development

The interviews lasted from 10 to 20 minutes. To address the scope of the study, three themes were developed that described the physical, spiritual, and mental experiences of the trekkers during their last Panch Kedar trek. The participants shared their experiences under (1) Physical Effects of the Trek, (2) Mental Effects of Trek, and (3) Spiritual Effects of Trek. An additional theme was also developed to describe other experiences during the trek. It is named (4) Other Trekking Experiences, which has three sub-themes that are (a) Challenges of Trek, (b) Experiences with Locals, and (c) Group Traveling.

3.2 Theme 1: Physical Effects of Trek

3.2.1 Major Findings

The theme covers both the physical experiences during and after the trek of the participants.

A very interesting finding from the study revealed that many participants felt physically exhausted during and after the completion of the trek. But despite this physical exhaustion, Participant 8, who trekked to Madhyamaheshwar, described his experience as,

> Jab trek complete kiya toh feel hua ki kaafi sahi laga. Pehle jo thoda muscle pain tha, woh sab dheere dheere chala gaya.

and he further added,

> same time challenging that par maza aaya.

when he described his physical experience during and after the trek. So, despite the participant feeling physically exhausted, he forgot his tiredness as soon as he reached the destination. Participant 9, who completed the Rudranath trek, said,

> Physically toh time laga thora, par uaas ki memory abhi tak hai mind me,

while describing his physical recovery. All the participants described that their body, especially legs, took anywhere from 2 to 10 days to heal completely. Participant 1, who hiked to Tungnath, described,

> It took 4–5 days for leg cramps to heal.

Apart from Tungnath, participants who trekked to other Panch Kedar temples felt really tired as the trekking routes were long. Participant 4, who trekked Kedarnath, described his experience during and after trek completion as,

> Vaha pauch ke halat aisi ho gyi thi ki vha gye, bed pakda or so gaye.

He also added,

> Physically, the entire body was fatigued. It felt like ki jahan bhi jaare hai bass vahin baith jaaye. Aisa rehta tha ki hotel mein gaye toh kahi Idhar udhar nahi jaana bass apne room pe rahe or so jaaye. Itna Jyada physically tiring tha

Expanding on the physical aftereffects after completing the trek and coming back home, Participant 4 said,

> physical effects toh main bta raha hu ki ek week tak feel hue,

and Participant 7 described,

> trek karne ke baad humne do din toh aaram kiya

after completing his Kedarnath trek. Participant 8 described,

> Physically toh ek hafta mein sab theek ho gaya.

Participant 9 said

> Jab trek complete hua, toh physically kaafi better feel ho raha tha, aur stamina bhi kaafi improve hua.

and it indicates improvement of physical abilities.

To summarize the physical effects during and after the trek, the participants faced physical exhaustion during the trek. Despite the physical challenges, the participants gained a sense of accomplishment after the completion of the trek. The recovery time for physical exhaustion varied from 2 to 10 days for different participants. Only one participant observed some physical benefit after the completion of the trek. Others simply reported exhaustion.

3.2.2 Discussion

The findings from the current study reveal that the trekking experience at Panch Kedar temples was physically demanding for all participants. Most trekkers experienced exhaustion, muscle pain, and overall fatigue. The recovery periods varied from 2 to 10 days. Despite the strenuous nature of the trek, an interesting psychological pattern emerged—participants often described their exhaustion as temporary and overshadowed by the sense of accomplishment and fulfillment upon reaching their destination.

From a psychological perspective, the findings align with the theory of cognitive appraisal (Lazarus & Folkman, 1984). In this particular case, individuals evaluate their experiences based on personal significance rather than just physical strain. Many participants, despite experiencing muscle pain and fatigue, recalled their trek with a positive emotional response. For instance, Participant 8, who completed the Madhyamaheshwar trek, mentioned that his physical exhaustion faded as soon as he reached the temple, emphasizing the psychological satisfaction of achieving his goal. Similarly, Participant 9 recalled his Rudranath trek, stating that despite the physical struggle, the memory of the journey remained strong in his mind. This suggests that the psychological impact of the trek was more enduring than the temporary discomfort of exhaustion.

Physiologically, the recovery time varied across participants, with some reporting complete physical recovery within a week while others took longer. This variability can be explained by differences in physical fitness levels, endurance capacity, and pre-existing physical conditioning.

Interestingly, only one participant (Participant 9) reported physical improvement in stamina post-trek. This suggests that while trekking has the potential to enhance physical endurance, most participants were focused on immediate exhaustion rather than long-term physiological benefits. Also, the findings from the study are not enough to conclude that trekking to Panch Kedar temples could enhance the physical well-being of individuals.

3.3 Theme 2: Mental Aftereffects of Trek

3.3.1 Major Findings

This theme captures the mental effects during and after the trek. Mental and psychological aspects like stress relief, sense of relaxation, positive vibes, and other aspects were taken into consideration under this theme. Participant 8 described their experience as,

> Har cheez mein shanti hoti hai. Koi noise, koi tension nahi hoti,
> bas bas khud mein rehta hoon aur nature ka enjoy karta hoon.

Participant 2 described,

> "Or mtlb bhut relaxed feel hota hai," explaining how the participant felt very much relaxed.

After reaching the Rudranath temple, Participant 9 described,

> Jab Rudranath ke mandir pahucha, toh pura tension bhool gaya tha.

Describing the mental aftereffects of the trek, Participant 2 described,

> mere ko lagta hai ki mental toh bhut time tak rehta hai kyuki jab bhi aap usko yaad karte ho toh aapko Accha feel aata hai.

Participant 4 described,

> agar mentally bola jaaye toh kaafi relief mila.

Participant 5 described,

> I felt a new energy and courage in my body, and I also became stronger mentally because you get to know about your capabilities.

Participant 8 described,

> Jab temple pahucha, toh ek peace mili, jo kaafi time tak sath raha.

Participant 10 described,

> Baki kaafi acha laga vaha jaa ke vo shanti jo vaha chandrashilla top me jaa ke feel hoti hai vo kahai ni hogi.

Participant 8 also described the trek as life changing by saying,

> It was life-changing, yaar.

Participant 3 described their experience after reaching the temple as,

> as soon as I reached Tungnath temple and sat for 2 minutes, I felt an invisible energy there and all my tiredness disappeared, then I completed the trek.

On the other hand, Participant 4 told his experience explaining,

> Maine Vaha jaake rudraksh dharan kiya or uski positivity mujhe har time feel hoti hai.

Another participant described on how trekking to Tunganath helped him break the stress of his work–life by saying,

> Maine jaise pehle bataya tha ki thoda getaway ho jaata hai. Jaise aap regularly call pe ho, meetings mein ho or kaam kar rahe ho toh aap kya hai ki ek cheej mein uljhe hue ho. Toh aap constantly us cheej ke baare mein soch rahe ho. Or fir aap ek baari free hoke nikal gaye to aap ghar, kaam or sabhi distractions se nikal gaye or ab aap apne time ko enjoy kar rahe ho. Toh ye ek getaway type ka hai ki aap out ho gaye or relax ho gaye. Toh Poora mind fresh ho jaata hai or stress mein bhit Accha relief milta hai. Bhut fresh lagta hai.

The majority of the participants reported feelings of relaxation, calmness, mental refreshment, peace, positive vibes, and stress relief during and after the completion of the trek. However, only Participant 5 described,

> After returning to my normal routine, it had an impact on me physically and mentally for many days,

which highlights the long-lasting mental effects. Others simply said that the memories from the trek are still with them, and they feel good remembering them.

3.3.2 Discussion

While the physical effects were short-lived, the psychological impact appeared to be more profound and enduring. Many participants reported feelings of accomplishment, mental clarity, and lasting positive memories associated with their trekking experience.

Participants reported experiencing deep relaxation, stress relief, and a sense of inner peace, which aligns with existing research on the mental health benefits of nature-based activities (Coventry et al., 2021). The trek provided a break from daily stressors, allowing individuals to feel mentally refreshed and emotionally uplifted. The sense of tranquility and calmness experienced during the trek suggests that immersion in natural and spiritual environments plays a crucial role in psychological well-being. Beyond the immediate sense of relaxation, many participants described long-lasting mental effects. The memories of the trek continued to evoke positive emotions even after returning to routine life, indicating a sustained psychological impact. Some participants also described a sense of newfound strength, energy, and courage, highlighting the transformative nature of the experience. This suggests that challenging treks not only offer temporary relief from stress but also contribute to personal growth, resilience, and self-awareness. Overall, the findings reinforce the idea that trekking, particularly in serene and sacred landscapes, offers substantial psychological benefits. Hence, trekking in natural settings can be used as an intervention for stress relief from the daily hectic work life of corporate employees.

3.4 Theme 3: Spiritual Aftereffects of Trek

3.4.1 Major Findings

This theme captures the spiritual effects that trekkers experience after trek completion. It also captures the spiritual experiences that the trekkers had during the trek. However, the results here are a bit mixed. While many trekkers did report that they did have spiritual and transformational experiences, few trekkers did describe feeling no spiritual experience at all. Participants 1, 5, and 10 reported no spiritual experiences during the trek. Participant 1 said,

> No, not at all,

while describing her spiritual experiences. Then, Participant 5 described,

> No, when I reached the temple, I did not experience any spirituality or any transformative moment.

Participant 10 described,

> Mai to trek karne gaya tha bss, to itna pta ni chala.

On the other hand, many participants did have spiritual and transformational experiences after trek completion. For instance, Participant 8 described,

> Mandir ka vibe aur wahan ka peace alag hi level pe tha.

Participant 3 said,

> Certainly, after returning from there, you feel very good for a few days, the body also feels a new energy, mentally you are also quite relaxed and the spirituality remains, if I say, then the effect remains for about 15–20 days.

Participant 8 also added,

> Lekin mental aur spiritual peace kaafi time tak rahi,

describing the long-lasting spiritual and mental aftereffects.

Participant 4 described a significant transformative experience as he said,

> main koi bhi kedar jaata hu toh Vaha jaake apni koi na koi ek buri aadat chor kar aata hu. Is yaatra ki baat Karu toh beech

> mein maine non veg Khaana start kiya tha toh Kedarnath jaake main bol kar a gya tha ki aaj ke baad main non veg nahi khaunga or tabse lekar aaj tak maine nahi khaaya toh vo ek buri aadat Maine chor di

Participant 6 also reported a transformative experience:

> But as soon as I reached near the temple, a new energy was felt inside me and all my tiredness went away.

Some participants also described the religious significance of the trek. Participant 10 said,

> Tunganath ka temple, jo duniya ka highest Shiva temple hai, wahan pahuchna ke baad apna alag ki feeling hai.

Participant 2 also described the same thing about Tunganath as being the highest temple of Lord Shiva and said,

> Toh ye hai ki Vha bheed bhi kam hai, Bhagwan ka sabse upar ka mandir hai or uske upar chandrashila bhi hai, vahan bhi kehte hai ki Bhagwan chandradev ne tapasya kari thi. To vo bhi main dekh ke aaya tha.

While some participants said that they did not have any spiritual or transformative experiences, the majority of the other participants did have such experiences. Participant 2 described,

> Or tunganath mein mujhe Accha feel hua Jaise main upar paucha,

which explains how he felt good after reaching the Tungnath temple. Participant 4 described,

> Fir jab subah uthe or mandir ke darshan hue toh vo cheej kaafi acchi lagi.

and he also added,

> Mere ko personally Bhut acchi feeling aayi or mere saath vaalon ko bhi aayi, vo bhi vahan baithe rahe. Humko late bhi ho raha tha tab bhi humne Kaha ki thodi der baith te hai.

Participant 6 described,

> But as soon as I reached near the temple, a new energy was felt inside me and all my tiredness went away.

Participant 8 described,

> Jab Madhyamaheshwar ke temple pahucha, toh ek spiritual connection feel hua.

Participant 9 said,

> Aur jo temples the, unka apna hi aura tha. Rudranath ke mandir mein, woh peace aur divine energy thi jo mujhe andar se feel hui.

All of these spiritual experiences are significant as they have a special value for each trekker. Many of the trekkers also reported a sense of connectedness to a higher power. Participant 7 described,

> Spiritual ye hai ki panch kedar mein se ek hai toh special hai.

Participant 8 described,

> Aur hn, Bhagwan se thora aur connect feel hua vaha jaa ke.

Participant 9 described,

> Especially vaha ke pujari se baat karna uaan se suan na mandir ki history aur ky importance hai uaas se eak alag he connection sa laga.

Overall, many trekkers did have spiritual experiences, and some didn't.

3.4.2 Discussion

The findings of this study reveal a nuanced and individualized experience of spirituality among trekkers completing the Panch Kedar trek. While many participants reported deep spiritual and transformative experiences, a few expressed no such feelings. This variance in experiences raises questions about the nature of spirituality, the psychological mechanisms underlying such experiences, and the role of external and internal factors in shaping them.

Spirituality is inherently subjective and varies based on an individual's beliefs, expectations, and psychological openness to transcendental experiences. James (1961) in *The Varieties of Religious Experience*, emphasized that spiritual experiences are deeply personal and shaped by prior conditioning. This aligns with the findings where some trekkers reported profound spiritual encounters, while others, such as Participants 1, 5, and 10, remained unaffected. Their lack of spiritual experience does not necessarily indicate an absence of spiritual elements in the trek but rather suggests that spirituality is an internal process that manifests differently in each individual. Another reason for this could be that some trekkers said that their main goal was trekking and not the Panch Kedar pilgrimage. Since they did not go with a spiritual mindset, they did not have any spiritual experiences. Another reason for this could be physical exhaustion. Since many participants reported physical exhaustion, it might be possible that they just got too focused on their physical exhaustion and missed the spiritual experiences. The sacredness of sites like Tungnath and Madhyamaheshwar, the temple atmosphere, and the energy associated with these places contributed to what participants described as an "aura" or a special "vibe" (Participants 8 and 9). Environmental psychology suggests that exposure to natural and sacred landscapes enhances mental well-being and fosters spiritual experiences (Md Sahak et al., 2024; Ningtyas et al., 2023). Many participants described a transformation that extended beyond the trek. For example, Participant 4 consciously gave up a habit (eating non-vegetarian food) after visiting Kedarnath, indicating a lasting impact. This aligns with research that suggests that deeply meaningful experiences can lead to long-term personal growth and habit change (Tedeschi & Calhoun, 2004). Several participants mentioned feeling a deeper connection to a higher power, particularly through interactions with temple priests or by reflecting on the historical and religious significance of the sites. The spiritual aftereffects of the Panch Kedar trek vary widely among trekkers, with some reporting profound spiritual transformations and others experiencing none. Overall, the spiritual experiences and aftereffects of the trek were widely subjective for every participant in the study. Further studies might be needed to make conclusive statements regarding the spiritual effects of trekking in Panch Kedar.

3.5 Theme 4: Other Trekking Experiences

This theme captures the experiences of participants beyond the scope of the study. These experiences are still helpful in understanding and gaining more insights about the Panch Kedar Trek.

3.5.1 Challenges of Trek

This sub-theme highlights all the physical and natural challenges of the trek in Panch Kedar. Participants who trekked Tunganath described dangerous roads to reach Chopta, which is the base camp of Tunganath. Then most participants reported having basic food and accommodation in all the Panch Kedar. Only Participant 4 described their food experience as bad saying,

> Or jo khaana mila vo toh bhut hi bura tha.

Participants also described that the trials in Rudranath and Madhyamaheshwar were quite risky as Participant seven described,

> Aapko bhut carefully chalna padta hai. Agar thoda bhi misstep hua toh Bhut acchi chot lag jyegi.

Overall, most participants reported extreme weather conditions be it monsoon, cold, or snow depending on the time they visited.

3.5.2 Experiences With Locals

This sub-theme explains the participants' experiences with locals. Most participants from the current study reported having pleasurable and good experiences with locals. Participant 1 said,

> People residing there are quite helpful and kind, living in such harsh conditions lets them know a lot of living hacks,

about locals. These were similar comments by all participants. They admired locals living in such harsh conditions and helping other people in need. However, Participant 4 described his experience with locals as bad by saying,

> As for the local people, their behavior is not good at all. Vo tourists ko tourists ki tarah hi treat karte hai. Vo ye nahi sochte ki hum itni acchi jagah par baithe hai toh trekkers ko thoda acche se treat kare. Vo unko aisa treat karte hai ki pucho Matt, bilkul bura.

But this could be a faulty interpretation as people on Kedarnath trekking routes come from all over India to do business, so there is a strong chance that they weren't locals.

3.5.3 Group Traveling

This theme highlights the importance of group traveling during Panch Kedar. Almost all the participants in the study traveled with a group and reported that group traveling helped them a lot to be motivated and also enjoy the trek throughout.

The Panch Kedar trek is an ideal case for understanding the interconnectedness of physical, mental, and spiritual well-being. It highlights how physically strenuous yet meaningful experiences can lead to deep psychological and spiritual transformations. The trek not only tested the endurance of the body but also provided an avenue for mental rejuvenation and, for many, a profound spiritual awakening.

Given the increasing stress levels in modern life, such experiences hold therapeutic potential. Trekking in natural and sacred landscapes can be leveraged as a holistic well-being intervention, particularly for individuals seeking stress relief, self-discovery, or spiritual fulfillment.

4. Implications and Recommendations

4.1 Academic Implications

The current research merges two different fields, tourism and psychology, and contributes to existing literature by bridging the gap between the two fields. This research can be used as a groundwork to expand both qualitative and quantitative approaches to tourism studies. Findings from the study can be used for new insights into the therapeutic potential of nature-based health tourism. Since the target population of the study was private sector employees, the current study also contributes to the existing literature on stress management strategies for private sector employees. It also offers a framework for future research on the intersection of physical, mental, and spiritual health. Furthermore, the current study strengthens academic discourse on the alignment of tourism research with UN SDGs, particularly SDG 3, SDG 8, SDG 12, and SDG 15.

4.2 Societal Implications

Findings from the study reveal that trekking is beneficial as it has the potential to be a holistic approach to health and well-being. For people looking to merge spirituality with physical activities, the Panch Kedar treks can be beneficial. Policymakers and planners in the private sector can also use the findings from the current study to develop trekking wellness programs for private sector employees. The findings from the current study also promote Panch Kedar as a destination for health tourism, potentially boosting the local economy.

4.3 Policy and Practical Recommendations

As of now, there is no official tourism board for the Panch Kedar pilgrimage, which makes the entire Panch Kedar pilgrimage circuit disorganized. The Uttarakhand government can establish a tourism board dedicated to the Panch Kedar circuit that will help promote these destinations all over India and the world and also help to create a better infrastructure around them. It is also important to note that the Panch Kedar temples are located in ecologically sensitive areas. Hence, infrastructure development should be done after considering all the environmental factors. Necessary steps must be taken to preserve the sanctity of these marvels and the natural environment around them.

For private sector policymakers, the managers and stakeholders can focus on organizing corporate-sponsored trekking retreats. Not only will it have a lasting positive mental effect but also allow the employees to spend time in nature and have transformational moments.

5. Conclusion

5.1 Summary of Key Findings

The three key themes developed for the current study are (1) Physical Effects of the Trek, (2) Mental Effects of Trek, and (3) Spiritual Effects of Trek. The first theme captures the physical effects during and after trek completion. Most participants reported having physical exhaustion that lasted between 2 to 10 days. But despite this physical exhaustion during the trek, the participants did have a sense of accomplishment after trek completion. The most significant findings from the study are related to the second theme, which captures the mental effects during and after the trek. Most participants reported feelings of accomplishment, mental calmness, and lasting positive memories associated with their trekking experience. This indicates that trekking can be a good intervention for stress relief and mental relaxation. The final main theme captured the spiritual experiences and transformations during and after the trek. Here, the findings differed, as many people did report having spiritual experiences and aftereffects, but some also did not have any spiritual experiences.

5.2 Limitations of the Study

(1) The study included only 10 participants, which is appropriate for qualitative research but limits the diversity of perspectives. While data saturation was reached, a larger sample could provide a broader range of experiences.
(2) Individual differences in stress levels, coping mechanisms, and outdoor activity preferences may influence the results. Additionally, those who voluntarily participated in the trek might already have an affinity for nature-based activities, leading to potential selection bias.
(3) The findings of the current study can't be generalized to a bigger population since it is qualitative in nature and has a small sample size with a lack of diversity.
(4) Since interviews were conducted sometime after the trek, participants' memories and reflections might have been influenced by other life experiences, leading to recall bias.
(5) The study relied on self-reported data, which is inherently subjective. Participants might have exaggerated positive effects or downplayed negative experiences.
(6) The study does not include follow-up assessments to determine whether the well-being benefits of the trek were sustained over time.
(7) Panch Kedar has deep spiritual significance in Hinduism. As a result, the spiritual benefits observed may not be universally applicable to participants from other religious backgrounds. The study does not explore how non-Hindu trekkers perceive the experience or whether they derive alternative forms of spiritual or psychological fulfillment.

(8) The study does not account for external factors such as personal fitness levels, past trekking experiences, or workplace dynamics, all of which could influence the extent to which trekking impacts stress relief and well-being.

5.3 Directions for Future Research

(1) Future studies should include a broader range of participants, such as government employees, freelancers, and entrepreneurs, to understand how trekking benefits individuals with different work dynamics.
(2) Future research should explore how different trekking destinations (e.g., Valley of Flowers, Chadar Trek, or Western Ghats) compare to Panch Kedar in terms of physical, mental, and spiritual benefits.
(3) Future research should adopt a mixed-methods approach, integrating qualitative insights with quantitative data (e.g., surveys and standardized stress measurement tools) for a more robust analysis.
(4) Wearable fitness trackers or mobile health apps can be used to measure real-time changes in participants' physiological states during and after trekking.
(5) Future studies should explore whether repeated trekking experiences lead to cumulative and long-term improvements in physical fitness, mental resilience, and stress management.
(6) Given the Hindu religious significance of Panch Kedar, future research should investigate how individuals from different religious and cultural backgrounds experience spirituality during treks.
(7) Future research should explore whether spiritual fulfillment contributes uniquely to mental health improvements beyond the physical and environmental factors of trekking.
(8) Studies can examine whether employer-sponsored trekking retreats result in improved productivity, reduced burnout, and better mental health among employees.

Funding

The current research did not have any funding from any source.

Author Contribution Statement

Siddhant Chaudhary—Conceptualization, Writing—original draft, Writingreview and editing, Data Curation, Methodology, Investigation, and Formal Analysis.

Saurav Uniyal—Conceptualization, Writing—original draft, Writing – review and editing, Data Curation, Methodology, Investigation, and Formal Analysis.

Prashant Kumar—Data Curation, Formal Investigation.

Raina—Investigation, Formal Analysis.

Rakesh Kumar—Conceptualization, Supervision, Methodology, and Writing—review.

Declaration of Competing Interest

The authors declare that they have no conflicts of interest related to this study.

Data Availability Statement

The transcripts of the interviews will be made available on request for research and learning purposes only.

Acknowledgments

We sincerely thank Dr. Arun Kumar, Head of the Department of Psychology at Gurukula Kangri (DU) for permitting us to conduct this study. We are also deeply grateful to all the participants for their valuable time and contributions. Additionally, we extend our heartfelt appreciation to the editors of the book for allowing us to contribute to this work.

References

Agarwal, P., & Parashar, A. (2024). Island and beach-based model: A nature-based health tourism practice at tourism destination. *International Journal of Health Management and Tourism*, *9*(2), 208–220. https://doi.org/10.31201/ijhmt.1494809

ANI. (2024, November 18). *Over 30-lakh pilgrims visit Badrinath-Kedarnath in 2024 yatra: Report*. Economic Times. https://economictimes.indiatimes.com/news/india/over-30-lakh-pilgrims-visit-badrinath-kedarnath-in-2024-yatra-report/articleshow/115402129.cms?from=mdr. Accessed on March 10, 2025.

Australian National University. (n.d.). *Physical wellbeing*. https://www.anu.edu.au/physical-wellbeing

Bhui, K., Dinos, S., Galant-Miecznikowska, M., de Jongh, B., & Stansfeld, S. (2016). Perceptions of work stress causes and effective interventions in employees working in public, private and non-governmental organisations: A qualitative study. *BJPsych Bulletin*, *40*(6), 318–325. https://doi.org/10.1192/pb.bp.115.050823

Biswas, J., & Kumar, S. (2021). Prevalence of work stress among private and public sector employees in Delhi: A differential study. *International Journal of Indian Psychology*, *9*(2), 1376–1387. https://doi.org/10.25215/0902.142

Braun, V., & Clarke, V. (2006). Using thematic analysis in psychology. *Qualitative Research in Psychology*, *3*(2), 77–101. https://doi.org/10.1191/1478088706qp063oa

Chang, C. C., Lin, B. B., Feng, X., Andersson, E., Gardner, J., & Astell-Burt, T. (2024). A lower connection to nature is related to lower mental health benefits from nature contact. *Scientific Reports*, *14*(1), 6705. https://doi.org/10.1038/s41598-024-56968-5

Coventry, P. A., Brown, J. V. E., Pervin, J., Brabyn, S., Pateman, R., Breedvelt, J., Gilbody, S., Stancliffe, R., McEachan, R., & White, P. C. (2021). Nature-based outdoor activities for mental and physical health: Systematic review and meta-analysis. *SSM - Population Health*, *16*. https://doi.org/10.1016/j.ssmph.2021.100934

Davis, D. M., & Hayes, J. A. (2012). The benefits of mindfulness: A wealth of new research has explored this age-old practice. *APA Monitor on Psychology*, *43*(7), 64.

Deloitte Global Report Team. (2022). *Mental health and well-being at the workplace: Insights into employee well-being trends worldwide*. https://www2.deloitte.com/in/en/pages/life-sciences-and-healthcare/articles/Mental-health-at-work-what-needs-to-change.html

Economic Times. (2023). *India emerging as major center for affordable medical tourism: President Murmu*. https://travel.economictimes.indiatimes.com/news/tourism/wellness/india-emerging-as-major-centre-for-affordable-medical-tourism-president-murmu/116421148

Environmental Change and Human Health. (n.d.). *Attention restoration theory: A systematic review*. https://www.ecehh.org/research/attention-restoration-theory-a-systematic-review/

Fazlan Nature's Nest. (n.d.). *5 reasons why you should go for a meditation retreat in India*. https://fazlaninaturesnest.com/reasons-why-you-should-go-for-a-meditation-retreat-in-india/

Gallup Workplace Report Team. (2024). *State of the global workplace report: Trends in employee productivity and stress management worldwide*. https://www.team-starter.com/en/blog/rapport-gallup

Gautam, S., Jain, A., Chaudhary, J., Gautam, M., Gaur, M., & Grover, S. (2024). Concept of mental health and mental well-being, its determinants and coping strategies. *Indian Journal of Psychiatry*, *66*(Suppl. 2), S231–S244. https://doi.org/10.4103/indianjpsychiatry.indianjpsychiatry_707_23

Geeta University. (n.d.). *The future of sustainable tourism: Trends and predictions*. https://blog.geetauniversity.edu.in/the-future-of-sustainable-tourism-trends-and-predictions/

Ghaderi, A., Tabatabaei, S. M., Nedjat, S., Javadi, M., & Larijani, B. (2018). Explanatory definition of the concept of spiritual health: A qualitative study in Iran. *Journal of Medical Ethics and History of Medicine*, *11*, 3. https://pmc.ncbi.nlm.nih.gov/articles/PMC6150917/

Global Wellness Institute. (n.d.). *What is wellness tourism?* https://globalwellnessinstitute.org/what-is-wellness/what-is-wellness-tourism/

Gounden, R., Munien, S., & Bob, U. (2024). COVID-19 impacts on nature-based tourism-dependent small towns: St Lucia in KwaZulu-Natal, South Africa. *Development Southern Africa*, *41*(4), 720–736. https://doi.org/10.1080/0376835X.2024.2371144

Government of Uttarakhand. (2024). *Kedarnath Yatra 2024*. District Rudraprayag. https://rudraprayag.gov.in/kedarnath-yatra-2/. Accessed on March 10, 2025.

Hernández, M., & Aguilera, A. (2011). The influence of religion on attitudes toward euthanasia. *Journal of Religion and Health*, *50*(2), 370–381. https://doi.org/10.1007/s10943-011-9540-2

India Hikes. (n.d.). *Panch Kedar Trek*. IndiaHikes. https://indiahikes.com/documented-trek/panch-kedar-trek

Institute of Human Development. (2020). *Uttarakhand Vision 2030*. https://www.ihdindia.org/pdf/Uttarakhand_Vision_2030.pdf

James, W. (1961). The varieties of religious experience. In W. James (Ed.), *A study in human nature*. Collier Books. https://csrs.nd.edu/assets/59930/williams_1902.pdf

Jayarajan, T. K., & Vasanthagopal, R. (2017). Causes and effects of occupational stress in private sector: An empirical study for Kerala. *Manthan: Journal of Commerce and Management*, *4*(2), 1–12. https://doi.org/10.17492/manthan.v4i02.11456

Jimenez, M. P., DeVille, N. V., Elliott, E. G., Schiff, J. E., Wilt, G. E., Hart, J. E., & James, P. (2021). Associations between nature exposure and health: A review of the evidence. *International Journal of Environmental Research and Public Health*, *18*(9), 4790. https://doi.org/10.3390/ijerph18094790

Johns Hopkins Medicine. (n.d.). *3 kinds of exercise that boost heart health*. https://www.hopkinsmedicine.org/health/wellness-and-prevention/3-kinds-of-exercise-that-boost-heart-health

Kang, S. J. (2014). Trekking exercise promotes cardiovascular health and fitness benefits in older obese women. *Journal of Exercise Rehabilitation*, *10*(4), 225–229. https://doi.org/10.12965/jer.140110

Keller, J., Kayira, J., Chawla, L., & Rhoades, J. L. (2023). Forest bathing increases adolescents' mental well-being: A mixed-methods study. *International Journal of Environmental Research and Public Health*, *21*(1), 8. https://doi.org/10.3390/ijerph21010008

Kil, N., Kim, J. G., Thornton, E., & Jeranek, A. (2023). Psychological and physiological health benefits of a structured forest therapy program for children and adolescents with mental health disorders. *International Journal of Mental Health Promotion*, *25*(10), 1117–1125. https://doi.org/10.32604/ijmhp.2023.022981

Knauf, S. (2024). *Water recreation: Health and fun—It must be summer*. https://www.thejoint.com/2024/06/05/water-recreation-health-and-fun-it-must-be-summer

Kobayashi, H., Song, C., Ikei, H., Park, B. J., Kagawa, T., & Miyazaki, Y. (2019). Combined effect of walking and forest environment on salivary cortisol concentration. *Frontiers in Public Health*, *7*, 376. https://doi.org/10.3389/fpubh.2019.00376

Lazarus, R. S., & Folkman, S. (1984). *Stress, appraisal, and coping*. Springer Publishing Company.

Li, C., Ahmad, S. F., Ayassrah, A. Y. A. B., Irshad, M., Telba, A. A., Awwad, E. M., & Majid, M. I. (2023). Green production and green technology for sustainability: The mediating role of waste reduction and energy use. *Heliyon*, *9*(12), e22496. https://doi.org/10.1016/j.heliyon.2023.e22496

Li, J., & Trivic, Z. (2024). Impact of "blue-green diet" on human health and well-being: A systematic review of potential determinants in shaping the effectiveness of blue-green infrastructure (BGI) in urban settings. *Science of The Total Environment*, *926*, 171397. https://doi.org/10.1016/j.scitotenv.2024.171397

Liu, Y., & Guo, Y. (2022). The effect of guided nature exposure on mental health and wellbeing in the mindful urban condition. *People and Nature*, *4*(3), 625–637. https://doi.org/10.1002/pan3.10744

Maniktala, J., & Sharma, A. (2024). Demand for green practices: Inception of sustainable tourism. In A. Sharma (Ed.), *International handbook of skill, education, learning, and research development in tourism and hospitality* (pp. 543–555). Springer International Handbooks of Education. https://doi.org/10.1007/978-981-97-4318-6_43

Marchiori, D. M., Mainardes, E. W., & Rodrigues, R. G. (2019). Do individual characteristics influence the types of technostress reported by workers?. *International Journal of Human-Computer Interaction, 35*(3), 218–230. https://doi.org/10.1080/10447318.2018.1449713

Mayo Clinic. (n.d.). *Exercise and stress: Get moving to manage stress*. https://www.mayoclinic.org/healthy-lifestyle/stress-management/in-depth/exercise-and-stress/art-20044469

Md Sahak, S. N., Roslan, S., Ahmad, N., & Zaremohzzabieh, Z. (2024). Spirituality and nature connectedness as mediators between exposure to nature and psychological well-being of school students. *Environment and Social Psychology, 9*(5). https://doi.org/10.54517/esp.v9i5.2346

Mensah, A. (2021). Job stress and mental well-being among working men and women in Europe: The mediating role of social support. *International Journal of Environmental Research and Public Health, 18*(5), 2494. https://doi.org/10.3390/ijerph18052494

Mitchel, H. (2025). *How stress impacts work productivity: 2025 insights*. Edstellar. https://www.edstellar.com/blog/how-stress-affects-employeeproductivity

Moxtain. (2023). *Waste management during trekking*. Moxtain. https://www.moxtain.com/blogs/waste-management-during-trekking

Munisi, V. I. (2025). Effects of workplace stress on employees' work performance: A case of Iringa Municipal Office in Tanzania. *Human Resource Management*, 1623–1630. https://doi.org/10.47772/IJRISS.2024.8120138

Ningtyas, R., Paddiyatu, N., Zani, B. N., & Herawati, X. (2023). The impact of nature exposure on mental health and well-being. *West Science Interdisciplinary Studies, 1*(8). https://doi.org/10.58812/wsis.v1i08.173

Physio-pedia. (n.d.). *Nature therapy*. https://www.physio-pedia.com/Nature_Therapy

Polus, R., & Carr, N. (2023). From pilgrimage to volunteer tourism: A spiritual journey in the contemporary world. *Anatolia, 35*(3), 607–620. https://doi.org/10.1080/13032917.2023.2289610

Program for the Endorsement of Forest Certification. (n.d.). *SDG 12: Responsible consumption and production.* . Program for the Endorsement of Forest Certification. https://pefc.org/what-we-do/sustainable-development-goals/sdg-12-responsible-consumption-and-production

Quaye, F. J. (2025). Digital detox tourism: Assessing tourist expectations and experiences. *Journal of Management, and Development Research, 2*(1), 11–21. https://doi.org/10.69739/jmdr.v2i1.220

Rook, G. A. (2013). Regulation of the immune system by biodiversity from the natural environment: An ecosystem service essential to health. *Proceedings of the National Academy of Sciences of the United States of America, 110*(46), 18360–18367. https://doi.org/10.1073/pnas.1313731110

Shapiro, S. L., Brown, K. W., & Astin, J. A. (2011). Toward the integration of meditation into higher education: A review of research evidence. *Teachers College Record: The Voice of Scholarship in Education, 113*, 493–528. https://doi.org/10.1177/016146811111300306

Somanchi, H. K., Rajput, H., M K, P., Rangnekar, S., & Sethumadhavan, R. (2023). Impact of nature-based tourism on physical & mental health of patients. *Journal for ReAttach Therapy and Developmental Diversities, 6*(10s), 347–357. https://jrtdd.com/index.php/journal/article/view/1123

Swastik Wellbeing. (n.d.). *Finding balance and harmony: The essence of spiritual wellness.* https://swastikwellbeing.com/blog/dimensions/spirituality/finding-balance-and-harmony-the-essence-of-spiritual-wellness-1

Talk to Angel. (n.d.). *Role of spirituality in psychological wellbeing.* https://www.talktoangel.com/blog/role-of-spirituality-in-psychological-wellbeing

Tandon, R. (2025). The silent killer: Work stress continues to claim lives of employees; what can be done? *The Economic Times.* https://economictimes.indiatimes.com/jobs/hr-policies-trends/the-silent-killer-work-stress-continues-to-claim-lives-of-employees-what-can-be-done/articleshow/113844750.cms?utm_source=contentofinterest&utm_medium=text&utm_campaign=cppst

Tedeschi, R. G., & Calhoun, L. G. (2004). Target article: "posttraumatic growth: Conceptual foundations and empirical evidence". *Psychological Inquiry, 15*(1). https://doi.org/10.1207/s15327965pli1501_01

Tetrick, L. E., & Winslow, C. J. (2015). Workplace stress management interventions and health promotion. *Annual Review of Organizational Psychology and Organizational Behavior, 2*, 583–603. https://doi.org/10.1146/annurev-orgpsych-032414-111341

Thapliyal, A. (2022, November 14). The mesmerising panch kedars. *The Times of India.* https://timesofindia.indiatimes.com/readersblog/vagabond-writer/the-mesmerising-panch-kedars-46614/. Accessed on March 12, 2025.

Times of India. (n.d.). Times travel. *Times of India.* https://timesofindia.indiatimes.com/travel/web-stories/tungnath-temple-the-highest-shiva-temple-in-the-world/photostory/108190148.cms

UC Davis Health. (2023). *3 ways getting outside into nature helps improve your health.* https://health.ucdavis.edu/blog/cultivating-health/3-ways-getting-outside-into-nature-helps-improve-your-health/2023/05

United Nations. (n.d.). *Goal 15: Life on land.* United Nations. https://sdgs.un.org/goals/goal15

University of Minnesota. (n.d.). *How does nature impact our wellbeing?.* https://www.takingcharge.csh.umn.edu/how-does-nature-impact-our-wellbeing

Uttarakhand Tourism. (n.d.a). *Chopta.* Uttarakhand Tourism. https://uttarakhandtourism.gov.in/destination/chopta

Uttarakhand Tourism. (n.d.b). *Madhyamaheshwar.* Uttarakhand Tourism. https://uttarakhandtourism.gov.in/destination/madhyamaheshwar

Uttarakhand Tourism. (n.d.c). *Uttarakhand tourism.* Uttarakhand Tourism. https://uttarakhandtourism.gov.in/tourism-circuit-details/panch-kedar-circuit. Accessed on March, 2025.

Vichhiya, P. H. (2017). A study of job stress in government and private employees. *The International Journal of Indian Psychology, 4*(5). https://ijip.in/articles/a-study-of-job-stress-in-government-and-private-employees/

Walking the Himalayas. (2021). *Exploring the divine: Best spiritual destinations in the Indian Himalayas.* https://www.walkingthehimalayas.com/post/exploring-the-divine-best-spiritual-destinations-in-the-indian-himalayas

Waterman, A. S., Schwartz, S. J., Zamboanga, B. L., Ravert, R. D., Williams, M. K., Agocha, V. B., Kim, S. Y., & Donnellan, M. B. (2010). The questionnaire for eudaimonic well-being: Psychometric properties, demographic comparisons, and evidence of validity. *The Journal of Positive Psychology, 5*(1), 41–61. https://doi.org/10.1080/17439760903435208

Weir, K. (2020). Nurtured by nature: Psychological research is advancing our understanding of how time in nature can improve our mental health and sharpen our cognition. *APA Monitor on Psychology*, *51*(3), 50.

White, M. P., Alcock, I., Grellier, J., Wheeler, B. W., Hartig, T., Warber, S. L., Bone, A., Depledge, M. H., & Fleming, L. E. (2019). Spending at least 120 minutes a week in nature is associated with good health and wellbeing. *Scientific Reports*, *9*(1), 7730. https://doi.org/10.1038/s41598-019-44097-3

World Health Organization. (2021). *Ambient (outdoor) air quality and health*. https://www.who.int/news-room/fact-sheets/detail/ambient-(outdoor)-air-quality-and-health

World Health Organization. (n.d.). *Health and well-being*. https://www.who.int/data/gho/data/major-themes/health-and-well-being

Yau, K. K. Y., & Loke, A. Y. (2020). Effects of forest bathing on pre-hypertensive and hypertensive adults: A review of the literature. *Environmental Health and Preventive Medicine*, *25*, 23. https://doi.org/10.1186/s12199-020-00856-7

Zhang, G., Huang, K., & Shen, S. (2023). Impact of spiritual values on tourists' psychological wellbeing: Evidence from China's Buddhist mountains. *Frontiers in Psychology*, *14*, 1136755. https://doi.org/10.3389/fpsyg.2023.1136755

Chapter 10

Sacred Valleys: 'The Intersection of Kullu's Cultural Heritage and Wellness Traditions'

Amrik Singh, Manoj Kumar and Nihal Kapoor

Central University of Himachal Pradesh, India

Abstract

The scenic valley of Kullu in the culturally rich state of Himachal Pradesh is renowned for its high cultural legacy and traditional healing practices, firmly embedded in its native communities. This chapter discusses how Kullu's spiritual traditions and holistic health systems – such as Ayurveda, folk herbal medicines and spiritual healing practices – interact. Local festivals and fairs such as Dussehra, Phagli and Fagli not only preserve its unique heritage but also include wellness practices that promote mental, physical and spiritual health. Vaids and Gurus, who are traditional healers, play significant roles in upholding community health through herbal treatment and traditional procedure methods. Employment of locally available herbs, Buransh, Rhododendron, Dhoop Himalayan Frankincense and Ashwagandha represents the eco-friendly and nature-based pattern of Kullu' curing process. Spiritual rituals like temple ceremonies and meditation in sacred groves also contribute to mental health. This chapter further discusses how modernisation and tourism influence these practices and thus present both opportunities and challenges. Despite growth in wellness tourism, with financial returns, it is also prone to risks of commercialisation and erosion of indigenous knowledge. Attempts at sustainability and by local communities to conserve and preserve these practices are crucial to sustaining their authenticity. Through documentation and analysis of Kullu's wellness and cultural heritage, research marks the need to integrate indigenous knowledge into contemporary wellness paradigms, ensuring that these invaluable practices are allowed to endure for generations ahead.

Nature, Wellness and Sustainability in Health Tourism, 251–279

doi:10.1108/978-1-83742-029-220261010

Keywords: Cultural heritage; custom wellness; Ayurveda; herbal solutions; fairs and festivals; sustainable tourism

1. Introduction

1.1 Overview of the Cultural Heritage and Traditional Well-Being

Traditional wellness as well as cultural heritage must be scrutinised to see how cultural beliefs, practices, and natural resources are been the root of the support of health and well-being by generations. Cultural heritage, as the inheritance of physical objects and intangible traits handed down from generation to generation, forms the core of traditional wellness systems (Smith, 2006). Cultural health, which is often based on traditional ancient knowledge and practices, includes various methods like spiritual healing, local ritual and herbal medicines, giving complete healthcare solutions that cover physical, spiritual and mental well-being (Ritu et al., 2020). Traditional health systems, which are widely prevalent in Himachal Pradesh, have remained relevant, as argued by Vidyarthi et al. (2013), because of the collaboration of 'Indigenous knowledge with the immediate natural environment. The necessity of conserving cultural heritage to facilitate community resilience and healthy practices in a sustainable form', Nocca (2017), 'while citing the interrelationship of local health implications and habits. Moreover, natural resource facets like the utilisation of hot springs and medicinal herbs have been cited in most of the above-discussed research papers, with one study being that of Sharma and Samant (2015)'. 'Acknowledge their healing value as an integral component of rural healthcare practices'. Around the world, traditional wellness systems and cultural heritage are regarded as being at the centre of contemporary paradigms in health since they provide complementary and alternative medicine (Rizvi et al., 2022).

1.2 History of Kullu Valley

'The history of Kullu Valley is thick and old, a testament to its centuries of significance in the cultural and religious life of Himachal Pradesh. The "Valley of Gods", to which the valley is famously referred, has been a hub of ancient civilisation with human settlement pre back to prehistoric periods' (Negi, 2022). 'Both Buddhist and Hindu elements have contributed to that region, where temples and monasteries have been part of the culture. There is good proof of the connection of Hindu mythology with Kullu, especially that of the God Lord Raghunath, and its subsequent existence as a part of its indigenous culture (Berti, 2009)'. 'The valley lies along the Beas River, which has historically served as a major trade route between regions such as Tibet, facilitating cross-cultural exchange of ideas, goods, and religious practices' (Gardner et al., 2002). 'The past of Kullu is also inextricably interconnected with the activities of the local monarchs and the revelation of lineal states, which have significantly contributed towards shaping the art and architectural heritage of that region' (Burchett & Rao, 2020). 'Manali is situated in the Himachal Pradesh district of Kullu, and according to Himachal tourist statistics of 2022 number of Indian tourists is 28,76,513 numbers which is the highest in the state, and foreigners are 3,706 (Kapoor & Singh, 2025).'

1.3 Evolution of Traditional Beliefs and Practices

'The origins of early practices and beliefs in the Kullu Valley reach far into its own rich historical and cultural past. Throughout the past, Kullu has worn a cultural melting pot of an oversupply of cultures stirred by the syncretism of the native traditions, Hinduism, Buddhism, and native mythology.' Given a geographic region conventionally controlled by the Himalayan Mountain range, the culture of Kullu then evolved along with the geography, including animistic ideas in addition to the resulting intermixing of Hindu and Buddhist spiritual practices (Kumar et al., 2022). The local Kulluans had their ancient healing and health practices, comprising herbal medicine and divine healing using rituals, appealing to gods associated with geography around them, for example, mountains and rivers (Kumar et al., 2021). Convergence of the Buddhist cultures, specifically with a spread of Tibetan Buddhism to the major area, brought with it a means of spiritual wellness that focused on meditation and being present, which complemented the previously practised health in the area (Manhas & Kour, 2014). Apart from that, there are traditional practices in Kullu which predominantly revolve around the festivals and ceremonies of the region, most such practices aiming to sustain the body's world and world of spirits euphony (Chundeli et al., 2021). These beliefs have been forged through not merely the indigenous habits but foreign cultural and religious flows, with impacts of Hindu temples and the immersion of Ayurveda (Sen & Chakraborty, 2015).

2. Cultural Influence in the Kullu Valley

2.1 Impact of Buddhism and Hinduism on Wellness Practices in Kullu Valley

'The impact of Buddhism or Hinduism on practices of well-being in the Kullu Valley is much wider because both of these prevalent religions have impacted not only beliefs and religion but also health and healing practices throughout the Kullu Valley.' Buddhism, whose emphasis lies in mindfulness, meditation and personal body health, greatly contributes towards overall well-being as well as mental well-being (Apollo et al, 2021). The monastic routines in Buddhist communities generally comprise yoga and pranayama, which have direct correlations with wellness routines, stressing harmony between body, spirit and mind (Namdul, 2021). Hinduism, with its broader interwoven rituals, temple healing and Ayurvedic philosophy as well, has historically conflicted with wellness routines in Kullu. Ayurveda, one of the ancient health systems rooted in Hindu philosophy, is a perfect submission to local practices where doctors practice massage therapy, natural medicine and diets for better health (Bhawana & Deepak, 2023).

2.2 Cultural Syncretism and Local Traditions

'Cultural syncretism within the Kullu Valley is a very interesting aspect of its historical and cultural development, where traditions indigenous to it are blended with other cultural roots, specifically through Hinduism's interaction with Buddhism and local folk traditions'. Cultural collaborations in Kullu have formed a separate cultural identity of sorts, with some of its arts, festivals and wellness routines showing evidence of such mixing. The region exhibits a rich and diverse cultural landscape. Halperin (2012) was a result of a blending of Hindu and Tibetan cultures, while Buddhism brought new medicinal practices. The blending is reflected in temple and monastery designs where Buddhist and Hindu symbolism blend, depicting coexistence among these two religions (Mehta et al., 2025). The local festivals, like the Kullu Dussehra, also witness this confluence of traditions where the local deity, Hindu Gods and Buddhist symbols all converge in the major and grand festival (Sharma, 2017). As Bhardwaj (2011) has also pointed out, the culture of the Kullu Valley has been shaped through centuries of trade, migration and religious contact and thus formed a space where various cultural practices converge and intersect. Other than that, traditional arts like music, handicrafts and dance decorate this gathering by bringing together Hindu and Tibetan motifs and patterns (Nayak, 2025). Syncretism has not only safeguarded the heritage of Kullu but has also enriched the people tradition, which remains a necessary remembrance in the wellness kingdom and the identity of that location.

3. Indigenous Knowledge and Traditional Wellness Practices

3.1 Definition and Scope of Traditional Wellness in Kullu Valley

'The State's Kullu valley is very diverse in terms of medicinal plants. There exists a vast scope for growth and conservation of medicinal plants, and hence integrated study on various areas of medicinal plants has yet to be done. Medicinal plants are finding applications in Unani, Ayurveda and other ancient systems of traditional medicine, and even in the pharma industries based on plants. The Himalayan species are also reliant on the Tibetan medicinal system. At least 90% of medicinal plant species have been obtained from wild sources, and up to a maximum of 69% of the material has been obtained by damaging means, an indicator that shows medicinal plants have been threatened' (Dhar et al., 2000). Oral traditions had distinct characteristics of their indigenous cultures. Medical and healing knowledge is transmitted orally from generation to generation. One of the significant factors in knowing the nature of traditional healing is witnessing healers and traditional healing in people. 'Indigenous languages and cultures around the world are rich and widely varied. It is possible that a local language understanding of traditional healing will not readily be translated into English or to other languages. Métis Elders in Canada, for a while, have described that the significance of their language (Michif) to Métis health is that it provides various views on how one sees oneself to the planet' (Robbins & Dewar, 2011). 'Canada, Australia, the United States, and New Zealand at first opposed the United Nations Declaration on the Rights of the Indigenous Peoples (UNDRIP) that recognises the right of Indigenous peoples to conserve and maintain traditional habits (Article 31). Later, however, the declaration was approved. Many projects and programs have appeared in the areas of traditional activity research since the adoption of UNDRIP' (Akbar et al., 2020). 'TEKW is recognised as being important to the preservation of global management, the biodiversity of regional resources, and the availability of locally relevant models for sustainable living. It is broadly acknowledged to apply to be equivalent to and supplementary to scientific knowledge' (Turner et al., n.d.). The total health understanding by the Aboriginal and Torres Strait Islander people puts land in high value and entails spiritual, mental, physical, cultural and cultural well-being. This overall construct is built upon the harmony between the makeup of cultural and spiritual well-being, i.e. environmental, intellectual, social, political, mental, economic and physical. It goes beyond an indication of the 'whole body' (Salmon et al., 2018). 'First search term (Aboriginal OR Indigenous OR Torres Strait Islander OR Koori OR Murri) AND (Health and Wellbeing) AND (Culture OR Law OR Country OR Community OR Elders OR Spirituality OR Language).' The second search Boolean string incorporates with first Nation, native, Inuit, Māori, or Metis. 'Culture, law, country, community, elders, spirituality, or language are also incorporated, as well as health and well-being' (Salmon et al., 2018). Both private and expedition cruise vessels regularly visit Aboriginal sites, including rock art and burial grounds, as outlined in research conducted by Smith and colleagues into the impacts of Aboriginal culture and spirituality on tourism in the Kimberley coastal waterways of North West Australia. Many business owners use Aboriginal aspects in advertising. Concerns of communities about coastal tourist activities are due to:

- the number of tourists;
- the lack of consultation with traditional owners;
- the refusal to seek permission to enter;
- the lack of knowledge about tourists' whereabouts and activities;
- the disrespect and tourist activities that damage the country.

3.2 Ayurveda and Folk Medicine Role in Kullu Valley

Around 3,500 higher plant species exist within the flora of Himachal Pradesh. Around 1,500 species are believed to possess which has therapeutic values. As Table 10.1 shows, the use of medicinal plants in the state of Himachal Pradesh and the northwest Himalayas as a whole has been the point of many studies. Some are the earlier studies from the ethnomedicine point of view are listed below.

Table 10.1. Herbal Plants of the Lug Valley, District Kullu of Himachal Pradesh.

Plants Name	**The Family**	**Common Name**	**Call it a Habit**	**Plant Part**	**Usage**
Wall Don's Trillidium govanianum Kunth	'Trilliaceae'	'Nag Chhatri'	H	Rhizome	Rhizome is eaten to treat diarrhoea and digestive issues.
(Forssk.) Polystichum setiferum Woyn	The family Dryopteridaceae	Baans	H	The Rhizome	To treat dysentery, the rhizome is wrapped around the child's neck.
Arboreum rhododendron Sm	The Ericaceae	Burnash	T	State flower	Flower juice is used to treat fever and nasal bleeding. Flower candy is also used to treat nosebleeds.
Wall, ex Roxb, is canescens by Viola	The Violaceae	Gugul phul	H	Leaf	To treat dysentery, consume 8–10 g of powdered dried leaves and flowers with tepid water in the morning on an empty stomach.
Wallr. Malva neglecta	The Malvaceae	Sunach	S	Leaf	Leaf decoration is used to treat cough and asthma.
The Hedera helix	The Araliaceae	Kermayie	C	Stem	Stem and leaf decoction is recommended for coughing.
Don 'Rumex hastatus'	The 'Polygonaceae'	Malore	H	Flower and stem	The stem and blossom juice are used to treat acne.

Source: Retrieved from Kumar et al. (2013).

3.3 Groves of Sacredness, Temples and Healing Rituals

'Tamil Nadu's sacred forests find their place in myths, folk songs, and records. Ward and Conner's memoirs, quoted in the Travancore state census of 1891, contain the earliest authentic description of the sacred groves. The Salem district's hill ranges of the Madras Presidency's sacred groves were enumerated by the Census Commissioner's Office, India, 1897, and Brandis, 1899, the country's first Inspector-General of Forests' (Ahmed et al., 2021). 'Sacred Groves to assess biodiversity's current status, various myths and beliefs concerning it, and their contribution to the conservation of biodiversity. Following oral prior informed consent initiation, semi-structured questionnaires were conducted to collect data from local study participants, particularly elderly members. Interviews were extracted from approximately 30% of the families of each SG. It is yet a matter of debate whether or not Guga was an actual person'. 'The cult's history remains mysterious. He is reported to have lived during the eleventh century, according to some sources. In the distant areas of the western Himalayas, Guga is highly venerated, for the most part, for his ability to ward off snake bites and heal bitten people. A major part, from Jammu to Siramur, is dedicated to his worship. His pictures are exhibited side by side with Nar Singh, Gugri, Pahariya, Bahmni, Bhajnoo, and Ratno at his temples, which he calls Guggamarhi. He is sometimes shown side by side with Shiva and Goarkhnath' (Thakur, 2019b).

3.3.1 Sacred Grove in the Kullu District

'Known as Dev Van (God's woodland), holy woods are sets of woods which are maintained due to religious beliefs. The stands are essential in the preservation of biodiversity because they are respected by the resident deities and fully preserved from deforestation'. Some popular Kullu holy groves include:

- '*Hidimba Devi Sacred Grove (Manali):* This ancient forest, surrounding the Hadimba Temple, is respected and untouched'.
- '*Shringa Rishi Grove in Tirthan Valley:* It is situated in Banjar (Tirthan), named after Sage Shringi, a legendary person in the mythology of Kullu '.
- '*Bijli Mahadev Temple:* Near Kullu on the Beas River's left bank is the Bijli Mahadev Sacred Grove and the famous Bijli Mahadev Temple, where lightning strikes the Shiva Lingam, meaning divine power'.

Temples and Their Spiritual Importance in Kullu:

Kullu is often referred to as the 'Valley of Gods' due to its numerous ancient temples, most of which have a close association with nature and healing traditions. Some of the famous temples include:

- '*Raghunath Temple Kullu:* The presiding deity of Kullu, Lord Raghunath, who is an avatar of Lord Rama, is revered at the Raghunath Temple in Kullu. The temple is a significant feature of the Dussehra celebrations'.

- *'Manali's Hadimba Devi Temple:* This temple is dedicated to Hadimba, wife of Mahabharata figure Bhima, and is believed to be a healing place and divine energy'.
- *'Mahadevi Tirth (Kullu):* is a powerful Shakti temple famous for its health and wellbeing prayers and spiritual healing'.
- *'Manali's Vashisht Temple & Hot Springs:* Manali is famous for its naturally occurring hot springs, which are believed to have medicinal properties for the treatment of joint and skin ailments'.
- *'Ringu Nag Forest Raila Sainj Valley*: The Forest is referred to as bun in local dialects. This is Famous for guarding trees because numerous medicinal plants are available here. A 'Hoom' festival is celebrated in this forest, which chases away negative energies'.

3.3.2 Healing Ritual and Customary Practices in Kullu

Local deities and spiritual healers (commonly known as 'Gur' in English, called Shaman or 'Malana Pujari') conduct rituals to heal diseases, ward off evil energies and attain prosperity. The significant healing rituals are as follows:

- *'Devi and Devta Shaman:* Gurs (Shamans) in some villages go into trance and deliver God's messages, guiding health and religion'.
- *'Hot Spring Therapy (Vashisht & Manikaran):* Individuals seeking a respite from illnesses are attracted to Kullu's geothermal springs, as they are believed to possess healing properties'.
- *'Animal Sacrifices and Offerings*: Even though they are diminishing in number, some temples still follow the old tradition of offering animals or symbolic symbols to the gods to appease them and ensure their protection and healing'.
- *'Dhooni (Sacred Fire Rituals*): Sages and devotees maintain sacred fires in temples and caves, which is believed to purify the body and soul. Local People also refer to it as Hoom. Example of some Popular Hoom, Raila Hoom, Dhaughi Hoom, and Nau Hoom'.
- *'Dham Healing Sacred food:* special Dham feasts are organised in certain villages as a ceremonial offering, and consuming this food is believed to have spiritual and health benefits'.

3.3.3 Ecological and Cultural Importance of Kullu

By maintaining woods and water sources, Kullu's temples and sacred groves conserve the environment as well as maintain long-standing traditions. These traditions' deep reverence for the natural world enhances the region's commitment to sustainable living.

3.3.4 Local Communities' Use of Plant-Based and Herbal Remedies

'Medicinal plants are being increasingly recognised in recent efforts for conservation and development at the international level. This can be seen in the mission and vision statement of the World Health Organisation (WHO) regarding improvement in health and community-based conservation efforts by international organisations, such as the World Bank, the International Development Research Centre (IDRC) and UNDP, for instance. The WHO's attempt to acknowledge and encourage the use of indigenous medicinal plant knowledge systems in the health industry, especially in developing nations, is noteworthy. The vocabulary regarding the use of plant medicine differed among numerous societies, states, and cultures. In its universally accepted report'. WHO defines 'traditional medicine' as 'diverse health practices, approaches, knowledge and beliefs incorporating plant, animal, and/or mineral based medicines, spiritual therapies, manual techniques, and exercises applied singly or in combination to maintain well-being, as well as to treat, diagnose, and promote health'.

Since the beginning of time, humans and plants have had a relationship. Plants have been and continue to be used by humans for fundamental everyday requirements such as clothing, food, shelter, hunting and nursing. Many societies have long placed a high value on plants, not only for their nutritional benefits but also for their therapeutic, ceremonial and magical properties – that is, their full ethnobotanical significance. Different civilisations have different applications for plants in ethnomedicine. There are an estimated 250,000 higher plant species (gymnosperms and angiosperms) on Earth (Gautam et al., 2011).

Local populations in Himachal Pradesh use a wide variety of herbs for therapeutic purposes, demonstrating the importance of traditional knowledge of medicinal plants in healthcare practices. Notable instances consist of:

- *The plant Aconitum heterophyllum,* also known as Atis or Ativisha, is native to Himachal Pradesh's sub-alpine and alpine regions. It is usually found at elevations ranging from 2,500 to 3,500 m. Its roots have long been used to cure colds, fevers, coughs, diarrhoea and dysentery. Fresh leaves are also utilised as a toothache remedy.
- *The stems, roots and fruits of the shrub Berberis aristata,* also known as tree turmeric or Indian barberry, are essential components of Ayurvedic medicine. This shrub is indigenous to the Himalayan region, which includes Himachal Pradesh. The alkaloid berberine, which has possible pharmacological effects, is found in the root bark. Traditional uses include treating skin and eye conditions, treating jaundice and using it as a natural supply of tannin and dye.
- *Saussurea species (Snow Lotus):* Several species in this genus are used in traditional Tibetan medicine. For example, Saussurea lappa is used as part of traditional Tibetan medicine, Padma 28. Studies show that Tibetan medicine practitioners in the Pin Valley of Himachal Pradesh use its roots to treat ulcers and dysentery.

- *Corylus jacquemontii (Himalayan Hazel):* The nuts are eaten by the local people, including the Pangwal and Bhot tribes of Himachal Pradesh. Aside from their edible value, the seed oil is used in traditional medicine as a massage oil to treat muscular aches.
- *Nicandra physalodes (Apple of Peru):* While non-native, it has been taken up in customary practices in Himachal Pradesh. Fresh leaves juice is utilised to treat amoebiasis, while seeds are used as an antipyretic and insecticide, treating fever, indigestion and constipation.

3.4 Spiritual Healing and the Role of Shamans

A metaphoric testament to its distinct religio-cultural and sociocultural identity is the Deity Institution of Himachal Pradesh. Originating in the Rigvedic era (1500 BC–1000 BC), the Deity or Devta system is frequently distinguished by the existence of a palanquin, also known as a Ratha, that holds an idol of the local Devta or Devi, who is seen as God's divine embodiment. In Himachal, every area or village has a resident god who is revered as the local centre of power and is seen as the presiding guardian of that particular territory. Regional communities engage in a shamanic oracle system wherein a medium, known as a Gur (shaman), serves as a conduit for invoking or channelling a Devic (divine) spirit. The Devta/Devi then speaks with His/Her subjects to either settle their grievances or bestow His/Her blessings. Since pre-modern times, Himachal Pradesh's Indigenous groups' sociocultural and religious-political structures have been significantly shaped by shamanism and deity institutions (Thakur, 2019a).

The shaman's job is to summon a good god and ward off evil spirits. He prevents the spirits from entering either his or the victims' bodies. He serves as a mediator during this procedure and is not possessed. The shaman does not experience altered states of consciousness; instead, he assists the afflicted in achieving such states. The following steps are involved in this healing process:

- Portions are made for deities and spirits to be occupied by the Shaman of specific deities.
- The other deities take their place after the Pahadiya, and the other deities look at their respective portion.
- The purpose of evil spirits is to escape.
- The victim experiences an altered state of awareness at the arrival of the deities (Daoli khel jaati hai).
- After telling Guga what happened, the victim begs for healing.
- The drum beats in time with this action, and a corresponding shift in pitch is heard.
- Until the person is cured, they are held at the temple.

4. Festivals, Rituals and Their Connection to Well-Being

Communities host festivals for several reasons, such as promoting their city, showcasing their cultural heritage, drawing tourists and giving locals access to more cultural entertainment options, all of which give them the chance to live better lives. Additionally, festivals might generate revenue to hold two communities, including increased employment, business prospects, tax revenues for governments and the creation of extra money for host towns. Additionally, the expenditure needed to organise these events can be justified by the development of new infrastructure, urban area revitalisation and facilities that locals can use for other purposes after the festival. Festivals can also aid in the growth of a destination's tourist sector by boosting visitor numbers, duration of stay and spending (Cudny, 2013; Yolal et al., 2016). These festivals and fairs give the leaders a chance to communicate with one another and give the residents of various communities a place to meet. Fairs are temporarily put up for special events at a shared location and are disassembled after the event. They serve as the main facilitators of identity consolidation and cultural preservation (Bhardwaj et al., 2017).

Festivals and rituals are an essential part of the cultural fabric of Kullu, Himachal Pradesh and have a big impact on both individual well-being and social cohesiveness.

Dussehra in Kullu

Kullu Dussehra is a popular festival that symbolises the triumph of virtue over evil and is celebrated in great splendour. The week-long Kullu celebration draws plenty of tourists, unlike in other places where the usual Dussehra celebration is a day affair. The celebration begins with a grand procession where deities from many valley temples are carried to the Dhalpur Maidan on elaborate palanquins. The different villages within the valley feel more integrated because of this celebration. The event offers a venue for cultural expression and community building through local fairs, traditional music and dance performances. By reaffirming a common cultural identity, such group participation improves social ties and enhances people's general well-being.

Maha Yagya Bhunda

Another major festival celebrated in Kullu is the Bhunda Maha Yagya, where people pray for protection from nature's wrath and prosperity. As a result of the flow of pilgrims and tourists, not only does it show the spirituality of the people but also the economic development of the region by boosting the hospitality and infrastructure industry. Social ties and a sense of belonging are strengthened by the group activity of organising and taking part in the Yagya, and these are essential components of mental and emotional well-being.

Benefits to the Social and Psychological

There are various advantages to taking part in these celebrations and customs:

Social Integration: Participating in group activities builds social networks and a sense of belonging both of which are essential for mental health.

Continuity: By commemorating customary holidays, communities can strengthen their sense of identity and ensure that cultural values and customs are passed down to future generations.

Economic Upliftment: By drawing tourists, festivals offer locals economic opportunities that improve their standard of living.

4.1 Major Festivals of Kullu and Their Significance

Festivals are a continually evolving phenomenon, which is why several sciences often study them. Because of their significant contribution to the growth of tourism, festivals should be thoroughly examined within the context of tourism geography. Festival tourism represents a distinct category of tourism that involves travel to attend cultural and religious festivals. In Kullu, a region in India, Dussehra is celebrated as a major cultural event. From a mythological perspective, it is a week-long annual congregation of Devi-Devta deities, held in mid-October. Traditionally observed throughout India, Dussehra is a religious holiday honouring two religious-mythological occurrences: the triumph of Rama over the 'demon' king Ravana and the victory of the goddess Durga over Mahishasura (Sarkar, 2023)

Kullu Dussehra: Celebrated on Vijayadashami, typically falling in October.

Significance: This week-long festival is among the most prominent cultural events in the Kullu region. No Ravana effigies are burned, in contrast to the rest of India. The deity that governs Kullu, Lord Raghunath, is revered instead. In massive processions, more than 200 village deities from different villages are transported to Dhalpur Maidan. It stands for both cultural unity and the assembly of gods. In the 17th century, Raja Jagat Singh initiated the celebration. When: February (the Hindu calendar month of Magh). Significance: Celebrated to honour the triumph of good over evil and the approach of spring. Men dance war while wearing traditional masks representing a demon being slain by the local deity.

Fagli (Faguli Festival):

When: Phalgun month, February/March. A harvest festival honouring the gods for a plentiful crop is significant. They perform traditional dances while donning elaborate costumes. Evil spirits are repelled by flaming torches and symbolic rituals.

4.2 The Role of Music, Dance and Art in Cultural Well-Being

For me, dance is an art form that is deeply significant and has a strong influence. The main issue of this book is raised by this intense passion for dance – indeed, for the arts in general – in what ways is dancing valuable? In what ways do the arts enhance human existence?

One must try to comprehend the significance of dance, whether they are committed to it for personal reasons or because they have professional responsibilities (such as being a student).

4.2.1 Music and Cultural Well-Being

Heritage Conservation: Cultural histories are conserved using old folk songs and musical instruments. Kullu's Himachal Nati music, for example, reflects the region's history and traditions.

Emotional and Mental Well-being: Two of the therapeutic advantages of music are relaxation and stress reduction. Folk and devotional music promote a sense of harmony and togetherness.

Community Bonding: Music deepens social ties as it is a common activity at festivals and ceremonies.

Identity Expression: The unique musical styles of several groups reflect their history and identity.

4.2.2 Dance and Cultural Well-Being

Festival of Life and Spirituality: Rituals and celebrations are not complete without dance. For example, the Kullu Nati dance serves as both a storytelling tool and a prayer.

Social Unity and Inclusion: At festivals like Kullu Dussehra, dance brings people together and fosters unity.

Benefits to Mental and Physical Health: Dancing releases endorphins, which improve well-being and physical health.

4.2.3 Art and Culture Well-Being

Preservation of Traditional Crafts: Handicrafts and paintings by Himachali Pahari are examples of traditional crafts that both guarantee livelihoods and preserve cultural heritage.

Therapeutic Expression: Visual arts such as painting and sculpture give people a way to express their emotions and experiences.

Education and Awareness: Art-based education ensures cultural continuity by teaching people about mythology, history and social values.

4.3 Community Gatherings and Their Social Benefits

Physical function, physical activity, social participation, self-rated health, instrumental activities of daily living (ADL), intellectual activities, frailty, functional disability, dementia and medical expenses are all linked to participation in community gathering places (Ide et al., 2023). A community that is endowed with a sizeable pool of social capital finds it easier to collaborate. This realisation turns out to have significant real-world ramifications for several issues on the American national agenda, such as how we might combat the violence and poverty in South Central Los Angeles, revive the Rust Belt's industrial sector, or support the emerging democracies of the former Soviet empire and the former Third World (Putnam, 1997).

Community gatherings are essential for fostering interpersonal relationships, upholding traditions and advancing the well-being of the whole community. They strengthen unity and support by bringing people together for social, religious or cultural purposes. 'The economic dependence on tourism can create vulnerabilities within local communities. When tourism is the primary source of income (Nag et al., 2025).'

Increasing Social Bonds: By uniting people from many communities, festivals like Kullu Dussehra allow for interactions and strengthen bonds, fostering a sense of belonging. Local fairs provide opportunities for networking, marriage alliances and business dealings.

Preservation of Cultural Heritage: Folklore, music, dance and rituals are all preserved from one generation to the next with the help of cultural gatherings. Events like temple festivals and Nati dance performances let people connect with their religious and cultural roots.

Financial Gains: Events in the community support local businesses, artists and travellers. Local economies are boosted by the opportunity for villages to sell their goods during seasonal markets and fairs.

Welfare of the Mind and Emotions: In addition to providing emotional support, social interactions during celebrations reduce stress and loneliness. Festivals provide joy, hope and group experiences, which improve mental health in general.

4.4 Traditional Healing Practices During Festivals

The goddess Ha-imb, also called Harimb, Hi-imb, or Hirm, has already been brought up about Kullu's Dasahr festival. The past monarchs and their descendants had five kul devis, including her. These five deities may be described as 'royally patronized local goddesses'. She is further regarded as the ultimate decision-maker. It is also asserted that Ha-limb 'is identical to the demon Ha-imb', the mother of Gha. 'Ithaca and the Pa%-ava hero Bh'ma's temporal consort. There are historical records to prove that a temple was built for R "j" Bahadur Singh Badani in the year 1553 between Dhungri hamlet and Manalghar, which is now known as Old Manali (Luchesi, n.d.). Traditional healing is usually practised in Kullu culture and is often integrated into celebrations. Spiritual rituals, medicinal herbs, and folk-based healing practices that have been passed down for generations are all part of Kullu's traditional healing practices'.

4.4.1 Spiritual Healing and Devta Practices

Local gods, devas, are taken out in grand parades during festivities such as Kullu Dussehra. Several approach the devta's guru (Shaman) for blessings and cures. Shamans (Gur or Chela) mediums provide advice and medical solutions, such as recital of mantras, rituals and purification methods.

4.4.2 Herbal and Ayurvedic Remedies

'Ayurvedic and herbal medicine have a long history in Himachal Pradesh, and during festivals, herbal practitioners, or vaidya, set up shops to vend natural medicines. For digestive issues, kutki and nagarmotha are used as common herbs. Shilajit with ashwagandha for strength and protection. Buransh (rhododendron) juice to maintain the heart's health'.

4.4.3 Conventional Massage and Therapy

Also, local therapists who specialise in oil massage, pressure-point therapy and bone setting are drawn to festivals. Particularly in rural regions, these therapies help people recover from joint pain and fatigue. Mustard oil and Himalayan herb massages that relax muscles are in demand.

4.4.4 Rituals Using Fire and Smoke to Purify

On occasions like Lohri and Phagli, bonfires are believed to sweep evil forces and diseases of this time out of the environment. It is common to smoke deodar, bhang (cannabis) and guggal (gum resin) to stay healthy in the lungs and not fall ill.

5. Natural Resources and How They Affect Health

Now, reframing the national health agenda relies almost entirely on well-being. Increasing amounts of proof have been found that contact with nature, exposure to it, can dramatically enhance human health. Human beings rely on nature for access to water or air (Brymer et al., 2010). 'Physical, mental and social well-being, rather than the absence of disease', was the initial definition of health proposed by the World Health Organisation (WHO, 1958, p. 1). The concept of well-being was developed by American physician Halbert Dunn in 1961 (Pechlaner & Fischer, 2006). 'Physical, mental, and spiritual health rely on natural resources.' From clean water and air to healing medicines and sacred landscapes, these resources heal, sustain and balance emotions. The high biodiversity in regions such as Kullu and the Seraj Valley sustains traditional medicine as well as general health.

Kutkii: used to promote liver and digestive health."

Ashwagandha: lowers stress and boosts immunity.

Shilajet: boosts strength and vitality levels.

Burah. helps us with blood pressure and heart health.

River Healing Water and Glaciers

'The Beas River is regarded as sacred and is traditionally used for spiritual purification in the Kullu Valley'. Beas Kund, the origin of the river Beas, is in the Kullu district of Himachal Pradesh. A mineral water from mountain springs is one of the traditional water treatments that aid in both digestion and cleansing.

Spiritual Well-Being and the Sacred Peak

The rejuvenating power of the Shrikhand Mahadev Kailash in the Kullu Valley summit. Places like Manimahesh and Chanderkhani Pass in Nager are spiritually charged. The pilgrims believe that walking and trekking in these mountains develops both physical stamina and spiritual peace, a fully physically active and young brain.

5.1 Kullu Medicinal Plants: Applications and Preservation

Herbal medicine is also practised extensively in rural areas, and most drugs continue to be locally prepared a home remedies for different diseases. More scientific evidence of the effectiveness of drugs and the fundamental principles of therapies should be demanded based on the increase in practice of traditional therapies (Vidyarthi et al., 2013). 'Indian Himalayan Region (IHR) stretches from northwestern Jammu & Kashmir to eastern Arunachal Pradesh and consists of There are eight biogeographic provinces and three biogeographic zones.' As Table 10.2, Table 10.3 and Table 10.4 showed the uses of medicinal plants are predominant in the Kullu Valley, the altitude given shows the uses of that plants, which has been utilised for thousands of years in Ayurvedic Conventional medicine. 'In Ayurveda and broader health systems, herbs constitute a central focus. However, due to overexploitation and the impacts of global warming, these valuable natural resources require urgent conservation'.

5.2 Rivers and Forests' Contribution to Traditional Health

The strongest determinant of life on the planet is likely cool water, supporting ecological health as well as each person's livelihood and way of life (Anderson et al., 2019). Mostly as a result of earlier unidimensional techniques' failure, well-being is now a concept and a proxy for the human condition (Agarwala et al., 2014). In regions of Kullu or Seraj Valley, society relies on nature for its body, feelings and soul; forests and streams have long been part of the common healthcare culture. Global well-being depends on the medical, religious and healing benefits arising from the contribution of such nature-based factors.

Table 10.2. Kullu High Altitude Medicine Plant.

Name of Application	Usage
The Jatamansi	Lowers stress and enhances memory
The Atis	Used to treat fever, coughing and stomach issues
Shilajit	Regarding strengths

Source: Author's Own Compilations.

Table 10.3. Kullu Mid-Altitude Medical Plant.

Name of Application	Usage
The Brahmi	Reduce anxiety, enhance cognitive function
The Guggul	Joint discomfort
The Ashwagandha	Utilised to alleviate tension

Source: Author's Own Compilations from various sources.

5.2.1 Forest Therapy for Physical and Emotional Health

Shinrin-Yuku (Woodland Bathing): Woodland bathing lowers blood pressure, improves mood and reduces stress. An Oxygen-Rich Setting: The deodar and pine forests release natural oils called phytoncides, which increase immunity and are extremely healthy. Peace and Quietness: The calming influence of forests promotes mental clarity and emotional balance.

5.2.2 Cultural and Spiritual Importance

Holly Groves (Dev woodland): Most of the Kullu forests are associated with local deities and are considered sacred. Rituals and Offerings: People offer prayers for health and well-being in the forest during festivals. The majority of medicinal herbs and their therapeutic benefits are based on myth and folklore.

6. The Impact of Cultural Tourism on Conventional Health Care

Culture tourism is increasingly becoming a central component of local development, especially in areas of heritage such as Kullu. Traditional wellness practices that are incorporated into the local cultural heritage have become trendy with more tourist interest in holistic and nature-based healing practices. However, the rapid increase in tourism also has its challenges, including commercialisation, loss combining customary wisdom and environmental stress (Kumar & Sharma, 2024).

Table 10.4. Kullu Low Altitude Medical Plant.

Plant of Application	Usage
The neem	Skin, blood purification
The tulsi	Reduction of stress
Aloe vera	Used to treat skin problems in humans

Source: Author's own compilations from various sources.

6.1 Growth in Kullu's Wellness and Heritage Tourism

The Kullu, abundant in spirituality and culture, has seen extraordinary heritage and well-being growth in tourism and draws in travellers with ancient temples, colourful festivities and local healing arts, such as Ayurveda and herbal antidote (Sharma, 2015). According to recent studies, tourists looking for a well-being experience in the Himalayas have seen an exponential increase thanks to global change in the direction of holistic and sustainable living (Manhas et al., 2019). Integrating cultural heritage into well-being tourism has been economically beneficial to the local populace while encouraging the conservation of traditional knowledge. Public capacity and private investment have also encouraged the growth of eco-friendly cottages and wellness retreats that offer indigenous recovery (Arora et al., 2023).

6.2 Ecotourism and Stays at Home' Contribution to Traditional Preservation

Homestays and ecotourism projects have become the main machinery for preserving Kullu's traditional wellness practices. By offering incredible experiences, homestays introduce tourists to first-hand involvement in indigenous healing practices, food and culture (Khatkar et al., 2024). Rural stays at home, owned and operated by friendly people engaged in traditional recovery practices or crafts, help maintain cultural knowledge while converting into a livelihood among locals (Saini & Singh, 2022). Eco-friendly tourism activities organised by NGOs or government schemes have encouraged organic farming, yoga and the production of herbal medicines to promote sustainable living. All these practices not only preserved traditional native means of well-being but also helped preserve the environment by embracing community-based tourism models (Sahani, 2019).

6.3 Difficulties With Commercialising Traditional Healing Methods

While wellness tourism has been promoting economic growth, commercialisation poses some threat to the authenticity and the long-term viability of conventional therapeutic methods. Tourism commercialisation is in odds with indigenous wellness practices at the cost of cultural purity in most instances. Most traditional healers are under pressure to change their practice to suit market needs, sacrificing their originality in the process (Zahra et al., 2020). Besides, 'Additionally, uncontrolled tourism growth has generated concerns regarding the overharvesting of medicinal plants, the disruption of sacred sites, and the increasing exploitation of local healers'. Moreover, there is a new wave of non-certified wellness centres diluting different kinds of common healing, reducing their efficacy and genuineness. Strong legislative frameworks that strike a balance between cultural preservation and tourism development are necessary to counter these concerns (Singh et al., 2021).

6.4 Wellness Facilities and Local Retreats

Many wellness centres and resorts in Kullu have been able to combine traditional healing with sustainable models of tourism (Oyo, 2024)..

6.4.1 Manuallaya in Manali

The Resort Spa resorts and wellness facilities in the Himalayas Luxury Manuallaya, a spa cottage in the heart of the magnificent Himalayas, offer holistic wellness programs that promote both physical and spiritual healing. Travellers can avail themselves of Ayurveda treatments, yoga and meditation and surround themselves with silence and enjoy breathtaking views of the Himalayas.

6.4.2 The Himalayan Iyengar Yoga Centre Kullu

Yogis of all ages are able to refine their practice of yoga under the tutelage of experienced teachers at the Himalayan Iyengar Yoga Centre. Situated amid a lush environment and serenity, the centre provides an environment that is supportive for novices and old timers alike to take their practice further.

6.4.3 Shreyas Yoga Resort

Escape to Shreyas Yoga Retreat and experience holistic well-being of body, mind and spirit. Personalised yoga and meditation lessons are tailored to fit specific needs, accompanied by vegetarian meals that are organic and supplemented to benefit the soul and body.

6.4.4 Ayurveda Kalmatia

Located in nature's lap, Ayurveda Kalmatia provides authentic Ayurvedic treatments and therapies for rejuvenation and healing. The peaceful atmosphere offers a serene retreat for relaxation and introduction, enabling visitors to indulge in the healing properties of Ayurveda to the fullest.

6.4.5 Ananda Himalayas Resort

Being one of the world's best luxury spa resorts, Ananda provides holistic wellness packages that combine yoga, meditation and Ayurveda. Its guests enjoy the breathtaking scenery of the Ganges River and rolling hills while adopting a holistic approach to well-being.

6.4.6 The Katoch Grand Retreat

Katoch Grand Resort offers a tranquil retreat with an emphasis on far-off well-being. There are yoga sessions, walks and other calming spa treatments offered to the guests within warm rooms furnished with the latest facilities.

6.4.7 Resort Svaastha

At Svaastha Resort, visitors can set out on a customised well-being odyssey suiting their requirements. From yoga and meditation to wellness workshops, each activity is designed for fostering equilibrium and rebirth in a relaxed ambience. Wholesome cuisine prepared from locally obtained organic foods adds to the experience in its entirety.

6.4.8 Himalayan Ayurvedic Massage Centre or Holistic Yoga School

Dive into yoga and Ayurveda tradition in the Himalayas at the Himalayan Holistic Yoga School and Ayurvedic Massage Centre. Study with certified instructors, hear about revitalising Ayurvedic massages and find the power of transformation within these ancient practices.

6.4.9 The Lama House

Get away to the Lama Home for a peaceful retreat amidst an apple garden and pine woodlands. Providing yoga and meditation sessions in a green setting, this hostel is a healthy retreat for self-awareness and relaxation. Indulge in vegetarian cuisine that is organic revives body and spirit.

6.4.10 Rainbow Home

Discover tranquillity in The Rainbow House, where Himalayan sunsets become the setting for yoga and meditation sessions. Blending in the domestic ambience with the bald landscape, this guesthouse provides the ideal location for de-stressing and rediscovery. These case studies illustrate how wellness centres are capable of aligning economic profitability with the preservation of conventional medical systems. They also illustrate the requirements for moral tourisms that ensure continued local involvement and environmental management.

7. Community Participation in Sustaining Cultural Heritage

7.1 Importance of Local Communities the Safeguarding Traditions

Local society plays a significant part in passing on cultural heritage through active involvement in local culture and knowledge transmission (Smith, 2006). Involvement of local people and indigenous groups in the conservation of heritage provides the feeling of ownership and tradition transmission (Ortiz & De Madariaga, 2021).

Community-based activities like festivals and oral history initiatives are significant in maintaining cultural practice continuity (Deacon & Smeets, 2013). Economic incentives as well as tourism planning can help enhance community involvement in cultural heritage conservation (Timothy & Nyaupane, 2009). Folk knowledge systems, conserved through local people's involvement, are vital towards safeguarding intangible cultural heritage (Harrison, 2010).

7.2 The Role of Women in Traditional Handicrafts and Wellness

'Women play a central role in maintaining and passing on Kullu's traditional wellness practices and handicrafts. Their involvement in local healing practices, such as the preparation of herbal remedies and midwifery, has maintained traditional local healthcare systems for centuries. Women artisans also play a significant role in the handicraft sector, particularly weaving the famous Kullu shawls, which are well accepted everywhere in the world for their designs and cultural significance" (Singh et al., 2019). "Handicrafts not only give economic freedom to women but also empower them socially and culturally' (Yadav & Unni, 2016). 'Conservation of weaving patterns and natural dyeing processes, controlled by women artisans, protects the art heritage of Kullu (Mehta et al., 2025). Additionally, women's participation in wellness tourism, like yoga retreats and organic herbal product manufacturing, aligns with the growing global trend towards sustainable wellness experiences' (Gupta & Roy, 2023). Although their contribution, however, is appreciated, their access to finances and markets is awkward. Policy interventions and collaborative frameworks are suggested as a mediation to enhance their participation in the heritage and tourism economy (Kumar, 2023).

7.3 Transmission of Knowledge Throughout All Generations

'Transmission of traditional knowledge in Kullu Valley is strongly rooted in oral traditional practices, apprenticeship systems, and communal rituals. Older members have a crucial role in passing wellness practices, like Ayurveda-based remedies, to younger members through casual learning and narrations' (Chattopadhyay et al., 2025). 'Similarly, handicraft skills, particularly wool weaving and handloom procedures, are transmitted through family-based workshops to sustain craftsmanship' (Thakur, 2019a). 'But modernisation and migration have interrupted this knowledge transfer chain, resulting in fears of cultural degradation' (Sharma, 2021). 'Formal education schemes and heritage documentation initiatives have been suggested as measures to fill this gap and incorporate traditional knowledge into modern learning systems' (Mandal & Mete, 2024). 'Attempts by researchers and residents to record and digitise folklore, use of medicine plants, and textile skill show the significance of indigenous knowledge systems being preserved' (Divekar et al., 2025). They facilitate intergenerational transmission and evoke the cultural awareness of the Kullu population.

7.4 Initiatives By the Government and Non-profits to Conserve Kullu Valley's Heritage

'Different government and nongovernment agencies have tried the preserve Kullu's natural as well as cultural heritage. The government of Himachal Pradesh, with the Department of Tourism, initiated programs in cultural tourism as well as handicraft promotion (Himachal Tourism, n.d.). State and central funding support heritage conservation efforts, such as the restoration of historic temples and traditional settlements' (NITI Aayog, 2023). 'NGOs such as the Himalayan Cultural Preservation Trust and women's cooperatives directly engage in upholding traditional traditions of wellness and handicraft through training and access to markets' (Ministry of Culture, n.d.). 'Intangible cultural heritage of the Himalayas has been identified as crucial by UNESCO and other global bodies, and they have also determined its importance regarding conservation policy' (UNESCO, n.d.). 'Community-based tourism systems, backed by NGOs, promote local wellness experts and artisans benefiting directly from heritage tourism while maintaining ecological harmony' (Das & Chatterjee, 2024). Despite this, issues like limited finance, untrained staff and commercialisation pressure still hinder conservation. Tackling these necessitates stronger collaboration between government agencies, NGOs and locals to develop long-term conservation programs.

8. Prospects for the Future and Sustainable Development

8.1 Using Innovation to Revive Traditional Wellness

Revitalising ancient well-being by incorporating old techniques with new science and technology entails merging ancient healing practices with new technologies and science. 'In regions such as Himachal Pradesh, this could entail the inclusion of Ayurveda, naturopathy, and indigenous herbalism into online wellness platforms, biotech research, and wellness tourism projects.' This can be realised through sustainable development by encouraging green wellness centres, organic cultivation of medicinal plants and regional community-based wellness initiatives. Evidence-based research, smart packaging and AI-based health monitoring can render it more accessible and credible. 'Integrating preservation of indigenous knowledge with innovation, traditional wellness can develop into a widely accepted, green industry that profits local communities as well as the world'.

8.2 Using Sustainable Tourism as a Cultural Preservation Instrument

Sustainable tourism plays a key role in conserving cultural heritage by encouraging ethical tourist behaviours with respect of the customs, architecture and traditions of a place. It encourages social interaction, ensuring that cultural destinations are preserved while also stimulating the local economy. 'By advocating authentic experiences, sustainable tourism aids greater appreciation for cultures, and loss of local identities due to mass tourism never happens. Activities such as green lodges, heritage trails, and artisan markets empower local craftsmen and preserve traditional knowledge. Furthermore, policies of sustainable tourism minimise the negative impacts so that cultural heritage is preserved for future generations and economic resilience is achieved among local populations'.

8.3 Digital Media's Function in Preserving and Promoting Heritage

Electronic media acts as a powerful tool in documenting and showcasing the rich cultural heritage of Kullu by conserving its cultural heritage, historical sites and folk arts. Media like websites, social networking sites and internet tours raise global visibility, attracting moral tourists and making people aware of local traditions and heritage. Electronic archives and oral histories through blogging and video make it possible to preserve oral folklore and traditions. Additionally, experiences such as AR experiences and heritage apps bring experiential education. Digital technology enables Kullu to sustain tourism, keeping culture alive and ensuring local economies greater involvement and respectful visitor engagement.

8.4 Suggestions for Researchers, Policymakers and Practitioners

'Kullu policymakers have to implement stringent waste management regulations, promote eco-tourism, and improve local cultural conservation. Incentives to sustainable business and sustainable tourism can optimise long-term economic returns'. Researchers have to research the environmental footprint of tourism, community involvement and optimal minimisation of waste. 'Practitioners like tour operators and hoteliers have to formulate environmentally friendly strategies, promote community-based tourism, and educate tourists about sustainability. Stakeholder collaboration is required to balance tourism development with nature and culture conservation to attain a sustainable and resilient tourism system that serves the environment and the people of Kullu'.

9. Conclusion

Kullu, Himachal Pradesh, is a living proof of the continued significance of cultural heritage and traditional wellness customs in framing community identity and sustainable tourism. The study has proven the complex interlinkages of sustaining cultural heritage and promoting well-being traditions in enhancing sustainable economic growth, environmental conservation and sociocultural robustness. The research lays special stress upon the fact that Kullu's cultural heritage is inescapably embedded with its religious festivities, rural handicrafts, ancient temples and traditional folklore. Such culture not only identifies the locale but also presents strong tourist attraction to individuals pursuing authentic experiences. Besides, Kullu's natural healing-based Ayurveda and yoga traditional wellness practices have been the focus of attraction in the global wellness tourism trend. 'Whole-person healing practices such as herbal therapy and meditation retreats' popularity has increased the destination as a popular health destination. The primary conclusion is that although tourism dominates the economy of Kullu, uncontrolled commercialisation and mass tourism pose critical challenges to its cultural and environmental sustainability. Cultural dilution, environmental degradation, and commodification of traditions have been reported. However, people-centric tourism enterprises, policy initiatives, and sustainable tourism practices are viable solutions for addressing such issues. Cultural Authenticity is Essential – Preservation of cultural authenticity is necessary for sustainable tourism.' Over-commercialisation reduces the purity of cultural expression and makes it less appealing to tourists who want authentic experiences. Preservation of traditional fairs, arts, and healthy living in their original state ensures their long-term sustainability. Local Community Involvement Encourages Sustainability – Direct engagement of the local community in tourism practices will enhance the conservation of healthy living and cultural traditions. 'The instant communities get involved in heritage and wellness tourism directly, they adopt these activities as their own, guaranteeing their survival and preventing outside exploitation. Kullu's rich cultural and wellness heritage offers a model for sustainable tourism that respects tradition as much as innovation. By developing cultural resilience, pro-responsible tourism, and community participation, Kullu can remain a role model for heritage conservation and wellness-focused tourism for India and the world. What is learned from this case study can be replicated in similar situations worldwide, showing that sustainable development is achievable when culture, wellness, and tourism come together synergistically'.

References

Agarwala, M., Atkinson, G., Fry, B., Homewood, K., Mourato, S., Rowcliffe, J. M., Wallace, G., & Milner-Gulland, E. (2014). Assessing the relationship between human well-being and ecosystem services: A review of frameworks. *Conservation and Society*, *12*(4), 437. https://doi.org/10.4103/0972-4923.155592

Ahmed, F., Zuk, A. M., & Tsuji, L. J. S. (2021). The impact of land-based physical activity interventions on self-reported health and well-being of Indigenous adults: A systematic review. *International Journal of Environmental Research and Public Health*, *18*(13), 7099. https://doi.org/10.3390/ijerph18137099

Akbar, L., Zuk, A. M., & Tsuji, L. J. S. (2020). Health and wellness impacts of traditional physical activity experiences on Indigenous youth: A systematic review. *International Journal of Environmental Research and Public Health*, *17*(21), 8275. https://doi.org/10.3390/ijerph17218275

Anderson, E. P., Jackson, S., Tharme, R. E., Douglas, M., Flotemersch, J. E., Zwarteveen, M., Lokgariwar, C., Montoya, M., Wali, A., Tipa, G. T., Jardine, T. D., Olden, J. D., Cheng, L., Conallin, J., Cosens, B., Dickens, C., Garrick, D., Groenfeldt, D., Kabogo, J., … Arthington, A. H. (2019). Understanding rivers and their social relations: A critical step to advance environmental water management. *WIREs Water*, *6*(6), e1381. https://doi.org/10.1002/wat2.1381

Apollo, M., Andreychouk, V., Mostowska, J., Jin, Z., Maciuk, K., Rettinger, R., & Jones, T. E. (2021). Himalayan nature-based tourism. Potential, regional diversity, nature conservation and touristic load. *International Journal of Conservation Science*, *12*(4), 1527–1546.

Arora, M., Dhiman, V., & Sharma, R. (2023). Exploring the dimensions of spirituality, wellness and value creation amidst himalayan regions promoting entrepreneurship and sustainability. *Journal of Tourismology*, *0*(0), 0. https://doi.org/10.26650/jot.2023.9.2.1327877

Berti, D. (2009). *Kings, gods, and political leaders in Kullu (Himachal Pradesh)*. ResearchGate. https://www.researchgate.net/publication/301652771_Kings_Gods_and_Political_Leaders_in_Kullu_Himachal_Pradesh

Bhardwaj, A., Pathak, R. K., & Sinha, A. K. (2017). Fairs and festivals of the Hatti community of district Sirmaur, Himachal Pradesh: An anthropological investigation. *Asian Journal of Research in Social Sciences and Humanities*, *7*(4), 359. https://doi.org/10.5958/2249-7315.2017.00290.8

Bhawana, M., & Deepak, P. (2023). Traditional ayurvedic treatment practices by vaidyas of the northern region of India. *Current Indian Science*, *1*. https://doi.org/10.2174/2210299x01666230120121801

Brymer, E., Cuddihy, T. F., & Sharma-Brymer, V. (2010). The role of nature-based experiences in the development and maintenance of wellness. *Asia-Pacific Journal of Health, Sport and Physical Education*, *1*(2), 21–27. https://doi.org/10.1080/18377122.2010.9730328

Burchett, P. E., & Rao, A. (2020). Ascetics, kings, and the 'triumphs' of Vaiṣṇavism in Mughal India: Myth and memory in the many lives of Krishnadās Payahārī from Rajasthan to the Western Himalayas. *South Asian History and Culture*, *12*(1), 53–74. https://doi.org/10.1080/19472498.2020.1843950

Chattopadhyay, K., Rana, N., Karki, S., Regmi, P., Gyanwali, P., Upadhyay, V., Bista, B., Tandon, N., Kinra, S., Biswas, T. K., Leonardi-Bee, J., Heinrich, M., Panniyammakal, J., Lewis, S. A., Greenfield, S. M., & Dhimal, M. (2025). Diabetes management using a clinical guideline versus usual practice: A feasibility trial-based qualitative study among Ayurvedic practitioners and patients in Nepal. *Therapeutic Advances in Endocrinology and Metabolism*, *17*. https://doi.org/10.1177/20420188261417088

Chundeli, F. A., Jain, M., Ramamurthy, A., & Singh, I. (2021). *Role of cultural heritage in conservation of natural environment amongst the Indigenous communities of... ResearchGate*. https://www.researchgate.net/publication/354853869_Role_of_Cultural_Heritage_in_Conservation_of_Natural_Environment_amongst_the_Indigenous_Communities_of_Kullu_Region_Himachal_Pradesh_India

Cudny, W. (2013). Festival tourism–the concept, key functions and dysfunctions in the context of tourism geography studies. *Geographical Journal*, *65*(2), 105–118.

Das, M., & Chatterjee, B. (2024). Ecotourism in Bhitarkanika wildlife sanctuary, India: Assessment of participation, economic benefits and conservation goals. *Journal of Ecotourism*, *23*(4), 589–608.

Deacon, H., & Smeets, R. (2013). Authenticity, value and community involvement in heritage management under the world heritage and intangible heritage conventions. *Heritage and Society*, *6*(2), 129–143. https://doi.org/10.1179/2159032x13z.0000000009

Dhar, U., Rawal, R. S., & Upreti, J. (2000). Setting priorities for conservation of medicinal plants — A case study in the Indian Himalaya. *Biological Conservation*, *95*(1), 57–65. https://doi.org/10.1016/s0006-3207(00)00010-0

Divekar, R., Chopra, K., Dange, P., & Mehendale, S. (Eds.). (2025). *Securing the future through sustainability, health, education, and technology*. Taylor & Francis.

Gardner, J., Sinclair, J., Berkes, F., & Singh, R. B. (2002). Accelerated tourism development and its impacts in Kullu-Manali, H.P., India. *Tourism Recreation Research*, *27*(3), 9–20. https://doi.org/10.1080/02508281.2002.11081370

Gautam, A. K., Bhatia, M. K., & Bhadauria, R. (2011). Diversity and usage custom of plants of south Western Himachal Pradesh, India - Part I. *Journal of Phytology*, *3*(2), 24–36.

Gupta, I., & Roy, A. (2023). What really empowers women? Taking another look at economic empowerment. *Journal of Social and Economic Development*, *25*(1), 17–31.

Halperin, E. (2012). *Hadimbā becoming herself: A himalayan goddess in change - ProQuest*. Columbia University.

Harrison, R. (2010). *The politics of heritage*. https://www.academia.edu/776646/The_politics_of_heritage

Himachal Tourism. (n.d.). *Culture heritage gallery - Himachal tourism official website*. Himachal Tourism Official Website. https://himachaltourism.gov.in/culture-heritage-gallery/

Ide, K., Nakagomi, A., Tsuji, T., Yamamoto, T., Watanabe, R., Yokoyama, M., Shirai, K., Kondo, K., & Shiba, K. (2023). Participation in community gathering places and subsequent health and well-being: An outcome-wide analysis. *Innovation in Aging*, *7*(9). https://doi.org/10.1093/geroni/igad084

Kapoor, N., & Singh, A. (2025). Tourism boom and environmental stress. In *Advances in hospitality, tourism and the services industry (AHTSI) book series* (pp. 133–156). https://doi.org/10.4018/979-8-3693-8347-6.ch007

Khatkar, P., Chauhan, S., & Bakshi, I. (2024). Homestays: Catalysts for eco-tourism promotion in Himachal Pradesh. *Cahiers Magellanes-NS*, *6*(2).

Kumar, S., Chand, G., & Sankhyan, P. (2013). Herbal Folk Remedies for Curing Various Ailments In Lug Valley Of District Kullu, Himachal Pradesh (N.W. Himalaya). *International Journal Of Ayurvedic And Herbal Medicine*, *3*(5), 1308–1314

Kumar, M., Rawat, S., Nagar, B., Kumar, A., Pala, N. A., Bhat, J. A., Bussmann, R. W., Cabral-Pinto, M., & Kunwar, R. (2021). Implementation of the use of ethnomedicinal plants for curing diseases in the Indian Himalayas and its role in sustainability of livelihoods and socioeconomic development. *International Journal of Environmental Research and Public Health*, *18*(4), 1509. https://doi.org/10.3390/ijerph18041509

Kumar, A., & Sharma, D. (2024). Adventure tourism development: A comparative study of Kullu and Bilaspur districts of Himachal Pradesh. *Journal of the School of Language, Literature and Culture Studies, Series*, *26*(19), 17.

Kumar, L., Sharma, V. R., & Sanu, S. K. (2022). Assessing the impact of land use land cover change in Kullu Valley: A remote sensing approaches from 1991-2021. *Uttar Pradesh Geographical Journal*, *27*(0975–4903). https://www.researchgate.net/

publication/366696705_Assessing_the_Impact_of_Land_Use_Land_Cover_Change_in_Kullu_Valley_A_Remote_Sensing_Approaches_From_1991-2021

Luchesi, B. (n.d.). *Fighting enemies and protecting territory: Deities as local rulers in Kullu, Himachal Pradesh.*

Mandal, R., & Mete, J. (2024). *A comparative study of Indian knowledge system in English textbooks of Central Board and West Bengal board….* ResearchGate. https://www.researchgate.net/publication/379054812_A_Comparative_Study_of_Indian_Knowledge_System_in_English_Textbooks_of_Central_Board_and_West_Bengal_Board_Schools

Manhas, P. S., Charak, N. S., & Sharma, P. (2019). Wellness and spa tourism: Finding space for Indian Himalayan spa resorts. *International Journal of Spa and Wellness*, *2*(3), 135–153. https://doi.org/10.1080/24721735.2020.1819705

Manhas, P. S., & Kour, P. (2014). Holistic approach to Wellness–A case study of himalayas. In *International CHRIE eBooks*. https://doi.org/10.4135/9781529710854

Mehta, R., Gale, F., Briskman, L., Wangmo, S., Cherian, S. T., & Edenborough, M. (2025). Doesn't matter if you stopped me, I've still got to chase my dream: Tibetan youth in NSW navigate racism and intergenerational differences. *Journal of Intercultural Studies*, *46*(1), 61–78.

Ministry of Culture. (n.d.). Scheme of financial assistance for the preservation and development of cultural heritage of the Himalayas. In *myScheme - One-Stop search and discovery platform of the government schemes*. https://www.myscheme.gov.in/schemes/sfapdchh#details

Nag, A., Kumar, V., Choudhary, V., Bhanu, U., Sharma, A., & Kapoor, N. (2025). Sustainable tourism in Ladakh. In *IGI Global eBooks* (pp. 317–344). https://doi.org/10.4018/979-8-3373-0427-4.ch014

Namdul, T. (2021). Re-Examining death: Doors to resilience and wellbeing in Tibetan Buddhist practice. *Religions*, *12*(7), 522. https://doi.org/10.3390/rel12070522

Nayak, S. (2025). Bridging tradition and modernity: Integrating Indian knowledge systems in higher education. *Indian Knowledge System: Interdisciplinary Approaches to Heritage, Sustainability, and Innovation*, *111*.

Negi, H. K. (2022). Linguistic demography of Himachal Pradesh. *Nepalese Linguistics*, 70–78. https://doi.org/10.3126/nl.v35i01.46563

NITI Aayog. (2023). *Improving heritage management in India*. Govt. of India. https://NITI.Gov.in

Nocca, F. (2017). The role of cultural heritage in sustainable development: Multidimensional indicators as decision-making tool. *Sustainability*, *9*(10), 1882. https://doi.org/10.3390/su9101882

Ortiz, S. L., & De Madariaga, C. J. (2021). The UNESCO convention for the safeguarding of the intangible cultural heritage: A critical analysis. *International Journal of Cultural Policy*, *28*(3), 327–341. https://doi.org/10.1080/10286632.2021.1941914

Oyo. (2024, April 15). Top 10 wellness retreats in Manali. *OYO*. https://www.oyorooms.com/travel-guide/top-10-wellness-retreats-in-manali/

Pechlaner, H., & Fischer, E. (2006).. *Alpine Well ness: A Resource-based View*, *31*(1).

Putnam, R. D. (1997). The prosperous community: Social capital and public life. *Frontier Issues in Economic Thought*, *3*, 211–212.

Ritu, N. S., GS, N. G., & MK, N. S. (2020). Traditional and Indigenous practices of some medicinal plants as immunity boosters by Folklore of Mandi district,

Himachal Pradesh. *International Journal of Ayurveda and Pharma Research*, 56–64. https://doi.org/10.47070/ijapr.v8i10.1573

Rizvi, S. a. A., Einstein, G. P., Tulp, O. L., Sainvil, F., & Branly, R. (2022). Introduction to traditional medicine and their role in prevention and treatment of emerging and Re-Emerging diseases. *Biomolecules*, *12*(10), 1442. https://doi.org/10.3390/biom12101442

Robbins, J. A., & Dewar, J. (2011). Traditional indigenous approaches to healing and the modern welfare of traditional knowledge, spirituality and lands: A critical reflection on practices and policies taken from the Canadian Indigenous Example. *International Indigenous Policy Journal*, *2*(4). https://doi.org/10.18584/iipj.2011.2.4.2

Sahani, N. (2019). Application of analytical hierarchy process and GIS for eco-tourism potentiality mapping in Kullu District, Himachal Pradesh, India. *Environment, Development and Sustainability*, *22*(7), 6187–6211. https://doi.org/10.1007/s10668-019-00470-w

Saini, N., & Singh, K. (2022). A study of determinants affecting homestay tourism in Kullu. *Specialusis Ugdymas*, *1*(43).

Salmon, M., Doery, K., Dance, P., Chapman, J., Gilbert, R., Williams, R., & Lovett, R. (2018). *Defining the indefinable: Descriptors of Aboriginal and Torres Strait Islander peoples' cultures and their links to health and wellbeing*. https://open-research-repository.anu.edu.au/items/e772daa7-ab69-45f8-a3c7-339d61055f9e

Sarkar, D. (2023). *Ritualizing politics and politicizing ritual: A Study of Kullu Dussehra*. Contemporary Voice of Dalit. https://doi.org/10.1177/2455328X231205396

Sen, S., & Chakraborty, R. (2015). Toward the integration and advancement of herbal medicine: A focus on traditional Indian medicine. *Botanics: Targets and Therapy*, *33*. https://doi.org/10.2147/btat.s66308

Sharma, A. (2015). *Exploring heritage of a hill state - Himachal Pradesh, in India*. DOAJ (DOAJ: Directory of Open Access Journals). https://doi.org/10.6092/issn.2036-5195/4840

Sharma, V. P. (2021). Displacement, environment and tribal life. *Development, Displacement & Tribal Life*, *65*.

Sharma, P., & Samant, S. (2015). Diversity, distribution and Indigenous uses of medicinal plants in Parbati Valley of Kullu district in Himachal Pradesh, Northwestern Himalaya. *Journal of Medical Biomedical & Applied Sciences*, *1*. https://doi.org/10.15520/.v1i0.6

Sharma, P., & Samant (2017). Diversity, distribution, Indigenous uses and conservation of orchids in Parvati Valley of Kullu District, Himachal Pradesh, Northwestern Himalaya. *Journal of Biodiversity & Endangered Species*, *05*(01). https://doi.org/10.4172/2332-2543.1000177

Singh, Anand, P., & Bhasin, A. (2019). Weaving social development: An exploratory study of adapting traditional textiles using Indigenous organic wool for the modern interior textiles market. *International Journal of Materials and Textile Engineering*, *13*(2). https://www.academia.edu/94589018/Weaving_Social_Development_An_Exploratory_Study_of_Adapting_Traditional_Textiles_Using_Indigenous_Organic_Wool_for_the_Modern_Interior_Textiles_Market

Singh, C., Chauhan, N., Upadhyay, S. K., Singh, R., & Rani, A. (2021). The Himalayan natural resources: Challenges and conservation for sustainable development. *Journal of Pharmacognosy and Phytochemistry*, 1643–1648.

Smith, L. (2006). *Uses of heritage*. Routledge.

Thakur, A. (2019a). Influence of deity institution and shamanic traditions on social structure of Himachal Pradesh. *Sociological Society, Himachal Pradesh (SSHP)*. https://www.academia.edu/40829113/Influence_of_Deity_Institution_and_Shamanic_Traditions_on_Social_Structure_of_Himachal_Pradesh

Thakur, D. (2019b). *Marginalisation, caste, and healing: A study of the Guga cult in Western Himachal Pradesh* (Bachelor's thesis). Panjab University.

Timothy, D. J., & Nyaupane, G. P. (Eds.). (2009). *Cultural heritage and tourism in the developing world*. Routledge.

Turner, N. J., Ignace, M. B., & Ignace, R. (n.d.). Traditional ecological knowledge and wisdom of aboriginal peoples in British Columbia. *Ecological Society of America*, *10*(5).

UNESCO. (n.d.). *UNESCO - Browse the lists of intangible cultural heritage and the register of good safeguarding practices*. https://ich.unesco.org/en/lists

Vidyarthi, S., Samant, S. S., & Sharma, P. (2013). Traditional and indigenous uses of medicinal plants by local residents in Himachal Pradesh, North Western Himalaya, India. *International Journal of Biodiversity Science, Ecosystem Services & Management*, *9*(3), 185–200. https://doi.org/10.1080/21513732.2013.823113

Yadav, V., & Unni, J. (2016). Women entrepreneurship: Research review and future directions. *Journal of Global Entrepreneurship Research*, *6*(1). https://doi.org/10.1186/s40497-016-0055-x

Yolal, M., Gursoy, D., Uysal, M., Kim, H. (Lina), & Karacaoğlu, S. (2016). Impacts of festivals and events on residents' well-being. *Annals of Tourism Research*, *61*, 1–18. https://doi.org/10.1016/j.annals.2016.07.008

Zahra, W., Rai, S. N., Birla, H., Singh, S. S., Rathore, A. S., Dilnashin, H., Keswani, C., & Singh, S. P. (2020). Economic importance of medicinal plants in Asian countries. *Bioeconomy for sustainable development*, 359–377.

Chapter 11

An Explorative Study on Traditional Wellness Practices Preserving and Promoting Cultural Heritage Tourism in Garhwal Mandal, Uttarakhand

Ashish Kumar[a], *Arunesh Parashar*[a], *Monika Pandey*[a], *Avanendu Parashar*[a] *and Ajay Bhardwaj*[b]

[a]Dev Sanskriti Vishwavidyalya, India
[b]Amity University Jaipur, India

Abstract

Uttarakhand's Garhwal region is believed to be the storehouse of traditional wellness practices, enriched with cultural heritage rooted in wisdom since centuries. This chapter studies the relationship between the indigenous wellness practices with the region's cultural heritage, popularizing their social, historical, and therapeutic importance at global level. After diving deep into the various cultural norms, traditional medicine systems, and spiritual activities of Garhwal, the study aims to underscore the significance of preservation of this heritage in the modern context. The conclusion gives a suggestion that uniting all these activities and practices into contemporary wellness context, it can offer holistic well-being tips, thereby sustaining the culture and preserving the Indigeneity of wellness tourism.

Keywords: Garhwal mandal; cultural heritage; wellness tourism; ayurveda; yoga and herbal medicine; sustainability; Himalayan traditions

Nature, Wellness and Sustainability in Health Tourism, 281–291

doi:10.1108/978-1-83742-029-220261011

1. Introduction

Nestled in the lap of the Himalayas, the origin point of many rivers, Garhwal region is not only famous for its scenic beauty but also for its cultural and spiritual significance (Negi, 2012). Uttarakhand is also known as "Land of Gods" (Devbhoomi). Garhwal being an important part of this Devbhoomi, it is Garh (confluence) of ancient temples, rituals, festivals, and traditional wellness tourism practices that continue to influence the lives of its inhabitants (Sharma, 2015). The aim of the chapter is to compile and do the analysis of the entire cultural heritage as well as the traditional wellness practices (yoga, Ayurveda and herbal medicines) of the region of Garhwal Himalayas, focusing its relevance in the modern society and its trends in current situations.

2. Traditional Wellness Practices

Traditional wellness practices include the healing of the entire body, mind, and soul. Traditional methods of wellness actually include a diverse range of holistic healing methods that help in maintaining the natural balance totally based on the strategies, which are natural and as per our life cycle. The balance between the three doshas (Vata, Pitta and Kapha) is what Ayurveda emphasizes, and this knowledge originated in India. It incorporates herbal medicine, yoga, and detox therapies like Panchakarma, naturopathy, and acupressure (Sharma, 2015). Traditional Ayurvedic Medicine (TAM) is based on the concept of Qi (vital energy) and Charak balance, utilizing acupuncture, herbal remedies, and spa treatments for overall well-being (Pant & Joshi, 2018). Unani medicine, with roots in Persia and Greece, focuses on balancing bodily humors through herbal treatments, diet regulation, and massage therapies (Negi, 2012). Naturopathy, influenced by various global traditions, promotes self-healing through natural methods like fasting, hydrotherapy, and lifestyle adjustments (Jain & Gupta, 2020). Yoga and meditation, deeply rooted in Indian tradition and Indian philosophy, enhances physical, mental, and spiritual health through postures, breath control, and mindfulness (Singh & Negi, 2020). Indigenous healing practices worldwide incorporate herbal medicine, spiritual rituals, and energy-based therapies such as Reiki and Shamanism (Gairola, 2019). Homeopathy, developed in Germany, uses highly diluted natural substances to stimulate the body's healing processes while Siddha medicine from South India relies on herbs, minerals, and yogic practices for holistic wellness (Pandey & Chauhan, 2022). These time-tested traditional practices continue to be valued for their natural and preventive approach to the health and well-being of individual tourists (Mishra, 2021).

3. Indigenous Medicine Systems

Garhwal's traditional wellness practices are rooted in Ayurveda and local herbal medicine systems. Various medicinal plants like Brahmi, Ashwagandha, Shilajit, etc. are found in majority in the region of Garhwal, which are actually the base of indigenous medicine system (Bisht, 2017). Local healers, known as Vaidyas, utilize these herbs to prepare remedies for various ailments (Pandey & Chauhan, 2022). The practice of Jaddi-Buti (herbal medicine) is a significant aspect of Garhwal's wellness culture, often accompanied by rituals and prayers, highlighting the spiritual dimension of healing (Gairola, 2019). In Indigenous medicine systems, both "Duwa" means blessings and "Dawa" means Medicine, and both work together. This is the beauty of Indigenous Medicine system.

4. Yoga and Spiritual Practices

Rishikesh, referred to as the "Yoga Capital of the World", is known for Yoga and meditation all over the globe. People Visit Garhwal regions' Rishikesh, especially to learn and experience yoga and meditation (Singh & Negi, 2020). The region's ashrams and spiritual retreats draw seekers from around the globe, offering practices that promote physical, mental, and spiritual well-being (Mishra, 2021). Meditation techniques taught in Garhwal often incorporate elements of mindfulness and nature therapy, leveraging the serene Himalayan environment to enhance their effectiveness. People get healed just by coming to this region of Garhwal and staying here for a few days in the lap of Nature and River Ganga (Chauhan, 2020).

5. Dietary Practices and Nutrition

The traditional diet of Garhwal, consisting of millets, lentils, and local greens, is inherently nutritious and eco-friendly, which totally supports the health and wellness of an individual visiting the place (Joshi & Sharma, 2020). Dishes like Mandua ki Roti (finger millet bread) and Jhangora ki Kheer (barnyard millet pudding) exemplify sustainable dietary habits that align with contemporary wellness trends (Negi, 2012). These trends actually boost the health and holistic wellness of tourists.

6. Interplay Between Culture and Wellness

Garhwal's cultural heritage and wellness practices are deeply interconnected. We can say both are assets of the same coin. Festivals often include rituals that promote physical and mental health, such as fasting and detoxification during Navratri. Fasting is also practiced during Ekadashi and various good occasions (Sharma, 2015). Similarly, local music and dance forms are not only entertainment but also therapeutic practices that foster community bonding and emotional well-being. Food, music, and environment all together constitute in making someone heal as if it's providing therapy to the individual tourists (Kapoor & Bhardwaj, 2021). Culture of Garhwal is so cooperative and filled with love and welcoming gestures that it automatically fosters wellness altogether. The spiritual ethos of Garhwal, emphasizing harmony with nature, aligns with modern principles of sustainable living and holistic health (Tripathi, 2019).

7. Cultural Heritage of Garhwal

In Garhwal, we can witness the mix of traditions, festivals, rituals, folklore, local art, dance, music, and all religious practices enclosed in the lap of Himalaya. When we talk about Himalaya, it's always taken with pride and with a spiritual importance as its home of all the four Dham of Uttarakhand (Yamunotri, Gangotri, Kedarnath, and Badrinath), which is actually the four important pillars of Uttarakhand Culture. Along with Hindu temples, it's home to Sikhs most important gurudwara Hemkunt Sahib. In Garhwal region, Local Folk traditions play an important role in preserving the actual essence of Garhwal by preserving the garhwali music, garhwali dance forms like Barada Nati, Pandav Nritya, Langvir Nritya, etc., which reflects the history of the region and its devotion to art and cultural forms. Festivals like Harela, Phool Dei, Ghee Sankranti, etc. depict the Garhwal rich cultural heritage, which marks the agricultural beginning and closing cycle and also explains the various seasonal changes being celebrated in the form of festivals related to environmental wellness. Men wear dhoti kurta, and women prefer Ghagri, which depicts the traditional attire of the region along with its unique jewelry items of silver, which reflects the identity of Garhwal culture. The authenticity of Himalaya as head of India is being preserved and sustained in the Garhwal region. This entire area is also famous for its handicrafts, particularly woolen weaved clothes as its colder region, the utensils made of brass and copper, wood carvings, etc. The unsung heroes of Uttarakhand, their folk tales, ballads, oral traditions, literature, and language all together further enhance the region's cultural identity. The roots are still alive in Garhwal region, and it can be felt despite the modern developments, which actually helps in the sustainable development of the region and the standard of life.

8. Spiritual and Ancient Importance

Culture and religion walk hand in hand, and it's interlinked as the traditions and rituals are intertwined. The spiritual ethos is being giantly standing as a protector of Garhwal, i.e. the Char dham.

The spiritual ethos is being giantly standing as a protector of garhwal i.e. the Char dham (Yamunotri, Gangotri, Kedarnath, and Badrinath) which attract millions of devotees annually (Singh, 2016). These destinations are not only religious sites but they actually bring the spiritual transformation when the tourists participate in the traditions and customs rituals, which are inherited from past generations till the present and will continue guiding the lights and wisdom to future. The absolutely amazing unique styles of architectural designs of the Katyuri and Chand dynasties are included in Kedarnath and Tungnath temples, which are built at highest altitudes of the Garhwal region. The creativity of the artisans of the region is showcased through the temple's design, and it is totally made from locally sourced materials and carvings (Rawat, 2019).

9. Festivals and Rituals

In Garhwal mandal, there are various local festivals and rituals celebrated by the local community in their own traditional way such as Holi, Diwali, and the most celebrated regional festival of Harela, providing a vast and impressive culture into the community's popular practices (Thapliyal, 2018). According to Kapoor and Bhardwaj (2021), these festivities are characterized by folk music, dance styles such as Langvir Nritya, and customs that represent the peaceful coexistence of people and Nature.

10. Challenges in Preservation

Garhwal's cultural and wellness practices are important, but they are threatened by migration, urbanization, and the impact of contemporary lifestyles (Devi & Singh, 2021). According to Rana and Singh (2017), the authenticity, dependability, and sustainability of these practices are in jeopardy due to the decline in interest in traditional knowledge among contemporary youths and the commercialization of heritage sites (see Table 11.1).

11. Sustainable Preservation Strategies

Sustainable preservation strategies focus on protecting cultural, natural, and historical resources while ensuring their longevity for future generations. These strategies integrate environmental, economic, and social considerations to maintain heritage sites, traditional knowledge, and ecosystems (Devi & Singh, 2021). To ensure cultural continuity and responsible tourism, an important key approach is community involvement, where local populations actively participate in conservation efforts.(Rawat, 2019). Eco-friendly tourism practices, such as limiting visitor numbers, using renewable energy, and promoting sustainable accommodations, help minimize the ecological footprint on heritage sites (Chauhan, 2020). Policy implementation and legal frameworks play a crucial role in preservation by enforcing heritage protection laws and promoting sustainable development policies (Uttarakhand Tourism Development Board, 2021). Documentation and digital preservation safeguard traditional knowledge, historical records, and architectural details through digital archives and virtual reconstructions (Tiwari, 2021). Using environmentally friendly resources, restoration with sustainable materials ensures that conservation work aligns with the original heritage (Thapliyal, 2018). Education and awareness programs foster a sense of responsibility among communities and tourists by highlighting the importance of heritage conservation (Bisht, 2017). Additionally, integrating traditional practices with modern technology helps in maintaining ecological balance while benefiting from scientific advancements (Pandey & Chauhan, 2022). By adopting these strategies, heritage conservation can be both sustainable and adaptive, ensuring that cultural and natural treasures remain intact for future generations (Tripathi, 2019).

Table 11.1. Challenges in Promoting Traditional Wellness Practices.

Category	Description	Proposed Solutions
Lack of awareness	Limited knowledge among tourists and locals	Awareness campaigns, workshops
Infrastructure issues	Poor access to remote wellness sites	Road improvement, eco-friendly transport
Environmental concerns	Degradation of natural resources	Sustainable tourism practices
Loss of traditional knowledge	Disappearance of traditional healing methods	Documentation, training new practitioners
Accountability issues	The prevalence of misinformation	Doing the job with honesty and credibility
Lack of accurate information	Excess of illusory knowledge	Intellectual seminar, workshops Person's awareness
Complexity of learning process	Lack of interest	Develop the habit of reading
Shortage of experts	Take studies in a normal way	Giving importance to specialization in any subject
To be suspicious	Different facts come to light	Finding the right sources of information
Lack of knowledge of true facts	Not checking different facts	Where to put authentic information
Proof of work available	Lack of exposure or different research	Publishing with small article and research papers
Geographical problems	Ge	Enhancing infrastructure
Sustainability issues	Sustainability not considered in setting up any small segment	Embracing sustainable tourism
Environmental problem	Loss of flora and fauna	Promotion of responsible tourism
Climate change issues	Different-different climate in each region	Climate conscious travel
Knowledge related problems	Lack of awareness about traditional knowledge	Promotion of traditional knowledge

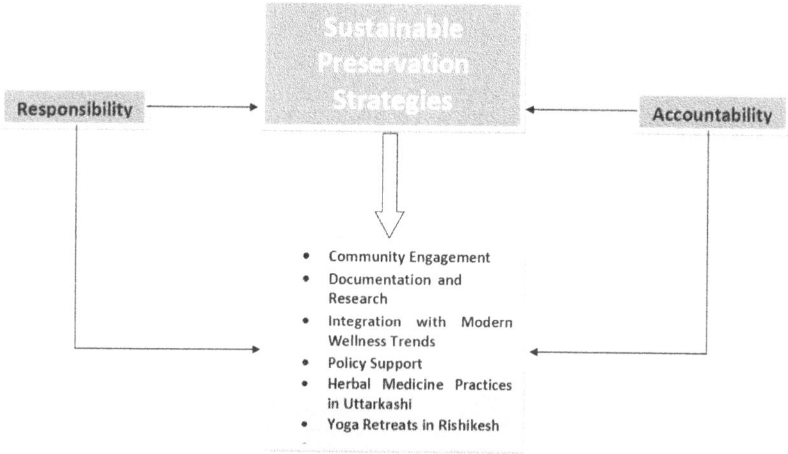

Fig. 11.1. Sustainable Prevention Strategies in Wellness Practices. *Source:* Own Elaboration.

Sustainable preservation strategies (see Fig. 11.1) involve initiatives that are long-lasting and enduring. Central to these strategies are concepts of responsibility and accountability. Supporting the preservation and promotion of wellness practices can be greatly enhanced through natural heritage tourism. Fostering the elements of nature is a critical necessity for our time, as many traditional wellness methods are fundamentally connected to natural environments. For a truly sustainable plan, it is essential to emphasize all aspects of the core elements. In the Garhwal region, traditional wellness practices are fundamentally integrated and represent a holistic sustainable heritage. The main components consist of community involvement, support from policies, herbal medicine traditions in Uttarakhand, yoga retreats available in Rishikesh, research and documentation efforts, and alignment with nature-focused wellness trends.

12. Community Engagement

There are lots of problems in empowering local communities to take pride in their cultural heritage and wellness practices. In order to solve the problem, few initiatives like workshops, storytelling sessions, and cultural festivals can help bridge the generational gap and foster a sense of ownership (Rawat, 2019).

13. Documentation and Research

One by one, person to person, object to subject, the documentation of Garhwal's cultural and wellness heritage is very important for its preservation. Collaborative research involving local scholars, anthropologists, and wellness experts can provide valuable insights and promote awareness (Jain & Gupta, 2020).

14. Integration With Modern Wellness Trends

The importance for traditional wellness strategies can be enhanced by integrating them into today's health and tourism sectors. As an example, promoting Garhwal's sustainable diets, yoga retreats, and herbal cures as wellness tourism can draw curiosity from all over the globe (Mishra, 2021).

15. Policy Support

Government initiatives that support ecotourism and give priority to the preservation of intangible cultural assets can be very helpful. The continuation of these customs may be promoted by offering incentives to regional craftspeople, Vaidyas, and wellness professionals (Uttarakhand Tourism Development Board, 2021).

16. Herbal Medicine Practices in Uttarkashi

The usefulness of traditional therapies for long-term illnesses is demonstrated by a case study of Uttarkashi's herbal medical practices (Bisht, 2017). Sustainable lifestyles have also been facilitated by local populations' participation in the cultivation and processing of medicinal plants (Kumar, 2018).

17. Yoga Retreats in Rishikesh

Yoga retreats in Rishikesh are a prime example of how Garhwal's spiritual history can be successfully incorporated with contemporary wellness trends. These retreats boost the local economy in addition to fostering emotional and physical well-being (Singh & Negi, 2020).

18. Research Methodology

The study is purely based on secondary data available in different research article, books, and papers. The study conducts an extensive review of ancient Indian texts such as the Vedas, Puranas, Dharma sutras, and classical Sanskrit literature. These texts provide insights into the rituals and customs associated with health and nature-based health tourism. The research identifies and analyzes key themes related to cultural background, environmental sensitivity, holistic well-being, and human and nature relationship. These themes are explored to understand how they can inform modern wellness practices. The research contextualizes the health practice of guest within the broader framework of Indian cultural impacts that have evolved over time and their relevance in today's health tourism industry.

19. Findings and Outcomes

Ancient wellness practices significantly contribute to the enrichment of cultural heritage. These practices promote cultural elements through various dimensions, including traditions, yoga, spirituality, customs, and rituals. Garhwal Division, located in Uttarakhand, is an ancient land and a hub for traditional wellness practices. The region's mountains, beauty, herbal flora, rivers, meadows, and more, offer new avenues for wellness tourism and trends, enhancing cultural richness. By combining ancient wellness practices with modern healthcare strategies, innovative initiatives can be developed. A nation's cultural richness can be showcased through health-promoting and happiness-inducing activities. These insights provide a deeper understanding of wellness and healthcare practices. Some examples like Yoga and meditation, herbal medicine and Ayurveda, traditional healing practices, and spiritual rituals and practices can be leveraged to promote cultural understanding via health tourism with modern health care strategies. Through this, we can develop wellness programs and cultural exchange opportunities and promote sustainable well-being practices to tourists.

This synergy can support the SDGs and overall traditional wellness practices to offer wealth of opportunities for cultural preservation, economic growth, and human well-being. By highlighting and discussing these practices, we can create a more holistic, sustainable, and accountable approach to health and wellness.

20. Conclusion

The holistic well-being of people and SDGs are profoundly infused into Garhwal Mandal's cultural heritage and traditional wellness practices, which serve as a wealth of information and insight. Local communities' lifestyles are still shaped by these generations-old customs, which include Ayurveda, yoga, herbal medicine, and spiritual healing. In today's wellness-driven world, they are extremely relevant because they not only provide a natural approach to health and wellness tourism but also stress harmony between people and nature. This heritage needs to be preserved and promoted through an all-encompassing approach that incorporates responsible tourism, academic research, community involvement, and policy support. Because local populations are the primary keepers of these traditions, community engagement is essential. They guarantee authenticity and long-term viability through their active participation in sustainable tourism initiatives and heritage conservation. Research and documentation initiatives can support the incorporation of these traditional practices into contemporary wellness paradigms by confirming their advantages.

Developments in technology also present chances to create enduring heritage experiences, digitally preserve cultural customs, and increase access to traditional wellness information. The acceptance and adoption of Garhwal's healing methods in the modern health and tourism sectors can be further enhanced by cooperation between regional practitioners and international wellness industries. By valuing and reviving its cultural and wellness heritage, Garhwal can establish itself as a global center for sustainable living and holistic tourism. Sustainable tourism initiatives that ensure minimal environmental impact and responsibly promote cultural heritage can draw wellness seekers. By ensuring that these age-old customs endure for upcoming generations, this strategy not only protects a priceless legacy but also makes a significant contribution to global tourism, cultural, and wellness discussions.

Acknowledgments

This research work has been supported by the Indian Council of Social Science Research (ICSSR), New Delhi, whose financial assistance has been invaluable in facilitating this study. We sincerely appreciate their commitment in promoting academic research and providing the necessary resources to undertake this work.

References

Bisht, D. S. (2017). Himalayan biodiversity and its role in Ayurveda. *Indian Journal of Traditional Medicine*, *1*(3), 200–210.

Chauhan, S. (2020). Nature-based wellness practices in Uttarakhand. *EcoHealth*, *17*(2), 170–184.

Devi, M., & Singh, P. (2021). Sustainability practices in Himalayan tourism. *Mountain Research and Development*, *41*(1), 90–100.

Gairola, R. (2019). Folk healing practices in Garhwal Himalayas. *Journal of Anthropology and Medicine*, *26*(3), 191–209.

Jain, A., & Gupta, R. (2020). Integrating local knowledge in sustainable tourism development. *Journal of Sustainable Tourism*, *28*(5), 736–752.

Joshi, P., & Sharma, D. (2020). Dietary practices and nutritional security in Himalayan regions. *Food and Nutrition Bulletin*, *41*(2), 205–216.

Kapoor, R., & Bhardwaj, V. (2021). The role of folk music in emotional well-being: Insights from Garhwal. *Journal of Ethnomusicology*, *14*(4), 298–312.

Kumar, R. (2018). Intergenerational knowledge transfer in traditional medicine. *Heritage Science*, *6*(1), 12–22.

Mishra, N. (2021). Challenges in sustaining yoga tourism in Rishikesh. *Tourism Review International*, *25*(3), 278–294.

Negi, B. S. (2012). *Cultural heritage of Uttarakhand*. Concept Publishing Company.

Pandey, A., & Chauhan, R. (2022). Role of herbal remedies in modern healthcare: Lessons from Garhwal. *Journal of Integrative Medicine*, *24*(1), 45–55.

Pant, G. B., & Joshi, S. C. (2018). Ayurvedic practices in Garhwal: An ethnobotanical perspective. *Journal of Medicinal Plants Research*, *12*(4), 112–120.

Rana, A., & Singh, R. (2017). Wellness tourism in Uttarakhand: Opportunities and challenges. *Tourism and Hospitality Research*, *17*(4), 342–357.

Rawat, S. P. (2019). Community participation in cultural heritage conservation in Uttarakhand. *Asian Journal of Heritage Studies*, *8**(1), 15–25.

Sharma, H. P. (2015). Traditional knowledge and practices in Himalayan regions. *International Journal of Himalayan Studies*, *7*(2), 45–60.

Singh, K. (2016). Spiritual practices in the Himalayas: A cultural perspective. *International Journal of Spiritual Studies*, *10*(1), 85–98.

Singh, M., & Negi, P. (2020). Yoga and spiritual tourism in Uttarakhand: Challenges and opportunities. *Tourism Management Perspectives*, *36*, 100749.

Thapliyal, U. (2018). Traditional festivals as a medium for cultural preservation in Garhwal. *Cultural Studies Review*, *12*(2), 67–83.

Tiwari, A. (2021). Ancient temples of Garhwal: A historical overview. *Archaeological Studies Quarterly*, *23*(2), 45–58.

Tripathi, M. (2019). Sacred groves of Garhwal: Biodiversity and cultural values. *Journal of Environmental Studies*, *15*(3), 88–97.

Uttarakhand Tourism Development Board. (2021). *Annual report on cultural and wellness tourism in Uttarakhand*. UTDB Publications.

Chapter 12

Wellness Tourism in Morocco's Mineral Healing Waters: The Case of Moulay Yacoub, Ain Allah, and Sidi Harazem

Chafik Bouchannafa and Mehdi Boukil

Faculty of Arts and Humanities Dahr al-Mahraz- Fes, Morocco

Abstract

Healing water tourism is a key aspect of Morocco's wellness and medical tourism, with destinations like Moulay Yacoub, Ain Allah, and Sidi Harazem offering therapeutic benefits and unique experiences. These thermal and mineral water sites are known for treating dermatological, rheumatic, and digestive ailments due to their mineral composition.

This chapter explores the healing properties of these waters, the services provided, such as hydrotherapy centers and spas, and their appeal through relaxation and natural landscapes. As wellness tourism becomes more competitive, customer satisfaction and loyalty are crucial for success. Based on 50 reviews from Booking.com, this study highlights key factors such as treatment effectiveness, spa ambiance, and staff professionalism, all of which impact visitors' emotional and physical well-being. Customer loyalty, reflected in return intentions and recommendations, emphasizes the need for continuous service and therapeutic improvements to maintain satisfaction and encourage repeat visits.

Keywords: Healing water; wellness tourism; Moulay Yacoub; thermal mineral water; therapeutic value

1. Introduction

Healing water tourism is a subset of medical and wellness tourism that has gained global recognition for its ability to combine therapeutic treatments with

Nature, Wellness and Sustainability in Health Tourism, 293–312

Published under exclusive licence by Emerald Publishing Limited
doi:10.1108/978-1-83742-029-220261012

leisure experiences. Morocco, with its rich hydrogeological resources, possesses a significant stock of mineral springs, estimated at 117 springs distributed across the national territory. These include 26 springs in the northeastern regions, 57 springs in the rural and southern rural areas, 13 springs in the central region, 7 springs in the Middle Atlas, 5 springs in the High Atlas, and 9 springs in the Little Atlas and Sahara regions (Meskali, 2007).

Despite this abundance, only six springs have developed into recognized mineral institutions that are regularly visited by tourists. These locations have the necessary infrastructure, equipment, and facilities to support hydrotherapy, making them focal points for healing water tourism. Notably, the Fez region holds the largest share of these institutions, reinforcing its role as a key player in Morocco's wellness tourism sector (Table 12.1).

Among the most renowned thermal and mineral water stations are Moulay Yacoub, Ain Allah, and Sidi Harazem, which have attracted visitors for centuries due to their reputed healing properties. These sites offer therapeutic benefits for dermatological, rheumatic, and digestive ailments while also providing diverse touristic experiences, including hydrotherapy centers, spas, accommodations, and cultural attractions. Additionally, the healing waters of Hamat, Sidi Harazem, Moulay Yacoub, and Ain Allah play a crucial role in attracting a significant number of tourists to these destinations, serving as key drivers of local economic and social development.

This study explores the potential of Morocco's healing water tourism by examining the mineral composition and medical benefits of its most visited springs, evaluating existing tourism infrastructure, and identifying opportunities for sustainable development within this sector while appreciating with gratitude the blessing of God, who has made water a source of healing and renewal.

2. Introducing the Field of Study

> If the location of a city influences its development, the expansion of its hospital center, and its functional transformations over time, the initial purpose for which it was founded is determined by the nature of the site on which it was established. (Wahbi, 1980, p. 70)

In this regard, the study area, encompassing Sidi Harazem, Moulay Yacoub, and Ain Allah, exemplifies this principle. Strategically located within the Fez region, it is renowned for its thermal springs and wellness tourism potential, as illustrated in the map below.

Sidi Harazem is located west of the city of Fez between latitudes 385° N and 380° S and longitudes 545° and 550°, bordered by the Sebou River to the north, Sidi Mouha Ben Waf to the south, the Kaada Plateau to the west, and Jebel Harisha to the east, 12 km from Fez on secondary road number 320, which connects Fez to Oujda. Moulay Yacoub (Map 12.1) is located 25 km from the

Table 12.1. The Share of the Fez Region as a Destination for Mineral Institutions Available in Morocco.

Mineral Enterprises	Method of Exploitation	Equipment in the Organization	Rated Hotel Establishments	Road Conditions on the Site	The Site's Tourism Potential	The Closest Tourist Center	Mineral Area
Sidi Hrazem	Sothermy Society	• Two barbecues • Two pools	• Hotel *3 • Hotel *1	Excellent	A picturesque nature characterized by palm trees—historical monuments	Fez	Rural and Rural South area
Moulay Yacoub	Sothermy Society	• Old station • Modern station	• Two hotels *4 • Two hotels *3 • Two hotels *1	Excellent connectivity via Fes, Meknes, and Ifran	Hama has a long history of traditional tourism	Fez	Rural and Rural South area
Ain Allah	A development company has been proposed to oversee the Hama.	• Old station • New modern station	First-class tourist accommodation	Good (connect via Fes, Meknes, and Ifran)	Diverse forest and resting space	Fez	Rural and Rural South area

Source: Monograph of the Territorial Communities of Sidi Harazem, Moulay Yacoub, and Ain Allah (2018).

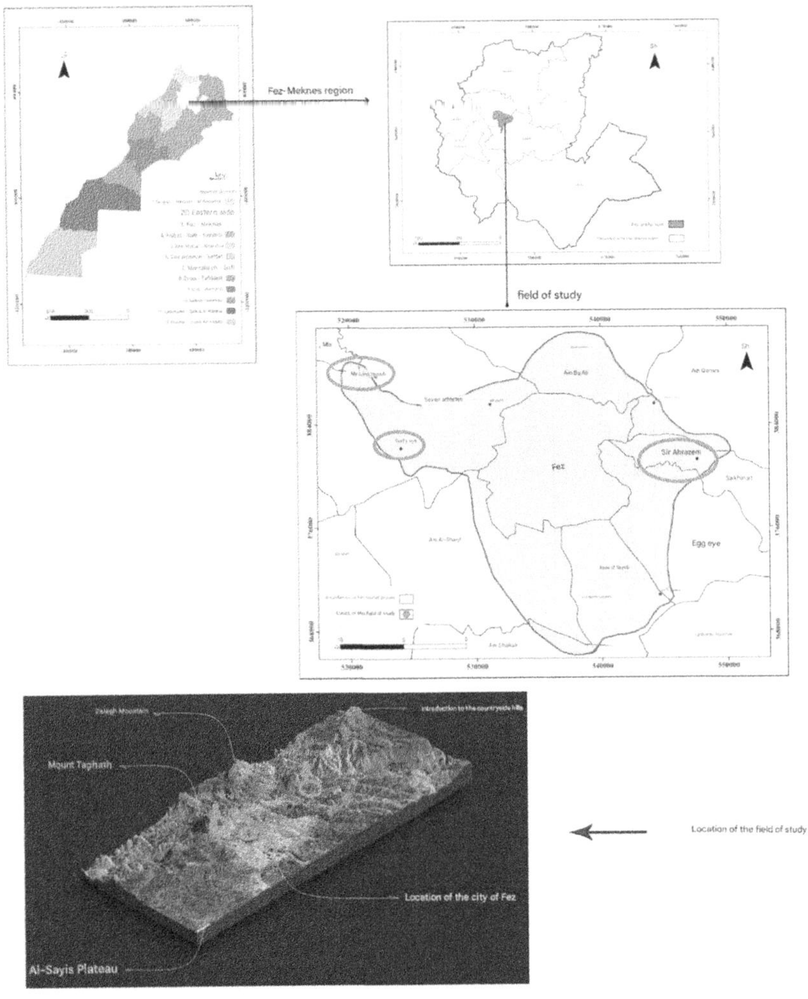

Map 12.1. The Strategic Location of the Study Area (Sidi Harazem, Moulay Yacoub, Ain Allah). *Source:* Prepared by the researcher based on the administrative division map of Morocco (2015) from the High Commission for Planning.

city of Fez, bordered on the east by Ain Bouali, on the north by the community of laajajra, on the west by the community of Mekkes, and on the south by the community of Ain El Chkef, and is located on secondary road No. 308 (Bouchnafa, 2008, pp. 11, 37). Finally, Ain Allah is located in the heart of the Saïs plateau, east of the Moulay Yacoub mineral station, within the community of Saba Rouadi, bordered by the north by the Ajajara community 'laajajra', the south by the Ain Chkef community and the Bensouda area, the east by the Sherrarda Ain Gadous area and the Ain Bouali community, and the west by the Mekkes community and the Mahia. It is about 14 km from the city of Fez, on the main road number 3 in the direction of Sidi Kacem. The site commonly known locally as Ain Lah (reflecting the phonetic rules of Tajweed) is formally referred to here as *Ain Allah*, acknowledging the divine source of these healing waters.

3. Results and Discussion

3.1 Thermal Mineral Water for Spa Tourism in Fez: Characteristics, Components, and Benefits

3.1.1 The Therapeutic Value of Sidi Harazem Water and Its Role in Attracting Wellness Tourism

This healing station is characterized by its high-quality hot mineral water, 12 km from the city of Fez in the direction of Oujda and 3 km from the Skhinat center (Lindner, 1998, p. 307), and this bath is a space for recreation and entertainment for the city's residents and visitors, especially internal tourists, represented by the waves of visitors who visit it every morning to exercise and refuel, as well as to enjoy its clean air and picturesque landscapes.

In terms of topography, Sidi Harazem is dominated by the plateau character, as it is located in the area between the hills of the Rif front and the Atlas Mountains, which made its warm springs rich in mineral waters of a healing nature, and it is noticeable that this area is characterized by a gradient in altitude from the south toward the south toward the Atlas Mountains. It is characterized by a gradient in altitude from the south toward the north of El Hamma, where the highest altitude reaches 530 m in the south (Benglig) while the lowest point is located in the north on the bank of the Sebou valley with a height of no more than 228 m, which gave it special natural qualities that impress visitors (Map 12.1).

From a medical and hospitalization point of view, analyses by the "Pharmacadyneraie" laboratory of the Scientific University of Bordeaux, France, have proven that the mineral waters of Sidi Harazem are of high quality and are suitable for all age groups, due to their purity and freedom from bacteria, as they contain substances necessary for the human body, such as calcium and magnesium, which resist fatigue and muscle spasms and their superior therapeutic ability (Bouchenafa & Hamdani, 2018, p. 180).

For further clarification, the following table has been included to highlight the health benefits of Sidi Harazem water, based on information from the Sothermy Society, a company responsible for bottling Sidi Harazem water in plastic bottles near the thermal spring.

Table 12.2 shows that Sidi Harazem's water is rich in mineral salts, especially calcium, sodium, and magnesium. According to Dr. Edmond Secret, this chemical composition makes Sidi Harazem's water occupy an intermediate position between Vittel and Evian, two mineral springs that enjoy great fame far

Table 12.2. Chemical Composition of Sidi Harazem Water. Mg/L.

Substances	Bicarbonate	Sulfate	Potassium	Sodium	Nitrate	Magnesium	Calcium	Chloride
Quantity (mg/L)	335	20	8	120	4	40	70	220

Source: Bouchnafa, Chafik. (2023). *Environmental tourism and sustainable development in the Fez destination* (Doctoral dissertation), p. 59.

beyond the borders of the French state and extend to various countries of the world (Bouchenafa & Hamdani, 2018, p. 181).

While laboratory tests have proven that Sidi Harazem's water is capable of enriching the human body with several essential substances that contribute to its activity and vitality. Dr. Edmond is keen to teach kidney and urinary tract patients the correct way to drink Sidi Harazem water, so that they can obtain satisfactory health benefits, as he urges them to drink the mineral water directly from the drinker in small doses (Fig. 12.1), during the morning before eating, or at the end of the evening after the end of the digestive process. For reference, the intake of these different amounts of water is determined by the doctor according to the condition of each patient in order to be treated properly.

In addition to its natural assets, the Sidi Harazem healing station is equipped with various tourist facilities, including accommodations at the Sidi Harazem Hotel, which play a significant role in attracting visitors from both within and outside Morocco. The station features several swimming pools, where many

Fig. 12.1. The Process of Consuming Sidi Harazem's Water by Tourists Directly From the Drinking Fountain. *Source:* Pictured By Chafiq Bouchannafa (August 2024).

residents of Fez are regular visitors. These pools are renowned for their therapeutic properties, particularly for those seeking relief from ailments such as joint pain, stress, and skin conditions. Visitors benefit not only from the healing properties of the mineral-rich waters but also from the opportunity to swim, which promotes physical relaxation and well-being.

3.1.2 Physical and Chemical Properties of Moulay Yacoub's Water and Its Therapeutic Value for Tourists

Moulay Yacoub station is about 25 km from the city of Fez, on the far western side, on secondary road No. 308, and is located in a steep terrain in the form of a concave shape with a high of 393 m and a low of 242 m. This made the region rich in its high-quality healing water, which is extracted at a depth of 1,500 m, with a temperature of 54 °Celsius (**Monograph of the Moulay Yacoub Territorial Commune, 2018**), and to know the physical and chemical properties of Moulay Yacoub water and its therapeutic value, the following table is included.

From the Table 12.3, you can conclude the medical importance of Moulay Yacoub's water, which is characterized by two key elements.

First, its *physical properties*, particularly its high temperature, affect the body. The rapid breathing that occurs during the bathing process enhances oxygen absorption by the body's tissues, leading to increased sweating, which helps cleanse the skin of parasites.

Second, its *chemical properties* include the presence of sulfur and sodium salts, which help stop germs from growing. They also help the skin heal, especially if someone has sores or infections that don't go away quickly.

Moulay Yacoub's thermal water is renowned for its unique composition and therapeutic properties. Initially, its pH is *6.2 (acidic)*, but upon contact with air, it rises to *7.2 (neutral)* within one minute. This thermal water is rich in essential minerals, contributing to its healing effects. Table 12.4 is the detailed *ionic composition* of this thermal water.

Moulay Yacoub's thermal water is exceptionally rich in sulfur, calcium, and sodium, all of which contribute to its renowned therapeutic benefits. Its naturally high temperature provides sedative, analgesic, and muscle-relaxing effects, making it particularly effective in the treatment of rheumatism and joint pain.

Table 12.3. Features of Moulay Yacoub's Mineral Water.

Water Characteristics	**Percentage**
• *Chemical contents*	57%
• *Physical contents:* Temperature	46%
• *Water radiation*	3.38%

Source: Elattaoui (1981, p. 18).

Table 12.4. Ionic Composition of Moulay Yacoub's Thermal Water.

Ion	Concentration (mEq/L)	Equivalent in Mg/L
Ca^{2+} (*calcium*)	56	1,125
Na^{+} (*sodium*)	408	9,400
Mg^{2+} (*magnesium*)	26	325
K^{+} (*potassium*)	8.5	332
Cl^{-} (*chloride*)	495	17,600
HCO_3^{-} (*bicarbonate*)	2.92	179
SiO_3^{2-} (*silicate*)	1.09	41.8
SO_4^{2-} (*sulfate*)	0.75	36

Source: Vichy Thermalia Spa Hotel (n.d.). *The thermal water of Moulay Yacoub*.

The water's sodium chloride content has antiseptic and anti-edematous properties while its significant sulfur concentration (33 mg/L) improves blood circulation, which enhances overall health and energy. Sulfur also helps kill germs to prevent infections and keep the skin clean. In addition, it promotes relaxation and helps regulate the skin's oil production, preventing it from becoming too oily or too dry.

Thermal treatments at Moulay Yacoub are especially recommended for respiratory conditions such as rhinitis, rhino-pharyngitis, sinusitis, bronchitis, and otitis, particularly when these ailments become chronic and lead to secondary infections (Abane, 2011).

Also according to an interview with the medical director of the thermal baths, "The unique chemical composition of Moulay Yacoub's water has remarkable effects on psoriatic skin, helping to eliminate scales. Additionally, due to its slight natural radioactivity, the water exhibits impressive anti-inflammatory virtues."

To attract visitors from different social classes, the thermal station was equipped with various facilities, including a newly established thermal complex in addition to the historic baths, which will be detailed in the following paragraphs.

3.1.2.1 The Old Thermal Baths of Moulay Yacoub. In 1962, Dr. François Cléret (former physician to Mohammed V and Hassan II), after demonstrating the effectiveness of the thermal waters in treating both dermatological and respiratory conditions, secured funding from Hassan II to modernize the site. This led to the construction of a large pool and a major borehole to increase the water flow from the source (Fig. 12.2).

That same year, two distinct pavilions were built: one dedicated to the treatment of respiratory diseases and the other to dermatological conditions. Additionally, 1962 marked the construction of the first hotels in the village of

Fig. 12.2. The Old Therm Pool. *Source:* Direction of Moulay Yacoub's station.

Moulay Yacoub, further enhancing its appeal as a health and wellness retreat (Moulay Yacoub, n.d. Vichy Thermalia Spa Hotel).

Second thermal bath: As part of the development of the Moulay Yacoub center and the diversification of tourism activity in Fez, this spa was opened in 1993 and *restored in 2016*, where it was equipped with four different wards, one for ear, nose, and throat diseases and respiratory diseases, another for skin diseases and oral diseases, in addition to a third ward specialized in gynecology, and a fourth for rheumatology, in addition to two departments, one related to cosmetic treatment and the other to the technical aspect.

Thus, this new project has become a prestigious attraction, drawing many visitors, mostly from the affluent class, particularly foreign tourists. This is due to the high prices, with a pool ticket at the new therm costing 80 dirhams and some treatment services reaching up to 1,000 dirhams (Fig. 12.3).

Third Thermal Station: Since *2016*, a third thermal facility has been established through the renovation of the ancient one, with the French company Vichy Spa International leading the project. The company has been responsible for repositioning the Moulay Yacoub thermal station as a prestigious tourist

Fig. 12.3. The Location of the Second Moulay Yacoub Station and Some of its Modern Equipment. *Source:* Direction of the new station of Moulay Yacoub.

destination, leveraging its expertise in both the hospitality and thermal sectors, along with its international commercial networks. Its objective is to enhance the commercial performance of both facilities and promote them in international markets, aiming to establish Moulay Yacoub as a globally renowned destination for wellness and health rehabilitation. This initiative also contributes to the economic development of the Fez-Meknes region.

In response to the lack of hotels in the area, the company built the 100-room, 4-star Vichy Thermalia Spa Moulay Yacoub, which opened in 2018 (Fig. 12.4). The hotel caters to visitors wishing to stay for days or even weeks to enjoy thermal treatments. The resort has partnered with specialists in thermal medicine, otorhinolaryngology, and dermatology to offer more specialized treatments, attracting visitors seeking an integrated wellness experience.

An interview with the director of the Vichy Thermal Center provided valuable insights into the hotel's operations, customer demographics, and service offerings. The findings highlight key aspects of the hotel's performance and market positioning.

The average length of stay at the Vichy Hotel is two nights, with 85% of guests being Moroccan nationals, primarily from major urban centers such as Casablanca, Rabat, and Tangier. The remaining 15% are international visitors. In 2024, the hotel's occupancy rate stands at 37%, highlighting the challenges of maintaining a steady influx of guests despite its strategic location and distinctive wellness offerings. This relatively low occupancy rate, along with the limited presence of international tourists, can be attributed to the perception of Fez—a nearby cultural and historical hub—as a transit destination for international travelers, who typically stay for only two days on average. As a result, Moulay Yacoub, where the hotel is located, remains largely dependent on Fez's tourism flow. The limited integration of Moulay Yacoub into Fez's broader tourism circuit further restricts its appeal, reducing the chances that short-stay visitors will venture beyond Fez to explore wellness experiences in the region. With international tourists spending only a brief period in Fez, their opportunities to discover nearby wellness destinations remain constrained.

The Vichy Hotel differentiates itself within the wellness tourism market by offering a range of specialized services tailored to the increasing demand for health and well-being experiences. These services include thermal baths, massages, traditional Moroccan hammam treatments, and outdoor activities such as hiking to Mount Lalla Chafia. Such offerings enhance the guest experience and align with broader trends in the global wellness tourism industry. The hotel caters to an upscale clientele, as evidenced by its premium pricing, with room rates reaching up to 1,800 MAD per night.

The Vichy Thermalia Resort is pioneering the development of thermal tourism in Morocco, strengthening the country's position as a leading wellness destination on the international stage. The resort represents a unique model of innovation and sustainability in the wellness tourism sector, addressing the specific needs of its visitors.

Fig. 12.4. Renovated Third Thermal Station of Moulay Yacoub and the Vichy Thermalia Spa Hotel. *Source:* Moulay Yacoub Vichy Thermalia Spa http://www.Booking.com

The programs offered include:

- *ENT Thermal Treatment (3 days, from 5,940 MAD, half-board):* Focused on respiratory health, targeting ear, nose, and throat conditions.
- *Rheumatology Program (6 days, from 8,580 MAD, half-board):* Specializing in the treatment of rheumatic diseases through hydrotherapy and mineral mud applications.
- *Wellness and Preventive Health Programs:* Designed to strengthen the immune system, improve skin health, promote relaxation, and alleviate stress.
- *Sports and Fitness Programs:* Offering group fitness classes and private training, ensuring a holistic approach to health through movement and therapy.
- *Hydrotherapy and Esthetic Care:* Combining water-based treatments with skincare therapies to promote relaxation, detoxification, and rejuvenation.
- *Therapeutic Mud Treatment:* Utilizing the healing properties of natural mud to stimulate circulation and support detoxification.
- *Berthollaix and Quartz Thermalia Treatments:* Innovative therapies that integrate modern technology with natural healing methods to target specific health concerns.

Each health stay includes a scheduled medical consultation with the spa doctor. Depending on the chosen program, there is also the option to consult with a doctor or physiotherapist to better understand specific health concerns and adjust spa treatments with the thermal waters of Moulay Yacoub accordingly. The main areas of focus are ENT diseases and rheumatological conditions as described on the Moulay Yacoub Vichy Thermalia Spa Hotel website (Vichy Thermalia Spa Hotel, n.d.).

Visitors can also enjoy access to the *thermal pool (200 MAD)*, alongside other wellness amenities such as a relaxing steam bath and personalized treatments, including manual lymphatic drainage and therapeutic massages.

3.1.3 The Hospitalization Importance of the Ain Allah Station and Its Tourism and Ecological Role

The station of Ain Allah is located at the confluence of the hills of the Rif front and the Sais plateau, on an area of about 14 hectares, and its topography is formed by hills with strong slopes, about 14 km from the city of Fez, on the main road N3 in the direction of Sidi Kassem, where its mineral waters were discovered in 1978 (El faid A, 1990, p. 37), and thus became a mineral station structured to develop and promote the center.

Since its creation, it has been very popular with visitors, especially during the winter season, due to its natural warm waters, but it has deteriorated over the past year (Fig. 12.5) prompting the authorities to restructure and equip it, preparing a new station that can compete with other hospital stations in attracting tourists (Fig. 12.6). It includes several modern facilities such as swimming pools,

Fig. 12.5. The Old Ain Allah Station in a Distinct Green Field. *Source:* Pictured by Chafiq Bouchannafa, 2014.

Fig. 12.6. The New Station of Ain Allah after Restoration. *Source:* Pictured by Chafiq Bouchannafa December 2024.

plunge pools, bathrooms and training rooms. A number of medical and laboratory studies carried out by Moroccan and foreign experts have shown that the water of the Ain Allah bath in Fez, Morocco, with its high heat and steam density, is useful for weight loss and pore cleansing.

As a reference, this station has a tourist complex called "Rim Aquatic", located at the intersection of the Fez-Meknes national road and the Ras El Maa Ain Allah secondary road, which includes several swimming pools, two open-air and one covered, as well as a swimming pool and a children's playground; this complex also includes a hotel, a garden, a restaurant, and a car park. From an environmental point of view, this center is characterized by its green area, which is represented by a large wooded area with different types of trees and shrubs (Fig. 12.7).

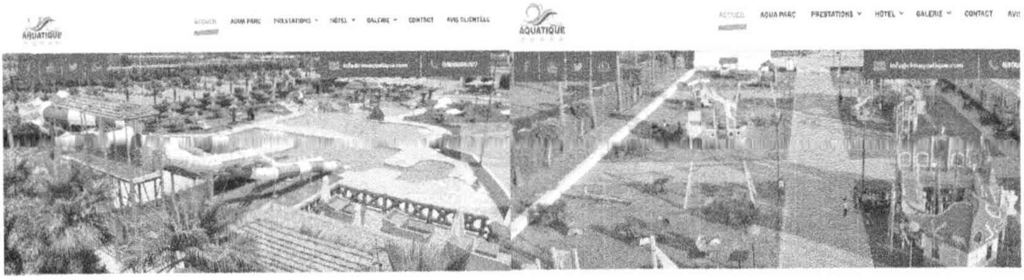

Fig. 12.7. Rim Aquatique Resort Near Ain Allah Station. *Source:* www.rimaquatique.com

3.2 Assessing the Environmental Status of the Hospital Baths in the Fes Tourist Destination and the Prospects for Valorization and Sustainability

Based on the importance of these baths and the important role they may play in the dynamism of hospital tourism, Map 12.2 was included to assess their environmental status to determine their contribution to sustainable tourism development in Fez.

In part of our PhD research focused on environmental tourism in the destination of Fez, we distributed *400* questionnaires. These were divided as follows: *100* for local tourists (focused on motivations, preferences, and expectations), *100* for international tourists (exploring perceptions, satisfaction, and experiences), and *200* for residents (examining the impact of tourism on the environment, economy, and daily life). Behind the questions were some items to assess aspects of health tourism in Moulay Yacoub, Ain Allah, and Sidi Harazem stations that we analyzed in this article.

The questionnaire was structured with standardized response options (*Good, Medium, Poor, Don't know*) to evaluate the potential impacts and environmental situation of proposed health tourism projects.

As illustrated in Map 12.2, the environmental condition of *Hama Sidi Harazem* is generally favorable, with 37% of respondents rating it as *acceptable* and 35% as *good*. Similarly, *Hama Moulay Yacoub* is perceived as *acceptable* by 39% and *good* by 37%. In contrast, *Hama Ainallah* faces a deteriorating environmental situation, with 39% of responses indicating *poor* and 22% *acceptable*. Our analysis focused on these percentages to accurately assess the environmental state of these centers and their impact on tourism development in the region.

Based on these findings, we conclude that the relatively stable environmental conditions of *Sidi Harazem* and *Moulay Yacoub* (*acceptable to good*) stem from local efforts to rehabilitate these sites. These efforts have transformed them into attractive destinations within an integrated tourism framework that combines natural and therapeutic experiences, ultimately fostering tourism development.

However, we noticed that Ain Allah fell short of tourist expectations due to its deteriorating environmental conditions and unresolved issues that delayed the opening of its new thermal baths at the time when we conducted our

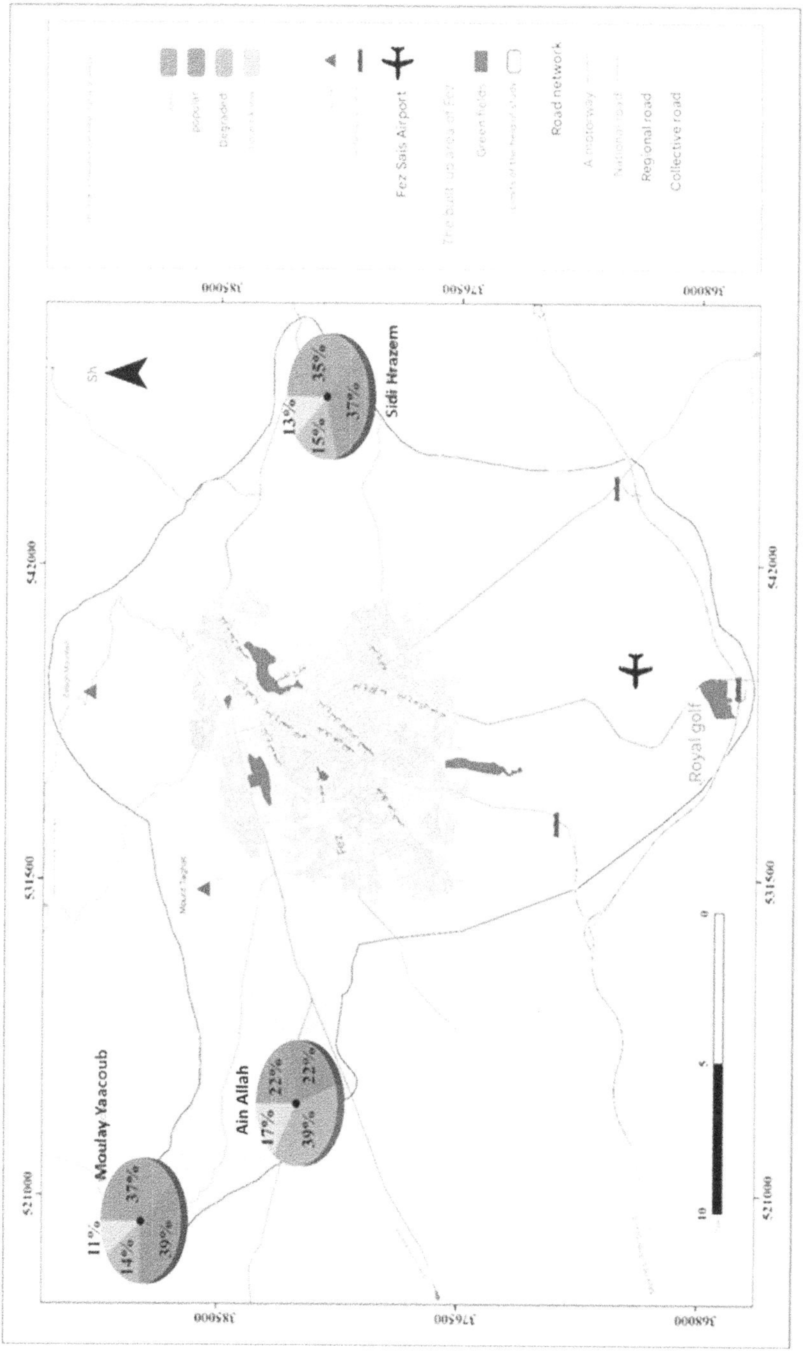

Map 12.2. Assessment of the Environmental Situation of the Hospital Baths in the Fes Tourist Destination.

inquiries. This setback has limited its potential contribution to health tourism and local development in the region although the future may hold new opportunities.

3.3 The Role of Customer Perceptions in Shaping Satisfaction and Loyalty in Wellness Tourism: Insights from Vichy Thermalia Spa Hotel

In today's competitive wellness tourism market, understanding the nuanced factors that drive customer satisfaction and loyalty is essential for sustainable business success. This study examines customer feedback from 50 reviews of the Vichy Thermalia Spa Hotel, exclusively sourced from Booking.com. We compiled these reviews and applied generative artificial intelligence (AI) tools, specifically ChatGPT, to conduct a qualitative thematic analysis aimed at identifying key factors shaping guests' experiences.

The analysis reveals critical dimensions including perceived service quality, emotional engagement with staff, value for money, infrastructure challenges, treatment effectiveness, and the quality of the spa environment (Fig. 12.8). By integrating human expertise with AI-assisted thematic coding, this approach uncovers how therapeutic benefits, staff professionalism, and ambiance collectively influence customer satisfaction and foster loyalty. These findings provide valuable insights for wellness tourism providers seeking to enhance guest experiences and promote repeat visitation.

3.3.1 Influence of Perceived Service Quality on Customer Loyalty

The reviews consistently praised certain elements, such as the cleanliness of the rooms (8.6/10), the quality of the staff (8.7/10), and the peacefulness of the location. These factors were highlighted as critical to overall guest satisfaction and play a significant role in fostering loyalty. Guests who enjoyed the high standard of service, the tranquil atmosphere, and the excellent spa facilities

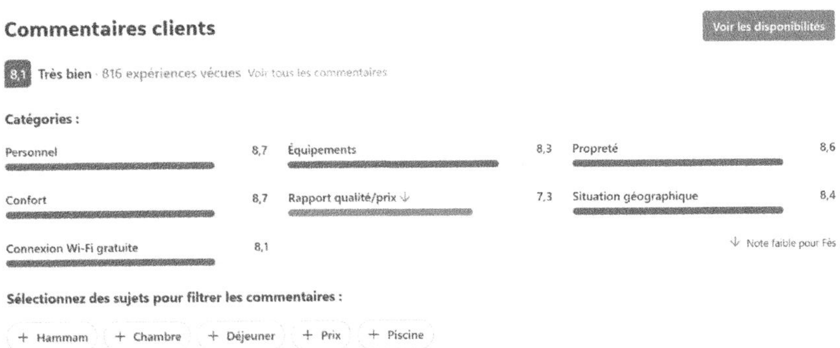

Fig. 12.8. Customer Feedback and Ratings About Hotel Vichy Moulay Yacoub.

expressed a strong desire to return. This connection between perceived service quality and customer retention aligns with customer satisfaction theories, which emphasize the importance of maintaining consistently high service standards to build lasting loyalty, especially in the wellness tourism sector.

3.3.2 The Importance of Emotional Aspects in Destination Choice for Thermal Treatments

Reviews revealed that emotional factors, especially the warmth and professionalism of the staff (with a rating of 8.7/10 for their welcome), significantly shape customer experiences. In wellness tourism, emotional expectations often take precedence over functional ones, with staff's ability to create a welcoming and soothing environment directly affecting guests' perceptions of well-being. This supports customer experience theories, which suggest that positive emotional engagement enhances customers' perceptions of a destination and encourages repeat visits. Guests frequently praised the staff's professionalism and expertise, with many noting how personalized service and tailored recommendations fostered trust and satisfaction. This highlights the importance of individualized attention in building customer loyalty. Additionally, guests shared their experiences of feeling revitalized, with improvements in mood, physical health, and general well-being, emphasizing the holistic benefits of the wellness services provided.

3.3.3 Perceived Value for Money in the Context of Thermal Treatments

While many guests praised the quality of the wellness services, several also raised concerns about the cost, particularly regarding room rates and spa services. The reviews suggest that customers evaluate the value of the services based on the balance between quality and price. This indicates that wellness establishments must strike a balance between providing luxury experiences and maintaining affordability. Exploring the quality-price relationship further could offer strategies for enhancing customer satisfaction while also safeguarding profitability, especially in the competitive luxury wellness market.

3.3.4 Continuous Improvement of Infrastructure and Services: Challenges and Customer Expectations

Certain reviews highlighted areas for improvement, such as the accessibility of the village and the quality of the Wi-Fi (rated 8.1/10). Although these aspects are not directly related to the therapeutic experience, they are important for certain customer groups, particularly those traveling with families or requiring reliable connectivity. These reviews suggest that addressing infrastructure challenges could improve the overall guest experience. In wellness tourism, where guests may stay for extended periods, it is essential to continuously improve both tangible (e.g., accessibility, internet) and intangible elements to meet evolving customer needs and expectations.

3.3.5 Effectiveness of Wellness Treatments

One of the most commonly discussed aspects in the reviews was the effectiveness of the spa's therapeutic treatments. Many guests reported significant relief from chronic conditions like joint pain and stress, often attributing their improvement to the spa's mineral-rich thermal waters. This therapeutic component is central to the wellness tourism experience, as it greatly affects customers' physical and emotional well-being. Guests expressed a high level of satisfaction with the benefits of the treatments, with several mentioning their intention to return for continued therapeutic benefits. This underscores the importance of maintaining high-quality wellness offerings that meet customer expectations and foster long-term loyalty.

3.3.6 Quality of the Spa Environment

The ambiance of the spa itself was another critical factor influencing customer satisfaction. Guests often described the spa as a peaceful, luxurious space, where attention to cleanliness, comfort, and design played a key role in enhancing the overall wellness experience. The serene atmosphere, combined with high standards of hygiene and design, contributed to the effectiveness of the treatments and helped guests feel more relaxed. This underscores the idea that the physical environment of wellness facilities significantly impacts customer satisfaction and their overall well-being.

4. Conclusion

The renowned mineral springs of Moulay Yacoub, Ain Allah, and Sidi Harazem position Morocco as a prominent destination in the global wellness tourism market, thanks to their scientifically recognized therapeutic benefits. These natural resources not only promote health and well-being but also play a vital role in advancing the country's economic and environmental sustainability. Central to this experience is the role of hospitality in thermal spas, where high-quality services—such as personalized treatment programs, tailored health advice, and integrated wellness solutions—significantly enhance the effectiveness of thermal therapies. Comfort, care, and well-being are inseparable from the healing process, underscoring the need for a holistic, guest-centered approach.

The combination of physical treatments, such as hydrotherapy, and emotional well-being, fostered by gratitude, can lead to more successful healing. By promoting relaxation and positive emotions, gratitude complements the therapeutic effects of treatments and accelerates recovery. The act of immersing oneself in mineral-rich waters becomes not just a physical cure but also a moment of spiritual renewal, reflection, and gratitude.

To fully capitalize on Morocco's wellness tourism potential, travel agencies, online travel agencies (OTAs), and specialized tour operators should develop attractive packages that highlight therapeutic stays. By offering well-structured wellness packages—combining accommodation, thermal treatments, wellness activities, and cultural experiences—stakeholders can effectively market these unique offerings to both domestic and international visitors. These strategic efforts will help establish Morocco as a premier destination for wellness tourism, fostering economic growth and sustainable development.

Moreover, the requirement for regular thermal treatments offers a key advantage: it encourages longer tourist stays and repeat visits. This naturally supports the development of higher-quality accommodations, infrastructure upgrades, and wellness-focused services. In turn, it creates jobs, strengthens local economies, and deepens the overall tourist experience.

In conclusion, the integration of wellness tourism with healing water treatments in Morocco represents a valuable opportunity for both the tourism industry and public health. By prioritizing customer satisfaction, enhancing hospitality services, and leveraging both digital and traditional distribution channels, Morocco can solidify its position as a leading wellness tourism destination for years to come. Furthermore, by acknowledging the spiritual aspects of healing, such as gratitude and the Qur'anic view of water as a divine blessing, the therapeutic experience becomes richer and more holistic, ensuring lasting impacts on both physical and emotional well-being.

References

Abane, I. (2011). *Thermalism in otorhinolaryngology* Doctoral thesis. Sidi Mohammed Ben Abdellah University, Faculty of Medicine and Pharmacy of Fez.

Bouchenafa, C., & Hamdani, N. (2018). Therapeutic tourism in Fez: Between resource abundance and territorial development challenges: Case study – Sidi Harazem and Moulay Yacoub. In *Territorial resources between fragility and sustainability prospects* (Al-Majalah al-Majali wal-Tanmiyah, Issue 2). Mediterranean Center for Regional, Social, and Environmental Research and Studies.

Bouchnafa, C. (2008). *Thermal tourism in the Fez-Boulemane region: The case of Sidi Hrazem and Moulay Yacoub*. Bachelor's thesis. University of Sidi Mohamed Ben Abdellah, Dhar El Mahraz, Fez.

Bouchnafa, C. (2023). *Environmental tourism and sustainable development in the Fez destination*. Doctoral dissertation, Faculty of Arts and Humanities, Dhar El Mahraz, Fez.

Elattaaoui, A. (1981). *Traditional thermalism in Moulay Yacoub: A study based on a survey of 460 spa-goers*. Medical thesis, Rabat. Faculty of Medicine Rabat.

Lindner, P. (1998). Lieux saints ou lieux de cures? Le processus de transformation des centres traditionnels de pèlerinage: cas de Sidi Harazem et de Moulay Yacoub (Maroc). In *Le tourisme au Magherb: Diversification du produit et devloppement local et régional* (Series Colloques et Seminaires N°79, p. 307). Université Mohammed V Agdal, Faculté des Lettres et des Sciences Humaines.

Meskali, A. (2007). *The role of tourism in local development: The case of Sidi Hrazem and Moulay Yacoub*. Doctoral research, Faculty of Arts and Humanities, Ibn Tofail University.

Vichy Thermalia Spa Hotel. *The thermal water of Moulay Yacoub*. www.moulay-yacoub-vichy-thermalia-spa-hotel.fr/en/lorem-ipsum-en-page-6. Accessed on March 31, 2025.

Wahbi, A. F. M. (1980). *In urban geography*. Dar Al-Nahda Al-Arabia for Printing and Publishing.

Chapter 13

The Symbiosis of Nature and Wellness Tourism: Sri Lanka's Journey to Nature-Based Healing

J. A. R. C. Sandaruwani[a] *and Amrik Singh*[b]

[a]Sabaragamuwa University of Sri Lanka, Sri Lanka
[b]Lovely Professional University, India

Abstract

Sri Lanka, as an island nation endorsed for its rich biodiversity, pristine landscapes, and ancient medicinal and healing traditions, has emerged as a prominent global hub for wellness tourism. This study explores the intricate interdependence between wellness tourism and natural ecosystems, emphasizing how natural ecosystems enhance well-being and the imperative for sustainable practices to preserve these vital resources. Drawing on qualitative data, the study underscores the interconnectedness of natural assets, traditional medicinal values, and wellness tourism practices. The findings emphasize that Sri Lanka's wellness tourism landscape is deeply enriched by the island's deep-rooted Ayurvedic heritage and its extraordinary ecological diversity. From ancient healing systems and endemic medicinal plants to serene hillscapes, biodiverse rainforests, and invigorating coastal zones, the country offers a cohesive ecosystem where physical health, mental clarity, and spiritual rejuvenation naturally converge. To sustain and expand this potential, it is crucial to protect the very ecosystems and cultural traditions that form the foundation of wellness tourism. This calls for an inclusive, community-centered approach that uplifts rural economies, safeguards intangible heritage, and reinforces environmental stewardship. With strategic investment and collaborative efforts, Sri Lanka can position itself not only as a sanctuary for healing and rejuvenation but also as a global exemplar for ethical, nature-aligned wellness tourism on the world stage.

Nature, Wellness and Sustainability in Health Tourism, 313–328

doi:10.1108/978-1-83742-029-220261013

Keywords: Ayurvedic heritage; natural ecosystems; nature-aligned wellness tourism; sustainability; Sri Lanka

1. Introduction

Wellness tourism prioritizes health-centric travel experiences, encompassing physical, mental, and spiritual rejuvenation (Global Wellness Institute, 2023). It emphasizes preventive and proactive care through activities such as yoga, meditation, spa therapies, and nature immersion (Smith et al., 2020). In the wake of the COVID-19 pandemic, global interest in wellness tourism has surged, with the sector projected to grow at an annual rate of 7.6%, reaching a market value of $1.3 trillion by 2025 (Global Wellness Institute, 2023). This burgeoning interest reflects a paradigm shift in travel motivations, as individuals increasingly prioritize health, rejuvenation, and holistic well-being. The demand for wellness tourism is driven by a complex interplay of health, environmental, and socioeconomic factors. Wellness tourism demand is driven by various factors, including rising health consciousness (Kessler, 2022; Talukder et al., 2024; Yeoman et al., 2014); escaping urban environments for restorative natural settings (Dillette et al., 2021); affluent seniors investing in longevity-focused travel (Hu et al., 2023; Kim & Kim, 2024); demand for digital detoxication and experiences in nature (Neuhofer & Celuch, 2020); social media and influencer culture (Neuhofer & Celuch, 2020), sustainability and eco-conscious travel, regenerative tourism (Dorji, 2021; Smith, 2023); cultural and spiritual reconnection (Curtin, 2021), and corporate wellness programs (Google Wellness, 2022).

Wellness tourism has historically drawn from nature's restorative capacities. From Japan's *shinrin-yoku* (forest bathing) to Iceland's geothermal spas, natural settings are integral to wellness interventions, leveraging biophilia—the innate human affinity for nature (Wilson, 1984)—to reduce stress, improve mood, and boost immunity (Li et al., 2010). These practices align with attention restoration theory, which posits that natural environments replenish cognitive resources depleted by urban stressors (Kaplan, 1995).

Nestled in the Indian Ocean, Sri Lanka, celebrated as a biodiversity hotspot, boasts an extraordinary wealth of natural ecosystems that in the process of positioning itself as a rising star in the global wellness tourism industry. From its mist-shrouded highland forests and golden coastal stretches to its verdant Ayurvedic herb gardens and sacred mountain peaks, Sri Lanka's landscapes are not just scenic marvels but living repositories of holistic healing traditions. Sri Lanka, with its millennia-old Ayurvedic heritage and unspoiled ecological diversity, epitomizes this synergy, offering a unique blueprint for leveraging natural assets to foster physical, mental, and spiritual rejuvenation.

This chapter explores how Sri Lanka's natural ecosystems underpin its wellness tourism appeal and harmonize wellness tourism development with environmental and cultural preservation. By doing so, it underscores Sri Lanka's potential to emerge as a global leader in nature-centric wellness tourism—a model where human well-being and planetary health thrive in tandem.

2. Literature Review

Wellness tourism roots to ancient Egyptian and Roman bath cultures and tie its modern rebirth to post-industrial lifestyle stress and the need for preventative health interventions. Kazakov and Oyner (2021) emphasize the historical evolution of wellness tourism from ancient spa practices to modern holistic travel. Wellness tourism compasses a broad spectrum of health-enhancing activities, ranging from physical, emotional, spiritual, and environmental wellness to lifestyle improvement programs. From a rationalist perspective, wellness tourism can be logically seen as a necessity rather than a luxury. This concept goes beyond curative health—it is a proactive, lifestyle-driven model rooted in self-responsibility and holistic health, integrating mind, body, and spirit (Stará & Peterson, 2017). Scholars such as Smith and Puczkó (2014) argue that wellness tourism emerges as a counterbalance to the stress and alienation caused by modern urban lifestyles, offering individuals opportunities to recalibrate through restorative experiences.

Recent academic and industry literature identifies several emerging trends in wellness tourism market. These trends highlight a paradigm shift in tourists' preferences. One notable trend is the rise of mental wellness tourism, which includes silent retreats, digital detox vacations, and mindfulness travel (Voigt et al., 2011). Additionally, local and authentic experiences have gained prominence. Post-COVID-19 travelers are increasingly looking for smaller, eco-conscious and culturally immersive wellness destinations (Smith, 2021) who provide sustainable, personalized, authentic, and distinctive wellness tourism offerings (Clerici et al., 2023) rather than large, commercial spas (Kelly, 2012; Smith & Kelly, 2006). This signals a philosophical shift from escapism to conscious, meaningful engagement. Local sourcing and cultural integration are viewed not only as ethical choices but as mechanisms to enhance the depth and credibility of the wellness experience (Csirmaz & Pető, 2015). Such services are not only therapeutic in nature but are also designed to fulfill the need for individualization and emotional resonance, which has become central to traveler motivation in the wellness domain.

Several countries have successfully capitalized on wellness tourism, adapting it to their unique cultural and environmental contexts. Thailand has become synonymous with affordable yet high-quality wellness retreats, offering a comprehensive package that includes traditional Thai massage, detox programs, Buddhist meditation, and holistic health services. Centers in Chiang Mai, Koh Samui, and Phuket serve both international wellness seekers and digital nomads looking for healing and rejuvenation (Wellness Tourism Magazine, 2024). Thailand's wellness industry benefits from strong government support, which recognizes wellness tourism as part of the national development strategy. As noted by Csirmaz and Pető (2015), Southeast Asia—including Thailand—has seen dynamic growth in spa and wellness offerings, particularly in the day spa and beauty sectors located in both tourist zones and urban centers. Thai massage, a UNESCO-recognized heritage, is often cited as a global benchmark for therapeutic touch practices (UNESCO, 2019).

India is widely acknowledged as the cradle of Ayurveda and yoga, making it one of the most authentic and spiritually resonant wellness destinations in the world. Kerala's Ayurvedic centers offer treatments based on centuries-old plant-based medical systems, while Rishikesh, often referred to as the "Yoga Capital of the World," attracts pilgrims and wellness tourists alike. According to Stará and Peterson (2017), India exemplifies a destination where Eastern philosophies and traditional healing systems form the foundation of the wellness offering. Practices such as Panchakarma therapy, meditation retreats, and spiritual discourses appeal to tourists seeking deeper, transformative experiences. These practices align with global wellness trends that emphasize spiritualization, mindfulness, and self-responsibility for health.

Iceland has effectively capitalized on its geothermal landscape to develop wellness tourism centered around natural hot springs and spa experiences, with the Blue Lagoon being the most iconic example. Located in a lava field, the Blue Lagoon offers silica- and mineral-rich waters with proven therapeutic properties for skin ailments such as psoriasis. Kazakov and Oyner (2021) identify such practices as an example of the rational use of environmental assets for wellness, linking naturally occurring features with contemporary health needs. Iceland also integrates wellness with environmental consciousness, positioning itself as a leader in eco-friendly tourism that respects and preserves its unique landscape.

Japan's wellness tourism draws its essence from traditional cultural rituals and healing practices. The onsen or hot springs offer a unique blend of communal and meditative therapeutic bathing often located in rural areas surrounded by mountains, forests, or coastal landscapes, further enhancing their restorative impact. In addition to onsen, Zen meditation retreats and Shinrin-yoku (forest bathing) are central to Japan's wellness offerings. As Csirmaz and Pető (2015) explain, Japan's wellness sector reflects a deep connection between natural environments and mental well-being, offering immersive experiences for stress relief, emotional balance, and spiritual clarity. Shinrin-yoku, in particular, is supported by scientific research validating its benefits in reducing cortisol levels and improving immune function making it an example of evidence-based nature therapy that blends ancient practice with modern wellness science. Shinrin-yoku has been institutionalized in Japan with certified forest therapy trails and guided experiences, making it a formally integrated health and tourism initiative that offers measurable mental and physiological benefits. Studies by the Japanese Forestry Agency and researchers such as Qing Li (2010) demonstrated that forest bathing reduces cortisol levels, a marker of stress; lowers blood pressure and heart rate, and enhances natural killer cell activity, improving immune function, mood, energy, and sleep quality.

In Morocco, retreats in the Sahara Desert—such as those organized by Riad Serai and NOSADE—offer minimalistic, eco-friendly settings that remove the distractions of modern life, creating space for introspection and transformation

(NOSADE, n.d.; Riad Serai, n.d.). These retreats emphasize the healing qualities of silence, stillness, and the immensity of the desert landscape, which are seen as natural facilitators for emotional detox and mental clarity (Gagnol & Landel, 2016). Similarly, in Arizona, luxury desert wellness resorts like Enchantment Resort in Sedona and Mii Amo Spa incorporate Native American spiritual traditions with modern wellness practices. Guests are often welcomed with smudging ceremonies, engage in sacred rituals, and participate in energy balancing therapies, reflecting an integrated approach to healing (Architectural Digest, n.d.; Condé Nast Traveler, 2007). These experiences promote resilience, inner healing, and self-discovery, making the harsh yet serene desert environment a powerful therapeutic landscape for many Western tourists seeking transformative travel rooted in both ancient wisdom and modern mindfulness.

The blue spaces (oceans, seas, and coastal environments) play a crucial role in mental and physical restoration. Ocean-based wellness practices include aqua yoga and floating meditation which leverage buoyancy for deep muscle relaxation, improved flexibility, and joint relief; snorkeling therapy which involves slow, mindful swimming enhanced by visual and tactile stimulation from marine life; and salt inhalation therapy (*halotherapy*) practiced in coastal caves or salt rooms, believed to improve respiratory function and skin health. Destinations such as Greece, the Maldives, and Costa Rica offer immersive oceanic wellness retreats where the rhythmic movement of water, saline air, and soothing ocean sounds create an environment conducive to nervous system regulation and emotional balance. As Stará and Peterson (2017) emphasize, wellness experiences involving natural water bodies are increasingly associated with reduced anxiety, improved mood, and enhanced clarity of thought. This is further supported by a growing body of environmental psychology research. Studies have found that exposure to coastal and aquatic environments—collectively referred to as *blue spaces*—can lead to lower stress hormone levels, enhanced psychological well-being, and faster mental recovery (Völker & Kistemann, 2011; White et al., 2010). These outcomes validate ocean therapy as a scientifically grounded component of nature-based wellness tourism.

The connection between wellness tourism and the natural environment is not only symbiotic but often essential. Natural settings have inherent therapeutic benefits, as demonstrated by Kaplan and Kaplan's (1989) Attention Restoration Theory, which posits that nature aids cognitive recovery and stress relief. Moreover, destinations offering forest retreats, mountain meditation, or beach yoga retreats leverage the biophilic principle—the innate human tendency to seek connection with nature. This logical link forms the cornerstone of nature-based wellness tourism, where the environment is both a setting and a participant in the healing process.

A rational critique, however, warns against over-commercialization. Excessive development in fragile ecosystems under the guise of wellness can erode the very natural assets that attract wellness tourists. Therefore, sustainable management practices must be integral to the planning of wellness experiences in natural environments.

Sri Lanka's Ayurvedic roots, spiritual landscape, and eco-diverse environment. While global wellness tourism has surged—estimated to be worth over $919 billion by 2022 (Kazakov & Oyner, 2021)—Sri Lanka remains an emerging player with underutilized assets. In the Sri Lanka Tourism Strategic Plan (2022–2025), wellness tourism is highlighted as part of the country's diversification strategy, emphasizing Ayurveda, meditation, and eco-retreats as authentic experiences that support sustainable, health-oriented travel (Sri Lanka Tourism Development Authority, 2022). Sri Lanka's wellness tourism offerings are largely grounded in Ayurveda, an ancient holistic medical system focused on balance between body, mind, and spirit (Government of Sri Lanka, Ministry of Development Strategies and International Trade, & Sri Lanka Export Development Board, 2018). Ayurveda in Sri Lanka is state-recognized, with licensed Ayurvedic hospitals and wellness centers regulated under the Ayurveda Act of 1961. The Department of Ayurveda, under the Ministry of Health, monitors practitioners, supporting the credibility of wellness services. Beyond Ayurveda, Buddhist meditation retreats, yoga, Siddha medicine, and natural therapies offer a multifaceted spiritual and physical healing environment. Retreat centers such as Nilambe Meditation Centre and Aranya Forest Hermitages cater to both locals and tourists seeking spiritual solace and mental clarity. Scholars such as De Silva (2013) argue that these traditional practices present an authentic, culturally rooted value proposition in a global market that increasingly seeks meaningful, sustainable wellness experiences. Kazakov and Oyner (2021) highlight the growing preference for nature-aligned wellness services, where the landscape itself becomes therapeutic. Sri Lanka's potential in this regard remains largely untapped, with few internationally recognized eco-wellness brands leveraging its biodiversity in structured tourism offerings.

3. Methodology

This study employed qualitative, exploratory research design to investigate how natural ecosystems underpin wellness tourism in Sri Lanka and to assess strategies for harmonizing tourism development with environmental and cultural sustainability. The exploratory nature of the study was justified by the emerging and context-specific nature (Stebbins, 2001) of wellness tourism in Sri Lanka, which has not yet been fully theorized or mapped in existing literature. This design is ideal for the flexible, in-depth exploration of stakeholders' perception, beliefs, and practices regarding the integration of natural environments into wellness tourism. To gain deeper multi-stakeholder insights, a focused group discussion was conducted including 10 purposively-selected participants, representing two from each categories—tourism operators, wellness tourists, ayurvedic doctors and wellness practitioners, environmentalists, and representatives from national tourism bodies. Focus groups are recognized for their ability to facilitate interactive, multi-perspective dialogue, often surfacing shared values, tensions, and innovative ideas through collective engagement (Morgan, 1997). The data were collected during the January 2025. A thematic analysis was conducted using manual coding, following Braun and Clarke's (2006) six-step framework. Thematic analysis, widely used in qualitative tourism research, provided the flexibility to unpack layered meanings and synthesize insights relevant to both academic inquiry and policy development (Braun & Clarke, 2006; Veal, 2018).

4. Results and Discussion

4.1 Sri Lanka's Ayurvedic Resources and Their Wellness Value

Sri Lanka is globally recognized for its rich Ayurvedic heritage, a holistic healing system that has been practiced on the island for over 2,000 years. Drawing from Deshiya Chikitsa (indigenous medicine) and classical Ayurveda from India, Sri Lankan Ayurveda emphasizes balance between body, mind, and environment, using natural remedies, diet, lifestyle changes, and therapeutic rituals. Sri Lanka's tropical climate supports over 1,400 species of medicinal plants used in Ayurvedic practices. Key Ayurvedic Herbs are Gotu Kola *(Centella asiatica-known for improving memory and skin health)*, Aralu *(Terminalia chebula—used in digestive tonics and cleansing formulations)*, Belimal *(Aegle marmelos—a common herbal tea ingredient for digestion and detox)*, and Venivel *(Coscinium fenestratum—antibacterial and used for fever, inflammation, and skin issues)*. These herbs are the basis for natural therapies that promote detoxification, immunity boosting, skin rejuvenation, stress relief, and overall vitality.

Across the island, from coastal towns like Wadduwa and Hikkaduwa to inland sanctuaries in Kandy, Dambulla, and Ella, visitors can find certified Ayurvedic resorts and hospitals offering immersive wellness experiences like Panchakarma Therapy—*A five-fold cleansing and rejuvenation process for detoxifying the body*, Abhyanga (Herbal Oil Massage)—*full-body massage using warm medicated oils to calm the nervous system and improve circulation*, Shirodhara—*a soothing treatment where warm oil is poured onto the forehead to relieve anxiety, insomnia, and mental fatigue*, and Herbal Steam Baths and Poultices *used to expel toxins and relieve muscular tension.*

> By the time, Sri Lanka has Ayurvedic centers, hospitals, and Ayurvedic resorts offering wellness experiences like Panchakarma Therapy, Abhyanga, Shirodhara, and Herbal Steam Baths and Poultices. These treatments provide detoxification, relaxation, and relief from anxiety, insomnia, and mental fatigue. Tourists can find these treatments in coastal and inland areas of the country. (Focus group discussion, personal communication, 18th March 2025)

Ayurveda in Sri Lanka is not limited to treatments but is a way of life. Many wellness programs emphasize the integration of Ayurvedic nutrition, daily routines (*Dinacharya*), and seasonal practices (*Ritucharya*) into guests' lives. Meals are tailored to individual *doshas* (Vata, Pitta, Kapha), focusing on balance, digestion, and nourishment using local organic produce and medicinal spices like turmeric, cumin, and coriander. Guests are guided in daily routines that include oil self-massage, yoga, meditation, herbal teas, and breathwork to align the body and mind with natural rhythms. These practices foster long-term health, stress reduction, improved metabolism, better sleep, and enhanced mental clarity.

4.2 Sri Lanka's Natural Assets and Their Wellness Value

Sri Lanka boasts an impressive array of natural environments that offer unique and scientifically supported wellness benefits. These assets serve not only as eco-tourism highlights but also as integral components of holistic well-being, attracting travelers seeking rejuvenation of the body, mind, and spirit. Sri Lanka's ecological richness contributes significantly to its wellness tourism appeal. Its diverse biomes from dense rainforests to serene beaches and lush highlands create immersive environments for natural healing and stress relief.

4.2.1 Interplay Between Rainforests and Wellness Tourism

Sri Lankan ancestors practiced forest bathing centuries ago. It is beautifully entrenched into rural Sri Lankans way of life. In Sri Lanka's rural villages, men, women and children still prefer to walk barefoot, hike barefoot and run barefoot. The forest is revered as a place of sustenance as well as healing. It is not a new form of ecotherapy in Sri Lanka. It's simply a way of life.

Guided forest bathing walks are available throughout the country and are led by local naturalists who know Sri Lanka's natural history. As the tourists walk through the forest floor, the crunch of dried twigs breaks the sound of the forest and travelers will glean insights into the ayurvedic properties of the barks and the benefit of it pressing onto their barefoot soles. Observations of wildlife and immersion in diverse forest landscapes activate the senses through the different landscapes and types of wild forests. The travelers emphasized the restorative and healing qualities of the experience, illustrating its therapeutic impact.

> The forest bathing experiences highlight the therapeutic and educational potential of tourists immersing with the natural world, contributing to the broader discourse on eco-therapy and biodiversity conservation. (Focus group discussion, personal communication, 18th March 2025)

Kanneliya Rainforest present an environment characterized by its lush vegetation and moisture-rich atmosphere. Its crisp cool air collectively contributes for enhancing alertness and refreshing the mind. Mindful walking within this ecosystem engages participants in a dynamic interaction with the terrain, which includes pebbles scattered along streams, lichen-covered rocky surfaces, and rocks submerged in water pools. These diverse textures and conditions necessitate heightened attention and balance, transforming the act of walking into a physically and mentally stimulating exercise. Such engagement with the natural environment not only underscores the intricate interplay between physical activity and sensory activation but also highlights the therapeutic potential of mindful practices in biodiversity-rich settings like Kanneliya. These observations contribute valuable insights to the broader discourse on eco-therapy and the restorative benefits of immersive natural experiences.

Horton Plains' is legendary for the true beauty of its cloud forest ecosystems in the intricate insight observed along a hike or a walk. The forest floor serves as a dynamic record, narrating stories of fluctuating weather patterns and the passage of previous travelers. Its vibrant colors and rich textures offer visual and tactile insights into the ecological wealth of the land. These sensory stimuli, combined with numerous opportunities for wildlife observation, contribute to heightened sensory awareness. The interplay of these elements highlights the holistic engagement that Horton Plains offers, positioning it as a site of both ecological significance and restorative potential. These findings underscore the role of immersive natural landscapes in fostering a deeper connection between individuals and their environment, offering valuable insights for both ecological research and conservation efforts.

The Talaimannar region, with its salty coastal air, offers a distinctive sensory experience, particularly within its mangrove forests. Forest bathing in this unique ecosystem engages participants on multiple levels, creating an interplay of tactile, auditory, and olfactory stimuli. The moisture-rich environment leaves the skin slightly damp, while immersion in the dark, muddy waters of the mangroves provides grounding and a physical connection to the terrain. The auditory dimension is enriched by the calls of the resident bird species, which present an opportunity to interpret ecological narratives through their diverse vocalizations. This highlights the sanctuary's avian biodiversity and its role in fostering environmental awareness. Moreover, tactile interactions within the mangrove pools, such as the gentle nibbling by wild baby fish pods or the delicate tickle of a hermit crab traversing the foot, add an element of spontaneity and intimacy with the ecosystem. Collectively, these experiences underline the therapeutic and educational potential of such engagements with the natural world. They emphasize the value of Talaimannar's mangrove forests as both a site for ecological study and a space for holistic restoration, contributing meaningful insights to the broader discourse on eco-therapy and biodiversity conservation.

The Sinharaja rainforest exemplifies a biodiversity hotspot, offering a rich tapestry of endemism and sensory experiences. Its ecological diversity is mirrored in the immersive interactions it facilitates, where the crushed leaves by resident gray langurs release a natural, untamed aromatherapy. The environment continuously heightens sensory engagement through the fragrant interplay of wildflowers, ripened fruit esters, and the earthy scents that shift across the terrain. These encounters underscore the intricate connection between biodiversity and sensory stimulation. Leaning against the roots of a centuries-old tree under the filtered golden sunlight streaming through the dense canopy creates moments of serene reflection, further emphasizing the rainforest's role as a sanctuary for both ecological appreciation and personal restoration. These findings contribute to the broader understanding of the therapeutic benefits associated with immersing oneself in biodiverse ecosystems.

Ritigala reserve exemplifies a sanctuary of wellness and connection, underscoring the intricate relationship between historical heritage and ecological richness. As a former monastery, its historical significance as a site of meditation, learning, and simplicity contributes to the pervasive sense of calm that envelops the area. The Reserve's base, rich in native herbs and medicinal plants, offers a distinctive olfactory landscape dominated by the presence of airborne essential oils or phytoncides, which are known to have rejuvenating and immune-boosting properties. The immersive sensory experience deepens as one ascends through the elevation, encountering shifting microclimates that transform both the physical and sensory landscape. These unique ecological and atmospheric variations illustrate the Reserve's multifaceted contribution to physical well-being and emotional restoration, positioning it as a critical subject for research in environmental therapy and biodiversity conservation.

4.2.2 Interplay Between Coastal Ecosystem and Wellness Tourism

Sri Lanka's 1,340 km-long coastline is not just a geographical asset but also a powerful driver of wellness tourism. It offers natural therapies, serene environments, and experiences rooted in both traditional healing and modern holistic practices. Sri Lanka's coastal ecosystems provide fertile ground for exploring the intersection of wellness practices and environmental benefits, particularly through thalassotherapy—an ancient approach that utilizes seawater and the marine climate for therapeutic purposes. The rhythmic soundscape of ocean waves and the mineral-rich composition of seawater are integral to this method, offering restorative experiences for both physical and mental well-being.

The warm waters of the Indian Ocean surrounding Sri Lanka are rich in minerals like magnesium, potassium, and iodine. These minerals, absorbed through the skin during swimming or treatments, have detoxifying and anti-inflammatory properties. Exposure to sea air, abundant in negative ions, has been scientifically associated with improved sleep quality, enhanced mood, and respiratory health. These factors position Sri Lanka's coastline as a natural setting for holistic wellness interventions. Examples from local practices further illustrate the application of these concepts. In Unawatuna, wellness resorts blend cultural and ecological elements through sunrise and sunset yoga sessions on the beach, incorporating breathwork that resonates with the calming soundscape of the ocean. Mirissa has emerged as a focal point for ocean-based mindfulness retreats, emphasizing the meditative aspects of the marine environment. Resorts in Mirissa and Bentota incorporate thalassotherapy pools, seawater baths, and seaweed wraps in their spa menus, promoting skin health, improved circulation, and muscular relaxation. Additionally, traditional spa treatments such as seawater immersion, salt scrubs, and mud masks grounded in local knowledge highlight the therapeutic potential of coastal resources. These examples underscore the significance of Sri Lanka's coastline not only as a site for relaxation and natural beauty but also as a subject of research on integrated wellness practices. Such studies contribute valuable insights to both ecological conservation and the development of sustainable wellness tourism. Proximity to water bodies (blue spaces) has been scientifically linked to reduced stress, anxiety, and depression. The soothing sounds of waves, the expanse of the horizon, and the slower pace of beach environments encourage mindfulness and emotional calm. Yoga and meditation retreats in coastal towns like Talalla and Arugam Bay often use open-air pavilions facing the sea to heighten this calming effect, enhancing breathwork and meditative focus. Ayurvedic beachside spas offer treatments using herbs grown in saline-adapted coastal areas, such as Coastal Neem and Lumnitzera, known for their antibacterial and anti-inflammatory properties. Ayurvedic nutrition programs also include seafood-based meals aligned with *dosha* balancing, combined with ocean-side dining to enhance sensory pleasure and digestion.

> Arugam Bay Wellness Retreats uses open-air pavilions, ayurvedic beachside spas, and Coastal Neem and Lumnitzera herbs for calming, meditative focus, and seafood-based nutrition programs for dosha balancing and sensory pleasure. (Focus group discussion, personal communication, 18th March 2025)

Sri Lanka's coastal mangroves, found in areas like Negombo and Kalpitiya, support unique ecosystems and provide quiet, shaded environments which is ideal for canoeing, birdwatching, and mindfulness walks. These nature-immersive activities are restorative and foster a deeper connection with the environment. Ecoresorts near mangroves often offer guided mindfulness paddling or sound healing sessions using natural soundscapes as background therapy.

Engagement in low-impact snorkeling and reef diving in areas like Hikkaduwa and Trincomalee connects tourists with vibrant marine life, enhancing feelings of awe and wonder—emotions shown to have lasting positive effects on well-being. Wellness itineraries include guided reef exploration combined with breathing techniques to promote lung function, focus, and relaxation.

4.2.3 Interplay Between Hill Country and Wellness Tourism

The high-altitude cities of Nuwara Eliya, Ella, and Haputale boasts cooler climates compared to lowlands, offering refreshing escape from tropical heat and humidity. The pristine air of these regions is rich with oxygen, and often infused with the fragrance of eucalyptus and wildflowers conducive for respiratory wellness. In Nuwara Eliya, wellness retreats capitalize on the climate to offer programs aimed at promoting deep rest, improving sleep quality, and enhancing respiratory health, especially beneficial for urban visitors from concrete environments or polluted environments. Nuwara Eliya's colonial-era gardens also offer botanical therapy sessions that include herbal walks and aromatherapy.

Trekking routes such as Horton Plains and Lipton's Seat transcend mere scenic adventures. They offer holistic wellness experiences involving aerobic activity, sensory immersion, and digital detox. Further, guided mindfulness treks through the Knuckles Range or Ella Rock are designed to combine cardiovascular exercise with meditative breathing techniques, encouraging stress relief and improved mental clarity which combine physical activity with mindfulness.

Tea plantations stretch across Sri Lanka hills, offering not only scenic views but also opportunities for detox-focused tourism. Ceylon green tea is renowned for its antioxidant properties and is often integrated into wellness packages as both a beverage and a spa ingredient. Wellness resorts and boutique tea estates offer tea-infused spa treatments including green tea body wraps, steam baths, and herbal compresses, promoting skin health and body detoxification. Tea tasting has been adapted into tea meditation sessions, where guests are guided through mindful tea preparation and slow sipping practices that encourage presence, gratitude, and sensory awareness.

> Ella as a tourist hotspot, offers mindful tea plucking, organic tasting, and treks to improve cardiovascular endurance and reduce mental fatigue. (Focus group discussion, personal communication, 18th March 2025)

The hill country of Sri Lanka is dotted with religious and spiritual landmarks, such as Sri Pada (*Adam's Peak*), which draws both pilgrims and spiritual tourists. The climb itself is a meditative journey, often undertaken at night to reach the summit by sunrise. Spiritual wellness retreats in areas such as Maskeliya and Hatton integrate pilgrimages with yoga, chanting, and reflective journaling for personal transformation. With its proximity to Buddhist temples and hermitages, the Hill Country supports meditation retreats, silent retreats, and Vipassana programs, often set in forest monasteries or remote ecolodges. For example, retreats in Bandarawela and Kandy's hill outskirts offer extended silent meditation, walking meditations in tea gardens, and Dhamma talks for mental purification and emotional balance.

4.2.4 Possible Interplay Between Hot-Water Springs and Wellness Tourism

Sri Lanka is blessed with hot water springs scattered across the island, e.g. Trincomalee, Polonnaruwa, Hambantota, and Ampara districts. They hold an ecological value but unfortunately it is still an untapped asset for wellness tourism in Sri Lanka.

> … Sri Lankan examples include the hot springs at Kanniya, Nelumwewa, Mahaoya, Wahawa, Madunagala, and which have cultural and historical importance alongside their natural allure. If these assets were introduced to Wellness Tourism in Sri Lanka, it would provide a unique therapeutic experience to the travelers

> as well as support in uplifting the livelihoods of the rural communities while preserving their historical legacy of Sri Lanka .... (Focus group discussion, personal communication, 18th March 2025)

Therefore, by recognizing and utilizing this geothermal wealth, Sri Lanka needs to strategically develop its potential combined with eco-conscious infrastructure in order for these hot water springs to enhance Sri Lanka's wellness tourism portfolio, providing unique experiences rooted in both natural and cultural heritage.

In conclusion, the integration of Ayurvedic therapies with immersive nature-based experiences, such as forest bathing in Sinharaja, mindful tea rituals in the Hill Country, or thalassotherapy along the southern coast, demonstrates how traditional knowledge and ecological assets can come together to create transformative wellness experiences in Sri Lanka. These multidimensional offerings not only serve the growing global demand for authentic, sustainable wellness travel but also reaffirm Sri Lanka's potential as a leading destination in the sector.

5. Conclusion and Recommendations

Sri Lanka's unique symbiosis of pristine natural ecosystems and millennia-old wellness traditions positions it as a transformative destination in the global wellness tourism landscape. The island's biodiversity hotspots; rainforests, coastal mangroves, hill country, and Ayurvedic heritage serve not merely scenic backdrops but active agents in holistic healing, offering scientifically validated benefits such as stress reduction, immune enhancement, and emotional restoration. By integrating immersive nature-based therapies from forest bathing to thalassotherapy with culturally rooted practices, Sri Lanka provides a blueprint for wellness tourism that harmonizes human well-being with environmental stewardship. By leveraging its ecological wealth alongside ancient traditions, the island can carve a niche in the global wellness market while championing sustainability. Future success hinges on collaborative, cross-sectoral efforts between policymakers, communities, and the tourism sector to protect the very resources that define Sri Lanka's wellness identity.

It is recommended to invest in infrastructure to connect rural wellness hubs, fostering inclusive growth and reducing urban–rural disparities. For example, market lesser-explored regions (e.g. Eastern Province, Ritigala Reserve) to alleviate overcrowding in hotspots like Ella and Unawatuna. Highlight unique offerings such as Talaimannar's mangrove therapy or Eastern Province's Ayurvedic herb trails. In order to establish community-led conservation initiatives, it is recommended to train local communities as wellness guides, herbalists, and cultural ambassadors, ensuring equitable revenue sharing. Safeguard intangible cultural heritage by supporting traditional healers and meditation masters through grants and global recognition programs. Integrate sustainability education into wellness itineraries, encouraging tourists to participate in conservation activities (e.g. coral reef restoration in Hikkaduwa). By adopting these strategies, Sri Lanka can leverage its ecological capital to establish a replicable framework for nature-based wellness tourism, which prioritize planetary health alongside human well-being.

References

Architectural Digest. (n.d.). *The 8 most beautiful desert spa destinations in America.* https://www.architecturaldigest.com/story/most-beautiful-desert-spas. Accessed on April 14, 2025.

Braun, V., & Clarke, V. (2006). Using thematic analysis in psychology. *Qualitative Research in Psychology*, *3*(2), 77–101. https://doi.org/10.1191/1478088706qp063oa

Clerici, A. P., Murphy, C., & Almeida, N. M. C. (2023). The future of wellness tourism after COVID-19. *European Spatial Research and Policy*, *30*(1), 103–122.

Condé Nast Traveler. (2007, May 2). *Native intelligence*. https://www.cntraveler.com/stories/2007-05-02/native-intelligence. Accessed on April 14, 2025.

Csirmaz, É., & Pető, K. (2015). International trends in recreational and wellness tourism. *Procedia Economics and Finance*, *32*, 755–762. https://doi.org/10.1016/S2212-5671(15)01458-6

Curtin, S. (2021). Exploring spiritual and cultural well-being in tourism: Sacred landscapes and mindful travel. *Tourism Recreation Research*, *46*(1), 52–66.

De Silva, N. (2013, April). Sri Lanka's traditional knowledge and traditional cultural expressions of health and wellbeing: History, present status and the need for safeguarding. In *SAARC regional seminar on traditional knowledge and traditional cultural expressions in south Asia* (pp. 40–56). https://www.researchgate.net/profile/Nirekha-De-Silva/publication/277558964_Sri_Lanka's_Traditional_Knowledge_about_Health_and_Wellbeing_History_Present_Status_and_Need_for_Safeguarding/links/556d098908aec22683054b8b/Sri-Lankas-Traditional-Knowledge-about-Health-and-Wellbeing-History-Present-Status-and-Need-for-Safeguarding.pdf. Accessed on March 30, 2025.

Dillette, A. K., Douglas, A. C., & Andrzejewski, C. (2021). Dimensions of holistic wellness as a result of international wellness tourism experiences. *Current Issues in Tourism*, *24*(6), 794–810.

Dorji, T. (2021). Regenerative tourism: A Bhutanese perspective. *Journal of Tourism Futures*, *7*(3), 333–344.

Gagnol, L., & Landel, P. A. (2016). Psammotourism: Desert sand as a specific resource and touristic experience (Merzouga, Southeast Morocco). *Via. Tourism Review*, *10*.

Global Wellness Institute. (2023). *Global wellness economy monitor*. Global Wellness Institute. https://globalwellnessinstitute.org/wp-content/uploads/2023/11/GWI-WE-Monitor-2023_FINAL.pdf. Accessed on March 15, 2025.

Google Wellness. (2022). *Google wellness program overview*. https://www.google.com/about/wellness

Government of Sri Lanka, Ministry of Development Strategies and International Trade, & Sri Lanka Export Development Board. (2018). *National export strategy of Sri Lanka: Wellness tourism strategy 2018–2022*. Government of Sri Lanka. https://www.srilankabusiness.com/pdf/nes/sri-lanka-wellness-4-2-web.pdf. Accessed on March 28, 2025.

Hu, F., Wen, J., Phau, I., Ying, T., Aston, J., & Wang, W. (2023). The role of tourism in healthy aging: An interdisciplinary literature review and conceptual model. *Journal of Hospitality and Tourism Management*, *56*, 356–366.

Kaplan, S. (1995). The restorative benefits of nature: Toward an integrative framework. *Journal of Environmental Psychology*, *15*(3), 169–182. https://doi.org/10.1016/0272-4944(95)90001-2

Kaplan, R., & Kaplan, S. (1989). *The experience of nature: A psychological perspective*. CUP Archive.

Kazakov, S., & Oyner, O. (2021). Wellness tourism: A perspective article. *Tourism Review*, *76*(1), 58–63.

Kelly, C. (2012). Wellness tourism: Retreat visitor motivations and experiences. *Tourism Recreation Research*. https://doi.org/10.1080/02508281.2012.11081709

Kessler, D. (2022). Motivations for wellness tourism in a post-COVID world. *Journal of Hospitality & Tourism*, *24*(2), 127–142.

Kim, B. H., & Kim, H. L. (2024). Effects of transformative tourism activity on the mitigation of menopause symptoms and life satisfaction. *International Journal of Tourism Research*, *26*(4), e2714.

Li, Q. (2010). *Effect of forest bathing on human immune function*. Environmental Health and Preventive Medicine.

Morgan, D. L. (1997). *Focus groups as qualitative research* (2nd ed.). Sage Publications.

Neuhofer, B., & Celuch, K. (2020). Social media and wellness tourism. *Journal of Travel & Tourism Marketing*, *37*(3), 289–303.

NOSADE. (n.d.). *Desert yoga retreats Morocco*. https://nosade.com/desert-yoga-retreats-morocco/. Accessed on April 14, 2025.

Riad Serai. (n.d.). *Yoga and retreats in the Sahara Desert*. https://riadserai.com/en/experiences/yoga-and-retreats-in-sahara-desert-morocco/. Accessed on April 14, 2025.

Smith, M. K. (2021). Creating wellness tourism experiences. In *Routledge handbook of the tourist experience* (pp. 364–377). Routledge.

Smith, M. K. (2023). New trends in wellness tourism: Restoration and regeneration. In *Routledge handbook of trends and issues in global tourism supply and demand* (pp. 480–496). Routledge.

Smith, M. K., & Kelly, C. (2006). Wellness tourism. *Tourism Recreation Research*, *31*(1), 1–4.

Smith, M., & Puczkó, L. (2014). *Health, tourism and hospitality: Spas, wellness and medical travel*. Routledge.

Sri Lanka Tourism Development Authority. (2022). *Sri Lanka tourism strategic plan 2022–2025*. Sri Lanka Tourism Development Authority. https://www.sltda.gov.lk/storage/common_media/Sri_Lanka-Final_V6_Edited850147500.pdf

Stará, J., & Peterson, C. (2017). Understanding the concept of wellness for the future of the tourism industry: A literature review. *Journal of Tourism & Services*, *8*(14), 18–29.

Stebbins, R. A. (2001). *Exploratory research in the social sciences*. Sage Publications.

Talukder, M. B., Hossain, S. E., Ferdous, F. A., & Khan, M. R. (2024). Exploring the rise of wellness tourism: Trends, benefits, and market potential. In *AI technologies and advancements for psychological well-being and healthcare* (pp. 351–377). IGI Global. https://doi.org/10.4018/979-8-3693-9158-7.ch013

United Nations Educational, Scientific and Cultural Organization (UNESCO). (2019). *Decision of the intergovernmental committee: 14.COM 10.B.37*. UNESCO.

Veal, A. J. (2018). *Research methods for leisure and tourism* (5th ed.). Pearson Education.

Voigt, C., Brown, G., & Howat, G. (2011). Wellness tourists: In search of transformation. *Tourism Review*, *66*(1/2), 16–30. https://doi.org/10.1108/16605371111127206

Völker, S., & Kistemann, T. (2011). The impact of blue space on human health and well-being – Salutogenetic health effects of inland surface waters: A review. *International Journal of Hygiene and Environmental Health*, *214*(6), 449–460.

Wellness Tourism Magazine. (n.d.). *Thailand's holistic approach to wellness: A complete guide to mind, body, and spirit*. https://www.wellnesstourism.com/article/thailands-holistic-approach-to-wellness-a-complete-guide-to-mind-body-and-spirit. Accessed on April 14, 2025.

White, M., Smith, A., Humphryes, K., Pahl, S., Snelling, D., & Depledge, M. (2010). Blue space: The importance of water for preference, affect, and restorativeness ratings of natural and built scenes. *Journal of Environmental Psychology*, *30*(4), 482–493.

Wilson, E. O. (1984). *Biophilia*. Harvard University Press.

Yeoman, I., McMahon-Beattie, U., & Findlay, K. (2014). The future of urban spas: A trend analysis of the UK market. *Tourism Recreation Research*, *39*(3), 397–413.

Index

Printed and bound by CPI Group (UK) Ltd, Croydon, CR0 4YY

24/09/2026

14969062-0001